Interactions I

Interactions I

A Cognitive Approach to Beginning Chinese

Margaret Mian Yan   **Jennifer Li-chia Liu**

嚴棉   劉力嘉

Illustrations by Chee Cheong Kung

Indiana University Press
Bloomington and Indianapolis

This book is a publication of

INDIANA UNIVERSITY PRESS
601 North Morton Street
Bloomington, IN 47404-3797 USA

http://www.indiana.edu/~iupress

Telephone orders 800-842-6796
Fax orders 812-855-7931
Orders by email iuporder@indiana.edu

The paper used in this publication meets the minimum
requirements of American National Standard for Information
Sciences—Permanence of Paper for Printed Library
Materials, ANSI Z39.48-1984.

MANUFACTURED IN THE UNITED STATES OF AMERICA

Cataloging information is available from the Library of Congress.

By Margaret Mian Yan and Jennifer Li-chia Liu
ISBN 978-0-253-21122-4 paperback (Interactions I)
ISBN 978-0-253-21202-3 paperback (Interactions I: Workbook)

By Jennifer Li-chia Liu and Margaret Mian Yan
ISBN 978-0-253-21123-1 paperback (Interactions II)
ISBN 978-0-253-21203-0 paperback (Interactions II: Workbook)
ISBN 978-0-253-21201-6 paperback (Interactions I & II: Teacher's Manual)

5 6 7 8   12 11 10

Contents

目錄

11.	Asking for and giving an opinion	不是…就是…construction Frequency expressions Manner or degree complements 要是…就…construction 一點兒也/都不…construction Question word 都(不)…construction 上/這/下(一)次 The prepositional phrase 在…上 The superlative marker 最 好像…似的 expression More on …的 N construction	子女懂像近 包男會真最 油餓己談次 牛別自所每
12.	Talking about the seasons and the weather Expressing likes and dislikes Talking about clothes Talking about colors Making a purchase	除了…(以外) construction 越…越…construction V來V去 expression The nominalizer 的 The situational 的 打幾折 expression Antonym compounds 號 as "size" 有什麼好V的! More on comparative construction	冷衣錢外號 貴毛塊除寫 短穿麵頭聽 長且球裏還
13.	Talking about the holidays Talking about transportation	坐…到/回…來/去 construction 是坐…到/回…來/去的 construction 從…坐…到…來/去 construction Pivotal construction 只要…就…construction 多/少 V 一點兒 O expressions …的時候 expression The suggestion and command particle 吧 Better not VO expression 再 vs. 又 Subject omission More on …的 N construction	口舍期難只 門宿星火市 行家假笑節 送回放玩鐘

Preface

Interactions I and *II* are intended for many different kinds of beginners, who may have very diverse interests and backgrounds in pursuing Chinese as a foreign language and varying degrees of exposure to the Chinese language and culture. Whether they are real beginners or advanced beginners who are strong in one or two language skills but lack others, they will find these two learner-centered textbooks accommodating, motivating, and thought-provoking.

I. Rationales and Instructional Design

We share a number of convictions that have motivated us since we first contemplated writing a beginning Chinese textbook. First, we believe in the cognitive approach to the design of language instruction. We are convinced that effective teaching of Chinese should go beyond simply providing language stimuli and linguistic information. By focusing on students' thought processes more than on rote practice, we believe language education can promote deeper, more active and meaningful learning. Thus we seek to design a textbook that enables learners to constructively *interact* with the language. For example, we explicate grammar by offering not just linguistic rules but also conceptual principles that relate to students' existing world knowledge. We advance character memorization by providing students with writing practice of meaningful compounds, sentences, or paragraphs rather than copying characters hundreds of times over. We supply real words and compounds instead of senseless syllables to help students practice pronunciation.

Second, we believe that the process of second-language acquisition can be enhanced if learners are given a central role in language instruction. This belief is based on the tenet that language input is best delivered from the perspective of the learner rather than that of the teacher. Therefore throughout the books we attempt to cover expressions and usages that are relevant and applicable to students' lives. The lesson topics revolve around the typical events occurring in a college setting over a year. Four personas that most learners of Chinese will run into and can identify with were created—a Chinese from mainland China, another from Taiwan, a non-Chinese American, and a Chinese American.

Third, we believe that learners of Chinese should acquire natural, appropriate, and contextualized language rather than simple textbook artifacts. Students should be exposed to not only the language structure but also its dynamic use in various sociocultural contexts. We weigh the significance of "appropriateness" over that of "standard" and present Chinese in variant forms (traditional vs. simplified characters) and usages (mainland China vs. Taiwan). Guided by the criteria of naturalness and frequency of use rather than the consideration of difficulty, we develop communication-driven rather than grammar-centered texts. Although some difficult yet common high-frequency linguistic structures have to be introduced early, we remedy the problem with a recycling strategy—complicated grammatical points are reintroduced in later chapters.

Fourth, we believe that language instruction should recognize each student as an individual with various needs and learning styles. Some learners seek to practice their literacy skills, whereas others desire aural-oral practice. Some are slow-paced, while others embrace challenges. Some prefer textual presentation, but others relate well to visuals. In the textbooks we address the diversity of learners with a balanced and multimodal treatment of the four language skills. We highlight the essential information while providing additional challenges in different styles, such as explanatory notes, diagrams, tables, and graphics.

Fifth, we contend that the dimension of culture is inseparable from language instruction. Therefore we have included in each lesson important cultural information (values, attitudes, behaviors) that can enlighten learners and help them develop a deeper understanding of the Chinese people and society.

Sixth, we believe that maximum learning effects can be achieved by studying not only hard but also smart. Throughout the textbooks we provide many tools, such as conventions and icons, to help students focus on key information; different groupings of lesson vocabulary, cross-references, and indexes to facilitate review and preview of vocabulary and grammar; and illuminating graphics and thought-provoking illustrations to maintain learning interest as well as promote character recognition and retention.

II. Organization of the Text
Introductory Chapters
The books begin with three introductory lessons that offer both conceptual and learning tools for the study of Chinese. Lesson 1 gives an overview of the Chinese languages and highlights their common characteristics and major differences. Lesson 2 introduces the components of the Chinese sound system (e.g., tones, initials, and finals) and discusses related linguistic phenomena (e.g., tone sandhi, stress and intonation, and dialectal differences). Useful classroom expressions are included as well. Lesson 3 examines important concepts related to the Chinese writing system. The topics included are stroke types, stroke order, six principles of character formation, transformation of writing styles, simplification of Chinese characters, Chinese radicals, and the use of dictionaries.

Core Lessons
Following the three introductory chapters are twenty core lessons, with 4 to 13 in *Interactions I* and 14 to 23 in *Interactions II*. These chapters cover topics of everyday life and situations in which functional language is introduced naturally. Lesson 4 deals with the notion of time and introduces usages related to numbers and dates. Lesson 5 focuses on a discussion of class schedules and reinforces time usages introduced earlier. Lesson 6 further discusses school work, with particular attention to conversation openers and closure. Shopping for school materials, expressing quantities, and using monetary terms are the focus of Lesson 7. Lessons 8 through 11 talk about meeting new friends, making phone calls, dining in a restaurant, and going to a movie. Major communicative functions are introduced and key concepts and usage are recycled. Lesson 12 centers on weather and clothing and Lesson 13 on holidays.

With the start of the spring semester, Lesson 14 discusses winter break. Lesson 15, about looking for a new apartment and moving in, introduces the concept of movement and relevant usages. Lesson 16, with its topic of going to a party, brings in expressions for giving directions and making comparisons. Lesson 17 highlights daily life usages and introduces terms about a person's temperament and personality. Lessons 18 through 20 revolve around the topics of music, sports, and health, respectively. Lesson 21 has its scenes set in a post office and a bank. Lesson 22, with its topic of driving, introduces the form and function of the passive voice in Chinese. As the semester draws to its end, Lesson 23 discusses various summer plans.

Each core lesson begins with a humorous illustration that provides an attention grabber to the chapter and stimulates learners to contemplate its contents. Then comes the Dialogue, which motivates learning through the natural use of language in diverse settings. The Dialogue is intended to provide comprehensible input and exposure to natural language. Its essential communicative functions are captured in the succeeding section, the Mini-Dialogue, which can be used for memorization and as a model for the student's own skit writing and performances. In the Vocabulary, Characters, and Grammar sections that follow the Mini-Dialogue, target language uses and structures are explained with diagrams, examples, notes, and visuals. Although we put stress on providing interesting and effective devices to intrigue learners, we equally value the teaching of language structures per se. Only by firmly grasping sentence structures can one perform in a functional way. Thus in the Grammar sections, aside from conceptual principles, we incorporate contrastive analyses of Chinese and English into the explanations of structures in order to help students see the differences from various perspectives. Each lesson ends with a section of Cultural Notes that aims to provide students with Chinese do's and don'ts so that they will be able to interact appropriately with native Chinese and can gain cross-cultural awareness.

Appendixes
Five appendixes are included in each book. The first one presents review lessons which summarize major grammatical points introduced in the core lessons. The second appendix lists supplementary characters (SC) that may be of interest to students who need more reading-writing practice. It also provides additional challenges for advanced beginners. The third appendix provides a list of radicals arranged by number of strokes. The fourth appendix presents a table on characters with two or more readings. The last one supplies a bibliography of sources used in the textbooks and refers students to other important resources.

Indexes
Each book concludes with four useful indexes: (1) lesson vocabulary, (2) lesson characters, (3) sentence patterns, and (4) measure words.

By designing and writing textbooks like these, we do not claim that we have discovered a solution to all the instructional challenges that many of us deal with on a daily basis. We only attempt to tackle some of the teaching and learning issues from a new perspective and hope to share insights that have come along over the years. We hope these books will inspire many more persons to come forth and help us march into a new era with pedagogical innovations and imagination.

The Authors

Acknowledgments

This textbook project was launched by Margaret M. Yan in 1986, after it was determined that Chinese language students needed a set of good, up-to-date basic textbooks. Originally entitled "Active Chinese," it was started with a review of all available materials concerning Chinese language teaching, including textbooks, workbooks, video tapes, and computer software. The literature survey was supported by a grant from the College of Arts and Sciences of Indiana University and resulted in the precursor of our book, the introductory chapters and two conversational lessons of the "Active Chinese." In 1995, Yan invited Jennifer L. C. Liu to join her in compiling the texts, now entitled ***Interactions I and II: A Cognitive Approach to Beginning Chinese***.

A project of this scope cannot succeed without institutional support and the help of many people. We would like to thank the College of Arts and Sciences of Indiana University for funding the preliminary literature review in 1986. Their support made it possible for the later collaborative work ***Interactions I and II*** to receive further funding for the partial editorial service and the cartoon illustrations in 1995. Special gratitude goes to Professor John Hou for his willingness to work with the drafts of these books at the 1996 Chinese School of the East Asian Summer Language Institute (EASLI) at Indiana University, as well as for his many valuable comments and suggestions. Thanks must also be extended to his students and teaching assistants as well as students and teaching assistants of 1996-97, 1997-98 First-year Chinese classes at IU who gave feedback that prompted us to perfect our books.

We would also like to thank Kenneth Goodall, Ruth I. Meserve, Virginia Harper Ho, William Moriarty, and Chih-kwang Sung for their editorial help, Chun-fang Bettina Hahn for her typing of the song Jasmine Flower, Kai-ping Hsu for writing the stroke orders of radicals, John Hollingsworth for his cartographic service, and Chang Kuang-yuan for his calligraphy of the bronze, oracle bone, and seal scripts. We thank Chee Cheong Kung for his willingness to take on the project of illustrations and to share his talents with us. His artwork has enriched our books. Thanks to Lung-sheng Sung for taking pictures for us in Taiwan and collecting relevant materials.

Jennifer Liu is especially grateful to Prof. James Chan for his inspiration during the development of this project, his excellent technical support and advice, his many comments on book layout and instructional design, as well as his generous critique of the pedagogical principles employed. She also thanks him for the wonderful electronic resources provided, which has made the creation of visuals and modification of clipart images possible. The clip arts used are from Corel Gallery by Corel Corporation (1994), ClipArt Library by Softkey International Corporation (1994), and Art Explosion 125,000 by Nova Development Corporation (1966).

Margaret Yan would like to express her sincere thanks to her mentor, the late Professor Yuen Ren Chao, of Cornell University, whose teaching and work on Chinese grammar and sound system have provided the basis and much of the inspiration for a major part of the second chapter and many grammatical points throughout the books as well as for the art of Chinese language instruction. Her hearty gratitude also goes to James H-Y. Tai for his brilliant invention of Temporal Sequence Principle (1989), which inspired her to propose the From Whole to Part Principle and the Principle of Simultaneous Existence (1993) and to apply these three conceptual principles in explaining many grammatical points in these books. If there are any errors or inadequacies in the grammar, Yan alone should be blamed for them.

Finally but not least, the patience and assistance of John Gallman, the Director of the Indiana University Press [1975–2000], and his staff is much appreciated.

A Note to Students

The following list captures a few essential qualities or attributes that we have found in many of our students who are successful in acquiring Chinese as a foreign language.   Though everyone has his/her own unique learning style, we hope you can make the most of this beginning Chinese course with an effort to:

1. **Be active and adventurous**
    Interactions I and *II* provide you with many resources and tools. However, you cannot benefit from the rich linguistic input or the learning environment we provide unless you are actively engaged in the learning process. By "active" we mean that you have to put in cognitive efforts to organize, connect, sort, construct, or de-construct knowledge for yourself rather than relying on rote memorization of fixed rules or information supplied. As a beginner, you may be intimidated by the amount of knowledge you have to absorb or the level of skill you need to attain. You may sometimes feel like a total fool when you speak up in class. However, as long as you are willing to venture out to explore this new language and culture and use it whenever you can (e.g., greeting your classmates in Chinese, writing a note to your teacher in pinyin, etc.), you will find yourself picking up the language in good time. As long as you are not afraid of making mistakes and are willing to take initiatives to test your own hypothesis, perhaps hundreds of times, you can master Chinese some day.

    As the subtitle of our books suggests, the cognitive aspect of language learning is emphasized. We do not want you to learn the language through passive reception and memorization of presented information and rules. There are, actually, many roads leading to the success of learning Chinese if you put in your own creative efforts and take on the challenge from many different angles and perspectives. We as textbook writers can design a wonderful stage and prepare intricate props for you to act upon; however, we cannot be the lead actors and actresses that all of you are in your study and your life.

2. **Be creative and playful**
    On the same note, you need to be creative with the learning tasks at hand so that you will not fall into the trap of thinking repetition alone will make magic. This is especially true with character learning. Although the traditional way of practicing writing in China is to copy characters as many times as possible, we want to encourage you to be different. Our experience tells us that you will learn and recall characters better if you can invent your own tricks and stories that facilitate character memorization.   To illustrate our points, we have provided visual

mnemonics throughout the books that may help register or anchor the image of a character in your mind. Remember that you are not studying the etymology of characters, though the knowledge of a character's history may deepen your understanding of the written language. You certainly do not have to be bound by the question of how each character originated. Your concern should be on how each character means or looks to you. Thus you should take your own notes and apply characters in a meaningful context.

In addition to being as creative as possible in all of your learning tasks, you need to be playful. We have found that a lighthearted attitude will ease any embarrassment you may bring upon yourself when you start practicing tones. A sense of humor will also help you through many frustrations that are part of your everyday life when you study Chinese. Certainly, the language is difficult, but you do not have to make it harder than it needs to be. If you can make things fun and relevant to you, we are sure you will be able to handle and even enjoy the many challenges that come with the study of Chinese. On this note, we encourage you to use the lesson dialogues and mini-dialogues as models, write your own skits, and role-play them in front of your class from time to time. If possible, you should also create a macro context for your study of Chinese, i.e., find a conversation partner, a pen pal, or a Chinese friend to make your study more meaningful and interesting.

3. **Be patient and realistic**
   By attempting to study a language as "foreign" or "difficult" as Chinese, you already possess an essential quality to be successful with your study—courage. However, there is another mindset that may contribute to your acquisition of the language: patience. This is particularly true with the study of characters if you have never been exposed to a nonalphabetic writing system before. As adult learners, you may understand and learn various grammatical structures quickly. Yet it is very unlikely that you can acquire many Chinese characters in a short time. In fact, the acquisition of characters will be painfully slow at the initial stage. You need to be patient and set a realistic goal for yourself. Your reading and writing competence probably won't progress at the same rate as your aural-oral skill. However, you should not avoid or delay the task of reading and writing and be content with your proficiency in listening and speaking.

In our books, we advocate the integrated practice of four language skills because we believe that all skills reinforce each other and because literacy skills are highly valued and respected in Chinese society. However, we also understand that the written language puts an enormous burden on students. Therefore we highlight twenty characters in each lesson to help you focus your study. We also enrich the vocabulary section with many useful and relevant lexical items so that you have enough words to communicate aural-orally in Chinese. If you prioritize the learning tasks and do not expect to "cram," over time you will acquire a base on which you can rapidly build and refine important skills in the future.

4. Be disciplined and flexible

The study of Chinese will test not only your patience but also your perseverance. You may be patient and realistic in terms of the goals you set for yourself. However, you also need to be disciplined in terms of the approach you take to studying the language. Using the study of characters as an example, if you want to learn twenty characters over five days, you have to study four per day; better still, you need to build a system of review for yourself. Without a disciplined approach, you will find yourself spending much time ineffectively and not making the most of your study. Passion and enthusiasm may get you started in your study of Chinese; however, it takes discipline to get you to the level of proficiency you desire.

You need to be aware that discipline does not imply that you have to be rigid. Rather, we encourage you to be flexible, especially in arranging your study schedule. Instead of spending three straight hours studying Chinese, it may be more effective for you to practice the language for shorter periods two or three times per day, making use of the odd hours that many of us find when we wait for a bus or a class, when we take an afternoon break, when we retire in the evening, etc.

5. Be tolerant and receptive

To be able to study Chinese well, it is also crucial for you to be tolerant of and receptive to differences, be they linguistic or cultural. You may feel disoriented or confused at the beginning, given the amount of differences between your native language and Chinese. And it is more than natural that you resort to your own culture and use it as a frame of reference to understand and interpret Chinese ways. Eventually you want to see things in the light of Chinese people and to obtain an insider's perspective. In this regard, our cultural notes may offer some assistance. You will certainly add many more notes of your own as you make contact with Chinese people and their culture.

It is important that you be tolerant not only of differences but also of ambiguities. In other words, it is best for you to study a lexical item or a grammatical structure in its context and to accept the fuzziness that sometimes comes with it. We have seen students who are so concerned with every single detail at each step of their study that their general comprehension suffers because of their hair-splitting efforts. If you can analyze the Chinese language system, that is fine. Yet it will prove to be far more productive if you learn to take in chunk of information rather than isolated details. The more you study Chinese, the better you will understand the significance of contextual cues, which play an important role in the use of this language.

6. Be resourceful and responsive

We can offer only a few general suggestions to guide your study of Chinese and provide only a limited number of exercises to help reinforce and consolidate your skills and understanding. You need to be resourceful and responsive to the questions and problems that emerge during your study of Chinese. You need to apply different learning strategies to various tasks and to identify or invent options and means to apply, internalize, and acquire this new language.

Abbreviations

Adj	Adjective	形容詞	xíngróngcí
Adv	Adverb	副詞	fùcí
Asp	Aspect Suffix	體貌詞尾	tǐmàocíwěi
AuxV	Auxiliary Verb	助動詞	zhùdòngcí
Comp	Complement	補語	bǔyǔ
Conj	Conjunction	連詞	liáncí
CV	Co-verb	輔動詞	fǔdòngcí
Dem	Demonstrative	指示詞	zhǐshìcí
Det	Determinative	定詞	dìngcí
EV	Equative Verb	對等動詞	duìděngdòngcí
Inter	Interjection	嘆詞	tàncí
IE	Idiomatic Expression	成語/習慣用語	chéngyǔ/xíguàn yòngyǔ
Loc	Localizer	方位詞	fāngwèicí
M	Measure Word	量詞	liàngcí
MA	Movable Adverb	可移副詞	kěyí fùcí
MTA	Movable Time Adverb	可移時間副詞	kěyí shíjiān fùcí
N	Noun	名詞	míngcí
Neg	Negative	否定詞	fǒudìngcí
No	Number	數詞	shùcí
NP	Noun Phrase	名詞	míngcí
O	Object	名詞詞組	míngcí cízǔ
O$_d$/O$_i$	Direct/indirect Object	直接/間接賓語	zhíjiē/jiānjiē bīnyǔ
Part	Particle	語助詞	yǔzhùcí
Place	Place Word	地方詞	dìfāngcí
Poss	Possesive	所有格	suǒyǒugé
PP	Prepositional Phrase	介詞詞組	jiècícízǔ
Pref	Prefix	詞頭	cítóu
P(rep)	Preposition	介詞	jiècí
Prog	Progressive Suffix	進行式詞尾	jìnxíngshì cíwěi
Pron	Pronoun	代名詞	dàimíngci
QW	Question Word	疑問詞	yíwèncí
QP	Question Particle	疑問語助詞	yíwèn yǔzhùcí
RE	Resultative Verb Ending	結果動詞補語	jiéguǒ dòngcí bǔyǔ
RV	Resultative Verb	結果動詞	jiéguǒ dòngcí
S	Subject	主詞	zhǔcí
SN	Surname	姓	xìng
Suf	Suffix	詞尾	cíwěi
SV	Stative Verb	靜態動詞	jìngtài dòngcí
TW	Time Word	時間詞	shíjiāncí
V	Verb	動詞	dòngcí
VO	Verb-Object Compound	動賓複詞	dòngbīn fùcí

Conventions

◎	This icon marks two subsections of Vocabulary in each lesson —one groups new words by their order of appearance in the main dialogue and the other by their grammatical categories.
✚	This icon introduces the subsection Supplementary Vocabulary in each lesson.
*	This symbol, in front of entries in the Vocabulary and Characters sections, calls the learner's attention to lexical items not used in the main dialogues but relevant to those used and possibly of interest for further study.
Ⓐ	This icon points out the first Grammar subsection, Major Sentence Patterns.
Ⓑ	This icon points out the second Grammar subsection, Usage of Common Phrases.
Ⓒ	This icon points out the third Grammar subsection, Reentry, the review of some major sentence patterns.
☼	This icon marks essential information and concise explanations for grammatical points.
↻	This icon indicates cross-references to grammatical points.
✗	This icon calls attention to commonly made errors or incorrect sentence formation.
👥	This icon, pointing to various mini-dialogues, highlights the major communication functions in each lesson.
今 jīn now 4 人 (person)	character the pronunciation of the character the meaning of the character the stroke number of the character radical the meaning of the radical

Cast of Characters
人物表 Rénwùbiǎo

高德中

	David Gore (Gāo Dézhōng)	
美國人	Měiguórén	American
研究生	Yánjiūshēng	Graduate student
專業：比較文學	Zhuānyè: bǐjiǎo wénxué	Major: Comparative Literature
年紀：二十七歲	Niánjì: èrshíqī suì	Age: 27
性別：男	Xìngbié: nán	Sex: male
個性：穩重、老實	Gèxìng: wěnzhòng, lǎoshí	Personality: focused
愛好：讀書、看電影	Aìhào: dúshū, kàn diànyǐng	Hobbies: studying, watching movies

高德中

李明

	Lǐ Míng	
中國人（大陸）	Zhōngguórén	Chinese (from the mainland)
大學生（大三）	Dàxuéshēng (dà sān)	Undergraduate (junior)
專業：商學	Zhuānyè: shāngxué	Major: Business
年紀：二十二歲	Niánjì: èrshí'èr suì	Age: 22
性別：男	Xìngbié: nán	Sex: male
個性：外向、好動	Gèxìng: wàixiàng, hàodòng	Personality: outgoing
愛好：旅行、拍照、美食	Aìhào: lǔxíng, pāizhào, měishí	Hobbies: traveling, photography, food

李明

林美英

林美英	Lín Měiyīng	
華裔美國人	Huáyì Měiguórén	Chinese American
大學生（大二）	Dàxuéshēng (dà'èr)	Undergraduate (sophomore)
專業：音樂	Zhuānyè: yīnyuè	Major: Music
年紀：二十歲	Niánjì: èrshí suì	Age: 20
性別：女	Xìngbié: nǚ	Sex: female
個性：外向、活潑	Gèxìng: wàixiàng, huópō	Personality: outgoing, active
愛好：唱歌、跳舞、運動	Aìhào: chànggē, tiàowǔ, yùndòng	Hobbies: singing, dancing, exercising

王華

王華	Wáng Huá	
中國人（台灣）	Zhōngguórén (Táiwān)	Chinese (from Taiwan)
大學生（大一）	Dàxuéshēng (dà'yī)	Undergraduate (freshman)
專業：電腦	Zhuānyè: diànnǎo	Major: Computer Science
年紀：十九歲	Niánjì: shíjiǔ suì	Age: 19
性別：女	Xìngbié: nǚ	Sex: female
個性：內向、文靜	Gèxìng: nèixiàng, wénjìng	Personality: reserved
愛好：看電視、球賽	Aìhào: kàn diànshì, qiúsài	Hobbies: watching TV, playing sports

第一課　緒論

Lesson 1. Introduction

I. The Chinese Language and Dialects

China, a multinational state, has fifty-six ethnic groups, each living within its own boundaries and each with its own language. Linguists have divided the languages spoken in China into several families.

Language	Where Spoken
1. Sino-Tibetan family (Indo-Chinese family) 漢藏語族 Hànzàng yǔzú: Chinese (or 漢語 Hànyǔ) Kam-Tai Miao-Yao Tibeto-Burman	 Throughout China Guangxi and Guizhou Hunan, Guizhou, Guangxi, Sichuan, Yunnan, and Guangdong Xizang (Tibet), Qinghai, and Sichuan
2. Austro-Asiatic family 南亞語族 Nányà yǔzú: Mon-Khmer	 Yunnan and Burma border
3. Altaic family 阿爾泰語族 A'ěrtài yǔzú: Turkish Mongolian Tunguz	 Xinjiang Inner Mongolia Heilongjiang, Jilin, and Liaoning
4. Indo-European family 印歐語族 In'ōu yǔzú: Tocharian (extinct)	 Formerly in Xinjiang
5. Austronesian family 南島語族 Nándǎo yǔzú: Polynesian Micronesian Melanesian Indonesian	 East Pacific islands West Pacific islands South Pacific islands Malaysia, Cham (Vietnam), Philippines, and Taiwan

As of 1992, the population of the People's Republic of China (the mainland; hereafter PRC) was 1,133,680,000. Of this number, 1,042,480,000 (92%) were Han-Chinese, or native speakers of Chinese dialects. Only 91,200,000 (8%) were non-Chinese, or non-Hànyǔ, speakers. [1] Within the Chinese language family, there are eight major dialect groups.

---

[1] The population figures are from 聯合報 *Lianhebao*, January 6, 1992.

Chinese Dialect 漢語方言 Hànyǔ fāngyán[2]	Population %	Where Spoken
1. Mandarin (the official language) 官話 Guānhuà: Northern Mandarin 北方官話 Běifāng Guānhuà	68.0	Hebei, Shanxi, Shaanxi, Gansu, Henan, Shandong, Xinjiang, Inner Mongolia, Heilongjiang, Jilin, Liaoning, Anhui, Qinghai, and Jiangsu
Eastern Mandarin 下江官話 Xiàjiāng Guānhuà		Anhui, Jiangsu
Southwestern Mandarin 西南官話 Xīnán Guānhuà		Sichuan, Yunnan, Guizhou, Hubei, and Guangxi
2. Wú 吳語 Wúyǔ	8.0	Zhejiang, Jiangsu, and part of Anhui, Jiangxi and Fujian
3. Hakka 客家話/客語 Kèjiāhuà/ Kèyǔ	4.3	Jiangxi, Guangdong, Taiwan, and Fujian
4. Gàn 贛語 Gànyǔ	1.7	Jiangxi and Guangdong
5. Mǐn 閩語 Mǐnyǔ: N. Mǐn 閩北 Mǐnběi	1.0	Northern part of Fujian
S. Mǐn 閩南 Mǐnnán	2.0	Southern part of Fujian, Taiwan (and Southeast Asia)
6. Yuè 粵語 Yuèyǔ (Cantonese)	5.0	Guangdong and Guangxi (and Southeast Asia, North America)
7. Xiāng 湘語 Xiāngyǔ	5.0	Hunan and Hubei
8. Other isolated groups		

The major Chinese dialects are all very different. The difference between any two dialects is as great as that between English and French; thus the dialects are mutually unintelligible.

---

[2] We have simplified the groupings of Chinese dialects here for introductory purposes. Those who want to know more about detailed subgroupings of the Chinese dialects may refer to Ramsey (1987), Norman (1988), and Wang (1991). See Appendix 5, Bibliography.

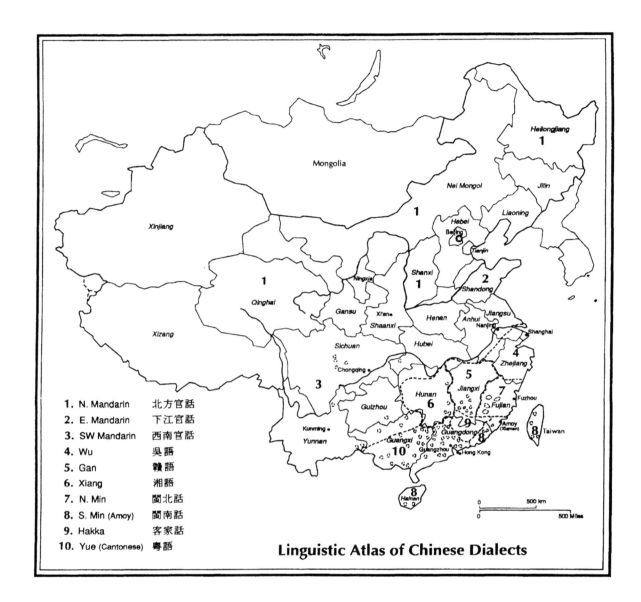

1. N. Mandarin	北方官話
2. E. Mandarin	下江官話
3. SW Mandarin	西南官話
4. Wu	吳語
5. Gan	贛語
6. Xiang	湘語
7. N. Min	閩北話
8. S. Min (Amoy)	閩南話
9. Hakka	客家話
10. Yue (Cantonese)	粵語

Linguistic Atlas of Chinese Dialects

II. Characteristics of the Chinese Language
Even though the spoken forms of Chinese dialects are remarkably different, several characteristics are shared by all dialects.

1. Chinese is a tonal language.

    Chinese is a language which uses pitch (音高 yīngāo) to distinguish different morphemes (語位 yǔwèi—a minimal unit of speech that is recurrent and meaningful). For example, 媽 mā (mother), 麻 má (hemp), 馬 mǎ (horse), 罵 mà (to scold).

2. Chinese is a monosyllabic language.

   In Chinese, the smallest meaningful unit (morpheme) is a single syllable. For example, 圖書館 túshūguǎn 'library' is a noun which consists of three syllables, where each syllable has its own lexical meaning: 圖 tú means 'chart or picture,' 書 shū means 'book,' and 館 guǎn means 'hall.'

3. Chinese is an analytic (or isolating) language.

   Typologically, Chinese is an analytic or isolating language in which each word consists of just one morpheme and cannot be further divided into component parts. Its grammatical relationships are indicated by using auxiliary words or word order. For example, 狗咬人 gǒu yǎo rén means 'Dogs bite people,' while 人咬狗 rén yǎo gǒu means 'People bite dogs.'

4. Chinese is a noninflectional language.

   Chinese does not undergo internal change; no prefixes or suffixes are used to indicate grammatical relationships as in English. Declensions are not used in Chinese nouns; for example, 書 shū can mean 'book' or 'books.' Also Chinese verbs are not inflected; for example, 買 mǎi can mean 'to buy,' 'buys,' or 'bought.'

5. The basic word order of Chinese is Subject-Verb-Object.

   The basic word order of Chinese is Subject-Verb-Object (SVO); however, modern Chinese is evolving from an SVO to an SOV word order.

6. The modifier precedes the modified.

   In Mandarin Chinese, the modifier usually comes before the thing modified. For example, 好 hǎo 'good' modifies 人 rén 'people' in 好人 hǎorén 'good people,' and 好 hǎo 'good' is modified by 很 hěn 'very' in 很好 hěn hǎo 'very good.'

7. The use of measure words (classifiers) with numerals is obligatory.

   When counting things in Chinese, numerals must be combined with measure words (classifiers) in order to modify nouns. For example, 一本書 yì běn shū means 'one book,' while 三個人 sān .ge rén means 'three people.'

8. Chinese is a topic-dominant language.

   Analysis of many sentence structures shows that Chinese people tend to present the topic that they are going to talk about first, then comment on it. For example, 煙我不抽 yān wǒ bù chōu '[As for] cigarettes, I don't smoke' —'I don't smoke cigarettes'; 酒我喝 jiǔ wǒ hē '[As for] wine, I drink'—'I drink wine.'

III. Variations of "Standard Chinese"

The three subdialects of Mandarin (Northern, Eastern, and Southwestern) are mutually intelligible. The Northern Mandarin pronunciation, or Beijing dialect (北京 Peking), was officially chosen as "standard Chinese" by the government in the 1930s because Mandarin speakers make up most of the population. Currently, "standard Chinese" is called 普通話 Pǔtōnghuà 'the common language' in the PRC, while it is called 國語 Guóyǔ 'the national language' in Taiwan. Outside of China proper, "standard Chinese" is called 中文 Zhōngwén 'the Chinese language,' or 華語 Huáyǔ 'the Chinese language.'

Because of the influence of local dialects, regional variations exist in the different forms of "standard Chinese." For example, in Beijing, "standard Chinese" is characterized by retroflex consonants ("r" sounds), while "standard Mandarin" in Taiwan, where Southern Min 閩南話 Mǐnnánhuà 'Amoy or Hokkien' is widely spoken, has no "r" sound because the local dialect is dominated by alveolar consonants. As a result, a merging of retroflex and alveolar consonants has occurred in Taiwanese Standard Mandarin, which is sometimes called 臺灣國語 Táiwān Guóyǔ. However, the different versions of "standard Chinese" (PRC and Taiwan) are still mutually intelligible and students of "standard Chinese" must be prepared to be exposed to "standard Chinese" with an accent. Since 1949, because of the different political and social developments in the PRC and Taiwan, some different usages or tones in vocabulary as well as idiomatic expressions have been found.

Despite these differences, the basic structures and vocabulary forms of "standard Mandarin" are largely the same, so you need not worry too much about the discrepancy. However, for the sake of convenience, we will hereafter refer to "standard Chinese" by the generic term "Chinese" because standard Chinese is the instructional language of all schools in China (in both the PRC and Taiwan), the United States, and the world.

Lesson 2. The Chinese Sound System

I. Overview

In the Chinese sound system, the components of a syllable are traditionally illustrated in the following way.

tone 聲調			
initial 聲母 (consonant)	final 韻母		
	medial 介音 (vowel on-glide)	rhyme 韻	
		nucleus (main vowel) 主要元音	coda 韻尾 (vowel off-glide/ nasal ending)

There are four basic tones (四聲 sìshēng), one neutral tone (輕聲 qīngshēng), twenty-one consonant initials (聲母 shēngmǔ) and thirty-six finals (韻母 yùnmǔ). Each final includes a medial (介音 jièyīn), a nucleus or main vowel (主要元音 zhǔyào yuányīn), and a coda (韻尾 yùnwěi). Among the components of a syllable, only the tone and main vowel are obligatory; the others are optional. In this text we use 漢語拼音 Hànyǔ Pīnyīn (the spelling system of Chinese), the official romanization implemented by the PRC government, which has also been adopted by the United Nations and the majority of countries in the world. Tables of spelling systems are provided merely as symbols and tools for learning Chinese pronunciation; they are not Chinese. When you use the appendixes for reference, it is important to remember, though, that all the spelling systems are aids to learning. Try to associate the spellings with Chinese sounds; do not think of them in English (or whatever your native language is).

Note: You are not expected to learn Chinese sounds in one lesson—or even in one year. But with repeated practice and use, in time you will be able to speak the language and be understood.

II. Tones

The four tones in Chinese are commonly called: 第一聲 dìyīshēng (first tone, hereafter 1T) , 第二聲 dìèrshēng (second tone, hereafter 2T), 第三聲 dìsānshēng (third tone, hereafter 3T), and 第四聲 dìsìshēng (fourth tone, hereafter 4T). Following Yuen-ren Chao (1933, 1968), the tone values (pitch) of these tones can be represented by the following graph and by the tone marks in the table.

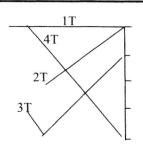

5 High pitch

4 Mid-high pitch

3 Middle pitch

2 Mid-low pitch

1 Low pitch

The vertical line stands for the pitch range of each person, starting from point 1 and going to point 5; the slant line or contour line stands for the pitch direction.

Table 1

Tone	Description	Pitch	Tone Mark	Example	Gloss
1T 第一聲 dìyīshēng	High-level	55	ā	mā 媽	mother
2T 第二聲 dìèrshēng	High-rising	35	á	má 麻	hemp
3T 第三聲 dìsānshēng	Low-dipping	214	ǎ	mǎ 馬	horse
4T 第四聲 dìsìshēng	High-falling	51	à	mà 罵	to scold
NT (輕聲) qīngshēng	Varies		.a	.ma 嗎	(interrogative particle)

The first tone's pitch starts at 5 (the highest point of your pitch range) and ends at 5. It is like the "ah" sound you make in a high pitch when a doctor checks your throat. The symbol for the first tone is a straight line placed above the main vowel, e.g., [ā].

The second tone's pitch starts at 3 (the midpoint of your pitch range), goes upward, and ends at 5. It is like "Mom" when you say it in a disbelieving or questioning manner. The symbol for the second tone is a slant line placed above the main vowel, e.g., [má].

The third tone's pitch starts at 2 (the second lowest point of your pitch range), falls to the lowest point of your pitch range, then goes upward to 4 (the second highest point of your pitch range). It is like "Mom" when you say it in a disapproving manner. The symbol for the third tone is a check mark placed above the main vowel, e.g., [mǎ].

The fourth tone's pitch starts at 5 and drops to 1 (the lowest point of your pitch range). It is like "No!" said to a child. The symbol for the fourth tone is a reverse slant line placed above the main vowel, e.g [mà].

Neutral tones (NT) are not stressed and have a short pitch range. The pitch of the neutral tone varies depending on the tones preceding it. A rule of thumb: When a neutral tone follows a half third tone, its pitch is high; when it follows other tones, its pitch is relatively low. (For an explanation of the half third tone, see section V of this lesson.)

Note: All tone marks are placed above the main vowel in a syllable. If a syllable has a medial /i/, /u/, or /yu/, the tone mark is placed above the following vowel, e.g., [xià, huā, yuè]. If a syllable doesn't have a medial, the tone mark is placed on the first vowel, e.g., [kāi, gěi, zǒu]. Neutral tones are marked with a dot (as in .ma) placed in front of the unstressed syllable, e.g., [wǒ.men], [tā.de].

III. Initials

The twenty-one consonant initials are as follows.

Table 2

	Type	Initial				
1	Labials/labiodental	b	p	m	f	
2	Alveolars	d	t	n	l	
3	Velars	g	k		h	
4	Alveolar affricates/fricative	z	c		s	
5	Retroflex affricates/fricative	zh	ch		sh	r
6	Palatal affricates/fricative	j	q		x	

They are classified into six main types.

Type 1. Bilabial Stops, Nasal and Labiodental Fricatives

Table 3

Hanyu Pinyin	IPA[1]	English Pronunciation Key
b	p	"p" as in "spy," but an unaspirated and voiceless "p"
p	p'	"p" as in "pie," but an aspirated and voiceless "p"
m	m	"m" as in "mother"
f	f	"f" in "father"

The symbol /b/ represents an *unaspirated voiceless* bilabial stop (不送氣雙唇清塞音 búsòngqì shuāngchún qīngsèyīn) and is equivalent to the [p] sound after the [s] in English words starting with "sp-."

The symbol /p/ is an *aspirated voiceless* bilabial stop (送氣雙唇清塞音 sòngqì shuāngchún qīngsèyīn) and is equivalent to the English [p'] sound in the word-initial position. It is produced with the release of a puff of air.

A. Examples

		Unaspirated			Aspirated	
八	bā	eight	趴	pā	to lie on one's face
拔	bá	to pull	爬	pá	to crawl
把	bǎ	to hold	跑	pǎo	to run
爸	bà	father	怕	pà	(to be) afraid

---

[1] International Phonetic Alphabet.

The symbols /m/ and /f/ are similar to their English counterparts. The symbol /m/ represents a bilabial nasal (雙唇鼻音 shuāngchún bíyīn), and the symbol /f/ represents a voiceless labiodental fricative (唇齒清擦音 chúnchǐ qīngcāyīn).

B. Examples

貓	māo	cat	飛	fēi	to fly
毛	máo	hair	肥	féi	(to be) fat
買	mǎi	to buy	匪	fěi	bandits
賣	mài	to sell	費	fèi	fee

Type 2. Alveolar Stops, Nasal and Lateral

Table 4

Hanyu Pinyin	IPA	English Pronunciation Key
d	t	"t" as in "steak," but an unaspirated and voiceless "t"
t	t'	"t" as in "take," but an aspirated and voiceless "t"
n	n	"n" as in "nice"
l	l	"l" as in "light"

The symbol /d/ represents an *unaspirated voiceless* alveolar stop (不送氣舌尖清塞音 búsòngqì shéjiān qīngsèyīn) and is equivalent to the [t] sound after the [s] in English words starting with "st-."

The symbol /t/ represents an *aspirated voiceless* alveolar stop (送氣舌尖清塞音 sòngqì shéjiān qīngsèyīn) which is equivalent to the English [t'] sound in the word-initial position. It is produced with the release of a puff of air.

A. Examples

	Unaspirated			Aspirated	
搭	dā	to build	他	tā	he, him, she, her, it
達	dá	to reach	談	tán	to talk
打	dǎ	to hit	塔	tǎ	pagoda
大	dà	(to be) big	踏	tà	to tread

The symbol /n/ represents an alveolar nasal (舌尖鼻音 shéjiān bíyīn) which is similar to its English counterpart. The symbol /l/ represents an alveolar lateral (舌尖邊音 shéjiān biānyīn) and is equivalent to the English [l] sound in the word initial position.

In Chinese, there is no "dark" [l] sound like the one that occurs in word-middle position in English (e.g., the [l] sound in 'little').

B. Examples

那	nā	a Chinese surname	拉	lā	to pull
拿	ná	to hold in hand	拉	lá	to cut
哪	nǎ	which?	喇	lǎ	trumpet
那	nà	that	辣	là	(to be) hot (of taste)

Type 3. Velar Stops and Fricatives

Table 5

Hanyu Pinyin	IPA	English Pronunciation Key
g	k	"k" as in "ski," but an unaspirated and voiceless "k"
k	k'	"k" as in 'key," but an aspirated and voiceless "k"
h	x	"h" as in "house"

The symbol /g/ represents an *unaspirated voiceless* velar stop (不送氣舌根清塞音 búsòngqì shégēn qīngsèyīn) and is equivalent to the [k] sound after the [s] in English words starting with "sk-."

The symbol /k/ represents an *aspirated voiceless* velar stop (送氣舌根清塞音 sòngqì shégēn qīngsèyīn) and is equivalent to the English [k'] sound in the word-initial position. It is produced with the release of a puff of air.

A. Examples

		Unaspirated			Aspirated
瓜	guā	melons	誇	kuā	to brag
古	gǔ	(to be) ancient	苦	kǔ	bitter
怪	guài	(to be) strange	快	kuài	(to be) quick

The symbol /h/ represents a velar fricative (舌根清擦音 shégēn qīngcāyīn) and is equivalent to the [h] sound in Enlgish words, such as "house" and " how."

B. Examples

		Unrounded			Rounded
黑	hēi	black	灰	huī	ash, gray
痕	hén	a stain	回	huí	to return
很	hěn	very	悔	huǐ	to regret
恨	hèn	to hate	會	huì	to know how

Type 4. Alveolar Affricates and Fricatives

Table 6

Hanyu Pinyin	IPA	English Pronunciation Key
z	ts	"ds" as in "cur<u>ds</u>," but voiceless and unaspirated
c	ts'	"ts" as in "ca<u>ts</u>"
s	s	"s" as in "<u>s</u>ay"

The symbol /z/ represents an *unaspirated voiceless* alveolar affricate (不送氣舌尖塞輕擦音 búsòngqì shéjiān qīngsècāyīn) and is equivalent to the "ds" in "cur<u>ds</u>," but it is voiceless (without the vibration of the vocal cords).

The symbol /c/ represents an *aspirated voiceless* alveolar affricate (送氣舌尖塞擦音 sòngqì shéjiān qīng sècāyīn) and is equivalent to the "ts" in "ca<u>ts</u>." It is produced with a puff of air.

A. Examples

Unrounded and unaspirated			Unrounded and aspirated		
資	zī	capital	疵	cī	flaw
子	zǐ	son, child	此	cǐ	this
早	zǎo	early	草	cǎo	grass

B. Examples

Rounded and unaspirated			Rounded and aspirated		
租	zū	to rent	粗	cū	coarse
坐	zuò	to sit	錯	cuò	(to be) wrong
最	zuì	the most	脆	cuì	(to be) crispy

The symbol /s/ represents a *voiceless* alveolar fricative (舌尖清擦音 shéjiān qīngcāyīn) and is equivalent to the "s" sound in "<u>s</u>ay."

C. Examples

Unrounded			Rounded		
思	sī	to think	酥	sū	crumbly
四	sì	four	宿	sù	to lodge
散	sàn	to disperse	算	suàn	to calculate

Type 5. Retroflex Affricates and Fricatives

Table 7

Hanyu Pinyin	IPA	English Pronunciation Key
zh	tʂ	"j" as in "jerk," but with the tip of the tongue curled farther back
ch	tʂ'	"ch" as in "church," but with the tip of the tongue curled farther back
sh	ʂ	"sh" as in "shirt," but with the tip of the tongue curled farther back
r	ʐ	"r" as in the "ring," but with lips unrounded, and the tip of the tongue curled farther back. Always pronounce the Chinese /r/ sound with a nice smile!

The symbol /zh/ represents an *unaspirated voiceless* retroflex affricate (不送氣捲 舌塞擦音 búsòngqì juǎnshé sècāyīn) and is equivalent to the "j" in "jerk," but with the tip of the tongue curled farther back.

The symbol /ch/ represents an *aspirated voiceless* retroflex affricate (送氣捲舌塞擦 音 sòngqì juǎnshé sècāyīn) and is equivalent to the "ch" sound in "church," but the tip of the tongue is curled farther back. It is produced with a puff of air.

A. Examples

Unrounded and unaspirated

知	zhī	to know		吃	chī	to eat
直	zhí	(to be) straight		遲	chí	(to be) late
只	zhǐ	only		齒	chǐ	tooth
制	zhì	a system		赤	chì	red

Unrounded and aspirated (column header over right group)

B. Examples

Rounded and unaspirated

豬	zhū	pig		出	chū	to go out
竹	zhú	bamboo		廚	chú	kitchen
煮	zhǔ	to cook		楚	chǔ	(to be) clear
住	zhù	to live		處	chù	place

Rounded and aspirated (column header over right group)

The symbol /sh/ represents a *voiceless* retroflex fricative (捲舌清擦音 juǎnshé qīngcāyīn) which is equivalent to the "sh" sound in "shirt," but with the tip of the tongue curled farther back.

C. Examples

	Unrounded			Rounded	
師	shī	teacher	書	shū	books
十	shí	ten	熟	shú	cooked
史	shǐ	history	暑	shǔ	the heat of summer
是	shì	to be	數	shù	number

The symbol /r/ represents a *voiced* retroflex fricative (捲舌濁擦音 juǎnshé zhuócāyīn) and is equivalent to the "r" sound in "ring," but the tip of the tongue is curled farther back with the lips *unrounded*. **Note**: Always pronounce the Chinese "r" sound with a nice *smile*. The only exception is when "r" precedes rounded vowel /o/ or /u/; then you should pronounce the "r" with lip rounding because of its assimilation to the following sound.

D. Examples

	Unrounded			Rounded	
日	rì	sun, day	容	róng	to allow
人	rén	people, man	柔	róu	(to be) gentle
忍	rěn	to endure	肉	ròu	meat, flesh
熱	rè	(to be) hot	如	rú	as
認	rèn	to recognize	入	rù	to enter
然	rán	still, however	軟	ruǎn	(to be) soft

A rule of thumb: Whenever you see a word spelled with *a consonant plus an "h,"* curl the tip of your tongue before you say the whole word. When you pronounce these four retroflex sounds, always curl the tip of your tongue as you do when you pronounce the /-er/ sound in English.

Type 6. Palatal Affricates and Fricatives

Table 8

Hanyu Pinyin	IPA	English Pronunciation Key
j	tɕ	"j" in "Jesus"
q	tɕ'	"ch" in "cheese"
x	ɕ	"s" in "see"

The symbol /j/ represents an *unaspirated voiceless* palatal affricate (不送氣舌面塞擦音 búsòngqì shémiàn sècāyīn) and is equivalent to the "j" sound in "Jesus."

The symbol /q/ represents an *aspirated voiceless* palatal affricate (送氣舌面塞擦音 sòngqì shémiàn sècāyīn) and is equivalent to the "ch" sound in "cheese."

A. Examples

Unrounded and unaspirated	Unrounded and aspirated

機	jī	machine	七	qī	seven
急	jí	(to be) urgent	奇	qí	(to be) strange
幾	jǐ	how many?	起	qǐ	to raise
寄	jì	to send	氣	qì	air

B. Examples

Rounded and unaspirated	Rounded and aspirated

居	jū	to reside	區	qū	district
橘	jú	tangerine	渠	qú	a ditch
舉	jǔ	to lift	娶	qǔ	to take a wife
句	jù	sentence	去	qù	to go

The symbol /x/ represents a *voiceless* palatal fricative (舌面擦音 shémiàn cāyīn) and is equivalent to the "s" sound in "<u>s</u>ee."

C. Examples

Unrounded	Rounded

西	xī	west	需	xū	to need
習	xí	to learn	徐	xú	a Chinese surname
洗	xǐ	to wash	許	xǔ	to permit; a Chinese surname
系	xì	(college) department	續	xù	to continue

Note: When pronouncing these three sounds, always place the front blade of your tongue against the hard palate and keep the tip of your tongue against the edge of your lower teeth.

IV. Finals (韻母 yùnmǔ)

The thirty-six finals are as follows.

Table 9

	Medial	Ending					
		Zero	*-i*	*-o/-u*	*-n*	*-ng*	*-r*
1	*Zero*	-i a e	ai ei	ao ou	an en	ang eng ong	er
2	*-i-*	i ia ie	iai	iao iu	ian in	iang ing iong	
3	*-u-*	u ua uo	uai ui		uan un	uang ueng	
4	*-ü-*	ü üe			üan ün		

They are classified into five main types. Some finals undergo phonetic changes under certain conditions.

Type 1. Single Vowels (單元音 dānyuányīn)

Table 10

Hanyu Pinyin	IPA	English Pronunciation Key
i, y-, yi	i	"ee" as in "s<u>ee</u>"
u, w-, wu	u	"oo" as in "w<u>oo</u>l"
ü, yu, yu-	y	"y" as in "<u>Y</u>vonne"
a	a	"a" as in "f<u>a</u>r"
o	o	"o" as in "h<u>o</u>e," the Chinese "o" is a single vowel
e	ɤ	"u" as in "<u>u</u>p," but with a little higher tongue position
e	e	"a" as in "ch<u>a</u>se"

When /i/ follows the consonant initials /z, c, or s/, it is pronounced as the prolonged /z, c, or s/, with the lips slightly spread. When /i/ follows the retroflex initials /zh, ch, sh, or r/, it is pronounced as the prolonged /zh, ch, sh, or r/, with the tip of the tongue curled back throughout the whole syllable. Elsewhere, the vowels /i/, /y-/, and /yi/ are all pronounced as an unrounded high front vowel [i] (展唇高前元音 zhǎnchún gāo qiányuányīn) and are equivalent to the "ee" sound in "s<u>ee</u>." The difference in the spelling depends on the sound's position in the syllable. When /i/ occurs in syllable-initial position, it is spelled as /y-/ and can be followed by other vowel(s); when it stands alone as a syllable, it is spelled as /yi/.

The vowels /u/, /w-/, /wu/ are all pronounced as a rounded high back vowel [u] (圓唇高後元音 yuánchún gāo hòuyuányīn) and are equivalent to the "oo" sound in "w<u>oo</u>l." The difference in the spelling depends on the sound's position in the syllable. When /u/ occurs in syllable-initial position, it is spelled as /w-/ and can be followed by other vowel(s); when it stands alone as a syllable, it is spelled as /wu/.

A. Examples

筆	bǐ	pen	補	bǔ	to mend
一	yī	one	屋	wū	house, room
頁	yè	page	味	wèi	taste
煙	yān	cigarette	灣	wān	bay

The vowels /ü/, /yu-/, and /yu/ are all pronounced as a rounded high front vowel [y] (圓唇高前元音 yuánchún gāo qiányuányīn) and are equivalent to the "y" sound in "<u>Y</u>vonne." The difference in the spelling depends on the sound's position in the syllable. When /ü/ follows consonant /j, q, x/, it is spelled as /u/. When it occurs in syllable-initial position, it is spelled as /yu/ if it stands alone as a syllable; it is spelled as /yu-/ if it is followed by other vowel(s). **Note:** Since there is no rounded high front vowel [y] sound in English, this sound is quite difficult for beginners. To practice this sound on your own, hold your tongue in the same position as you pronounce an [i]

sound and just round your lips. Or you can prolong the "sh" of the "shush" sound.
Two dots are written over /u/ only after /l/ and /n/, where they are needed to
distinguish /lu/ and /nu/ from /lü/ and /nü/.

B. Examples

雨	yǔ	rain	曲	qǔ	song
月	yuè	moon, month	確	què	firmly
雲	yún	cloud	裙	qún	skirt
居	jū	to inhabit	需	xū	to need
覺	jué	to feel	學	xué	to learn
俊	jùn	handsome	訊	xùn	information
卷	juàn	test paper	選	xuǎn	to choose

The symbol /o/ represents a rounded mid-high back vowel [o] (圓唇半高後元音
yuánchún bàngāo hòuyuányīn) and is similar to the "o" sound in "hoe," but it is a
single vowel, not a diphthong. However, /o/ never occurs alone; it is always either
preceded or followed by /u/. **Note:** When /o/ occurs after the bilabial/labiodental
consonants /b, p, m, f/, it represents a diphthong [uo].

C. Examples

	/o/ represents [o]			/o/ represents [uo]	
多	duō	many	撥	bō	to dial
都	dōu	all	波	pō	waves
狗	gǒu	dog	摸	mō	to touch
果	guǒ	fruit	佛	fó	Buddha

The symbol /e/ represents two sounds. (1) When it is preceded or followed by /i/ or
/y/, it represents an unrounded mid-high front vowel [e] (展唇半高前元音 zhǎnchún
bàn gāo qiányuányīn) and is pronounced like the "a" sound in "chase," but it is a single
vowel, not a diphthong. (2) When /e/ occurs alone or is preceded by other consonants,
it represents the unrounded mid-low back vowel [ɤ] (展唇半高後元音 zhǎnchún
bàngāo hòuyuányīn) and is pronounced like the "u" in "up," but with a little higher
tongue position.

D. Examples

	/e/ represents [e]			/e/ represents [ɤ] ʊ - up	
美	měi	(to be) pretty	鵝	é	goose
得	děi	must	餓	è	(to be) hungry
碟	dié	a small dish	哥	gē	older brother
寫	xiě	to write	德	dé	virtue
切	qiē	to cut	和	hé	and
缺	quē	to lack	課	kè	lesson
塞	sè	to stop	社	shè	society
責	zé	responsibility	折	zhé	to discount

Type 2. Diphthongs (複元音 fùyuányīn) and Finals without Medials

Table 11

Hanyu Pinyin	IPA	English Pronunciation Key
ai	ai	"I" as in "like"
ei	ei	"ay" as in "say"
ao	au	"ow" as in "how"
ou	ou	"o" as in "host"
an	an/	"an" as in "ant," but the Chinese vowel is lower
	ɛn	"en" as in "yen"
en	ən	"on" as in "London"
ang	aŋ	"ong" as in "tongue," but the Chinese vowel is lower
eng	əŋ	"eng" as in "length," but the Chinese vowel is higher and central
ong	ɔŋ	"ong" as in "thong"

A. Examples

愛	ài	to love	包	bāo	to wrap
臺	tái	platform	到	dào	to arrive
杯	bēi	cup	頭	tóu	head
給	gěi	to give	後	hòu	behind
談	tán	to talk	贈	zèng	to offer
漢	hàn	Han, Chinese	蒸	zhēng	to steam
很	hěn	very	湯	tāng	soup
本	běn	origin	當	dāng	ought to
森	sēn	forest	張	zhāng	a surname
身	shēn	body	昌	chāng	prosperous
怎	zěn	how	商	shāng	business
診	zhěn	to diagnose	中	zhōng	middle
曾	zēng	a surname	充	chōng	to fill
成	chéng	to complete	送	sòng	to deliver

Type 3. Triphthongs (三合元音 sānhéyuányīn) and Finals with Medial /i-/

Table 12

Hanyu Pinyin	IPA	English Pronunciation Key
ia, ya	ia	"ya" as in "yacht"
iao, yao	iau	"yahw" as in "Yahweh"
ie, ye	ie	"ye" as in "yes"
iu, you	iou	"you" as in "you," but the Chinese vowel is diphthong and longer
ian, yan	iɛn	"yen" as in "yen," but the Chinese vowel is lower
in, yin	in	"in" as in "inn"

iang, yang	iɑŋ	"yan" as in "Yankee"
ing, ying	iŋ	"ing" as in "sing"
iong, yong	yœŋ	"young" as in "young", but the Chinese vowel is lip-rounding and higher

When a syllable starts with an /i/ sound, then spell it as "y." When /iu/ stands alone as a syllable, then spell it as "you."

A. Examples

牙	yá	tooth	業	yè	profession
家	jiā	home	街	jiē	street
咬	yǎo	to bite	別	bié	don't
藥	yào	medicine	姐	jiě	older sister
小	xiǎo	little	鞋	xié	shoes
鳥	niǎo	bird	借	jiè	to borrow, to lend

B. Examples

		/iu/ represents [iou]			/you/ represents [iou]
流	liú	to flow	優	yōu	excellent
酒	jiǔ	wine, liqour	游	yóu	to swim
球	qiú	ball	有	yǒu	to have
休	xiū	to rest	又	yòu	again

C. Examples

年	nián	year	兩	liǎng	two
天	tiān	day, sky	想	xiǎng	to think
嚴	yán	(to be) strict	洋	yáng	ocean
今	jīn	today	講	jiǎng	to talk
民	mín	people	樣	yàng	pattern
音	yīn	sound	姓	xìng	surname
明	míng	bright	用	yòng	to use
應	yìng	to answer	窮	qióng	(to be) poor
影	yǐng	shadow	熊	xióng	bear

Type 4. Triphthongs (三合元音 sānhéyuányīn) and Finals with Medial /u-/

Table 13

Hanyu Pinyin	IPA	English Pronunciation Key
ua, wa	ua	"wa'" as in "Hawaii"
uo, wo	uo	"wa" as in "waltz"
uai, wai	uai	"wi" as in "wide"
ui, wei	uei	"way" as in "way"
uan, wan	uan	"won" as in "want," but the Chinese sound is fronted

un, wen	uən	"wen" as in "went," but the Chinese sound is higher and centered
uang, wang	uɑŋ	"won" as in "wonky"
ueng, weng	uəŋ	"wan" as in "wangler" but the Chinese sound is higher and centered

When a syllable starts with a /u/ sound, spell it as "w."
When /ui/ or /un/ stands alone as a syllable, spell it as "wei" or "wen."

A. Examples

花	huā	flower		我	wǒ	I, me
話	huà	language		握	wò	to grasp
挖	wā	to dig		筷	kuài	chopsticks
襪	wà	socks		壞	huài	(to be) bad
國	guó	country		歪	wāi	slanted
過	guò	to pass		外	wài	outside

B. Examples

/ui/ represents [uei] *way*

對	duì	(to be) correct		吹	chuī	to blow
醉	zuì	to be drunk		追	zhuī	to chase
脆	cuī *ts*	(to be) crispy		睡	shuì	to sleep
隨	suí	to follow		銳	ruì	(to be) sharp

C. Examples

/wei/ represents [uei]

危	wēi	(to be) dangerous
圍	wéi	to encircle
尾	wěi	tail
胃	wèi	stomach

D. Examples

專	zhuān	to specialize		彎	wān	curved
穿	chuān	to wear		玩	wán	to play
閂	shuān	to shut (the door)		晚	wǎn	(to be) late
短	duǎn	(to be) short		萬	wàn	ten thousands

E. Examples

	/un/ represents [uən]			/wen/ represents [uən]	
準	zhǔn	(to be) accurate	溫	wēn	(to be) warm
春	chūn	spring	文	wén	language
順	shùn	in the same direction	穩	wěn	(to be) stable
婚	hūn	marriage	問	wèn	to ask

F. Examples

黃	huáng	yellow, a surname	汪	wāng	deep and vast (ocean)
裝	zhuāng	to make up	王	wáng	king, a surname
床	chuáng	bed	網	wǎng	net
雙	shuāng	a pair	忘	wàng	to forget
翁	wēng	old man	甕	wèng	earthen jar

Type 5. Finals with Medial / ü-/~ /yu-/

Table 14

Hanyu Pinyin	IPA	English Pronunciation Key
üe, yue	ye	"y" as in "Yvonne" plus "e"
üan, yuan	yan	"y" as in "Yvonne" plus "an"
ün, yun	yn	"y" as in "Yvonne" plus "n"

When a syllable starts with a /ü/ sound, spell it as "yu."

A. Examples

	/üe/ represents [ye]			/yue/ represents [ye]	
決	jué	to decide	約	yuē	to make an appointment
雀	què	sparrow	樂	yuè	music
靴	xuē	boots	閱	yuè	to read
學	xué	to learn	越	yuè	to climb over

B. Examples

	/üan/ represents [yan]			/yuan/ represents [yan]	
捐	juān	to donate	冤	yuān	(to be) falsely accused
全	quán	(to be) complete	元	yuán	beginning; dollar
選	xuǎn	to choose	遠	yuǎn	(to be) far
倦	juàn	(to be) tired	院	yuàn	a courtyard

C. Examples

	/ün/ represents [yn]			/yun/ represents [yn]	
軍	jūn	military	暈	yūn	to feel dizzy
裙	qún	skirt	允	yǔn	to permit
訊	xùn	information	運	yùn	to move

Phonetic Changes of Retroflex Endings

In typical Beijing Mandarin, some words are pronounced with a diminutive suffix "-r" which is a part of the syllable ér 兒 and sounds like the "ur" in the English word "fur." When a syllable combines with the "-r" sound, the final word may undergo a phonetic change because of the incompatibility of the vowel ending with the "-r" sound (Chao 1968:46). For simplicity, we list a few important rules to help students to be familiar with the modification.

Rule 1. If a syllable has a diphthong -ai , -ei, -an, or -en as final: When it combines with suffix "-r," the "-i" or "-n" is deleted.

Syllable Final	Suffix -r	Phonetic Change	Example
-ai, -ei	+ r →	-ar, -er	牌 pái → pár 牌兒 杯 bēi → bēr 杯兒
-an, -en	+ r →	-ar, -er	館 guǎn → guǎr 館兒 玩 wán → wár 玩兒 份 fèn → fèr 份兒

Rule 2. If a syllable ends with a velar nasal [ng]: When it combines with suffix "-r," the "-ng" is deleted and the preceding vowel or vowels become nasalized.

Syllable Final	Suffix -r	Phonetic Change	Example
-ing	+ r →	-i^n	影 yǐng → yǐ^n 影兒
-ong	+ r →	-o^n	空 kòng → kò^n 空兒

Rule 3. If a syllable has -i , -yu, or -in as final: When it combines with suffix "-r," an -e must be inserted between them and the -n deleted.

Syllable Final	Suffix -r	Phonetic Change	Example
-i	+ r →	- ier	雞 jī → jīer 雞兒
yu	+ r →	-yuer	魚 yú → yúer 魚兒
-in	+ r →	-ier	巾 jīn → jīer 巾兒

Rule 4. If a syllable ends with -a, -o, -e, or -u: There is no phonetic change when it combines with suffix "-r."

Syllable Final	Suffix -r	Example
-a	+ r →	pá 耙 → pár 耙兒
-o	+ r →	dāo 刀 → dāor 刀兒
-e	+ r →	gē 歌 → gēr 歌兒
-u	+ r →	dòu 豆 → dòur 豆兒

V. Full Tones in Combination, Tone Sandhi, One and No

1. Full Tones in Combination

When two or more syllables are combined into a word or phrase, most tones do not change, as shown in the next three tables. The numerals stand for tones.

Examples—First Tone

1 + 1	fāyīn	pronunciation	發音
	xīngqī	week	星期
	jiāoshū	to teach	教書
	kāichē	to drive a car	開車
	cāntīng	dining hall; canteen	餐廳
	kāfēi	coffee	咖啡
	yī.shēng	doctor	醫生
1 + 2	Zhōng.guó	China	中國
	Zhōngwén	Chinese	中文
	Yīngwén	English	英文
	shēngcí	new words	生詞
	wēnxí	to review	溫習
	hēchá	to drink tea	喝茶
1 + 3	tīngxiě	dictation	聽寫
	zhōng.wǔ	noon, midday	中午
	qiānbǐ	pencil	鉛筆
	gāngbǐ	pen	鋼筆
	hēibǎn	blackboard	黑板
	kāishǐ	to begin	開始
1 + 4	shēngdiào	tone	聲調
	gōngkè	homework	功課
	gōngzuò	work, to work	工作
	zhōumò	weekend	週末
	shūdiàn	bookstore	書店
	gāo.xìng	(to be) glad, happy	高興
1 + .	mā.mā	mother	媽媽
	gē.gē	elder brother	哥哥
	tā.men	they, them	他們
	xiān.shēng	Mr.	先生
	zhuō.zi	table, desk	桌子
	xiū.xí	to rest	休息

Examples—Second Tone

2 + 1	míng.tiān	tomorrow	明天
	zuó.tiān	yesterday	昨天
	qián.tiān	the day before yesterday	前天
	chéngjī	result, achievement	成績
	chénggōng	success	成功
	Táiwān	Taiwan	台灣
2 + 2	xuéxí	to learn	學習
	huídá	to answer	回答
	lánqiú	basketball	籃球
	zúqiú	football	足球
	yóujú	post office	郵局
	yínháng	bank	銀行
2 + 3	yóuyǒng	to swim	游泳
	niúnǎi	milk	牛奶
	píjiǔ	beer	啤酒
	píngguǒ	apple	蘋果
	máobǐ	Chinese brush pen	毛筆
	chuántǒng	tradition	傳統
2 + 4	xuéxiào	school	學校
	cídài	cassette tape	磁帶
	zázhì	magazine	雜誌
	liúlì	(to be) fluent	流利
	qíguài	(to be) strange	奇怪
	chídào	(to be) (come/arrive) late	遲到
2 + .	xué.shēng	student	學生
	péng.yǒu	friend	朋友
	míng.zì	name	名字
	hái.zi	child	孩子
	xié.zi	shoes	鞋子
	qún.zi	skirt	裙子

Examples—Fourth Tone

4 + 1	niànshū	to study	念書
	yònggōng	to work hard	用功
	lùyīn	to record	錄音
	hòu.tiān	the day after tomorrow	後天
	miànbāo	bread	麵包
	diàndēng	electric light	電燈

4 + 2	liàn.xí	to practice	練習
	yùxí	to prepare lessons before class	預習
	fùxí	to review	復習
	wèntí	question, problem	問題
	kèwén	text	課文
	dàxué	university	大學
4 + 3	Hànyǔ	Chinese language	漢語
	Rìyǔ	Japanese language	日語
	diànnǎo	computer	電腦
	diànyǐng	movie	電影
	bàozhǐ	newspaper	報紙
4 + 4	jiàoshòu	professor	教授
	zhùjiào	teaching assistant	助教
	sùshè	dormitory	宿舍
	diànshì	TV	電視
	diànhuà	telephone	電話
	duìhuà	dialogue	對話
4 + .	bà.bà	father	爸爸
	mèi.mèi	younger sister	妹妹
	dì.dì	younger brother	弟弟
	tài.tài	Mrs.	太太
	gù.shì	story	故事
	kè.qì	(to be) polite	客氣

2. Tone Sandhi

When a third-tone syllable combines with another syllable, the tone value undergoes a tone change (or tone sandhi 變調 biàndiào), as shown in the next two tables. When a third tone is followed by a first, second, fourth, or neutral tone, the pitch drops and does not rise (i.e., only the first half of the third tone is pronounced); it is called "half third tone" (半上聲 bànshǎngshēng).

Examples —Third Tone

3 (half 3 + 1)	lǎoshī	teacher	老師
	zǎocān	breakfast	早餐
	Běijīng	Beijing	北京
	měitiān	every day	每天
	jǐn.zhāng	(to be) nervous	緊張
	hǎochī	(to be) tasty, delicious	好吃

3 (half 3 + 2)	yǔyán	language	語言
	Měi.guó	the States	美國
	Fǎ.guó	France	法國
	dǎqiú	to play a ball game	打球
	lǚxíng	to travel	旅行
	hǎowán	(to be) fun	好玩
3 (half 3 + 4)	wǎnfàn	dinner	晚飯
	wǎnhuì	evening party	晚會
	zhǔnbèi	to prepare	準備
	nǔlì	to work hard	努力
	hǎokàn	(to be) good-looking, interesting	好看
	hǎoxiào	(to be) funny	好笑
3 (half 3 + .)	wǒ.men	we, us	我們
	nǐ.men	you (plural)	你們
	zǎo.shàng	(early) morning	早上
	wǎn.shàng	evening	晚上
	jiě.jiě	elder sister	姐姐
	yǐ.zi	chair	椅子

When a third tone is followed by another third tone, the first syllable changes into the second tone.

Examples—Third Tone

3 + 3 → 2 + 3	yǔfǎ	grammar	語法
(→ stands for	xiǎokǎo	quiz	小考
"change into")	fǔdǎo	to coach, to guide, to tutor	輔導
	biǎoyǎn	to perform	表演
	hěn hǎo	(to be) very good	很好
	kě.yǐ	can, may	可以

3. One and No

When the number 一 (yī 'one') and the negative marker 不 (bù 'not') precede a first, second, or third tone, they change into a fourth tone; when they precede a fourth tone, they change into a second tone.

Examples

| Used alone | yī | one, a | 一 |
| | bù | no, not | 不 |

With 1, 2, 3 → 4	yì tiān	one day	一天
	yì nián	one year	一年
	yì.diǎnr	a little	一點兒
	bù shuō	not say	不說
	bù nán	not difficult	不難
	bù hǎo	not good	不好
With 4 → 2	yíyàng	alike	一樣
	yídìng	certainly, necessarily	一定
	bú mài	not sell	不賣
	bù yíyàng	not the same	不一樣
	bù yídìng	not necessarily	不一定

Note: In the typical Beijing dialect, the numerals 七 qī 'seven' and 八 bā 'eight' follow the same rule of tone changes as the number 'one,' but in Putonghua and Taiwanese Mandarin these two numerals don't change in tone.

VI. Stress and Intonation

1. Stress

According to Y. R. Chao (1968: 35-36), stress in Chinese is primarily an enlargement in pitch range and time duration and only secondarily in loudness. There are three degrees of stress: normal, contrastive, and weak. With the exception of syllables that have contrastive or weak stress, all syllables have normal stress. When a compound, phrase, or sentence consists of two or more syllables, the last syllable has the strongest stress, the first syllable has the next strongest, and the intermediate syllable has the least stress. For example:

圖書館 ²tú ³shū ¹guǎn 'library'
飛機場 ²fēi ³jī ¹chǎng 'airport'
打電話 ²dǎ ³diàn ¹huà 'to make a phone call'

When one intends to show a contrast between two syllables, the stress will be placed on the contrasted syllable no matter where in the expression it is located As in English, contrastive stress sounds higher, longer, and louder than a normal stress.

Neutral tone syllables have weak stress. The pitch of a weak stress is usually much shorter and flatter.

2. Intonation

In Chinese, sentences with different styles have different intonations. For a statement, the sentence usually starts with normal pitch and tends to trail off toward the end. For a complex sentence which consists of two clauses, the intonation of the first clause tends to end with suspension, while the second clause tends to end slightly downward.

Questions usually have higher pitch than statements and tend to accelerate and elevate toward the end of the sentence.

Strong commands always have a stronger and louder pitch, and sometimes they end with a sharp downward pitch, while mild commands tend to have softer tones and slight acceleration toward the end of the sentence.

VII. Sound Variations and Dialectal Differences

Owing to the long geographical and political separation of Chinese living in the PRC and Taiwan, regional sound variations are found on both sides of the Taiwan Straits. Students may find differences in pronunciation and stress.

1. Some variations affect tones, e.g., 星期 xīngqī (PRC)/xīngqí (Taiwan) 'week.' In such cases, the lessons provide both pronunciations to note the difference.

2. Some lexical items (mostly nouns) are pronounced with or without the retroflex "-r" sound at the end of the word, e.g., 飯館兒 fànguǎnr (PRC)/fànguǎn (Taiwan) 'restaurant.' In these cases, we will use "fànguǎnr." Students are advised to be aware of these regional differences and to speak with or without the "-r" sound in appropriate social contexts.

3. Some lexical items are pronounced with or without neutral tones, e.g., 東西 dōng.xi (PRC)/dōngxī (Taiwan) 'thing.' In cases such as these, we place a neutral tone symbol (a dot) in front of the syllable and mark the original tone as well to show the difference.

VIII. Classroom Expressions

1. Common Expressions

• Greetings

1.	How do you do! How are you?	Nǐ hǎo!	你好！
2.	Hello, everyone!	Nǐ.men hǎo! Dàjiā hǎo!	你們好！大家好！
3.	Hello, teacher!	Lǎoshī hǎo!	老師好！
4.	Good-bye.	Zàijiàn!	再見！
5.	See you tomorrow.	Míng.tiān jiàn!	明天見！
6.	See you next time.	Xià.cì jiàn!	下次見！
7.	See you later.	Huítóu jiàn!	回頭見！
8.	See you on Thursday.	Xīngqīsì jiàn!	星期四見！

• Formulas of courtesy

1.	Please come in.	Qǐng jìn!	請進。
2.	Please sit down.	Qǐng zuò!	請坐。
3.	Thanks.	Xiè.xiè!	謝謝！
4.	You are welcome.	Bú kè.qì! / Bié kè.qì!/ Béng kè.qì!	不客氣。/別客氣。/ 甭客氣。
5.	Sorry. Excuse me.	Duì.buqǐ.	對不起。
6.	Never mind.	Méi guān.xi.	沒關係。

2. Students' Expressions

• Asking for name

1.	What's your name?	Nǐ jiào shén.me míng.zì?	你叫什麼名字？
2.	My name is X.	Wǒ .de míng.zì jiào X.	我的名字叫X。

• Asking for help

1.	How do you say X in Chinese?	X, Zhōngwén zěn.me shuō?	X, 中文怎麼說？
2.	How do you write X in Chinese?	X, Zhōngwén zěn.me xiě?	X, 中文怎麼寫？
3.	How do you pronounce this character?	Zhè .ge zì zěn.me niàn?	這個字怎麼念？

• Request

1.	Please say it again.	Qǐng nǐ zài shuō yícì. Qǐng nǐ zài shuō yíbiàn.	請你再說一次。 請你再說一遍。
2.	Please say it louder.	Qǐng nǐ shuō dàshēng yì.diǎnr.	請你說大聲一點兒。
3.	Please say it slower.	Qǐng nǐ shuō màn yì.diǎnr.	請你說慢一點兒。

● Response

1.	I don't know.	Wǒ bù zhī.dào.	我不知道。
2.	I don't understand.	Wǒ bù dǒng.	我不懂。
3.	I forgot.	Wǒ wàng .le.	我忘了。
4.	I don't remember.	Wǒ bú jì.de.	我不記得。
5.	I can't hear.	Wǒ tīng.bujiàn.	我聽不見。
6.	I don't have a pen.	Wǒ méi.yǒu bǐ.	我沒有筆。
7.	I don't have paper.	Wǒ méi.yǒu zhǐ.	我沒有紙。

3. Teachers' Expressions

● Instruction

1.	Let's start class now.	Xiànzài shàngkè.	現在上課。
2.	Class is over.	Xiànzài xiàkè.	現在下課。
3.	Please pay attention.	Qǐng zhùyì.	請注意。
4.	Attention, everyone.	Dàjiā zhùyì.	大家注意。
5.	Listen to me.	Tīng wǒ shuō.	聽我說。
6.	Say after me.	Gēn wǒ shuō.	跟我說。
7.	Say together.	Dàjiā shuō.	大家說。
8.	All the boys.	Nánshēng shuō.	男生說。
9.	All the girls.	Nǚshēng shuō.	女生說。
10.	Please answer the question.	Qǐng huídá wèntí.	請回答問題。
11.	Please ask a question.	Qǐng wèn wèntí.	請問問題。
12.	Stand up.	Zhàn.qǐlái.	站起來。
13.	Sit down.	Zuò.xià.	坐下。
14.	Sit in a circle.	Zuòchéng yí .ge quānr.	坐成一個圈兒。
15.	Come up in front of the class.	Dào qiánmiàn lái.	到前面來。
16.	Go back to your seat.	Qǐng huí.qù.	請回去。
17.	Put away your book.	Bǎ shū shōu.qǐlái.	把書收起來。
18.	Open your book.	Bǎ shū dǎ.kāi.	把書打開。
19.	Turn to page X.	Fāndào dì X yè.	翻到第X頁。
20.	Look at page X.	Kàn dì X yè.	看第X頁。
21.	Next we'll practice dialogue.	Xiàmiàn wǒ.men yào liàn.xí duìhuà.	下面我們要練習對話。
22.	Next we'll practice vocabulary.	Xiàmiàn wǒ.men yào liàn.xí shēngcí.	下面我們要練習生詞。
23.	Next we'll practice sentence patterns.	Xiàmiàn wǒ.men yào liàn.xí jùxíng.	下面我們要練習句型。
24.	Next we'll practice characters.	Xiàmiàn wǒ.men yào liàn.xí hànzì.	下面我們要練習漢字。
25.	Next we'll do team work.	Xiàmiàn wǒ.men yào fēnzǔ liàn.xí.	下面我們要分組練習。
26.	Let's start the test.	Wǒ.men kāishǐ kǎoshì.	我們開始考試。
27.	Let's start the dictation.	Wǒ.men kāishǐ tīngxiě.	我們開始聽寫。

28.	There will be a quiz tomorrow.	Míng.tiān yǒu xiǎokǎo.	明天有小考。
29.	There will be an exam next week.	Xià xīngqī yǒu dàkǎo.	下星期有大考。
30.	Please turn in your homework.	Qǐng jiāo zuòyè.	請交作業。
31.	Please turn in your test.	Qǐng jiāo juàn.zi.	請交卷子。

• Questions

1.	Do you understand?	Míng.bái .ma? Dǒng .ma? Dǒng .budǒng?	明白嗎？懂嗎？懂不懂？
2.	Do you have any questions?	Yǒu .méiyǒu wèntí?	有没有問題？
3.	Is this clear?	Qīng.chǔ .buqīng.chǔ?	清楚不清楚？
4.	Are you ready?	Hǎo .le méi.yǒu?	好了没有？
5.	What is she/he saying?	Tā shuō shén.me?	他說什麼？

• Feedback

1.	Right.	Duì.	對。
2.	Incorrect.	Bú duì.	不對。
3.	Very good.	Fēicháng hǎo. Hěn hǎo.	非常好。很好。
4.	Good./OK.	Hǎo.	好。
5.	OK./Not bad.	Búcuò.	不錯。

4. Others

• Titles

1.	Madame	nǔshì	女士
2.	Miss	xiǎo.jiě	小姐
3.	Mr., Sir	xiān.shēng	先生
4.	Mrs.	tài.tài	太太
5.	Professor	jiàoshòu	教授
6.	Student	xué.shēng	學生
7.	Teacher	lǎoshī	老師
8.	Teaching assistant	zhùjiào	助教

• Audiovisual equipment

1.	blackboard	hēibǎn	黑板
2.	cassette tape	lùyīndài	錄音帶
3.	cassette tape recorder	lùyīnjī	錄音機
4.	computer	diànnǎo	電腦
5.	extension cord	yánchángxiàn	延長線
6.	overhead projector	tóuyǐngjī	投影機
7.	video cassette recorder	lùxiàngjī	錄像機
8.	video tape	lùxiàngdài	錄像帶

• Colors

1.	black	hēi(sè)	黑(色)
2.	blue	lán(sè)	藍(色)
3.	green	lǜ(sè)	綠(色)
4.	red	hóng(sè)	紅(色)
5.	white	bái(sè)	白(色)
6.	yellow	huáng(sè)	黃(色)

• Stationery

1.	book	shū	書
2.	notebook	běn.zi	本子
3.	paper	zhǐ	紙
4.	pen	bǐ	筆

第三課 漢字簡介

Lesson 3. The Chinese Writing System

I. Overview

Linguistically, the Chinese language can be subclassified into 口語 kǒuyǔ 'the spoken language' and 書面語 shūmiànyǔ 'the written language.' *Kǒuyǔ* is the language that people speak in everyday life, while *shūmiànyǔ* is the language that people write (or print) on paper. People now write in 白話文 báihuàwén 'vernacular language' style rather than in 文言文 wényánwén 'classical Chinese' style, and there are some differences in the usages of lexical items and sentence structures in these two forms of the Chinese language.

In Chinese, the writing (or script) system is called 文字 wénzì. 文 wén 'a writing, literature' originally denoted simple noncomposite graphs (see examples 1, 4, and 5 below), and 字 zì 'character' originally denoted composite graphs which consist of more than one 文 wén (see examples 2, 3, and 6). Unlike the English writing system, which is an alphabetic script, the Chinese writing system is in ideographic form, with Chinese characters being basically combinations of pictograms, ideograms, and phonograms. Each Chinese character, or Hànzì (漢字 'Han-character'), consists of one to thirty-three strokes, but most characters have fewer than fifteen strokes.

Examples
1. 木 mù 'tree, wood'
2. 木 + 木 → 林 lín 'grove'
3. 木 + 木 + 木 → 森 sēn 'forest'
4. 白 bái 'white'
5. 巾 jīn 'towel, handkerchief'
6. 木 + 白 + 巾 → 棉 mián 'cotton—the white fibrous substance (used to make towels, etc.) that grows on a tree or bush.

Each Chinese character includes three aspects: a form (形 xíng), a sound (聲 shēng), and a meaning (義 yì). Traditionally, Chinese characters are classified into categories, with each category falling under a radical (部首 bùshǒu), which is the component by which lexicographers arrange characters in Chinese dictionaries. Most radicals bear a clue to the meaning of the character. For example, 棉 mián 'cotton' includes the radical 木 mù 'tree.' Thus what makes Chinese script unique is that even if you don't know how to pronounce a character, you can still guess the meaning if you know the radical. In English, by contrast, if you know the spelling of the word "grove," for example, you cannot guess its meaning from any of the letters that make up the word. Instead you can only guess the pronunciation of the word because English script is phonetic.

II. Stroke Types

Each Chinese character is formed with one or more of eight types of strokes (筆劃 bǐhuà).

Stroke Type				Examples					
1. Horizontal	héng	橫	一	五	wǔ	five	三	sān	three
2. Vertical	shù	豎	丨	山	shān	mountain	十	shí	ten
3. Left Stroke	piě	撇	丿	手	shǒu	hand	八	bā	eight
4. Right Stroke	nà	捺	㇏	水	shuǐ	water	走	zǒu	to walk
5. Dot	diǎn	點	丶	下	xià	down	六	liù	six
6. Hook	gōu	鉤	乙	九	jiǔ	nine	七	qī	seven
7. Turning Stroke	zhé	折	㇇	女	nǚ	woman	是	shì	to be
8. Rising Stroke	tí	提	丿	打	dǎ	to play	刁	diāo	naughty

Chinese characters can be classified into three types of form.

Type	Character Form	Examples
1		們 .men
		謝 xiè
		語 yǔ
		送 sòng
2		賣 mài
		家 jiā
		宿 sù
		能 néng
3		因 yīn

To analyze and count the number of strokes a character has, use the following rules.

Rule	Examples					
1. Left → right	他	tā	he	說	shuō	to say
2. Top → bottom	買	mǎi	to buy	星	xīng	star
3. Outside → inside	回	huí	to return	國	guó	country

III. Stroke Order

Chinese characters are designed in an elegant and balanced way so that all characters can fit into identical square spaces. When using a brush or pen to write characters, it is very important to learn and follow the correct stroke order (筆順 bǐshùn) so that you can write quickly and smoothly. Learning how to count the strokes of a character is also very important, because if you don't know the pronunciation or meaning of a character, you can use the "stroke number index" in a dictionary to look it up.

Strokes are written according to the following order.

Stroke Order	Examples			
1. From top to bottom	立	lì	to stand	` 丶 亠 宀 立 立
	雨	yǔ	rain	
	馬	mǎ	horse	
2. From left to right	竹	zhú	bamboo	ノ ト ケ ケ 竹 竹
	日	rì	sun	
	狗	gǒu	dog	
3. Middle first, then both sides	小	xiǎo	small	亅 亅丶 小
	你	nǐ	you	
	木	mù	wood	
4. First horizontally, then vertically	士	shì	scholar	一 十 士
	下	xià	down	
	土	tǔ	soil	
5. From outside to inside	月	yuè	moon	丿 冂 月 月
	高	gāo	tall	
	包	bāo	to wrap	
6. Finish the inside first, then enclose it	日	rì	sun	丨 冂 日 日
	西	xī	west	
	國	guó	country	

Take a look at the following characters and figure out their stroke order. Note that the first column gives the character's Pinyin spelling, an English meaning, and the total number of strokes.

yī one 1 stroke	一	¹⟋一	liù six 4 strokes	六	六
èr two 2 strokes	二	¹⟋二 ²⟋	qī seven 2 strokes	七	七
sān three 3 strokes	三	三	bā eight 2 strokes	八	八
sì four 5 strokes	四	四	jiǔ nine 2 strokes	九	九
wǔ five 4 strokes	五	五	shí ten 2 strokes	十	十

IV. Six Principles of Character Formation

According to Xǔ Shèn's (許慎) *Shuō wén jiě zì* (說文解字 The Explanation of Writing and Analysis of Words) written during the Later Han dynasty (A.D. 25-220), Chinese characters can be divided into six categories (六書 liùshū).

Character Category			Examples					
1. Pictographs Imitative drafts	象形	xiàngxíng	日	rì	sun	月	yuè	moon
2. Indicatives Indicative symbols	指事	zhǐshì	上	shàng	up	下	xià	down
3. Ideatives Logical aggregates	會意	huìyì	從	cóng	to follow			
4. Harmonics Phonetic compounds	形聲	xíngshēng	清	qīng	clear (water)	晴	qíng	clear (sky)
5. Transmissives Derived meanings	轉注	zhuǎnzhù	網	wǎng	net			
6. Phonetic loan words Arbitrary meanings	假借	jiǎjiè	哥	gē	elder brother			

The first four categories are based on the structure of the characters, while the last two are based on their usage. Of the 9,353 characters included in *Shuō wén jiě zì,* about 7,697 are formed by phonetic compounds, constituting 82% of the total. Therefore, when you see a new character, for example 沐 mù 'to bathe,' which shares the same phonetic component with the character 木 mù 'tree or wood,' you can use the phonetic clue to make an educated guess about the pronunciation of the new character 沐 mù 'to bathe.' (Section VII helps you distinguish the radical and phonetic components.)

V. Transformation of Writing Styles

A recent study (Chang Kuang-yuan 1995: 9-27) indicates that the development of Chinese script can be divided into three stages: (1) the creation period (草創時期 cǎochuàng shíqī), representened by pottery inscriptions (16C-14C BC); (2) the formative period (演進時期 yǎnjìn shíqī), represented by bronze inscriptions (金文 jīnwén), which date from the Shang dynasty (16C-11C BC); and (3) the standardization period (定型時期 dìngxíng shíqī), represented by the small seal (小篆 xiǎozhuàn) and regular standard (楷書 kǎishū) scripts. In contrast to earlier theories, Chang believes that bronze inscriptions show the first written script of the second period, whereas oracle bone inscriptions (甲骨文 jiǎgǔwén) on cattle bones and tortoise shells, which date from the late Shang dynasty (14C-11C BC), should be considered as the first instance of simplification of the Chinese script. As time went by, Chinese script developed from picturelike lines to rounder, smoother forms and then to straight, linear strokes. Before the Chinese invention of paper, animal-figure characters were drawn vertically owing to the rough quality of the material used (bones, shells, and bamboo).

The following table shows the development of Chinese script in chronological order, from bronze and oracle bone script to seal script and then modern standard script.

Meaning	金文 Bronze script 16C-11C BC	甲骨文 Oracle bone script 14C-11C BC	小篆 Seal script 211-207 BC	楷書 Standard script 25 AD-present
Sun				日
Moon				月
Mountain				山
Man				人
Mouth				口
Eye				目
Hand				手
Woman				女
Child				子
Dog				犬
Horse				馬
Tree				木

VI. Simplification of Chinese Characters

Traditionally, in formal settings, such as texts, official announcements, tests, newspapers, and teaching, Chinese write (with a writing brush) or print 正體字 zhèngtǐzì 'correct characters' or 繁體字 fántǐzì 'complicated characters.' The words run vertically from top to bottom and right to left across the paper. In informal settings, such as personal correspondence, notes, bookkeeping, menus, and even when teaching subjects other than Chinese language at high schools or colleges, Chinese people tend to use shortened forms, 簡體字 jiǎntǐzì 'simplified characters.' Even so, because many Chinese characters have over fifteen strokes and are hard to memorize, the PRC government launched a character simplification movement to promote the literacy of the common people (90% of Chinese were peasants prior to 1949). In 1956, a list of 515 simplified characters was issued and then in 1964 a new list of 2,238. A majority of these simplified characters are the shortened forms which have been used for centuries; others are derived from the traditional (or complicated) characters. Simplified characters are now used in modern publications in the PRC and in some Chinese communities in Southeast Asia, such as Singapore and Malaysia. Traditional characters are still used in Taiwan and Chinese communities in North America and in classical Chinese publications in the PRC.

Students of Chinese eventually must learn both the traditional and the simplified characters; it is a question of which should be learned first. In this textbook, we introduce the traditional characters first, then provide their simplified counterparts where applicable. You can apply some corresponding rules in switching from the traditional form to the simplified one. No matter which form you learn first, when you practice reading, you will run into certain characters that you can't recognize. Don't panic; always try to guess the meaning of a character from the context. As for writing, you may write whichever form you like, but you must make sure it is the correct one in any case.

VII. Chinese Radicals

The concept of the radical was introduced in Xǔ Shèn's *Shuō wén jiě zì*, the first Chinese etymological dictionary. It arranged Chinese characters under 540 radicals. The number of standard radicals was reduced to 214 in the dictionary 字匯 *Zìhuì*, compiled during the Ming dynasty (1358-1644). These standard radicals have been used by Chinese lexicographers up to the present time. Characters that are classified under the same radical include this radical in their graphical structure and incorporate its meaning. For instance, characters related to human beings, such as 你 nǐ 'you (singular),' 他 tā 'he/she/it,' and 信 xìn '[human-language] letter,' are classified under the 人 rén 'man, person' radical (人 changes its form to 亻 when used as a radical). Characters related to girls or women, such as 媽 mā 'mother,' 姐 jiě 'older sister,' and 婦 fù 'woman' fall under the 女 nǚ 'female' radical.

Four general rules will help you locate the radical in a character.

1. If a character consists of a left-hand, a middle, and a right-hand component, the left-hand component is the radical in most cases.
2. If a character consists of top and bottom components, then in most cases the top component is the radical.
3. If a character consists of an outside enclosure with components inside, then in most cases the outside component is the radical.
4. If a character cannot be broken down into clear components, then the highest part or stroke is the radical.

These rules by no means apply to all characters, but at least they provide you with a foundation upon which you can build your knowledge of the radicals.

Over the centuries, more than 50,000 characters have been used in the Chinese language (Norman 1988:72), but the number of commonly used characters in modern publications is between 6,000 and 7,000. After studying Chinese for two years, you will have learned about 1,500 to 2,000 characters, which is not quite enough to encompass the range of modern Chinese writing. Thus it is very important for you to learn the radicals well so that you can use a Chinese dictionary to look up unfamiliar characters on your own. Radicals provide a hint of the meaning of a character and help you learn characters in a much quicker and easier way. For quick consultation, the complete radical list is presented in Appendix 3.

Following is a list of the most commonly used radicals arranged according to their semantic domain.[1] Use this shortened, meaning-based list to start to familiarize yourself with radicals.

Radicals Arranged by Categories

Radical	Pinyin	English	Examples					
People								
人	rén	person	你	nǐ	you	信	xīn	letter
心 忄	xīn	heart	念	niàn	to read	情	qíng	affection
手 扌	shǒu	hand	打	dǎ	to hit	推	tuī	to push
口	kǒu	mouth	吃	chī	to eat	喝	hē	to drink
目	mù	eye	眼	yǎn	eye	睡	shuì	to sleep
足	zú	foot	跟	gēn	heel	路	lù	road
肉 月	ròu	flesh	肌	jī	muscle	肚	dù	stomach
女	nǔ	woman	好	hǎo	be good	妹	mèi	younger sister
疒	chuáng	sickness	病	bìng	be sick	疼	téng	ache
力	lì	power	加	jiā	to add	助	zhù	to help

---

[1] There is a Chinese input system called 倉頡 cāngjié which arranges some of the radicals based on their general categories, e.g., human bodies, animals, etc.

Animals

牛	niú	ox	物	wù	thing	犀	xī	rhinoceros
馬	mǎ	horse	騎	qí	ride	駕	jià	harness
犬	quǎn	dog	狗	gǒu	dog	獸	shòu	beast
魚	yú	fish	鮮	xiān	fresh	鯊	shā	shark
虫	chóng	insect	蚊	wén	mosquito	蜜	mì	honey
鳥	niǎo	bird	鳴	míng	chirp	鳳	fèng	phoenix

Actions

彳	chì	left step	後	hòu	behind	很	hěn	very
攵	pū	tap	放	fàng	put	敲	qiāo	knock
辶	chuò	run and stop	這	zhè	this	過	guò	pass
食	shí	eat	飯	fàn	cooked rice	養	yǎng	raise

Nature

日	rì	sun	明	míng	bright	春	chūn	spring (season)
月	yuè	moon	有	yǒu	to have	期	qī	period
金	jīn	gold, metal	錢	qián	money	釜	fǔ	cauldron
木	mù	wood	枝	zhī	branch	本	běn	root
水 氵	shuǐ	water	河	hé	river	泉	quán	spring (water)
火 灬	huǒ	fire	煙	yān	smoke	照	zhào	to shine
土	tǔ	soil	地	dì	land	在	zài	exist
山	shān	mountain	岩	yán	rock	島	dǎo	island
石	shí	stone	砂	shā	sand	磨	mó	polish
阜	fù	mound	院	yuàn	yard	防	fáng	defense
玉	yù	jade	玩	wán	play	璧	bì	jade
田	tián	field	男	nán	man	留	liú	remain
禾	hé	grain	種	zhǒng	seed	秀	xiù	elegant
米	mǐ	rice	粉	fěn	powder	粒	lì	grain
竹	zhú	bamboo	筆	bǐ	pen	笑	xiào	laugh
艹	cǎo	grass	花	huā	flower	草	cǎo	grass
糸	mì	silk	紙	zhǐ	paper	紫	zǐ	purple
雨	yǔ	rain	雪	xuě	snow	電	diàn	snow

Materials

衣	yī	clothing	裏	lǐ	inside	裡	lǐ	inside
巾	jīn	napkin	帽	mào	hat	布	bù	cloth
刀	dāo	knife	刻	kè	to engrave	切	qiē	cut
宀	mián	roof	家	jiā	home	安	ān	peaceful
广	yǎn	shelter	店	diàn	shop	廟	miào	temple
門	mén	door	門	mén	door	關	guān	close

Miscellaneous

口	wéi	enclosure	四	sì	four	國	guó	country
大	dà	large	天	tiān	sky	奇	qí	rare
言	yán	word	說	shuō	say	警	jǐng	to warn

貝	bèi	cowrie	貴	guì	expensive	賑	zhàng	account
車	chē	vehicle	輕	qīng	light	軍	jūn	army
邑	yì	village	郊	jiāo	suburbs	鄉	xiāng	countryside
頁	yè	a page	頭	tóu	head	願	yuàn	hope

VIII. The Use of Dictionaries

1. Types of Dictionaries

Traditionally, there are two types of Chinese dictionaries.

- 字典 zìdiǎn 'character dictionary' This type contains only single-character entries. No words or phrases of more than one character are included.

- 辭典／詞典 (辞典／词典) cídiǎn 'word dictionary' This type lists single characters as the major entries. Under each major entry, compound words and phrases which begin with the major entry are listed. Since modern Chinese has many homonyms, Chinese speakers have created numerous disyllabic or polysyllabic words in order to avoid ambiguity. Consequently, a cídiǎn 'word dictionary' will be more useful than a zìdiǎn 'character dictionary,' even for the beginning learner of Chinese.

2. Indexes Used in Dictionaries

Chinese dictionaries usually include one to four of the following indexes to help the user look up a character.

- (Hanyu) Pinyin index

  Pinyin is a phonetic spelling system devised to denote the sounds of Chinese characters. It was implemented by the PRC government in 1958. Dictionaries with the Pinyin index arrange the entries in alphabetical order, as in English.

- Wade-Giles romanization index

  Wade-Giles romanization is a spelling system for Chinese characters designed by British diplomat Thomas Wade and modified by another British diplomat, Herbert A. Giles, during the nineteenth century. Prior to the implementation of the Pinyin system, the Wade-Giles system was the most popular form for transliteration of Chinese and was used by sinologists around the world. The Library of Congress, most libraries and post offices in the world, and Chinese-English dictionaries published in Taiwan still use this system. Like the Pinyin index, the Wade-Giles system arranges entries alphabetically.

- Mandarin Phonetic Symbols index

  Devised by a language unification committee in 1919, Mandarin Phonetic Symbols, 國語注音符號 Guóyǔ zhùyīn fúhào (or BoPoMoFo), is a set of official phonetic scripts which are partly alphabetic and partly syllabic. All Chinese dictionaries published in Taiwan are arranged according to these phonetic symbols; some also include the National Romanization, 國語羅馬字 Guóyǔ Luómǎzì. Some Chinese dictionaries published in the PRC include the Mandarin Phonetic Symbols along with Pinyin spellings.

- Radical index

  Most Chinese dictionaries include a radical index in which entries are listed under their respective radicals. Characters sharing the same radical are arranged according to the ascending number of strokes.

- Total stroke number index

  Dictionaries using the total stroke number index list entries according to the ascending order of strokes in the characters.

- First stroke-type index

  Some Chinese dictionaries arrange entries by the starting stroke of the characters: 橫 héng 'horizontal stroke,' 直 zhí 'vertical stroke,' 撇 piě 'left slant stroke,' 點 diǎn 'dot,' and 折 zhé 'turning stroke.'

- Four-Corner Coding index

  Four-Corner Coding (四角號碼檢字法 sìjiǎo hàomǎ jiǎnzìfǎ) was invented by Wang Yun-wu (王雲五) in 1928. He used the numerals from 0 to 9 to represent ten different categories of stroke components for coding characters. 0 represents 頭 tóu 'head,' 1 for 橫 héng 'horizontal,' 2 for 垂 chuí 'vertical,' 3 for 點 diǎn 'dot,' 4 for 叉 chā 'cross,' 5 for 插 chā 'to pierce,' 6 for 方 fāng 'square,' 7 for 角 jiǎo 'angle,' 8 for 八 bā 'eight,' and 9 for 小 xiǎo 'small.' For each character, the coding order runs in the same direction as the letter "Z," from the stroke component of the upper-left corner, to the upper-right corner, to the lower-left corner, and then to the lower-right corner (Wang 1967).

第四課　今天是幾月幾號？

對話

〔高德中是研究生，李明是大學生。他們都在印大學習。
　印大八月三十號開學。〕

小高：　嘿！小李，你哪一天
　　　　註册？

小李：　我明天註册。你呢？
　　　　今天（註册）嗎？

小高：　不，我後天註册，下
　　　　星期一上課。

小李：　下星期一是不是八月
　　　　三十一號？

小高：　不（是），下星期一是八月三十號，不是三十一號。

小李：　八月三十號不是你的生日
　　　　嗎？

小高：　不（是），我的生日是八
　　　　月二十三號，前天。你的
　　　　生日是幾月幾號？

小李：　（我）也是八月。八月二
　　　　十六號，明天。

小高：　生日快樂！

对话

〔高德中是研究生，李明是大学生。他们都在印大学习。
印大八月三十号开学。〕

小高：　嘿！小李，你哪一天注册？

小李：　我明天注册。你呢？今天（注册）吗？

小高：　不，我后天注册，下星期一上课。

小李：　下星期一是不是八月三十一号？

小高：　不（是），下星期一是八月三十号，不是三十一号。

小李：　八月三十号不是你的生日吗？

小高：　不（是），我的生日是八月二十三号，前天。你的生日是
　　　　几月几号？

小李：　（我）也是八月。八月二十六号，明天。

小高：　生日快乐！

My questions:

Duìhuà

(Gāo Dézhōng shì yánjiūshēng, Lǐ Míng shì dàxué.shēng. Tā.men dōu
zài Yìndà xuéxí. Yìndà bāyuè sānshíhào kāixué.)

Xiǎo Gāo:	Hēi! Xiǎo Lǐ, nǐ něiyìtiān zhùcè?
Xiǎo Lǐ:	Wǒ míng.tiān zhùcè, nǐ .ne? Jīn.tiān (zhùcè) .ma?
Xiǎo Gāo:	Bù, wǒ hòu.tiān zhùcè, xià xīngqīyī shàngkè.
Xiǎo Lǐ:	Xià xīngqīyī shì .búshì bāyuè sānshíyīhào?
Xiǎo Gāo:	Bú (shì), xià xīngqīyī shì bāyuè sānshíhào.
Xiǎo Lǐ:	Bāyuè sānshíhào búshì nǐ .de shēng.rì .ma?
Xiǎo Gāo:	Bú (shì), wǒ .de shēng.rì shì bāyuè èrshísānhào, qián.tiān. Nǐ .de shēng.rì shì jǐ yuè jǐ hào?
Xiǎo Lǐ:	(Wǒ) yě shì bāyuè, èrshíliùhào, míng.tiān.
Xiǎo Gāo:	Shēng.rì kuàilè!

Sunday	Monday	Tuesday	Wednesday	Thursday	Friday	Saturday
1	2	3	4	5	6	7
8	9	10	11	12	13	14
15	16	17	18	19	20	21
22	23 ☺ 高	24	(25) Today	26 ☺ 李	27	28
29	30 📖	31	28	29	30	

Dialogue

(Gāo Dézhōng is a graduate student; Lǐ Míng is an undergraduate student. They are both studying at Indiana University, where school starts on August 30.)

Xiǎo Gāo: Hi! Xiǎo Lǐ, when are you going to register?

Xiǎo Lǐ: I will register tomorrow. How about you? Do you register today?

Xiǎo Gāo: No, I will register the day after tomorrow, (and my) classes start next Monday.

Xiǎo Lǐ: Is next Monday August 31st?

Xiǎo Gāo: No, next Monday is August 30th, (it) is not (August) 31st.

Xiǎo Lǐ: Isn't August 30th your birthday?

Xiǎo Gāo: No, my birthday is August 23rd, (it was) the day before yesterday. When is your birthday?

Xiǎo Lǐ: (It) is also in August. (It is) tomorrow, August 26th.

Xiǎo Gāo: Happy birthday!

Mini-Dialogue
小對話 Xiǎoduìhuà

Talking about days

1. A: 你哪一天開學？

    Nǐ nǎyìtiān kāixué?
    On which day do you start school?

    B: 我明天開學。

    Wǒ míng.tiān kāixué.
    I start school tomorrow.

2. A: 你不是今天註冊嗎？

    Nǐ búshì jīn.tiān zhùcè .ma?
    You register today, don't you?

    B: 不，我後天註冊。

    Bù, wǒ hòu.tiān zhùcè.
    No, I register the day after tomorrow.

Talking about dates

1. A: 下星期一是不是八月三十
        一號？

    Xià xīngqīyī shì .búshì bāyuè sānshíyī hào?
    Is next Monday August 31st?

    B: 對，下星期一是八月三十
        一號。

    Duì, xià xīngqīyī shì bāyuè sānshíyī hào.
    Yes, next Monday is August 31st.

2. A: 你的生日是幾月幾號？

    Nǐ .de shēng.rì shì jǐ yuè jǐ hào?
    What date is your birthday on?

    B: 我的生日是五月二十號。

    Wǒ .de shēng.rì shì wǔyuè èrshíhào.
    My birthday is May 20th.

Vocabulary
生詞 Shēngcí

◎ **By Order of Appearance**

	今天		jīn.tiān	N/MTA	[present-day] today
	是		shì	EV	to be (is, was, are, were)
	幾	几	jǐ	QW	how many, how much
	月		yuè	N	[moon] month
	號	号	hào	N	number, day of month (colloquial), size (clothing only)
*	年		nián	N/MTA	year
*	日		rì	N	[sun] day of the month (written form)
	一		yī	N	one
	二		èr	N	two
	三		sān	N	three
	四		sì	N	four
	五		wǔ	N	five
	六		liù	N	six
	七		qī	N	seven
	八		bā	N	eight
	九		jiǔ	N	nine
	十		shí	N	ten
*	零		líng	N	zero
*	第		dì	Prefix	an ordinalizing prefix which attaches to numerals to form ordinal numbers
*	第一		dìyī	Adj	[prefix-one] the first
	高		Gāo	SN/Adj	surname, high, tall
	李		Lǐ	SN	[plums] surname
	大		dà	SV	(to be) big, large, old (age)
	小		xiǎo	SV	(to be) small, little (size), young (age)
	他們	他们	tā.men	Pron	[s/he/it-PL] they, them
*	他		tā	Pron	he, she, him, her
*	她		tā	Pron	she, her
*	它		tā	Pron	it
	開學	开学	kāixué	VO	[open-school] to start school/classes
*	學校	学校	xuéxiào	N	[learn-school] school
*	學生	学生	xué.shēng	N	[learn-birth] student
	嘿		hèi	Inter	an interjection
	你		nǐ	Pron	you (sing.)
*	你們	你们	nǐ.men	Pron	[you-PL] you (pl.)
*	誰	谁	shéi	QW	who, whoever, whom, whomever

哪一天		nǎyìtiān/ něiyìtiān	NP	[which-one-day] which day?
* 哪		nǎ/něi	Inter/Det	which
* 天		tiān	N/M	day, sky
註冊	注册	zhùcè	VO	[register-notebook] to register (at school)
我		wǒ	Pron	I, me
* 我們	我们	wǒ.men	Pron	[I-PL] we, us
明天		míng.tiān	N/MTA	[bright-day] tomorrow
呢		.ne	QP	particle for interest in additional information; how about…?
嗎	吗	.ma	QP	particle for yes-or-no question
不		bù	Neg/Adv	no, not
* 對	对	duì	SV	(to be) right, to face
後天	后天	hòu.tiān	N/MTA	[back-day] the day after tomorrow
* 昨天		zuó.tiān	N/MTA	[yesterday-day] yesterday
星期		xīngqī/qí	N	[star-period] week (literary)
* 禮拜	礼拜	lǐbài	N	[ritual-worship] week (colloquial)
上課	上课	shàngkè	VO	to go to class; to attend class
* 上		shàng	V	to ascend; to go to (street/school/class/work)
* 下		xià	V	to descend, to go down; to get off (class/work)
* 課	课	kè	N	lesson, course
* 下課	下课	xiàkè	VO	class dismissed
的		.de	Poss Part	possessive marker
* 誰的	谁的	shéi .de	QW	[who-Poss Part] whose
你的		nǐ .de	Pron	[you-Poss Part] your
我的		wǒ .de	Pron	[I-Poss Part] my
* 他的		tā .de	Pron	[s/he/it-Poss Part] his/her
生日		shēng.rì	N	[birth-day] birthday
前天		qián.tiān	N/MTA	[front-day] the day before yesterday
也		yě	Adv	also, too
快樂	快乐	kuàilè	N/Adj	[fast-happy] happiness; happy
* 祝		zhù	V	to wish

◎ By Grammatical Categories

Nouns/Pronouns

*	天		tiān	N/M	day, sky
	今天		jīn.tiān	N/MTA	[present-day] today
*	昨天		zuó.tiān	N/MTA	[yesterday-day] yesterday
	前天		qián.tiān	N/MTA	[front-day] the day before yesterday
	明天		míng.tiān	N/MTA	[bright-day] tomorrow
	後天	后天	hòu.tiān	N/MTA	[back-day] the day after tomorrow
*	年		nián	N/MTA	year
	月		yuè	N	[moon] month
	號	号	hào	N	number, day of the month (colloquial), size (clothing only)
*	日		rì	N	[sun] day of the month (written form)
	星期		xīngqī/qí	N	[star-period] week (literary)
*	禮拜	礼拜	lǐbài	N	[ritual-worship] week (colloquial)
	哪一天		nǎyìtiān/ něiyìtiān	NP	[which-one-day] which day?
	一		yī	N	one
	二		èr	N	two
	三		sān	N	three
	四		sì	N	four
	五		wǔ	N	five
	六		liù	N	six
	七		qī	N	seven
	八		bā	N	eight
	九		jiǔ	N	nine
	十		shí	N	ten
*	零		líng	N	zero
*	課	课	kè	N	lesson, course
*	學校	学校	xuéxiào	N	[learn-school] school
*	學生	学生	xué.shēng	N	[learn-birth] student
	生日		shēng.rì	N	[birth-day] birthday
	快樂	快乐	kuàilè	N/Adj	[fast-happy] happiness; happy
	我		wǒ	Pron	I, me
*	我們	我们	wǒ.men	Pron	[I-PL] we, us
	你		nǐ	Pron	you (sing.)
*	你們	你们	nǐ.men	Pron	[you-PL] you (pl.)
*	他		tā	Pron	he, she, him, her
*	她		tā	Pron	she, her
*	它		tā	Pron	it
	他們	他们	tā.men	Pron	[s/he/it-PL] they, them
	的		.de	Poss Part	possessive marker

我的		wǒ .de	Pron	[I-Poss Part] my
你的		nǐ .de	Pron	[you-Poss Part] your
* 他的		tā .de	Pron	[s/he/it-Poss Part] his/her/its
高		Gāo	SN/Adj	surname, high, tall
李		Lǐ	SN	[plums] surname

Verbs/Stative Verbs/Adjectives

是		shì	EV	to be (is, was, are, were)
* 對	对	duì	SV	(to be) right, to face
大		dà	SV	(to be) big, large, old (age)
小		xiǎo	SV	(to be) small, little (size), young (age)
* 第一		dìyī	Adj	[prefix-one] the first
註冊	注册	zhùcè	VO	[register-notebook] to register (at school)
開學	开学	kāixué	VO	[open-school] to start school/classes
* 上		shàng	V	to ascend; to go to (street/school/class/work)
上課	上课	shàngkè	VO	to go to class; to attend class
* 下		xià	V	to descend, to go down; to get off (class/work)
* 下課	下课	xiàkè	VO	class dismissed
* 祝		zhù	V	to wish

Adverbs

不		bù	Neg/Adv	no, not
也		yě	Adv	also, too

Particles

呢		.ne	QP	particle for interest in additional information; how about...?
嗎	吗	.ma	QP	particle for yes-or-no question

Question Words

幾	几	jǐ	QW	how many, how much
* 哪		nǎ/ něi	Inter/Det	which
* 誰	谁	shéi	QW	who, whoever, whom, whomever
* 誰的	谁的	shéi .de	QW	[who-Poss Part] whose

Others

嘿		hèi	Inter	an interjection
* 第		dì	Prefix	an ordinalizing prefix which attaches to numerals to form ordinal numbers

✚ Supplementary Vocabulary

1. Vocabulary for Classroom Instructions

日曆		rìlì	N	[day-calendar] calendar
對話	对话	duìhuà	N	[to face-talk] dialogue
生詞	生词	shēngcí	N	[raw-word] new words
句型		jùxíng	N	[sentence-pattern] sentence pattern

2. Months of the Year

一月	yīyuè	N	[one-month] January
二月	èryuè	N	[two-month] February
三月	sānyuè	N	[three-month] March
四月	sìyuè	N	[four-month] April
五月	wǔyuè	N	[five-month] May
六月	liùyuè	N	[six-month] June
七月	qīyuè	N	[seven-month] July
八月	bāyuè	N	[eight-month] August
九月	jiǔyuè	N	[nine-month] September
十月	shíyuè	N	[ten-month] October
十一月	shíyīyuè	N	[eleven-month] November
十二月	shí'èryuè	N	[twelve-month] December

3. Days of the Week

For both spoken and written:

星期一	xīngqīyī	N	[week-one] Monday
星期二	xīngqī'èr	N	[week-two] Tuesday
星期三	xīngqīsān	N	[week-three] Wednesday
星期四	xīngqīsì	N	[week-four] Thursday
星期五	xīngqīwǔ	N	[week-five] Friday
星期六	xīngqīliù	N	[week-six] Saturday
星期日	xīngqīrì	N	[week-day] Sunday

For spoken only:

星期天		xīngqītiān	N	[week-day] Sunday
禮拜一	礼拜一	lǐbàiyī	N	[week-one] Monday
禮拜二	礼拜二	lǐbài'èr	N	[week-two] Tuesday
禮拜三	礼拜三	lǐbàisān	N	[week-three] Wednesday
禮拜四	礼拜四	lǐbàisì	N	[week-four] Thursday
禮拜五	礼拜五	lǐbàiwǔ	N	[week-five] Friday
禮拜六	礼拜六	lǐbàiliù	N	[week-six] Saturday
禮拜天	礼拜天	lǐbàitiān	N	[week-day] Sunday
禮拜日	礼拜日	lǐbàirì	N	[week-day] Sunday

Characters
漢字 Hànzì

nǐ
you 亻 radical
7 strokes (person)

你們	nǐ.men	you (pl.)
你的	nǐ .de	your (sg.)
你們的	nǐ.men .de	yours (pl.)

A: **你**是小學生嗎？
B: 是，我是小學生。

wǒ
I, me 戈
7 (weapon)

我們	wǒ.men	we, us
我的	wǒ .de	my
我們的	wǒ.men .de	our

A: 你是學生嗎？
B: 是，**我**是學生，是大學生。

shì
to be 日
9 (sun)

A: 你**是不是**學生？
B: **是**，我**是**學生。

bù
not 一
4 (one)

不是	bú shì	to be not
不對	bú duì	not correct
*不錯	búcuò	not bad

A: 你是學生嗎？
B: **不**，我**不是**學生。

繁簡對照：	其他漢字：	✎ **My notes:**
	*您 SC1[1]	

---
[1] Supplementary Character 1: See Appendix 2.

大

dà
big   大
3   (big)

大學	dàxué	university
*大小	dàxiǎo	size
*大人	dàrén	adult

A: 你是**大學生**嗎？
B: 是，我是**大學生**。

小

xiǎo
small   小
3   (small)

| 小學 | xiǎoxué | primary school |
| 小學生 | xiǎoxué.shēng | primary school student |

A: 你是學生嗎？
B: 是，我是學生，是**小學生**。

學

xué
to study   子
16   (son)

學生	xué.shēng	student
大學生	dàxué.shēng	university student
中學生	zhōngxué.shēng	middle school student

A: 你是不是**中學生**？
B: 不，我不是**中學生**，是**大學生**。

生

shēng
be born   生
5   (be born)

| 生日 | shēng.rì | birthday |
| *生活 | shēnghuó | life |

A: 你是**學生**嗎？
B: 是，我是**學生**。

繁簡對照：	其他漢字：	✎ **My notes:**
學学	*人 SC2 中 L5²	

上 學　　shàngxué　　to go to school
上 課　　shàngkè　　to go to classes
*上 班　　shàngbān　　to go to work

shàng
up 　　一
3　　(one)

A: 你**上大學**嗎？
B: 對，我**上大學**，我是大學生。

下 課　　xiàkè　　class dismissed
*下 班　　xiàbān　　to get off from work

xià
down 　　一
3　　(one)

我們現在**下課**。

*課文　　kèwén　　text
中文課　　Zhōngwén kè　　Chinese class

kè
lesson 　　言
15　　(speech)

A: 你上不上**中文課**？
B: 上。

.ma
particle 　　口
13　　(mouth)

A: 今天是九月三號**嗎**？
B: 不是。

繁簡對照：	其他漢字：	✎ My notes:
課课 嗎吗		

的

.de
particle   白
8   (white)

我的	wǒ .de	my
你的	nǐ .de	your
他的	tā .de	his

A: 他是**你的**學生嗎？
B: 是，他是**我的**學生。

日

rì
sun, day   日
3   (sun)

| 生日 | shēng.rì | birthday |
| *日記 | rìjì | diary |

我的**生日**是五月五號。

月

yuè
month   月
4   (moon)

五月	wǔyuè	May
九月	jiǔyuè	September
*月亮	yuèliàng	moon

今天是**五月**五號。

幾

jǐ
how many 幺
12 (one, small)

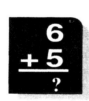

| 幾月幾號 | jǐ yuè jǐ hào | when (what month? what day?) |

A: 你的生日是**幾月幾號**？
B: 我的生日是**六月八號**。

繁簡對照：	其他漢字：	✎ **My notes:**
幾几		

明

míng
bright 日
8 (sun)

| 明天 | míng.tiān | tomorrow |
| *明白 | míng.bái | to understand |

A: 你**明天**上不上課？
B: 我**明天**不上課，後天上課。

天

tiān
sky 大
4 (big)

昨天	zuó.tiān	yesterday
前天	qián.tiān	the day before yesterday
*大前天	dàqián.tiān	two days before yesterday

A: 你**今天**上中文課嗎？
B: 我**昨天**上中文課，**今天**不上中文課。

他

tā
he, him 亻
5 (person)

他們	tā.men	they, them
他的	tā .de	his, her
他們的	tā.men .de	their

A: **他**明天上課嗎？
B: **他**明天不上課，大後天上課。

哪

nǎ, něi
which 口
10 (mouth)

| 哪一天 | něiyītiān | which day |
| *哪個人 | něi .ge rén | which one (person) |

A: **哪一天**是你的生日？
B: 五月五號是我的生日。

繁簡對照：	其他漢字：	✎ **My notes:**
	*她 SC3	
	*它 SC4	
	那 L7	

+

Grammar
語法 yǔfǎ

Ⓐ Major Sentence Patterns 主要句型 zhǔyào jùxíng

1. From Whole to Part Principle

> Whole 》 Part
> (largest unit 》 smallest unit)

1. Personal Names
    The family name comes first.
    高德中   Gāo, Dézhōng
                                               family name, given name

2. Time Expressions
    The year comes first.
    一九九六年九月十八號星期六   Yījiǔjiǔliù nián jiǔyuè shíbāhào xīngqīliù
                                               Saturday, September 18, 1996

3. Addresses
    The name of the country comes first.
    美國印地安那州布城第一街三號   Měiguó Yìndì'ānnàzhōu Bùchéng dìyījiē
                                               sānhào
                                               3 First Street, Bloomington, Indiana, USA

 In Chinese, the word order of some noun phrases begins with the largest picture (the whole) and progresses down into the whole's parts (e.g., personal names, time expressions, and addresses) (Chao 1968, Tai 1989, Yan 1993).

2. Equational sentences

> S + Equative Verb + O
> (N/NP)   (EV)   (N/NP)

The word order of an equational sentence in Chinese is the same as in a sentence with the verb "to be" in English: subject, verb, object.

2.1 Affirmative and negative sentences

> S   是   O
> S 不是   O

1.　昨天是八月二十四號。

Zuó.tiān shì bāyuè èrshísìhào.
Yesterday was August 24th.

2.　明天是星期六。

Míng.tiān shì xīngqīliù.
Tomorrow is Saturday.

3.　今天不是八月二十四號。

Jīn.tiān bú shì bāyuè èrshísìhào.
Today is not August 24th.

4.　星期二不是八月二十八號。

Xīngqī'èr bú shì bāyuè èrshíbāhào.
Tuesday is not August 28th.

In Chinese, a negative adverb must precede the verb to form a negative sentence.

2.2 Sentences with adverb 也 and negative adverb 不

S	也是	O
S	也不是	O

1.　八月二十七號是星期天，九月
　　三號也是星期天。

Bāyuè èrshíqīhào shì xīngqītiān. Jiǔyuè sānhào yě shì xīngqītiān.
August 27th is Sunday. September 3rd is Sunday, too.

2.　我的生日是十月五號，他的生
　　日也是十月五號。

Wǒ .de shēng.rì shì shíyuè wǔhào, tā .de shēng.rì yě shì shíyuè wǔhào.
My birthday is October 5th; his birthday is October 5th, too.

3.　二十二號不是星期一，二十九
　　號也不是星期一。

Èrshí'èrhào bú shì xīngqīyī, èrshíjiǔhào yě bú shì xīngqīyī.
The 22nd is not Monday; the 29th is not Monday, either.

4.　你的生日不是十二月，我的生
　　日也不是十二月。

Nǐ .de shēng.rì bú shì shí'èryuè, wǒ .de shēng.rì yě bú shì shí'èryuè.
Your birthday is not in December; my birthday is not in December, either.

An adverb is a form which modifies a verb or an adjective. In Chinese, the adverb 也 yě 'also, too' must precede the verb. To say "A is not X; B is not X, either," 也 yě must precede 不是 búshì in the second phrase.

3. Choice-type (A-not-A) questions

Question	Answer
S　是不是　O？	是/對了，S　　是　O 不/不是，S　不是　O

1.　八月十三號是不是星期天？

　　Bāyuè shísānhào shì .búshì xīngqītiān?
　　Is August 13th Sunday?

　　是/對了，八月十三號是星期天。

　　Shì/duì.le, bāyuè shísānhào shì xīngqītiān.
　　(You are) right/Yes, August 13th is/was Sunday.

　　不/不是，(八月十三號) 不是星期天。

　　Bù/búshì, (bāyuè shísānhào) bú shì xīngqītiān.
　　No, (August 13th) is/was not Sunday.

　　不/不是，是星期四，不是星期天。

　　Bù/búshì, shì xīngqīsì, bú shì xīngqītiān.
　　No, (it) is/was Thursday, not Sunday.

2.　前天是不是九月十三號？

　　Qián.tiān shì .búshì jiǔyuè shísānhào?
　　Was the day before yesterday September 13th?

　　不/不是，前天不是九月十三號。

　　Bù/búshì, qián.tiān bú shì jiǔyuè shísānhào.
　　No, the day before yesterday was not September 13th.

A choice-type question (called an A-not-A question by some linguists) is formed by combining the affirmative verb and its negative counterpart into a verb phrase. This type of question is equivalent to the "yes-no question" in English.

When the answer to the question is affirmative, one can say, 是 /對 了 shì/duì.le and then repeat the whole affirmative sentence or just the affirmative verbal expression. When the answer to the question is negative, one should first say the negative form of verb, 不/不是 bù/búshì, which indicates the negating, then say the whole negative sentence or the negative verbal expression without the subject. One can also say the affirmative answer/the real fact, then the negative verbal expression without the subject.

4. 嗎 questions

Question	Answer
S　是　O　嗎？	是/對了，S　　是　O 不/不是，S　不是　O

1. 十月十號是星期二嗎？

   Shíyuè shíhào shì xīngqī'èr .ma?
   Is October 10th Tuesday?

   是/對了，十月十號是星期二。

   Shì/duì.le, Shíyuè shíhào shì xīngqī'èr.
   Yes/that's right, October 10th is Tuesday.

   不/不是，十月十號不是星期二。

   Bù/búshì, Shíyuè shíhào bú shì xīngqī'èr.
   No, October 10th is not Tuesday.

2. 下星期三是九月二十號嗎？

   Xià xīngqīsān shì jiǔyuè èrshíhào .ma?
   Is next Wednesday September 20th?

   是/對了，下星期三是九月二十號。

   Shì/duì.le, xià xīngqīsān shì jiǔyuè èrshíhào.
   Yes/that's right, next Wednesday is September 20th.

   不/不是，下星期三不是九月二十號。

   Bù/búshì, xià xīngqīsān bú shì jiǔyuè èrshíhào.
   No, next Wednesday is not September 20th.

In Chinese, there is another common "yes-no" question which is formed by adding an interrogative particle 嗎 .ma (unstressed and in neutral tone) to the end of a statement. The function of 嗎 .ma is to change a statement into a question. If the verb in the sentence is positive and the answer is positive, then you say 是/對 (了) shì/duì.le 'yes/that's right' and repeat the positive statement. If the answer is negative, then you first say 不/不是 bù/búshì 'no/it is not the case that' and repeat a negative statement. An affirmative 嗎 question implies an affirmative presupposition of the speaker, while a negative one implies a negative presupposition.

5. Question-word questions
5.1 Sentences with question word 星期幾

Question	Answer
S 是 星期幾？	S 是 星期 no.

1. 今天是星期幾？

   Jīn.tiān shì xīngqījǐ?
   What day is today?

   今天是星期五。

   Jīn.tiān shì xīngqīwǔ.
   Today is Friday.

2. 九月二十八號是星期幾？

   Jiǔyuè èrshíbāhào shì xīngqījǐ?
   What day is September 28th?

   九月二十八號是星期四。

   Jiǔyuè èrshíbāhào shì xīngqīsì.
   September 28th is Thursday.

In Chinese, the word order of an interrogative sentence remains the same as in a narrative sentence. In a question-word question, a question word occupies the same position as the word which replaces it in the answer.

5.2 Sentences with question word 幾月幾號

Question	Answer
S 是 幾月幾號？	S 是 no. 月no. 號

1. 明天是幾月幾號？

    明天是八月二十六號。

    Míng.tiān shì jǐ yuè jǐ hào?
    What day of which month is tomorrow?

    Míng.tiān shì bāyuè èrshíliùhào.
    Tomorrow is August 26th.

2. 星期五是幾月幾號？

    星期五是八月二十五號。

    Xīngqīwǔ shì jǐ yuè jǐ hào?
    What day of which month is Friday?

    Xīngqīwǔ shì bāyuè èrshíwǔhào.
    Friday is August 25th.

5.3 Sentences with question word 哪一天

Question	Answer
S 哪一天 V O？	S Time When V O

1. 你們哪一天註冊？

    我們明天註冊。

    Nǐ.men něiyìtiān zhùcè?
    What day do you register?

    Wǒ.men míng.tiān zhùcè.
    We will register tomorrow.

2. 他們哪一天開學？

    他們九月五號開學。

    Tā.men něiyìtiān kāixué?
    What day does their school start?

    Tā.men jiǔyuè wǔhào kāixué.
    Their school will start on September 5th.

When a Chinese sentence denotes an action, the actor (subject) comes first, then the time when the action occurs, then the action itself. A sentence with the question word 哪一天 něiyìtiān 'which day? when?' expresses "time when" and therefore this phrase occurs right after the actor (subject).

5.4 Sentences with question word 誰

Question	Answer
S 是 誰？	S 是 X
# 月 # 號 是 誰 的 生日？	no. 月 no. 號 是 X 的 生日

1. 他是誰？

   Tā shì shéi?
   Who is he/she?

   他是李老師。

   Tā shì Lǐ lǎoshī.
   He/She is Teacher Li.

2. 九月二十八號是誰的生日？

   Jiǔyuè èrshíbāhào shì shéi .de shēng.rì?
   September 28th is whose birthday?

   九月二十八號是孔子的生日。

   Jiǔyuè èrshíbāhào shì Kǒngzǐ .de shēng.rì.
   September 28th is Confucius' birthday.

6. Stative verbs/adjectives

Structure	Example	Grammatical Function	Gloss
S + (adv) + SV	他 (很) 老。 Tā (hěn) lǎo.	lǎo as a verb	He is (very) old.
Adj + N	老學校 lǎo xuéxiào	lǎo as an adjective	old school

In Chinese, stative verbs (SV) form a subclass of verbs. Like other verbs, they may be modified by adverbs. Stative verbs describe a quality or status and are equivalent to adjectives in English. But note that they function as verbs when they follow a subject (S) and occupy the predicate position. When they occur before a noun as a modifier, they function as adjectives. The major difference between Chinese and English adjectives is that Chinese "adjectives" have a built-in "to be." Thus there is no need to use the verb 是 'to be' when you translate an English adjective into a Chinese stative verb.

✗ When you wish to say "He is very old" in Chinese, do *not* say 他是很老。

  See L7–A1 for more on adjectives.

ⓑ Usage of Common Phrases 詞組用法 cízǔ yòngfǎ

1. The question particle 呢

Question	Gloss
S₁ 是 X, S₂ 呢？	S₁ is X, how about S₂?
S₁ Time When V O, S₂ 呢？	S₁ Time When V O, how about S₂?

1. 我的生日是八月五號，你的   Wǒ .de shēng.rì shì bāyuè wǔhào, nǐ .de .ne?
    呢？
                                     My birthday is August 5th; how about yours?

    我的生日是七月三號。   Wǒ .de shēng.rì shì qīyuè sānhào.
                                     My birthday is July 3rd.

2. 他們今天註冊，你們呢？   Tā.men jīn.tiān zhùcè, nǐ.men .ne?
                                     They will register today; how about you?

    我們後天註冊。   Wǒ.men hòu.tiān zhùcè.
                                     We will register the day after tomorrow.

The question particle 呢 .ne has several uses. In this lesson, it takes the place of some words in the statement immediately preceding it.

See L6–A1.4, A5, L8–A4 for more on 呢 .ne.

2. Verb-object compounds

| Verb + Object → VO compound |

1. 小高哪一天註冊？   Xiǎo Gāo něitiān zhùcè?
                                     When will Xiao Gao register?

    他明天註冊。   Tā míng.tiān zhùcè.
                                     Xiao Gao will register tomorrow.

2. 你們九月五號開學嗎？   Nǐ.men jiǔyuè wǔhào kāixué .ma?
                                     Will your (school) start on September 5?

    不，我們九月二號開學。   Bù, wǒ.men jiǔyuè èrhào kāixué.
                                     No, our (school) will start on September 2.

In Chinese, a verb plus a noun may form a verb-object compound (or VO compound). Various types of VO compounds serve different functions. In this lesson, VO compounds such as 註冊 zhùcè 'to register' and 開學 kāixué 'to start school' function as intransitive verbs.

Cultural Notes
文化點滴 wénhuà diǎndī

1. Chinese people use two kinds of calendars:

Yánglì 陽曆 [yáng-calendar] Western calendar
Yīnlì　陰曆 [yīn-calendar] lunar calendar, also called Nónglì 農曆 [farmer-calender] farmer's calendar

Yīnlì/nónglì is the traditional Chinese calendar in which the seasonal terms for farming are provided so that farmers will be able to plant their crops according to the seasons. The first day of each month of the lunar calendar is always at the beginning of the crescent moon; the fifteenth day is the full moon. Because the days follow the movement of the moon, the Chinese use the character 月 yuè 'moon' for month. Therefore you can look at the phases of the moon and guess the day of the month in the lunar calendar.

2. Chinese people use the character 日 rì 'sun' for day because they consider that the day starts when the sun rises and ends when the sun sets. A day passes as the sun moves across the sky. Two famous Chinese sayings describe the farmer's life: 日出而作 rì chū ér zuò 'to start work at daybreak' and 日落而息 rì luò ér xí 'and retire at sunset.'

3. Lǐbài 'week' originally meant 'worship' and is used to refer to Christian worship. That is why the Chinese call Sunday lǐbàitiān—the worship day.

4. In China, people observe the rule of seniority. For direct address among close friends or colleagues, one may use "老 Lǎo + surname" to address seniors and "小 Xiǎo + surname" to address juniors. But when you address your teachers/mentors, don't use either of these terms. Their use is considered disrespectful to teachers/mentors. Instead, you should always address a teacher/mentor as "Surname + 老師 Lǎoshī 'Teacher'" to show proper respect.

5. In China, people traditionally eat 壽麵 shòumiàn 'longevity noodles' and/or 壽桃 shòutáo 'longevity peaches' to celebrate someone's birthday. In the Southern Min speaking areas, people eat 麵線 miànxiàn '(longevity) rice noodles' and 豬腳 zhūjiǎo 'pig's feet.' The length of noodles symbolizes long life. The pig's feet symbolize strength— to wish a person strong legs on which to walk and to have good health. Nowadays, people also adopt the Western tradition of serving birthday cakes.

6. September 28 is celebrated as the birthday of Confucius, the early Chinese philosopher (551-479 BC). Chinese greatly respect Confucius and his teaching, so the government chose his birthday to be 教師節 Jiàoshījié 'Teachers Day,' a national holiday to honor teachers.

7. Chinese has acronyms, just as English does (NASA, OPEC, PhysEd, etc.). Since each Chinese character consists of one syllable, a Chinese acronym is made up of the first syllables of a compound or a phrase. 台大 Táidà stands for 台灣大學 Táiwān dàxué '(National) Taiwan University,' 北大 Běidà stands for 北京大學 Běijīng dàxué 'Beijing University,' and 印大 Yìndà stands for 印地安那大學 Yìndì'ānnà dàxué 'Indiana University.' Here are the acronyms for six other U.S. universites.

University			Acronym
Columbia University	哥倫比亞大學	Gēlúnbǐyà dàxué	Gēdà
Ohio State University	俄亥俄州立大學	Éhàié zhōulì dàxué	Édà
Princeton University	普林斯頓大學	Pǔlínsīdùn dàxué	Pǔdà
University of Michigan	密西根大學	Mìxīgēn dàxué	Mìdà
University of Washington	華盛頓大學	Huáshèngdùn dàxué	Huádà
Yale University	耶魯大學	Yēlǔ dàxué	Yēdà (or Yēlǔ)

8. In Taiwan, people use 1911, the year the Republic of China (ROC) was founded, as the first year of their modern calendar. When Chinese newspapers or magazines there give the date as 中華民國八十六年 Zhōnghuá mínguó bāshí liù nián 'the 86th year of ROC,' you can figure out the year in the Western calendar by using the formula "1911 + 86 = 1997."

第五課 你今天有沒有課？

對話

〔小李，小高在學校裡，兩人在討論他們上的課。〕

小李： 小高，你今天有沒有課？

小高： 有，上午有一堂中文課。

小李： 下午呢？

小高： 下午有兩堂課。

小李： 你下午上什麼課？

小高： 一堂日文跟一堂英文。

小李： 你每天都有課嗎？

小高： 我一、三、五有課。二、四沒（有）課。你呢？

小李： 我天天都有課，週末沒（有）課。你週末做什麼呢？

小高： 我星期六休息，星期天預備功課。你呢？

小李： 我週末得打工。

对话

〔小李，小高在学校裡，两人在讨论他们上的课。〕

小李： 小高，你今天有没有课？

小高： 有，上午有一堂中文课。

小李： 下午呢？

小高： 下午有两堂课。

小李： 你下午上什么课？

小高： 一堂日文跟一堂英文。

小李： 你每天都有课吗？

小高： 我一、三、五有课。二、四没（有）课。你呢？

小李： 我天天都有课，周末没（有）课。你周末做什么呢？

小高： 我星期六休息，星期天预备功课。你呢？

小李： 我周末得打工。

My questions:

Duìhuà

(Xiǎo Lǐ , Xiǎo Gāo zài xuéxiào .lǐ, liǎng rén zài tǎolùn tā.men shàng .de kè.)

AaBbCcDdEeFfGgHhIiJjKkLlMmNnOoPpQqRrSs

Xiǎo Lǐ:	Xiǎo Gāo, nǐ jīn.tiān yǒu .méiyǒu kè?
Xiǎo Gāo:	Yǒu, shàng.wǔ yǒu yì táng Zhōngwén kè.
Xiǎo Lǐ:	Xià.wǔ .ne?
Xiǎo Gāo:	Xià.wǔ yǒu liǎng táng kè.
Xiǎo Lǐ:	Nǐ xià.wǔ shàng shén.me kè?
Xiǎo Gāo:	Yì táng Rìwén gēn yì táng Yīngwén.
Xiǎo Lǐ:	Nǐ měitiān dōu yǒu kè .ma?
Xiǎo Gāo:	Wǒ yī-sān-wǔ yǒu kè, èr-sì méi(.yǒu) kè. Nǐ .ne?
Xiǎo Lǐ:	Wǒ tiāntiān dōu yǒu kè. Zhōumò méi(.yǒu) kè. Nǐ zhōumò zuò shén.me .ne?
Xiǎo Gāo:	Wǒ xīngqīliù xiū.xí, xīngqītiān yù.bèi gōngkè. Nǐ .ne?
Xiǎo Lǐ:	Wǒ zhōumò děi dǎgōng.

Dialogue

(Xiǎo Lǐ and Xiǎo Gāo are on campus discussing their class schedules.)

Xiǎo Lǐ: Xiǎo Gāo, do you have class today?

Xiǎo Gāo: Yes, (I) have one Chinese class in the morning.

Xiǎo Lǐ: (How about) the afternoon?

Xiǎo Gāo: (I) have two classes in the afternoon.

Xiǎo Lǐ: What classes do you have in the afternoon?

Xiǎo Gāo: (I have) one Japanese class and one English class.

Xiǎo Lǐ: Do you have class every day?

Xiǎo Gāo: I have class on Mondays, Wednesdays, (and) Fridays.
                No class on Tuesdays (and) Thursdays. (How about) you?

Xiǎo Lǐ: I have class every day. No class on weekends. What do you
                do on weekends?

Xiǎo Gāo: I take a break on Saturdays (and) prepare for my
                classes on Sundays. (How about) you?

Xiǎo Lǐ: I have to work on weekends.

Mini-Dialogue
小對話 Xiǎoduìhuà

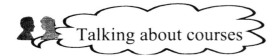
Talking about courses

1. A: 你今天上幾堂課？

    Nǐ jīn.tiān shàng jǐ táng kè?
    How many classes do you have today?

    B: 三堂。中文、日文、和英
        文。你呢？

    Sān táng: Zhōngwén, Rìwén, hé
    Yīngwén. Nǐ .ne?
    Three: Chinese, Japanese, and English.
    How about you?

    A: 我今天上兩堂課。

    Wǒ jīn.tiān shàng liǎng táng kè.
    I have two classes today.

2. A: 你明天上午有什麼課？

    Nǐ míng.tiān shàng.wǔ yǒu shén.me kè?
    What class do you have tomorrow
    morning?

    B: 我明天上午有中文課。

    Wǒ míng.tiān shàng.wǔ yǒu Zhōngwén kè.
    I have Chinese class tomorrow morning.

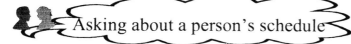
Asking about a person's schedule

1. A: 你星期一有課嗎？

    Nǐ xīngqíyī yǒu kè .ma?
    Do you have classes on Monday?

    B: 不，我星期一沒有課，二
        、四有課。

    Bù, wǒ xīngqíyī méi.yǒu kè, èr-sì yǒu
    kè.
    No, I have no classes on Mondays. I have
    classes on Tuesdays and Thursdays.

2. A: 你週末打工嗎？

    Nǐ zhōumò dǎgōng .ma?
    Do you work during the weekend?

    B: 對，我上午打工，下午預
        備功課。

    Duì, wǒ shàng.wǔ dǎgōng, xià.wǔ
    yù.bèi gōngkè.

    Yes, I work in the morning and prepare
    my homework in the afternoon.

Vocabulary
生詞 Shēngcí

◎ **By Order of Appearance**

有		yǒu	V	to have
沒(有)		méi (.yǒu)	V	to not have
上午		shàng.wǔ	N	[upper-noon] morning, forenoon
* 中午		zhōng.wǔ	N	[mid-noon] noon
堂		táng	M	[hall] measure word for classes
* 節	节	jié	M	[section] measure word for classes
* 個	个	.ge	M	measure word for persons and things
中文		Zhōngwén	N	[Chinese-language] Chinese
下午		xià.wǔ	N	[lower-noon] afternoon
* 晚上		wǎn.shàng	N	[late-upper] evening, night
* 早上		zǎo.shàng	N	[early-upper] morning, forenoon (= 上午)
兩	两	liǎng	N	two (occurs only before a measure word)
日文		Rìwén	N	[Japanese-language] Japanese
跟		gēn	Conj	[to follow] and
* 和		hé/hàn	Conj	and (= 跟)
英文		Yīngwén	N	[English-language] English
每天		měitiān	MTA/N	[every-day] every day
天天		tiāntiān	MTA/N	[day-day] every day (=每天)
* 去年		qù.nián	N	[go-year] last year
* 今年		jīn.nián	N	[now-year] this year
* 明年		míng.nián	N	[bright-year] next year
都		dōu	Adv	all, both
週末	周末	zhōumò	N	[week-end] weekend
做		zuò	V	to do, to make
什麼/甚麼	什么	shén.me	QW	what?
休息		xiū.xí	V	[rest-rest] to take a rest, to rest from work
預備	预备	yù.bèi	V	[beforehand-prepare] to prepare
功課	功课	gōngkè	N	[merit-lesson] homework
得		děi	Aux V	must, to have to
* 不用		búyòng	Aux V	doesn't have to, need not
* 不必		búbì	Aux V	doesn't have to, need not (=不用)
打工		dǎgōng	V	[hit-work] to work (at a temporary job)
* 工作		gōngzuò	V/N	[labor-do] to work
* 學	学	xué	V	to learn, to study (=學習)
* 學習	学习	xuéxí	V	to learn, to study
* 教		jiāo	V	to teach
* 朋友		péng.yǒu	N	[friend-friend] friend

◎ **By Grammatical Categories**

Nouns/Pronouns

* 早上		zǎo.shàng	N	[early-upper] morning, forenoon (= 上午)
上午		shàng.wǔ	N	[upper-noon] morning, forenoon
* 中午		zhōng.wǔ	N	[mid-noon] noon
下午		xià.wǔ	N	[lower-noon] afternoon
* 晚上		wǎn.shàng	N	[late-upper] evening, night
兩	两	liǎng	N	two (occurs only before a measure word)
每天		měitiān	MTA/N	[every-day] every day
天天		tiāntiān	MTA/N	[day-day] every day (=每天)
* 去年		qù.nián	N	[go-year] last year
* 今年		jīn.nián	N	[now-year] this year
* 明年		míng.nián	N	[bright-year] next year
週末	周末	zhōumò	N	[week-end] weekend
中文		Zhōngwén	N	[Chinese-language] Chinese
日文		Rìwén	N	[Japanese-language] Japanese
英文		Yīngwén	N	[English-language] English
功課	功课	gōngkè	N	[merit-lesson] homework
* 朋友		péng.yǒu	N	[friend-friend] friend

Measure Words

* 個	个	.ge	M	measure word for persons and things
堂		táng	M	[hall] measure word for classes
* 節	节	jié	M	[section] measure word for classes

Auxiliary Verbs

得		děi	Aux V	must, to have to
* 不用		búyòng	Aux V	doesn't have to, need not
* 不必		búbì	Aux V	doesn't have to, need not (=不用)

Verbs/Stative Verbs/Adjectives

有		yǒu	V	to have
沒(有)		méi (.yǒu)	V	to not have
做		zuò	V	to do, to make
* 工作		gōngzuò	V/N	[labor-do] to work
打工		dǎgōng	V	[hit-work] to work (at a temporary job)
休息		xiū.xí	V	[rest-rest] to take a rest, to rest from work
預備	预备	yù.bèi	V	[beforehand-prepare] to prepare

* 學	学	xué	V	to learn, to study (=學習)
* 學習	学习	xuéxí	V	to learn, to study
* 教		jiāo	V	to teach

Adverbs

都		dōu	Adv	all, both

Conjunctions

跟		gēn	Conj	[to follow] and
* 和		hé/hàn	Conj	and (= 跟)

Question Words

什麼/甚麼	什么	shén.me	QW	what?

➕ **Supplementary Vocabulary**
Countries and Languages

中國	中国	Zhōng.guó	N	[middle-country] China
台灣	台湾	Táiwān	N	[platform-bay] Taiwan
美國	美国	Měi.guó	N	[beautiful-country] America
英國	英国	Yīng.guó	N	[outstanding-country] England
英文		Yīngwén	N	[English-language] English
日本	日本	Rìběn	N	[sun-origin] Japan
日文		Rìwén	N	[Japanese-language] Japanese
韓國	韩国	Hán.guó	N	[Korea-country] Korea
韓文	韩文	Hánwén	N	[Korea-language] Korean
越南		Yuènán	N	[surpass-south] Vietnam
越南文		Yuènánwén	N	[Vietnam-language] Vietnamese
法國	法国	Fǎ.guó	N	[law-country] France
法文		Fǎwén	N	[France-language] French
德國	德国	Dé.guó	N	[virtue-country] Germany
德文		Déwén	N	[Germany-language] German
俄國	俄国	È.guó	N	[Russia-country] Russia
俄文		Èwén	N	[Russia-language] Russian
西班牙		Xībānyá	N	[west-group-tooth] Spain
西班牙文		Xībānyáwén	N	[Spain-language] Spanish
意大利		Yìdàlì	N	[meaning-big-profit] Italy
意大利文		Yìdàlìwén	N	[Italy-language] Italian
印度		Yìndù	N	[print-degree] India
印尼		Yìnní	N	[print-nun] Indonesia
馬來西亞	马来西亚	Mǎláixīyà	N	[horse-come-west-Asia] Malaysia
泰國	泰国	Tài.guó	N	[great-country] Thailand

Characters
漢字 Hànzì

今

jīn
now
4　　人
　　(person)

| 今天 | jīn.tiān | today (spoken) |
| 今年 | jīn.nián | this year |

A: 你**今天**上課嗎？
B: 不，我**今天**不上課。

年

nián
year
6　　干
　　(a stem)

2001

| 明年 | míng.nián | next year |
| 去年 | qù.nián | last year |

A: 你**今年**上中文課嗎？
B: 對，我**今年**上中文課。

有

yǒu
to have
there is　　月
6　　(moon)

有課	yǒu kè	to have classes
沒有課	méi.yǒu kè	to have no classes
有沒有	yǒu .méi.yǒu	to have or not have

A: 你今天**有沒有**課？
B: 有，我今天**有課**。

沒

méi
did not
have not　　氵
7　　(water)

| 沒有 | méi.yǒu | to not have |
| 沒課 | méi kè | to have no classes |

A: 你今天有課**沒有**？
B: **沒有**，我今天**沒有課**。

繁簡對照：	其他漢字： 昨 L19	✎ **My notes:**

中

中午	zhōngwǔ	noon
中國	zhōng.guó	China
中文	zhōngwén	Chinese language

zhōng
middle
center   丨
4   (vertical line)

A: 你今天**中午**有沒有**中文**課？
B: 沒有，我上午有**中文**課。

午

| 上午 | shàng.wǔ | morning |
| 下午 | xià.wǔ | afternoon |

wǔ
noon   十
4   (ten)

A: 你今天**下午**有幾堂課？
B: 我**下午**有三堂課。

國

美國	Měi.guó	United States
*英國	Yīng.guó	Great Britian
*法國	Fǎ.guó	France

guó
nation
state   囗
11   (boundary)

A: 他是不是**美國人**？
B: 不，他是**英國人**，不是**美國人**。

文

英文	Yīngwén	English
日文	Rìwén	Japanese
*法文	Fǎwén	French
*德文	Déwén	German

wén
language
literature   文
4   (literature)

A: 你學**日文**嗎？
B: 不，我不學**日文**，我學**中文**。

繁簡對照：	其他漢字：	✎ **My notes:**

兩

liǎng
two　　入
8　　(enter)

兩年	liǎng nián	two years
兩天	liǎng tiān	two days
兩堂課	liǎng táng kè	two classes

A: 你有幾個中國朋友？
B: 我有**兩個**中國朋友。

個

.ge
Measure　　亻
10　　(person)

| 一個學生 | yī .ge xué.shēng | one student |
| 兩個月 | liǎng .ge yuè | two months |

A: 你的朋友是**個**大學生嗎？
B: 是，他是大學生，印大的學生。

朋

péng
friend　　月
8　　(moon)

| 朋友 | péng.yǒu | friends |
| *小朋友 | xiǎopéng.yǒu | little friends (to address kids) |

A: 他是你的**朋友**嗎？
B: 是，他是我的**朋友**。

友

yǒu
friend　　又
4　　(again)

A: 你的**朋友**的生日是幾月幾號？
B: 他的生日是五月五號。

繁簡對照：	其他漢字：	✎ **My notes:**
兩 两 個 个		

早

zǎo
early   日
6   (sun)

早上   zǎo.shàng   morning
*早晚   zǎowǎn   sooner or later (lit. early-
                                  late)

A: 他今天**早上**有沒有課？
B: 他今天**早上**沒課，明天**早上**有課。

做

zuò
to do   亻
11   (person)

做功課   zuò gōngkè   to do homework
做什麼   zuò shén.me   to do what?
*做事   zuòshì   to do things
*做工   zuògōng   to work (manual labor)

A: 你明天早上**做什麼**？
B: 我明天早上有課，有中文課、英文課。

什

?

shén
what   亻
4   (person)

什麼   shén.me   what
*爲什麼   wèishén.me   why

A: 你今天下午做**什麼**？
B: 休息，我今天下午沒有課。

麼

?

.me
suffix for
interrogative
and adverbs 麻
14   (hemp)

*怎麼   zěn.me   how; why
*怎麼樣   zěn.meyàng   how
*這麼   zhè.me   this way; so

A: 你星期天早上做**什麼**？
B: 我星期天早上學中文。

繁簡對照：	其他漢字：	✎ **My notes:**
什=甚 麼=么	晚 L17 作 L9	

跟

gēn
follow
with   足
13   (foot)

A: **你跟你的朋友**星期天都做什麼呢？
B: 我們做功課。

也

yě
also
too   乙
3   (second)

A: 她是中國人，你呢？
B: 我**也是**中國人。

都

dōu
in all cases
all   阝
11   (city)

A: 你跟她**都是**中國人嗎？
B: 對，我們都是中國人。

呢

.ne
particle   口
8   (mouth)

A: 你星期六打工，星期天做什麼**呢**？
B: 我星期天也打工。

繁簡對照：	其他漢字： 和 L9	✎ **My notes:**

Grammar
語法 yǔfǎ

ⒶMajor Sentence Patterns 主要句型 zhǔyào jùxíng

1. Noun phrases

1.1 Noun plus noun

Noun Phrase (NP) → Noun (N) + Noun (N)

1. 中文課 → 中文 + 課   Zhōngwén kè → Zhōngwén + kè
                                        Chinese classes → Chinese + classes

2. 日文課 → 日文 + 課   Rìwén kè → Rìwén + kè
                                        Japanese classes → Japanese + classes

In Chinese, a noun phrase may consist of two nouns (N); the first noun modifies the second one.

1.2 Noun (time) plus noun (time)

	Whole		Part
NP →	Day	+	Forenoon/afternoon/evening

1. 今天下午   jīn.tiān xià.wǔ
                                        [today-afternoon] this afternoon

2. 昨天晚上   zuó.tiān wǎn.shàng
                                        yesterday evening

If a noun phrase consists of two nouns that denote time, then the word order follows the From Whole to Part Principle. For example, since 上午 shàng.wǔ 'morning' is a part of a day, for "this morning" you should say 今天上午 jīn.tiān shàng.wǔ 'today-morning.'

1.3 Noun phrases with measure words

NP → No. + Measure Word (M) + N

1. 一堂課   yì táng kè
                                        [one-period-class] one class

2. 兩個星期   liǎng .ge xīngqī
                                        [two-unit-week] two weeks

In Chinese, individual nouns are always associated with their specfic measure words (M) when they are preceded by numbers for counting objects. Measure words function as classifiers of nouns. They are used according to the shape, length, kind, or other property associated with them. Thus a noun phrase may consist of a number, a measure word, and a noun. From now on, whenever a countable noun appears in a lesson, there will be an appropriate measure word to go with it.

Note: If a noun itself denotes a measure, e.g., 天 tiān 'day' and 年 nián 'year,' then it will be preceded immediately by a number without another measure word.

NP → No. + 天/年

1. 四天/五年   sì tiān/ wǔ nián
four days/ five years

2. The possessive verb 有 — 嗎 form

2.1 Verb 有

Question	Answer
S MTA 有 O .ma ?	對(了), S MTA 有 O 不, S MTA 沒(有) O

1. 你今天下午有課嗎?/
今天下午你有課嗎?

Nǐ jīn.tiān xià.wǔ yǒu kè .ma?/
Jīn.tiān xià.wǔ nǐ yǒu kè .ma?
Do you have class this afternoon?

對(了), 我今天下午有課。/
今天下午我有課。

Duì.le, wǒ jīn.tiān xià.wǔ yǒu kè./
jīn.tiān xià.wǔ wǒ yǒu kè.
Yes, I have class this afternoon.

不, 我今天下午沒(有)課。/
今天下午我沒(有)課。

Bù, wǒ jīn.tiān xià.wǔ méi.yǒu kè./
jīn.tiān xià.wǔ wǒ méi.yǒu kè.
No, I don't have class this afternoon.

2. 你星期一上午有中文課嗎?/
星期一上午你有中文課嗎?

Nǐ xīngqīyī shàng.wǔ yǒu Zhōngwén kè
.ma?/ Xīngqīyī shàng.wǔ nǐ yǒu Zhōngwén
kè .ma?
Do you have Chinese class on Monday
morning?

對(了),我星期一上午有中文課。/
星期一上午我有中文課。

Duì.le, wǒ xīngqīyī shàng.wǔ yǒu Zhōngwén kè./
xīngqīyī shàng.wǔ wǒ yǒu Zhōngwén kè.

Yes, I have Chinese class on Monday morning.

不，我星期一上午没(有)中文課。/
星期一上午我没(有)中文課。

Bù, wǒ xīngqīyī shàng.wǔ méi.yǒu Zhōngwén kè/
xīngqīyī shàng.wǔ wǒ méi.yǒu Zhōngwén kè.
No, I don't have Chinese class on Monday morning.

When the subject of a sentence with the transitive verb 有 yǒu is animate, then 有 means "to have," which carries a noun/noun phrase as an object. The question particle 嗎 can be added to the end of 有 sentence to transform it to a question meaning "Does X have...?" If the answer is positive, you should say 對(了) duì(.le) 'that's right,' then repeat the positive statement. If the answer is negative, you say 不 bù 'no' first, then X 没(有) méi (.yǒu) Obj. **Note:** 有 can be negated only by 没 méi. It cannot be negated by 不.

The *Principle of Simultaneous Existence* governs two grammatical units that exist simultaneously (Yan 1993). In the real world, we human beings grow old as time goes by; in other words, we and the time are simultaneously existent. In a Chinese sentence, the word order of the subject (S—the actor) and the movable time adverb (MTA—the time when the action occurs) are interchangeable. This is a reflection of the reality of their simultaneous existence. Thus you may say 我今天... or 今天我....

2.2 Verb 有 plus 也 and 都

Question	Answer
S MTA (也)(都) 有 O .ma?	對(了), S MTA (也)(都) 有 O 不, S Time When (也)(都) 没(有) O

1. 你明天下午也有課嗎？

    Nǐ míng.tiān xià.wǔ yě yǒu kè .ma?
    Do you also have class tomorrow afternoon?

    對(了)，我明天下午也有課。

    Duì(.le), wǒ míng.tiān xià.wǔ yě yǒu kè.
    Yes, I have class tomorrow afternoon, too.

    不，我明天下午没(有)課。

    Bù, wǒ míng.tiān xià.wǔ méi(.yǒu) kè.
    No, I don't have class tomorrow afternoon.

2. 你今天下午跟明天下午都没有課嗎？

    Nǐ jīn.tiān xià.wǔ gēn míng.tiān xià.wǔ dōu méi(.yǒu) kè .ma?
    Is it true that you don't have class this afternoon or tomorrow afternoon?

    對(了), 我今天下午跟明天下午都没(有)課。

    Duì(.le), wǒ jīn.tiān xià.wǔ gēn míng.tiān xià.wǔ dōu méi(.yǒu) kè.

(You are) right, I don't have class this afternoon or tomorrow afternoon.

3.　他們每天都有課嗎？

Tā.men měitiān dōu yǒu kè .ma?
Do they have class every day?

對(了), 他們每天都有課。
我們每天也都有課。

Duì(.le), tā.men měitiān dōu yǒu kè.
Wǒ.men měitiān yě dōu yǒu kè.
Yes, they have class every day. We have class every day, too.

不, 他們每天都沒(有)課。
我們每天也都沒(有)課。

Bù, tā.men měitiān dōu méi(.yǒu) kè.
Wǒ.men měitiān yě dōu méi(.yǒu) kè.
No, they don't have class any day. We don't have class any day, either.

Since both 也 yě and 都 dōu are adverbs, they occur only in front of the verb. If they both occur in front of the verb 有, then the order must be 也都有 '(plural N) also have...,' or 也都沒(有) '(plural N) don't have ...either.'

See L11–A5, A6 for more on 都.

2.3 The difference between 也 and 跟、和

| S (MTA) (Neg) V O,　也 (Neg) V O |
| S (MTA) (不) 是 A,　也 (不) 是　B |

1.　我今天有中文課，也有日文課。

Wǒ jīn.tiān yǒu Zhōngwén kè, yě yǒu Rìwén kè.
Today I have Chinese class, (and I) also have Japanese class.

2.　他星期六休息，星期天也休息。

Tā xīngqīliù xiū.xí, xīngqītiān yě xiū.xí.
He doesn't work on Saturday, (and he) doesn't work on Sunday, either.

3.　小高昨天上午沒有中文課，也沒有英文課。

Xiǎo Gāo zuó.tiān shàng.wǔ méi.yǒu Zhōngwén kè, yě méi.yǒu Yīngwén kè.
Xiao Gao didn't have Chinese class yesterday morning, (and he) didn't have English class, either.

4.　十月七號不是星期四，也不是星期五。

Shíyuè qíhào bú shì xīngqīsì, yě bú shì xīngqīwǔ.

October 7th is not Thursday; (it) is not Friday, either.

 也 yě is an adverb that occurs only before a verb or an adverb, but it can also connect two or more verbs/verbal phrases and functions as a conjunction equivalent to "and" in English.

> S (MTA) (Neg) VO₁ 跟/和 O₂
> A 跟/和 B (Time When) 都 (Neg) V O

1. 小李明天有日文課和英文課。
    Xiǎo Lǐ míng.tiān yǒu Rìwén kè hé Yīngwén kè.
    Xiao Li has Japanese and English classes tomorrow.

2. 小高跟/和他的朋友星期六都沒課。
    Xiǎo Gāo gēn/hé tā .de péng.yǒu xīngqīliù dōu méi kè.
    Neither Xiao Gao nor his friend has class on Saturday.

3. 我跟/和他每天上午都有中文課。
    Wǒ gēn/hé tā měitiān shàng.wǔ dōu yǒu Zhōngwén kè.
    He and I have Chinese class every morning.

跟 gēn 'and' and 和 hé 'and' are conjunctions that can connect two or more nominal expressions (nouns or pronouns). When they join more than one element together and serve as the subject of a sentence, the whole subject must be followed by an adverb 都 'all' for the plurality.

See L14–A7, L19–B3 for more on 跟、和、也.

3. The possessive verb 有 — choice-type (A-not-A) form

Question	Answer
S （MTA） 有沒有 O？	有， S （MTA） 有 O
S （MTA） 有 O 沒有？	沒有，S （MTA） 沒(有) O

1. 你一、三、五有沒有課？/
    你一、三、五有課沒有？
    Nǐ yī-sān-wǔ yǒu méi.yǒu kè?/
    Nǐ yī-sān-wǔ yǒu kè méi.yǒu?
    Do you have class on Mondays, Wednesdays, and Fridays?

	我一、三、五沒有課，二、四 有課。	Wǒ yī-sān-wǔ méi.yǒu kè, èr-sì yǒu kè. I don't have class on Mondays, Wednesdays, and Fridays; (I) have class on Tuesdays and Thursdays.
2.	小李有沒有中國朋友？/ 小李有中國朋友沒有？	Xiǎo Lǐ yǒu méi.yǒu Zhōng.guó péng.yǒu?/ Xiǎo Lǐ yǒu Zhōng.guó péng.yǒu méi.yǒu? Does Xiao Li have Chinese friends?
	小李有中國朋友。	Xiǎo Lǐ yǒu Zhōng.guó péng.yǒu. Xiao Li has Chinese friends.
	小李沒有中國朋友。	Xiǎo Lǐ méi.yǒu Zhōng.guó péng.yǒu. Xiao Li doesn't have Chinese friends.

 A choice-type (A-not-A) question with the transitive verb 有 'to have' is formed by combining the affirmative verb 有 and its negative counterpart 沒有 'doesn't have' into a verb phrase. This type of question is equivalent to the 'yes-no question' in English. However, if the answer is positive, you must say the verb 有 first, then repeat the positive statement. If the answer is negative, you must say 沒有, then repeat the negative statement.

4. The question word 什麼 / 甚麼

Question	Answer
S MTA 有什麼 N?	S MTA 有 N/NP
S MTA 上 什麼 課？	S MTA 上 X 課
S MTA 做什麼？	S MTA VO

1.	你星期四下午有什麼課？	Nǐ xīngqīsì xià.wǔ yǒu shén.me kè? What classes do you have on Thursday afternoon?
	我星期四下午有英文課。	Wǒ xīngqīsì xià.wǔ yǒu Yīngwén kè. I have English class on Thursday afternoon.
2.	小高後天上午上什麼課？	Xiǎo Gāo hòu.tiān shàng.wǔ shàng shén.me kè? What class does Xiao Gao attend in the morning of the day after tomorrow?
	他後天上午上日文課。	Tā hòu.tiān shàng.wǔ shàng Rìwén kè. He attends Japanese class in the morning of the day after tomorrow.

3.　你星期六晚上做什麼？

Nǐ xīngqīliù wǎn.shàng zuò shén.me?
What do you do on Saturday night?

　　我星期六晚上休息。

Wǒ xīngqīliù wǎn.shàng xiū.xí.
I rest on Saturday night.

什麼 shén.me is an interrogative pronoun for things that one would like to ask in a question. It can occur as a subject or an object. In this lesson, 什麼 is used only to modify a nominal expression or as an object of an action verb. In the answer, you use a noun or a verb phrase in place of 什麼.

上課 shàngkè 'to attend class' is a VO compound. In this pattern, between the verb 上 shàng and the object 課 kè you can insert a modifier X to describe what kind of class you are going to attend.

5. The question word 幾

Question	Answer
S MTA 有 幾 M N?	S MTA 有 No. M N

1.　他一個星期有幾堂課？

Tā yí .ge xīngqī yǒu jǐ táng kè?
How many classes does he have each week?

　　他一個星期有十堂課。

Tā yí .ge xīngqī yǒu shí táng kè.
He has ten classes each week.

2.　小高昨天上午有幾堂課？

Xiǎo Gāo zuó.tiān shàng.wǔ yǒu jǐ táng kè?
How many classes did he have yesterday morning?

　　他昨天上午有四堂課。

Tā zuó.tiān shàng.wǔ yǒu sì táng kè.
He had four classes yesterday morning.

幾 jǐ is an interrogative for numerals. When a question asks "how many X?" you should use 幾 to replace the numeral, which always precedes a measure when it modifies a noun.

6. The auxiliary verb 得

Question	Answer
S MTA 得 V O 嗎？ (AuxV)	對，S MTA 得 V O 不，S MTA 不必／不用 V O

1. 他週末得打工嗎？

   Tā zhōumò děi dǎgōng .ma?
   Does he have to work on weekends?

   對，他週末得打工。

   Duì, tā zhōumò děi dǎgōng.
   Yes, he has to work on weekends.

   不，他週末不必打工。

   Bù, tā zhōumò búbì dǎgōng.
   No, he doesn't have to work on weekends.

2. 你星期六得上課嗎？

   Nǐ xīngqīliù děi shàngkè .ma?
   Do you have to go to class on Saturday?

   對，我星期六得上課。

   Duì, wǒ xīngqīliù děi shàngkè.
   Yes, I have to go to class on Saturday.

   不，我星期六不用上課。

   Bù, wǒ xīngqīliù búyòng shàngkè.
   No, I don't have to go to class on Saturday.

 得 děi 'have to, must' is an auxiliary verb which always follows the subject. In general, the negative marker for an auxiliary verb is 不 bù 'not.' But note that in the case of 得 , the negative form is 不必 búbì or 不用 búyòng 'need not to, doesn't have to.'

ⓑ Usage of Common Phrases 詞組用法 cízǔ yòngfǎ

1. X 也是 expression

Structure	Gloss
S₁ MTA V O	S₁ Time V O
S₂ 也是	S₂ too

1. 他週末得打工。

   Tā zhōumò děi dǎgōng.
   He has to work on weekends.

   我也是。

   Wǒ yě shì.
   I (do) too.

2. 小李星期一星期三有課。

   Xiǎo Lǐ xīngqīyī xīngqīsān yǒu kè.
   Xiao Li has classes on Monday and Wednesday.

   他也是。

   Tā yě shì.
   He (does) too.

 X也是 X yě shì 'X too' is an idiomatic expression which denotes that X is in the same situation/case as the subject in the previous sentence. It is wrong to say just "X也."

Cultural Notes
文化點滴 wénhuà diǎndī

1. In China and Taiwan, students in elementary schools, middle schools, and high schools have classes on Saturday mornings. Teachers usually give extra homework assignments to students on weekends and holidays and during winter and summer vacations because students have more time then to do homework.

2. The most common temporary work that college students do is serving

as 家教 jiājiào 'family tutors' for middle and high school students who need 補習 bǔxí '[supplement-learning] private tutoring to supplement regular schooling.' In China and Taiwan, the examinations for getting into good schools are very difficult, so parents always hire tutors to teach their children at home or send them to 補習班 bǔxíbān '[supplement-learning-class] extended schools' to prepare them for the tough competition.

3. Learning the number of days of each month is not an easy task for young children, so Chinese have invented an easy way to help their kids learn which month has how many days:

   * Make a fist of your hand.
   * Use the index finger of the other hand to point to the first knuckle and say, 一月大 yíyuè dà '[first-month-big] January (is a) big (month)', then point to the place in between the first knuckle and the second knuckle and say 二月小 èryuè xiǎo '[second-month-small] February (is a) small (month),' and so on.
   * If a month is "big," then it has 31 days. If a month is "small," then it has 30 days, except for the second month, which has 28/29 days.

第六課　你上哪兒去？

對話

〔小李要去書店買 書。 小高要去圖書館借書。小李 在 路
上遇見小高〕

小李 ： 小高，你上哪兒去？

小高 ： 我上 圖書館去。你
呢？

小李 ： 我要到書店去買 幾本
書。我不喜歡法文課
，退了（ 那門課），
加選了一門日文課。

小高 ： 日文課怎麼樣？

小李 ： 很不錯，可是得念很多書，功課也很多，很累！你怎麼
樣？

小高 ： 還好。選了四門課，十二個學分。這一個學期課不太重。
對了，你決定主修什麼？
國貿還是日文？

小李 ： 主修國貿，副修日文。對
不起，已經 五點（ 鐘）
了，我得去買書了，書店快
（ 要） 關門了。再見！

小高 ： 我也得去圖書館借書了。
再見！

对话

〔小李要去书店买书。小高要去图书馆借书。小李在路上遇见小高〕

小李 ： 小高，你上哪儿去 ？

小高 ： 我上图书馆去。你呢 ？

小李 ： 我要到书店去买几本书。我不喜欢法文课，退了（那门课），加选了一门日文课。

小高 ： 日文课怎么样 ？

小李 ： 很不错，可是得念很多书，功课也很多，很累！你怎么样 ？

小高 ： 还好。选了四门课，十二个学分。这一个学期课不太重。对了，你决定主修什么？国贸还是日文 ？

小李 ： 主修国贸，副修日文。对不起，已经五点（钟）了，我得去买书了，书店快（要）关门了。再见！

小高 ： 我也得去图书馆借书了。再见！

My questions:

Duìhuà

(Xiǎo Lǐ yào qù shūdiàn mǎi shū. Xiǎo Gāo yào qù túshūguǎn jièshū.
  Xiǎo Lǐ zài lù .shàng yù.jiàn Xiǎo Gāo.)

Xiǎo Lǐ: Xiǎo Gāo, nǐ shàng nǎr qù?

Xiǎo Gāo: Wǒ shàng túshūguǎn qù. Nǐ .ne?

Xiǎo Lǐ: Wǒ yào dào shūdiàn qù mǎi jǐ běn shū. Wǒ bù
             xǐ.huān Fàwén kè, tuì .le (nà mén kè), jiā xuǎn .le yì
             mén Rìwén kè.

Xiǎo Gāo: Rìwén kè zěn.meyàng?

Xiǎo Lǐ: Hěn búcuò, kě.shì děi niàn hěn duō shū, gōngkè yě
             hěn duō, hěn lèi! Nǐ zěn.meyàng?

Xiǎo Gāo: Hái hǎo. Xuǎn .le sì mén kè, shí'èr .ge xuéfēn. Zhèi
             .ge xuéqī kè bútài zhòng. Duì.le, nǐ juédìng zhǔxiū
             shén.me? Guómào hái.shì Rìwén?

Xiǎo Lǐ: Zhǔxiū guómào, fùxiū Rìwén. Duì.buqǐ, yǐ.jīng wǔ
             diǎn(zhōng) .le, wǒ děi qù mǎishū .le, shūdiàn kuài
             (yào) guānmén .le. Zàijiàn!

Xiǎo Gāo: Wǒ yě děi qù túshūguǎn jièshū .le. Zàijiàn!

Dialogue

(Xiǎo Lǐ is going to the bookstore to buy some books. Xiǎo Gāo is going to the library to check out some books. Xiǎo Lǐ runs into Xiǎo Gāo on the street.)

Xiǎo Lǐ: Xiao Gao, where are you going?

Xiǎo Gāo: I am going to the library; how about you?

Xiǎo Lǐ: I am going to the bookstore to buy some books. I don't like the French class; (I have) dropped that course and have added a Japanese course.

Xiǎo Gāo: How is the Japanese course?

Xiǎo Lǐ: It's pretty good, but (we) have to read a lot of books (and there is) a lot of homework too; (it's) very tiresome! How about you?

Xiǎo Gāo: It's O.K. (I) am taking four courses, twelve credits. This semester (my) course load is not too heavy. Oh, have you decided your major yet? (Is it) international business or Japanese?

Xiǎo Lǐ: (My) major (is) in international business, minor in Japanese. Excuse me, (it's) already five o'clock. I've got to buy the books; the bookstore is going to close soon. Bye!

Xiǎo Gāo: I've got to go to the library to check out books, too. Goodbye!

Mini-Dialogue
小對話 Xiǎoduìhuà

Greeting on the street
Asking about destination

1. A: 你上哪兒去？

    Nǐ shàng nǎr qù?
    Where are you going?

    B: 我上圖書館去。你也去嗎？

    Wǒ shàng túshūguǎn qù. Nǐ yě qù .ma?
    I am going to the library. Are you?

    A: 不，我得到書店去。

    Bù, wǒ děi dào shūdiàn qù.
    No, I have to go to the bookstore.

Telling time

1. A: 對不起，現在幾點？

    Duì.buqǐ, xiànzài jǐ diǎn?
    Excuse me, what time is it now?

    B: 五點差一刻。

    Wǔ diǎn chà yí kè.
    A quarter to five.

2. A: 現在幾點？

    Xiànzài jǐ diǎn?
    What time is it now?

    B: 對不起，我没帶錶。

    Duì.buqǐ, wǒ méi dài biǎo.
    Sorry, I don't have a watch.

Ending a conversation

1. A: 對不起，已經六點了。我
        得去書店買書了。再見！

    Duì.buqǐ, yǐ.jīng liù diǎn .le. Wǒ děi
    qù shūdiàn mǎi shū .le. Zàijiàn!

    Excuse me, (it's) already six o'clock.
    I've got to go to the bookstore to buy
    books. Bye!

    B: 我也得去打工了。再見！

    Wǒ yě děi qù dǎgōng .le. Zàijiàn!
    I've got to work, too. Bye!

Vocabulary
生詞 Shēngcí

◎ By Order of Appearance

上…去/來	上…去/来	shàng…qù/lái	V	[up…go/come] to go there/come here
到…去/來	到…去/来	dào…qù/lái	V	[arrive…go/come] to go there/come here
* 去		qù	V	to go
* 來	来	lái	V	to come
* 回		huí	V	to return (to a place; from a trip; to original state), to go back
哪兒	哪儿	nǎr	QW	where?
* 什麼地方	什么地方	shén.me dì.fāng	QW	what place? where?
圖書館	图书馆	túshūguǎn	N	[picture-book-hall] library (M: 個.ge)
書店	书店	shūdiàn	N	[book-store] bookstore (M: 家 jiā)
* 家		jiā	M/N	measure word for stores, restaurants, cinema; home
買	买	mǎi	V	to buy
* 賣	卖	mài	V	to sell
幾	几	jǐ	Adj	few, some (+M+N) (indefinite)
本		běn	M	[origin] measure word for books, notebooks
書	书	shū	N	book
喜歡	喜欢	xǐ.huān	V	[happy-happy] to like
退		tuì	V	to drop (a course), to withdraw (from school), to return (something to the store)
了		.le	Asp	aspect marker for completed action
那		nà/nèi	Det	that
* 這	这	zhè/zhèi	Det	this
門	门	mén	M	[door] measure word for courses
加	加	jiā	V	to add
選	选	xuǎn	V	to take (a course), to elect
怎麼樣	怎么样	zěn.meyàng	QW	how is it?
很		hěn	Adv	very
* 非常		fēicháng	Adv	[not-often] unusually, extraordinarily
不錯	不错	búcuò	SV	[not-bad] (to be) not bad, quite good
可是		kě.shì	Conj	but
念		niàn	V	to study (a subject)
多		duō	SV	(to be) much; many
* 少		shǎo	SV	(to be) little (quantity), few
累		lèi	SV	(to be) tired

* 忙		máng	SV	(to be) busy
* 用功		yònggōng	SV	[use-work] (to be) diligent
還	还	hái	Adv	still
好		hǎo	SV	(to be) good
個	个	.ge	M	measure word for persons or things
學分	学分	xuéfēn	N	[learn-point] credits (M: 個 .ge)
學期	学期	xuéqī	N	[learn-period] semester (M: 個 .ge)
不太		bútài	Adv	not quite, not very
重		zhòng	SV	(to be) heavy (course load, taste, weight)
* 輕	轻	qīng	SV	(to be) light (course load, weight)
決定	决定	juédìng	V	to decide
主修		zhǔxiū	N/V	[main-study] major, to major in
* 專業	专业	zhuānyè	N	[specialize-profession] specialty, major
國貿	国贸	guómào	N	[country-trade] international business
還是	还是	hái.shì	Conj	[still-is] or
副修		fùxiū	N/V	[secondary-study] minor, to minor in
對不起	对不起	duì.buqǐ	IE	[face-not-up] (I am) sorry
已經	已经	yǐ.jīng	Adv	[already-pass through] already
點(鐘)	点(钟)	diǎn(zhōng)	N	[point-clock] o'clock
* 刻		kè	N	quarter
* 分		fēn	N	minute
* 秒		miǎo	N	second
* 時候	时候	shí.hòu	N	[time-wait] time
* 現在	现在	xiànzài	N	[appear-at] now
* 過	过	guò	V	to pass
* 差		chà	V	to be short of, lack
* 什麼時候	什么时候	shén.me shí.hòu	QW	what time? when?
* 幾點鐘	几点钟	jǐ diǎnzhōng	QW	what time?
快(要)		kuài(yào)	Adv	soon, before long
要		yào	V/ Aux V	to want; will, shall
關門	关门	guānmén	VO	[close-door] to close the door
* 開門	开门	kāimén	VO	[open-door] to open the door
再見	再见	zàijiàn	V	[again-see] goodbye
借		jiè	V	to borrow
* 還	还	huán	V	to return (something)

◎ **By Grammatical Categories**

Nouns/Pronouns

書	书	shū	N	book
書店	书店	shūdiàn	N	[book-store] bookstore (M: 家 jiā)
圖書館	图书馆	túshūguǎn	N	[picture-book-hall] library (M: 個 .ge)
學分	学分	xuéfēn	N	[learn-point] credits (M: 個)
學期	学期	xuéqī	N	[learn-period] semester (M: 個)
點(鐘)	点 (钟)	diǎn(zhōng)	N	[point-clock] o'clock
* 刻		kè	N	quarter
* 分		fēn	N	minute
* 秒		miǎo	N	second
* 時候	时候	shí.hòu	N	[time-wait] time
* 現在	现在	xiànzài	N	[appear-at] now
主修		zhǔxiū	N/V	[main-study] major, to major in
* 專業	专业	zhuānyè	N	[specialize-profession] specialty, major
副修		fùxiū	N/V	[secondary-study] minor, to minor in
國貿	国贸	guómào	N	[country-trade] international business

Measure Words

本		běn	M	[origin] measure word for books, notebooks
門	门	mén	M	[door] measure word for courses
個	个	.ge	M	measure word for persons or things
* 家		jiā	M/N	measure word for stores, restaurants, cinema; home

Verbs/Stative Verbs/Adjectives

* 去		qù	V	to go
* 來	来	lái	V	to come
上...去/來	上...去 / 来	shàng...qù/lái	V	[up...go/come] to go there/come here
到...去/來	到...去 / 来	dào...qù/lái	V	[arrive...go/come] to go there/come here
* 回		huí	V	to return (to a place; from a trip; to original state), go back
要		yào	V/ Aux V	to want; will, shall
買	买	mǎi	V	to buy
* 賣	卖	mài	V	to sell

喜歡	喜欢	xǐ.huān	V	[happy-happy] to like
念		niàn	V	to study (a subject)
退		tuì	V	to drop (a course), to withdraw (from school), to return (something to the store)
加	加	jiā	V	to add
選	选	xuǎn	V	to take (a course) , to elect
不錯	不错	búcuò	SV	[not-bad] (to be) not bad, quite good
多		duō	SV	(to be) much; many
* 少		shǎo	SV	(to be) little (quantity), few
幾	几	jǐ	Adj	few, some (+M+N) (indefinite)
累		lèi	SV	(to be) tired
* 忙		máng	SV	(to be) busy
好		hǎo	SV	(to be) good
重		zhòng	SV	(to be) heavy (course load, taste, weight)
* 輕	轻	qīng	SV	(to be) light (course load, weight)
* 用功		yònggōng	SV	[use-work] (to be) diligent
決定	决定	juédìng	V	to decide
關門	关门	guānmén	VO	[close-door] to close the door
* 開門	开门	kāimén	VO	[open-door] to open the door
再見	再见	zàijiàn	V	[again-see] goodbye
借		jiè	V	to borrow
* 還	还	huán	V	to return (something)
* 過	过	guò	V	to pass
* 差		chà	V	to be short of, lack
了		.le	Asp	aspect marker for completed action

Adverbs

很		hěn	Adv	very
* 非常		fēicháng	Adv	[not-often] unusually, extraordinarily
不太		bútài	Adv	not quite, not very
還	还	hái	Adv	still
已經	已经	yǐ.jīng	Adv	[already-pass through] already
快(要)		kuài(yào)	Adv	soon, before long

Conjunctions

| 可是 | | kě.shì | Conj | but |
| 還是 | 还是 | hái.shì | Conj | [still-is] or |

Question Words

哪兒	哪儿	nǎr	QW	where?
* 什麼地方	什么地方	shén.me dì.fāng	QW	what place? where?
* 什麼時候	什么时候	shén.me shí.hòu	QW	what time? when?
* 幾點鐘	几点钟	jǐ diǎnzhōng	QW	what time?
怎麼樣	怎么样	zěn.meyàng	QW	how is it?

Idiomatic Expressions

對不起	对不起	duì.buqǐ	IE	[face-not-up] (I am) sorry

Others

那		nà/nèi	Det	that
* 這	这	zhè/zhèi	Det	this

✚ **Supplementary Vocabulary**

1. Odds and Ends

參考書	参考书	cānkǎoshū	N	reference books
查書	查书	chá shū	VO	[check-book] to look up information in books
找資料	找资料	zhǎo zīliào	VO	[look for-material] to search for reference

2. Places

宿舍		sùshè	N	[stay-hut] dormitory (M: 棟 dòng, 間 jiān)
屋子		wū.zi	N	[house-Suf] room (M: 間)
辦公室	办公室	bàngōngshì	N	[manage-public-room] office
餐廳	餐厅	cāntīng	N	[meal-hall] cafeteria (M: 個)
食堂		shítáng	N	[eat-hall] dining hall (M: 個)
餐館兒	餐馆儿	cānguǎnr	N	[meal-hall] restaurant (M: 家)
酒吧		jiǔbā	N	[wine-bar] bar (M: 家)
洗衣房		xǐyīfáng	N	[wash-clothes-room] laundry room (M: 間)
活動中心	活动中心	huódòng zhōngxīn	N	[live-move-middle-heart] student union, activity center (M: 個)
體育館	体育馆	tǐyùguǎn	N	[body-nourish-hall] gymnasium (M: 個)
博物館	博物馆	bówùguǎn	N	[broad-thing-hall] museum (M: 個)
理髮廳	理髮厅	lǐfàtīng	N	[cut-hair-hall] a barbershop (M: 家)
美容院		měiróngyuàn	N	[beauty-face-court] beauty parlor (M: 家)

購物中心	购物中心	gòuwù zhōngxīn	N	[purchase-thing-center] shopping mall (M: 個)
商店		shāngdiàn	N	[commerce-store] store (M: 家)
藥店	药店	yàodiàn	N	[medicine-store] drugstore (M: 家)
藥房	药房	yàofáng	N	[medicine-room] drugstore (M: 家)
保健中心		bǎojiàn zhōngxīn	N	[protect-health-center] health center (M: 個)
醫務所	医务所	yīwùsuǒ	N	[medical-business-house] clinic (M: 間)
公園	公园	gōngyuán	N	[public-garden] a park (M: 個)
教室		jiàoshì	N	[teach-room] classroom (M: 間)
錄音室	录音室	lùyīnshì	N	[record-sound-room] audio laboratory (M: 間)
禮堂	礼堂	lǐtáng	N	auditorium (M: 個)

3. Majors and Subjects

Humanities and Social Sciences 人文科學和 社會科學 rénwén kēxué hé shèhuì kēxué	Anthropology 人類學 rénlèixué Archeology 考古學 kǎogǔxué Comparative Literature 比較文學 bǐjiǎo wénxué East Asian Studies 東亞研究 dōngyà yánjiù Folklore 民俗學 mínsúxué Foreign Languages 外語 wàiyǔ Geography 地理 dìlǐ History 歷史 lìshǐ Journalism 新聞學 xīnwénxué Library Science 圖書館學 túshūguǎn xué Linguistics 語言學 yǔyánxué Mass Communication 大眾傳播 dàzhòng chuánbō Philosophy 哲學 zhéxué Political Science 政治學 zhèngzhìxué Religious Studies 宗教研究 zōngjiào yánjiù
Natural Sciences 理科 lǐkē	Biology 生物學 shēngwùxué Chemistry 化學 huàxué Earth Science 地球科學 dìqiú kēxué Geology 地質學 dìzhìxué Mathematics 數學 shùxué Physics 物理 wùlǐ Psychology 心理學 xīnlǐxué
Law 法科 fǎkē	Law 法律 fǎlǜ Public Administration 公共行政 gōnggòng xíngzhèng

Business 商科 shāngkē	Accounting 會計學 kuàijìxué
	Business Management 商業管理 shāngyè guǎnlǐ
	Economics 經濟學 jīngjìxué
	Finance 財政學 cáizhèngxué
	International Business 國際貿易 guójì màoyì
	Marketing 市場學 shìchǎngxué
Agriculture 農科 nóngkē	Botany 植物學 zhíwùxué
	Zoology 動物學 dòngwùxué
Engineering 工科 gōngkē	Computer Science 電腦/電子計算機 diànnǎo/diànzǐ jìsuànjī
	Electrical Engineering 電機工程 diànjī gōngchéng
	Mechanical Engineering 機械工程 jīxiè gōngchéng
Medical Sciences 醫科 yīkē	Dentistry 牙科 yákē
	Medicine 醫學 yīxué
	Nursing 護理 hùlǐ
	Optometry 眼科 yǎnkē
	Pathology 病理學 bìnglǐxué
	Pharmacology 藥學 yàoxué
Education 教育 jiàoyù	Language Education 語言教育 yǔyán jiàoyù
	Physical Education 體育 tǐyù
	Special Education 特殊教育 tèshū jiàoyù
Arts 藝術 yìshù	Dance 舞蹈 wǔdǎo
	Fine Arts 美術 měishù
	Music 音樂 yīnyuè
	Theatre 戲劇 xìjù

Characters
漢字 Hànzì

去	到	書	店
好	得	買	了
誰	很	太	忙
多	少	快	要
點	分	這	兒

上…去　　　shàng…qù　　　to go there
上…來　　　shàng…lái　　　to come here

A: 你上哪兒**去**？
B: 我上學校**去**。

去
qù
to go　　ム
5

到…去　　　dào…qù　　　to go there
到…來　　　dào…lái　　　to come here

A: 他上午**到**哪兒去？
B: 他上午**到**學校去。

到
dào
to arrive
8　　(knife)

中文書　　Zhōngwénshū　　Chinese books
日文書　　Rìwénshū　　　Japanese books
英文書　　Yīngwénshū　　English books

A: 你要買什麼？
B: 我要買兩本**中文書**。

書
shū
book　　曰
10　　(to say)

書店　　　shūdiàn　　　bookstore
*花店　　huādiàn　　　floral shop
*鞋店　　xiédiàn　　　shoe store

A: 這兒有**書店**嗎？
B: 有，有一個很大的**書店**。

店
diàn
store　　广
8

繁簡對照：	其他漢字：	✎ **My notes:**
書书	*畫 SC5 *筆 SC6 *紙 SC7	

好

還好	háihǎo	still O.K., fine
很好	hěn hǎo	very good
*好人	hǎorén	good guy
*好朋友	hǎopéng.yǒu	good friends

hǎo
good, well　女
6　　(woman)

A: 這家書店的書**好**嗎？
B: **很好**，我昨天買了三本呢！

得

得 V	děi V	must V
*覺得	jué.de	to feel; think

dé, děi
to obtain, must
彳
11

A: 你上哪兒去？
B: 我上書店去，**得買**本中文書。

買

買書	mǎi shū	to buy books
*買賣	mǎimài	to buy and sell; business

mǎi
to buy　　貝
12　　(shells)

A: 你**買書**了沒有？
B: 還沒有，我明天**買**。

了

liǎo, le
finish, particle
亅
2

A: 你吃**了**飯沒有？
B: 吃**了**。

繁簡對照：	其他漢字：	✎ **My notes:**
買 买	*壞 SC8 *賣 SC9	

shéi
who, whom 言
15　　(speech)

A: 他的朋友眞多。
B: 對，**誰**他都認識。

很好	hěn hǎo	very good
很忙	hěn máng	very busy
很累	hěn lèi	very tired

hěn
very　彳
9

A: 你今天忙不忙？
B: **很忙**，我得上四門課。

太累	tài lèi	too tired
太忙	tài máng	too busy
太重	tài zhòng	too heavy

tài
excessively 大
4　　(big)

A: 你今天要不要到學校去？
B: 不要，我**太累**了。

máng
busy　忄
6　　(heart)

A: 你今天**忙**嗎？
B: 忙，天天都**很忙**。

繁簡對照：	其他漢字：	✎ **My notes:**
誰谁	累 L15	

*多少　　　　duōshǎo　　　　how many, how much

duō
much, many 夕
6　　(evening)

A: 這兒有**多少**個學生？
B: 有十二個學生。

很少　　　　hěn shǎo　　　　very few, very little

shǎo
few　　小
4　　(small)

A: 你的中國朋友多不多？
B: 不多，**很少**。

快要　　　　kuàiyào　　　　soon, before long

kuài
fast　　忄
7　　(heart)

A: 書店**快要**關門了，我得走了。
B: 再見。

yào
to want, will 西
9

A: 你**要**買幾本書？
B: 五本。

繁簡對照：	其他漢字：	✎ **My notes:**
	慢 L17 想 L8	

點
diǎn
a dot, little　黑
17　　(black)

四點	sì diǎn	four o'clock
*一點兒	yì.diǎnr	a little

A: 現在**幾點**？
B: **四點**。

分
fēn
minute, cent 刀
4　　(knife)

學分	xuéfēn	credits
*五分	wǔ fēn	five minutes, five points

A: 現在幾點？
B: 兩點**五分**。

這
zhè, zhèi
this, these　辶
11

這 M	zhèi M	this
*這兒	zhèr	here
*這裏	zhèlǐ	here

A: **這家**書店有沒有中文書？
B: 沒有，可是他們有日文書。

兒
ér
child　　儿
8

哪兒	nǎr	where
*兒子	ér.zi	son
*女兒	nǚ'ér	daughter

A: 你上**哪兒**去？
B: 我上圖書館去。

繁簡對照：	其他漢字：	✎ **My notes:**
點 点 這 这 兒 儿	那 L7	

Grammar
語法 yǔfǎ

Ⓐ Major Sentence Patterns 主要句型 zhǔyào jùxíng

1. The aspect marker 了

1.1 Completed action with 了

	Structure	Gloss
Question	S V 了 O 嗎 ? S V 了 O 沒有 ?	Did S V O ? Has S V-ed O ?
Answer	S V 了 O (了) S 還沒 V (O) 呢 !	S did V O S hasn't V-ed O yet

1. 他退了法文課嗎？

    他退了法文課了。

    Tā tuì .le Fàwén kè .ma?
    Did he drop the French course?

    Tā tuì .le Fàwén kè .le.
    He dropped the French course.

2. 你買了書沒有？

    我買了書了。

    我還沒買呢！

    Nǐ mǎi .le shū méi.yǒu?
    Have you bought the book yet?

    Wǒ mǎi .le shū .le.
    I have bought the book.

    Wǒ hái méi mǎi .ne!
    I haven't bought (it) yet.

3. 你退了日文課沒有？

    我已經退了日文課了。

    我還沒退呢！

    Nǐ tuì .le Rìwén kè méi.yǒu?
    Have you dropped the Japanese language course?

    Wǒ yǐ.jīng tuì .le Rìwén kè .le.
    I have dropped the Japanese language course.

    Wǒ hái méi tuì .ne!
    I haven't dropped it yet.

Chinese doesn't have tense markers, but it has aspect particles. 了 is a perfective aspect particle that has a meaning of "completed action" when it is suffixed to a verb. But 了 has other grammatical functions as well.

Note: The negative form for V+了 is 沒有. 沒(有) V means "didn't V" and 還沒(有) V means "hasn't V-ed yet." There are two ways of forming a question with the perfective aspect suffix 了. You can add a question particle 嗎 at the end of a sentence with the structure of V (O) + 了. Or you can combine the affirmative form V+ 了 and the negative form 沒有 to form a choice type/yes-no question. When the object is understood in the conversational context, there is no need to mention the object in the answer at all. In the negative answer, the sentence particle 呢 denotes the suspense of an action.

See L4–B1, L8–A4 for more on 呢.

1.2 Change status with 了

	Structure	Gloss
Question	S V O 了 嗎？ S V O 了 沒有？	Has S V-ed O ?
Answer	S 已 經 V (O) 了 S 還 沒 V (O) 呢！	S has already V-ed O S hasn't V-ed O yet

1. 圖書館已經關門了嗎？

   Túshūguǎn yǐ.jīng guānmén .le .ma?
   Has the library closed yet?

   圖書館已經關門了。

   Túshūguǎn yǐ.jīng guānmén .le.
   The library has already closed.

   圖書館還沒關門。

   Túshūguǎn hái méi guānmén.
   The library hasn't closed yet.

2. (現在) 幾點鐘了？

   (Xiànzài) yǐ diǎnzhōng .le?
   What time is it now?

   (現在) 已經五點鐘了。

   (Xiànzài) yǐ.jīng wǔ diǎnzhōng .le.
   (It's) already five o'clock (now).

3. 你買了書嗎？

   Nǐ mǎi .le shū .ma?
   Have you bought the books yet?

   我 (今天上午) 已經買了(書了)。

   Wǒ (jīn.tiān shàng.wǔ) yǐ.jīng mǎi .le (shū .le).
   I bought the books this morning.

   我還沒買呢。

   Wǒ hái méi mǎi .ne.
   I haven't bought the books yet.

When 了 occurs at the end of a sentence or in the structure of 已 經...了, it denotes a change of status or situation.

1.3 Imminent action with 了

Structure	Gloss
S 快要 V(O) 了	S is about to V O

1. 書店快要開門了嗎？

   Shūdiàn kuàiyào kāimén .le .ma?
   Is the bookstore about to open?

   對，書店快要開門了。

   Duì, shūdiàn kuàiyào kāimén .le.
   Yes, the bookstore is about to open.

2. 你們學校快要開學了嗎？

   Nǐ.men xuéxiào kuàiyào kāixué .le .ma?
   Is your school about to start soon?

   不，我們學校還沒開學呢。

   Bù, wǒ.men xuéxiào hái méi kāixué .ne.
   No, our school is not about to start.

 When 了 occurs in the structure of 快要...了, it means that a certain action or event is about to happen.

2. V...來/去 construction

2.1 Questions with question words 哪兒 and 什麼地方

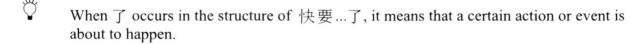

Question	Answer
S (MTA) (要) 上/到 哪兒　　來/去？ 上/到 甚麼地方來/去？	S (MTA) (要) 上/到　Place 來/去 S (MTA)　　　上/到　Place 來/去了

1. 今天上午他到甚麼地方去了？

   Jīn.tiān shàng.wǔ tā dào shén.me dì.fāng qù .le?
   Where did he go this morning?

   今天上午他到圖書館去了。

   Jīn.tiān shàng.wǔ tā dào túshūguǎn qù .le.
   He went to the library this morning.

2. 後天誰要上這兒來？

   Hòu.tiān shéi yào shàng zhèr lái?
   Who will come here the day after tomorrow?

   後天我的朋友要上這兒來。

   Hòu.tiān wǒ .de péng.yǒu yào shàng zhèr lái.
   My friend is coming here the day after tomorrow.

 In Chinese, when motion verbs such as 上 shàng '(to go) up to/toward' and 到 dào 'to arrive at/in, (go) toward' combine with a verb of direction, 來 lái 'to come' or 去 qù 'to go,' they denote the motion of a person going toward the narrator or away from the narrator respectively. 上 shàng and 到 dào function like the prepositions 'to, toward' in English, but they are called co-verbs in Chinese.

In Chinese, there are no specific markers to indicate the tense, that is, the time relation of an event with respect to speech time. To express actions that will occur in the future, Chinese uses an auxiliary verb 要 yào 'will, going to' in front of the verb. Thus 不要 V means "won't V" and 不 V means "don't V."

2.2 Questions with particle 嗎

Question	Answer
S (MTA) 要 上／到 Place 來／去 嗎？	S (MTA)（不）要 上／到 Place 來／去
S (MTA) 上／到 Place 來／去 了 嗎？	S (MTA) 上／到 Place 來／去 了
	S (MTA) 沒 上／到 Place 來／去

1. 小高昨天到中國去了嗎？

    Xiǎo Gāo zuó.tiān dào Zhōng.guó qù .le .ma?
    Did Xiao Gao go to China yesterday?

    對了，小高昨天到中國去了。

    Duì.le, Xiǎo Gāo zuó.tiān dào Zhōng.guó qù .le.
    Yes, Xiao Gao went to China yesterday.

    不，小高昨天沒到中國去。

    Bù, Xiǎo Gāo zuó.tiān méi dào Zhōng.guó qù.
    No, Xiao Gao didn't go to China yesterday.

2. 小李明天要上你家來嗎？

    Xiáo Lǐ míng.tiān yào shàng nǐ jiā lái .ma?
    Will Xiao Li come to your home tomorrow?

    對了，小李明天要上我家來。

    Duì.le, Xiáo Lǐ míng.tiān yào shàng wǒ jiā lái.
    Yes, Xiao Li will come to my home tomorrow.

    不，小李明天不要上我家來。

    Bù, Xiáo Lǐ míng.tiān bú yào shàng wǒ jiā lái.
    No, Xiao Li won't come to my home tomorrow.

3. V...來／去 VO construction

Q.	S (MTA) （要）上／到 Place 來／去 VO 嗎？
A.	S (MTA)（不）（要）上／到 Place 來／去 VO
	S (MTA)（沒） 上／到 Place 來／去 VO

1. 他明年要到美國來念書嗎？

    Tā míngnián yào dào Měi.guó lái niànshū .ma?
    Will he come to America to study next year?

對了，他明年要到美國來念書。 Duì.le, tā míngnián yào dào Měi.guó lái niànshū.
Yes, he will come to America to study next year.

不，他明年不要到美國來念書。 Bù, tā míngnián bú yào dào Měi.guó lái niànshū.
No, he won't come to America to study next year.

2. 小高今天下午要到書店去買書嗎？ Xiǎo Gāo jīn.tiān xià.wǔ yào dào shūdiàn qù mǎi shū .ma?
Is Xiao Gao going to the bookstore to buy books this afternoon?

對了，小高今天下午要到書店去買書。 Duì.le, Xiǎo Gāo jīn.tiān xià.wǔ yào dào shūdiàn qù mǎi shū.
Yes, Xiao Gao is going to the bookstore to buy books this afternoon.

不，小高今天下午不要到書店去買書。 Bù, Xiǎo Gāo jīn.tiān xià.wǔ búyào dào shūdiàn qù mǎi shū.
No, Xiao Gao is not going to the bookstore to buy books this afternoon.

 In Chinese, the relative word order between two syntactic units is determined by the temporal order of the states or events which they represent in the conceptual world; this is called the *Temporal Sequence Principle* (Tai 1985). When a person goes to a place to do something, she or he has to go to that place and then perform the action; the word order of the sentence thus maps the temporal order of the events.

4. Time when expressions

Question	Answer
S 幾點鐘　V (O)？ S 甚麼時候 V (O)？	S　Time When　V(O)

1. 圖書館幾點鐘開門？

Túshūguǎn jǐ diǎnzhōng kāimén?
When does the library open?

圖書館八點鐘開門。

Túshūguǎn bā diǎnzhōng kāimén.
The library opens at eight o'clock.

2. 你什麼時候上中文課？

Nǐ shén.me shí.hòu shàng Zhōngwén kè?
When do you go to Chinese class?

我十點鐘上中文課。

Wǒ shí diǎnzhōng shàng Zhōngwén kè.
I go to Chinese class at ten o'clock.

In Chinese, when a time expression occurs before the verb, it denotes a punctual time when an event or action occurred. In the grammatical structure, this kind of time expression is called "time when." Since telling time with "o'clock" employs numerical expressions, you can use the question words 幾點鐘 or 甚麼時候 to make a question. In the answer, you replace the question words with numerals.

5. A 還是 B construction

Question	Answer
S (AuxV) V O₁ 還是 VO₂ (呢)?	S (AuxV) V (O)
S (AuxV) V A 還是 B (呢)?	S (AuxV) V A/ S V B

1. 你決定主修國貿還是日文？

Nǐ juédìng zhǔxiū guómào hái.shì Rìwén?
Have you decided to major in International Business or Japanese (yet)?

我決定主修國貿，不要主修日文。

Wǒ juédìng zhǔxiū guómào, búyào zhǔxiū Rìwén.
I have decided to major in International Business, not to major in Japanese.

2. 你要上圖書館去還是上書店去呢？

Nǐ yào shàng túshūguǎn qù hái.shì shàng shūdiàn qù .ne?
Do you want to go to the library or bookstore?

我要上圖書館去，不要上書店去。

Wǒ yào shàng túshūguǎn qù, búyào shàng shūdiàn qù.
I want to go to the library, not to the bookstore.

In Chinese, 還是 hái.shì 'or' can be either a disjunctive (as the "or" of "whether or" or an alternative (as the "or" of "either/or"). The sentence particle 呢 .ne may be added to the end of a choice-type question.

See L4–B1, L6–A1.4, L8–A4 for more on 呢.

B Usage of Common Phrases 詞組用法 cízǔ yòngfǎ

1. Telling the time by the clock

Gloss	O'clock		Quarter	Minute	Second
	點(鐘)		刻	分	秒
6:15	六點(鐘)		一刻		
4:15:07	四點			十五分	七秒
8:06	八點	(零)		六分	
10:03	十點	過		三分	
8:58	九點	差		兩分	

When telling the time by the clock, Chinese follow the From Whole to Part Principle—from the largest to the smallest unit. When telling even hours, you may use 點鐘 or just 點 if it is understood in the conversational context that you are talking about time. But when telling fractional hours, you use the number + 點 to denote "hour."

2. 上、下、這 in time expressions

Gloss	Year	Month	Week	Weekend	Day
Last	去年	上個月	上個星期	上個週末	昨天
This	今年	這個月	這個星期	這個週末	今天
Next	明年	下個月	下個星期	下個週末	明天

The notions of "this," "last," and "next" in time expressions are very different in Chinese from those in English. Terms for years and days are compound nouns that are formed by adding one modifier to 年 and 天 respectively. But terms for months, weeks, and weekends are expressed in the following form of noun phrase:

[上/這/下] + [個] + [月/星期/週末]

In Chinese, Monday is the first day of the week and Sunday is the last. If, on a Wednesday, you wish to mention "last Monday," in Chinese you would say 這個星期一; you speak of *this* week even though the day you mention was before the narrative time (i.e., in the past). If you wish to speak of "next Friday (of this week)," you say 這個星期五, since it too is a day within this week. If you wish to mention "next Friday (of next week)," you say 下個星期五.

In contrast to English, Chinese uses the vertical spatial relation above-below 上 - 下 to denote past and future. Imagine a calendar hanging on a wall; you turn "last month" 上個月 *up* so that "this month" 這個月 is right in front of your eyes and "next month" 下個月 is *below*. The same concept holds true for "last week" and "next week."

Cultural Notes
文化點滴 wénhuà diǎndī

1. Chinese has numerous homonyms—words that are pronounced exactly alike but have different meanings—owing to countless sound changes over the centuries and a limited number of syllables. In China, people commonly apply the semantic ambiguity of homonyms, using homophonous tokens in expressing their culture-oriented desires for happiness, wealth, longevity, happy marriage, and the proliferation of male children and in expressing their fear of ill omens. The phrase 送鐘 sòngzhōng 'to give a clock as a gift' is homophonic with 送終 sòngzhōng 'to prepare for the burial of one's parent—to wish someone to die.' Therefore it is taboo to give someone a clock as a gift for auspicious occasions, such as weddings, birthdays, or moves into new homes (Sung 1979).

2. In Chinese culture, the home of your parents is forever your own home even if you have grown up and live separately. When talking about going back to one's parents' home, one says 回家 huíjiā '[return-home] go home,' not 去家 qùjiā 'go home.' After a girl gets married, she says 回娘家 huí niángjiā '[return-mother-home] go back to one's maiden home.'

3. When you run into your friends on the street in China, you may use either of these two most commonly used Chinese greetings: (1) 你上哪兒去？ 'Where are you going?' But don't expect your friends to tell you exactly where they are going; most people give a vague answer. (2) 吃了飯沒有？ chī.le fàn méi.you? 'Have (you) eaten yet?' The long-term poverty of most Chinese peasants made having enough food of great concern, so asking this question became a common greeting. Some Chinese-language textbooks published for Westerners, seeking to meet the need for a Western-style greeting, coined the expression 你好嗎？ Nǐ hǎo .ma? 'How are you?' Try not to use it; native Chinese consider it very "foreign."

4. The geographical and political separation of mainland China and other Chinese communities has given rise to differing lexical items and expressions.

Gloss	Mainland China	Taiwan
major (field)	专业 zhuānyè	主修 zhǔxiū
computer	电子计算机 diànzǐ jìsuànjī	電腦 diànnǎo
laser disk	激光唱片 jíguāngchàngpiàn	雷射唱盤 léishèchàngpán
disco	迪斯科 dísīkē	的士高 díshìgāo
service person	服务员 fúwùyuán	服務生 fúwùshēng
postman	邮递员 yóudìyuán	郵差 yóuchāi
ball pen	圆珠笔 yuánzhūbǐ	原子筆 yuánzǐbǐ

Don't be discouraged by these variant terms; just try to apply them in the appropriate sociocultural context.

第七課　一共多少錢？

對話

〔小李在書店買東西。〕

小李：請問，你們這兒有沒有「中國小說」這本書？

店員：我查一下電腦看看。有，就在那兒（手指書架）。

小李：（翻書）才兩百多頁就要四十塊，太貴了！有沒有便宜（一）點兒的舊書？

店員：舊書早就賣完了，你可以去別的書店問問。

小李：好吧！可是我還要買些別的東西。我也覺得有（一）點兒累，先坐一下，喝杯咖啡再說（喝完咖啡，拿東西去付錢）。

店員：就要這些嗎？

小李：沒錯，一本漢英字典，一個隨身聽，五卷錄音帶，兩片光碟，四個本子，三枝筆（一枝紅的，一枝藍的，一枝黑的）。一共多少錢？

店員：九十八塊二毛五。

小李：（付錢）

店員：謝謝！

小李：（自言自語）身上的錢
都給了你，我的「中國
飯」也泡湯了，只好回
宿舍去吃漢堡、三明治
了。

My questions:

对话

〔小李在书店买东西。〕

小李：请问，你们这儿有没有「中国小说」这本书？

店员：我查一下电脑看看。有，就在那儿（手指书架）。

小李：（翻书）才两百多页就要四十块，太贵了！有没有便宜（一）点儿的旧书？

店员：旧书早就卖完了，你可以去别的书店问问。

小李：好吧！可是我还要买些别的东西。我也觉得有（一）点儿累，先坐一下，喝杯咖啡再说（喝完咖啡，拿东西去付钱）。

店员：就要这些吗？

小李：没错，一本汉英字典，一个随身听，五卷录音带，两片光碟，四个本子，三枝笔（一枝红的，一枝蓝的，一枝黑的）。一共多少钱？

店员：九十八块二毛五。

小李：（付钱）

店员：谢谢！

小李：（自言自语）身上的钱都给了你，我的「中国饭」也泡汤了，只好回宿舍去吃汉堡、三明治了。

Duìhuà

(Xiǎo Lǐ zài shūdiàn mǎi dōng.xī.)

Xiǎo Lǐ: Qǐngwèn, nǐ.men zhèr yǒu .méiyǒu "Zhōng.guó Xiǎoshuō" zhè běn shū?

Diànyuán: Wǒ chá.yíxià diànnǎo kàn.kàn. Yǒu, jiù zài nàr (Shǒu zhǐ shūjià).

Xiǎo Lǐ: (Fān shū) Cái liǎngbǎi duō yè jiùyào sìshí kuài, tài guì .le! Yǒu .méiyǒu pián.yí (yì).diǎnr .de jiùshū?

Diànyuán: Jiùshū zǎo jiù màiwán .le, nǐ kě.yǐ qù bié .de shūdiàn wèn.wèn.

Xiǎo Lǐ: Hǎo .ba! Kě.shì wǒ hái yào mǎi xiē bié .de dōng.xi. Wǒ yě jué.de yǒu (yì).diǎnr lèi, xiān zuò.yíxià, hē bēi kāfēi zài shuō (hēwán kāfēi, ná dōng.xī qù fùqián).

Diànyuán: Jiù yào zhè xiē .ma?

Xiǎo Lǐ: Méicuò, yì běn Hànyīng zìdiǎn, yí .ge suíshēntīng, wǔ juǎn lùyīndài, liǎng piàn guāngdié, sì .ge běn.zi, sān zhī bǐ (yì zhī hóng.de, yì zhī lán.de, yì zhī hēi.de). Yígòng duō.shǎo qián?

Diànyuán: Jiǔshíbā kuài èr máo wǔ.

Xiǎo Lǐ: (Fùqián)

Diànyuán: Xiè.xie!

Xiǎo Lǐ: (Zì yán zì yǔ) Shēnshàng .de qián dōu gěi .le nǐ, wǒ .de "Zhōng.guó fàn" yě pàotāng .le, zhǐhǎo huí sùshè qù chī hànbǎo, sānmíngzhì .le.

Dialogue

(Xiǎo Lǐ is shopping at the bookstore.)

Xiǎo Lǐ: Excuse me, do you have the book *Chinese Novels*?

Clerk: Let me check the computer and see. Yes, (we) do. It's there (pointing at the bookshelf).

Xiǎo Lǐ: (Browsing through the books.) (It) costs forty dollars for only two hundred pages. It's too expensive! Do you have used books that are less expensive?

Clerk: The used books are sold out. You can go to another bookstore to ask.

Xiǎo Lǐ: All right! But I still need something else. I also feel a bit tired. Let me sit down for a while and have a cup of coffee first. (After drinking the coffee, he takes his things and goes to pay at the register.)

Clerk: Do you just want these?

Xiǎo Lǐ: That's it: one Chinese-English dictionary, one Walkman, five tapes, two CDs, four notebooks, and three pens, one red, one blue, one black. How much is it altogether?

Clerk: Ninety-eight dollars and twenty-five cents.

Xiǎo Lǐ: (Pays for the merchandise.)

Clerk: Thanks.

Xiǎo Lǐ: (Talking to himself:) All my money is gone; so is my Chinese cuisine. (Now) I can only go back to the dorm and have hamburgers and sandwiches.

Mini-Dialogue
小對話 Xiǎoduìhuà

Asking for help in a store

1. A: 請問，你們這兒有沒有
　　「中國」這本書？

Qǐngwèn, nǐ.men zhèr yǒu .méiyǒu "Zhōng.guó" zhè běn shū?
Excuse me, do you have the book *China*?

B: 有，就在那兒。

Yǒu, jiù zài nàr.
Yes, (we) do. It's there.

Expressing quantity

1. A: 請問，你要買什麼？

Qǐngwèn, nǐ yào mǎi shén.me?
Excuse me, what do you want to buy?

B: 我要三枝筆、五本本子、
　　和一卷錄音帶。

Wǒ yào sān zhī bǐ, wǔ běn běn.zǐ, hé yì juǎn lùyīndài.
I want three pens, five notebooks, and one tape.

Talking about prices

1. A: 請問，這本書多少錢？

Qǐngwèn, zhè běn shū duō.shǎo qián?
Excuse me, how much is this book?

B: 二十四塊八毛三。

Èrshísì kuài bā máo sān.
Twenty-four dollars and eighty-three cents.

A: 太貴了！

Tài guì .le!
That's too expensive!

Vocabulary
生詞 Shēngcí

◎ **By Order of Appearance**

一共		yígòng	Adv	altogether
多少		duō.shǎo	QW	how much, how many?
錢	钱	qián	N	money
* 圓	圆	yuán	N	dollar (as printed on real money)
* 元		yuán	N	dollar (written form)
塊 (錢)	块钱	kuài (qián)	N	[lump-money] dollar (colloquial)
* 角	角	jiǎo	N	[angle] dime (as printed on real money)
毛(錢)	毛 (钱)	máo (qián)	N	[hair-money] dime (colloquial)
* 分(錢)	分 (钱)	fēn (qián)	N	[divide-money] cent
請問	请问	qǐngwèn	IE	may I ask?
* 請	请	qǐng	V	please, to request
* 問	问	wèn	V	to ask
這兒	这儿	zhèr	Loc	here
小說	小说	xiǎoshuō	N	[small-talk] novel, fiction (M: 本 běn)
查		chá	V	to check
V 一下		….yíxià	V	[one-down] just V...
電腦	电脑	diànnǎo	N	[electric-brain] computer (M: 個)
(VO) 看看		...kàn.kàn	Part	[look-look] just VO and see what happens
就		jiù	Adv	just, precisely, then
在		zài	V	(be) located at, in, on
那兒	那儿	nàr	Loc	there
才		cái	Adv	only
百		bǎi	N	hundred
頁	页	yè	M/N	page
貴	贵	guì	SV	(to be) expensive
便宜		pián.yí	SV	[cheap-proper] (to be) cheap
一點兒	一点儿	yì.diǎnr	Adv	[one-dot-son] a little bit
舊	旧	jiù	Adj	old (for things), used
* 新		xīn	Adj	new
早就		zǎo jiù	Adv	[early-then] to have already
賣完	卖完	màiwán	RV	[sell-finish] sold out
* 完		wán	V	to finish
可以		kě.yǐ	Aux V	[may-by means of] may
別的		bié.de	Adj	[other-Part] other
* 有的		yǒu.de	Adj	[have-Part] some (+N)
吧		.ba	Part	particle for agreement
些		xiē	M	measure word for plural nouns; some

這些	这些	zhèixiē	Dem Pron	these
* 那些		nèixiē	Dem Pron	those
東西	东西	dōng.xī	N	[east-west] thing
覺得	觉得	jué.de	V	to feel, think
先		xiān	Adv	first
坐		zuò	V	to sit
* 站		zhàn	V	to stand
喝		hē	V	to drink
杯		bēi	M/N	cup; measure word for tea, wine, coffee
咖啡		kāfēi	N	coffee
再		zài	Adv	then
說	说	shuō	V	to say
沒錯	没错	méicuò	IE	[not-wrong] (you are) right
字典		zìdiǎn	N	[character-literary canon] dictionary (M: 本)
隨身聽	随身听	suíshēntīng	N	[follow-body-listen] portable stereo, Walkman (M: 個)
錄音帶	录音带	lùyīndài	N	[record-sound-belt] audio tape (M: 卷 juǎn)
磁帶	磁带	cídài	N	[magnetic-belt] audio tape (M: 盤 pán) (China)
光碟		guāngdié	N	[light-plate] CD (compact disc)
本子		běn.zi	N	[origin-son] notebook (M: 本、個)
筆	笔	bǐ	N	pen (M: 枝 zhī)
謝謝	谢谢	xiè.xie	V	[thank-thank] thank (you)
* 不謝	不谢	búxiè	V	[no-thank] you're welcome
身上		shēn.shàng	NP	[body-upper] on one's body, with one's self
給	给	gěi	V	to give
飯	饭	fàn	N	rice, meal (M: 頓 dùn)
泡湯	泡汤	pàotāng	VO	[soak-soup] to be gone, finish
只好		zhǐhǎo	Adv	[only-good] the only alternative is
宿舍		sùshè	N	[stay-hut] dormitory (M: 棟 dòng, 間 jiān)
吃		chī	V	to eat
漢堡	汉堡包	hànbǎo(bāo)	N	hamburger (M: 個)
三明治		sānmíngzhì	N	[three-bright-govern] sandwich (M: 個)

◎ **By Grammatical Categories**

Nouns/Pronouns

小說	小说	xiǎoshuō	N	[small-talk] novel, fiction (M: 本 běn)
電腦	电脑	diànnǎo	N	[electric-brain] computer (M: 個)
百		bǎi	N	hundred
錢	钱	qián	N	money
* 圓	圆	yuán	N	dollar (as printed on real money)
* 元		yuán	N	dollar (written form)
塊 (錢)	块钱	kuài (qián)	N	[lump-money] dollar (colloquial)
* 角	角	jiǎo	N	[angle] dime (as printed on real money)
毛(錢)	毛 (钱)	máo (qián)	N	[hair-money] dime (colloquial)
* 分(錢)	分(钱)	fēn (qián)	N	[divide-money] cent
東西	东西	dōng.xī	N	[east-west] thing
咖啡		kāfēi	N	coffee
宿舍		sùshè	N	[stay-hut] dormitory (M: 棟 dòng, 間 jiān)
字典		zìdiǎn	N	[character-literary canon] dictionary (M: 本)
隨身聽	随身听	suíshēntīng	N	[follow-body-listen] portable stereo, Walkman (M: 個)
錄音帶	录音带	lùyīndài	N	[record-sound-belt] audio tape (M: 卷 juǎn)
磁帶	磁带	cídài	N	[magnetic-belt] audio tape (M: 盤 pán) (China)
光碟		guāngdié	N	[light-plate] CD (compact disc)
本子		běn.zi	N	[origin-son] notebook (M: 本、個)
筆	笔	bǐ	N	pen (M: 枝 zhī)
身上		shēn.shàng	NP	[body-upper] on one's body, with one's self
飯	饭	fàn	N	rice, meal (M: 頓 dùn)
漢堡	汉堡包	hànbǎo(bāo)	N	hamburger (M: 個)
三明治		sānmíngzhì	N	[three-bright-govern] sandwich (M: 個)
這些	这些	zhèixiē	Dem Pron	these
* 那些		nèixiē	Dem Pron	those

Measure Words

頁	页	yè	M/N	page
杯		bēi	M/N	cup; measure word for tea, wine, coffee
些		xiē	M	measure word for plural nouns; some

Auxiliary Verbs

可以		kě.yǐ	Aux V	[may-by means of] may

Verbs/Stative Verbs/Adjectives

*	請	请	qǐng	V	please, to request
*	問	问	wèn	V	to ask
	查		chá	V	to check
	V 一下		....yíxià	V	[one-down] just V...
	(VO) 看看		...kàn.kàn	Part	[look-look] just VO and see what happens
	在		zài	V	(be) located at, in, on
	賣完	卖完	màiwán	RV	[sell-finish] sold out
*	完		wán	V	to finish
	坐		zuò	V	to sit
*	站		zhàn	V	to stand
	喝		hē	V	to drink
	覺得	觉得	jué.de	V	to feel, think
	說	说	shuō	V	to say
	給	给	gěi	V	to give
	吃		chī	V	to eat
	謝謝	谢谢	xiè.xie	V	[thank-thank] thank (you)
*	不謝	不谢	búxiè	V	[no-thank] you're welcome
	泡湯	泡汤	pàotāng	VO	[soak-soup] to be gone, finish
	舊	旧	jiù	Adj	old (for things), used
*	新		xīn	Adj	new
	貴	贵	guì	SV	(to be) expensive
	便宜		pián.yí	SV	[cheap-proper] (to be) cheap
	別的		bié.de	Adj	[other-Part] other
*	有的		yǒu.de	Adj	[have-Part] some (+N)

Adverbs

才		cái	Adv	only
就		jiù	Adv	just, precisely, then
早就		zǎo jiù	Adv	[early-then] to have already
先		xiān	Adv	first
再		zài	Adv	then
一點兒	一点儿	yì.diǎnr	Adv	[one-dot-son] a little bit
一共		yígòng	Adv	altogether
只好		zhǐhǎo	Adv	[only-good] the only alternative is

Particles

吧	.ba	Part	particle for agreement

Localizers

| 這兒 | 这儿 | zhèr | Loc. | here |
| 那兒 | 那儿 | nàr | Loc. | there |

Question Words

| 多少 | | duō.shǎo | QW | how much, how many? |

Idiomatic Expressions

| 請問 | 请问 | qǐngwèn | IE | may I ask? |
| 沒錯 | 没错 | méicuò | IE | [not-wrong] (you are) right |

✚ Supplementary Vocabulary

1. Odds and Ends

手		shǒu	N	hand
指		zhǐ	V/N	to point, finger
書架	书架	shūjià	N	[book-frame] bookcase (M: 個)
翻書	翻书	fānshū	VO	[to turn-book] to thumb through a book
找錢	找钱	zhǎoqián	V	[to return-money] to give change
付錢	付钱	fùqián	V	[to pay-money] to pay
自言自語	自言自语	zì yán zì yǔ	IE	[self-language-self language] to talk to oneself

2. Stationery

文具		wénjù	N	stationery
毛筆	毛笔	máobǐ	N	[hair-pen] brush pen
鉛筆	铅笔	qiānbǐ	N	[lead-pen] pencil
原子筆	原子笔	yuánzibǐ	N	[atom-pen] ball pen
圓珠筆	圆珠笔	yuánzhūbǐ	N	[round-pearl-pen] ball pen
鋼筆	钢笔	gāngbǐ	N	[steel-pen] fountain pen
粉筆	粉笔	fěnbǐ	N	[powder-pen] chalk
紙	纸	zhǐ	N	paper
講義夾	讲义夹	jiǎngyìjiá	N	[handouts-folder] folders
雜誌	杂志	zázhì	N	magazine (M: 本)
畫報	画报	huàbào	N	[picture-newspaper] pictorial (M: 本)
報紙	报纸	bàozhǐ	N	newspaper (M: 份 fèn, 張 zhāng)
電子計算機	电子计算机	diànzǐ jìsuàn jī	N	[electronic-calculator] computer (M: 個)

Characters
漢字 Hànzì

請	問	說	坐
可	以	看	完
先	吃	飯	吧
再	給	東	西
才	就	在	那

請

qǐng
to request; invite
please   言
15   (speech)

請問	qǐngwèn	may I ask...
請坐	qǐngzuò	please sit down
*請客	qǐngkè	to treat (people)

A: **請問**，你們這兒有沒有中文書？
B: 没有，我們只有英文書。

問

wèn
to ask   門
11   (door)

| *問題 | wèntí | question, problem |

A: 你到大學書店**問問**。
B: 大學書店在哪兒？

説

shuō
to speak, say,
tell   言
14   (speech)

| 小說 | xiǎoshuō | novel |
| *說話 | shuōhuà | to say |

A: 你看不看**小説**？
B: 不看，我太忙了。

坐

zuò
to sit, ride 土
7   (soil)

| 坐下 | zuò.xià | to sit down |

A: 你**坐一下**吧，忙什麼？
B: 我得去上課。

繁簡對照：	其他漢字：	✎ **My notes:**
請 请	聽 L12	
問 问	站 L15	
說 说		

可

kě
may, able　口
5　　(mouth)

可是　　　kě.shì　　　but
可以　　　kě.yǐ　　　can

A: 我**可以不可以**說英文？
B: **不可以**，上中文課得說中文。

以

yǐ
(and with it), by
means of　人
5　　(person)

*所以　　　suǒ.yǐ　　　therefore

A: 我**可以**出去一下嗎？
B: 好，可是你得快點兒回來 。

看

kàn
to see, look at
目
9　　(the eye)

*好看　　　hǎokàn　　　good-looking (good to see)
*看見　　　kàn.jiàn　　　to see
*看到　　　kàn.dào　　　to see

A: 請你**看看**這個有沒有問題。
B: 沒有問題，很好 。

完

wán
to finish　宀
7

賣完　　　màiwán　　　sold out
*做完　　　zuòwán　　　to finish doing (things)
*看完　　　kànwán　　　to finish reading/seeing (things)

A: 你功課**做完**了沒有？
B: 還沒有，老師給的功課太多了。

繁簡對照：	其他漢字：	✎ **My notes:**
	見 L9	

先

先…再   xiān…zài   first…then
*先生   xiān.shēng   Mr.; teacher

xiān
first, in advance
            儿
6

A: 我**先**歇會兒**再**打掃。
B: 你可別睡著了。

吃

吃飯   chīfàn   to eat meals
*好吃   hǎochī   delicious (good to eat)

chī
to eat   口
6   (mouth)

A: 你今天中午**吃飯**了沒有？
B: 吃了，我在家**吃中國飯**。

飯

中國飯   Zhōng.guófàn   Chinese food
*早飯   zǎofàn   breakfast
*中飯   zhōngfàn   lunch
*晚飯   wǎnfàn   dinner

fàn
cooked rice,
food   食
12   (to eat)

A: 你**早飯**吃什麼？
B: 我不吃東西，我喝咖啡。

吧

.ba
particle for
agreement 口
7   (mouth)

A: 你坐下來吃飯**吧**！
B: **好吧**！

繁簡對照：	其他漢字：	✎ **My notes:**
飯饭	後 L9 喝 L10 *頓 SC10	

再
zài
again　冂
6

再見　　zàijiàn　　to see again, goodbye
*再說　　zàishuō　　to say again

A: 我們今天就上到這兒，星期三**再見**。
B: 星期三見。

給
gěi
to give, for the
benefit of　糸
12

A: 他**給**你多少錢？
B: 不多，就三塊錢。

東
dōng
east　　　木
8　　　(tree)

東西　　dōng.xi　　thing; object
*東邊　　dōngbiān　　east side
*東方　　dōngfāng　　east

A: 你到書店買了什麼**東西**？
B: 我買了一本書。

西
xī
west　　　西
6

*西邊　　xībiān　　west side
*西方　　xīfāng　　west

A: 請問，你要喝點兒什麼**東西**？
B: 給我一杯咖啡。

繁簡對照：	其他漢字：	✎ **My notes:**
給给 東东		

才

cái
only, then, just
手
3   (hand)

A: **才**三枝筆就要二十塊？
B: 沒有錢就不要買。

就

jiù
then, at once,
only   尢
12

早就   zǎo jiù   to have already…

A: 我得到大學書店買東西。
B: 那家店**早就**關了。

在

zài
in, at, etc.
土
6   (soil)

*現在   xiànzài   now

A: 你**在哪兒**學中文？
B: 我**在美國**學中文。

那

nà, nèi
that, those   阝
7   (city)

那兒   nàr   there
*那些   nàxiē   those

A: **那些**錢是你的嗎？
B: 不是，是他的，他要去買東西。

繁簡對照：	其他漢字： 這 L6	✎ **My notes:**

Grammar
語法 yǔfǎ

ⓐ Major Sentence Patterns 主要句型 zhǔyào jùxíng

1. Place words

Place Words
Pron /N + localizer

1. 我們這兒   wǒ.men zhèr
                                        [we-here] where we are.

    請你明天到我們這兒來。   Qǐng nǐ míng.tiān dào wǒ.men zhèr lái.
                                        Please come to (where we are) our place
                                        tomorrow.

2. 書架那兒   shūjià nàr
                                        [bookcase-there] where the bookcase is.

    他到書架那兒去拿書。   Tā dào shūjià nàr qù ná shū.
                                        He goes to the bookcase to fetch the book.

 In Chinese, there are special kinds of lexical items called localizers. A localizer is a form/morpheme which forms a place word when preceded by a pronoun or a noun. Besides place names (such as city names, country names), pronouns and nouns may be used as place words *only* when they are combined with a general localizer: either 這兒 zhèr 'here' or 那兒 nàr 'there,' depending on whether the location of reference is centered on the speaker or away from the speaker.

✗ Although it is O.K. to say "come to me" in English, it is wrong to say 到我來 in Chinese. Instead, you must say 到我這兒來.

2. The main verb 在

Question	Answer
S (MTA) 在 哪兒/什麼地方？	S (MTA)　在 Place
S (MTA) 在不在 Place？	S (MTA)不在 Place
S (MTA) 在 Place 嗎？	

1. 漢英字典在哪兒/甚麼地方？   Hànyīng zìdiǎn zài nǎr /shén.me dì.fāng?
                                        Where is the Chinese-English dictionary?

    漢英字典在這兒。   Hànyīng zìdiǎn zài zhèr.
                                        The Chinese-English dictionary is over here.

漢英字典不在那兒。

Hànyīng zìdiǎn bú zài nàr.
The Chinese-English dictionary is not over there.

2. 小高今天上午在家嗎？

Xiǎo Gāo jīn.tiān shàng.wǔ zài jiā .ma?
Was Xiao Gao at home this morning?

小高今天上午不在家。

Xiǎo Gāo jīn.tiān shàng.wǔ bú zài jiā.
Xiao Gao was not at home this morning.

小高今天上午在學校。

Xiǎo Gāo jīn.tiān shàng.wǔ zài xuéxiào.
Xiao Gao was at school this morning.

在 has three different grammatical functions. In the preceding examples, it serves as a main verb and means "to be located in, at, on." As a main verb, it may also denote "existence," but in most cases it is used in a negative sense, e.g., 他媽媽還在 Tā mā.mā hái zài 'His mother is still existent—His mother is alive'; 他爸爸不在了 Tā bà.bà bú zài .le 'His father is not existent—His father has passed away.'

See L8–A4; L9–A3, L11–B2, L14–A1 for more on 在.

3. The existential verb 有

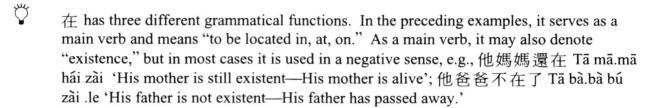

Structure	Grammatical Meaning	Gloss
Place 有沒有 X?	existence of X	Is there X at Place?
Place 有 X		There is X at Place
Place 沒有 X		There is no X at Place

1. 你家有沒有漢英字典？

Nǐ jiā yǒu méi.yǒu Hànyīng zìdiǎn?
Is there a Chinese-English dictionary in your home?

我家有漢英字典。

Wǒ jiā yǒu Hànyīng zìdiǎn.
There is a Chinese-English dictionary in my home.

我家沒有漢英字典。

Wǒ jiā méi.yǒu Hànyīng zìdiǎn.
There is no Chinese-English dictionary in my home.

2. 你們學校有沒有電腦？

Nǐ.men xuéxiào yǒu méi.yǒu diànnǎo?
Are there any computers at your school?

有，我們學校有電腦。

Yǒu, wǒ.men xuéxiào yǒu diànnǎo.
Yes, there are computers at our school.

没有，我們學校没有電腦。	Méi.yǒu, wǒ.men xuéxiào méi.yǒu diànnǎo. No, there isn't a computer at our school.

If the subject of a sentence is a place and the verb is 有 yǒu, then the verb denotes the existence of the object.

See L5–A1, A2, A3, and L7–A3 for more on 有.

4. The adverb 就

Structure	Grammatical Meaning	Gloss
X 就在 Place	adverb	X is right over at Place
才 No. M 就要 No. 塊(錢)	conjunction	(It's) only No. M and (it) costs No. dollars
早就... 了	adverb	(It) has already...

4.1 X 就在 Place

1. 錄音帶在哪兒？

   Lùyīndài zài nǎr?
   Where is the tape ?

   錄音帶就在那兒。

   Lùyīndài jiù zài nàr.
   The tape is right over there.

2. 隨身聽在哪兒？

   Suíshēntīng zài nǎr?
   Where is the portable stereo?

   隨身聽就在我這兒。

   Suíshēntīng jiù zài wǒ zhèr.
   The portable stereo is right over here (where I am).

4.2 才 No. M 就要 No. 塊(錢)

1. 這本書多少錢？

   Zhè běn shū duō.shǎo qián?
   How much is this book?

   二十塊(錢)。

   Èrshí kuài (qián).
   Twenty dollars.

   這本書才五十頁就要二十塊(錢)。

   Zhè běn shū cái wǔshí yè jiù yào èrshí kuài (qián).
   This book (has) only fifty pages and (it) costs twenty dollars.

2. 三枝筆多少錢？   Sān zhī bǐ duō.shǎo qián?
                                            How much are these three pens?

    四十塊(錢)。   Sìshí kuài (qián).
                                            Forty dollars.

    才三枝筆就要四十塊(錢)。   Cái sān zhī bǐ jiù yào sìshí kuài (qián).
                                            (There are) only three pens and (they)
                                            cost forty dollars.

4.3 早就 ... 了

1. 書店關門了嗎？   Shūdiàn guānmén .le .ma?
                                            Has the bookstore closed yet?

    書店早就關門了。   Shūdiàn zǎo jiù guānmén .le.
                                            The bookstore has already closed.

2. 電腦賣完了嗎？   Diànnǎo zǎo jiù màiwán .le .ma?
                                            Have the computers sold out yet?

    電腦早就賣完了。   Diànnǎo zǎo jiù màiwán .le.
                                            The computers have already sold out.

就 jiù has several meanings. The interpretation of its meaning depends on the
conversational context.

See L9–A5 for more on 才.

5. 先 ... 再 construction

Structure	Gloss
S 先 $V_1 O_1$, 再 $V_2 O_2$	S will $V_1 O_1$ first, (and) then $V_2 O_2$

1. 他先做什麼，再休息？   Tā xiān zuò shén.me, zài xiū.xí?
                                            What will he do first, before he takes a
                                            rest?

    他先預備功課，再休息。   Tā xiān yù.bèi gōngkè, zài xiū.xí.
                                            He will prepare his homework first, (and)
                                            then take a rest.

2. 你要先到日本去，再到哪兒去？

Nǐ yào xiān dào Rìběn qù, zài dào nǎr qù?
You will go to Japan first, (and) then where will you go?

我要先到日本去，再到中國去。

Wǒ yào xiān dào Rìběn qù, zài dào Zhōng.guó qù.
I will go to Japan first, (and) then go to China.

先…, 再… '…first, (and) then…' construction denotes two actions in sequence. Note that both 先 and 再 are adverbs, thus they always precede the verbs.

See L9–A5, L23–A1 for more on actions in sequence.

6. Resultative verbs — actual form

Structure	Gloss
V + RE 完 + 了	finished Ving
(還) 沒 V + RE 完 (呢)	(still) haven't finished Ving (yet)

1. 小李喝完咖啡了嗎？

Xiǎo Lǐ hēwán kāfēi .le .ma?
Has Xiao Li finished drinking coffee?

小李喝完咖啡了。

Xiǎo Lǐ hēwán kāfēi .le.
Xiao Li has finished drinking coffee.

小李還沒喝完咖啡呢。

Xiǎo Lǐ hái méi hēwán kāfēi .ne.
Xiao Li still hasn't finished drinking coffee.

2. 舊書已經賣完了嗎？

Jiùshū yǐ.jīng màiwán .le .ma?
Have the used books been sold out yet?

舊書已經賣完了。

Jiùshū yǐ.jīng màiwán .le.
The used books have already been sold out.

舊書還沒賣完呢。

Jiùshū hái méi màiwán .ne.
The used books haven't been sold out yet.

3. 這本小說你看完了嗎？

Zhèi běn xiǎoshuō nǐ kànwán .le .ma?
Have you finished reading this novel yet?

這本小說我還沒看完呢。

Zhèi běn xiǎoshuō wǒ hái méi kànwán .ne.
I haven't finished reading this novel yet.

Resultative verbs (RV) are compound verbs that consist of an action verb plus a resultative verb ending (RE), which denotes the result/state of the action. In this lesson, you are learning the actual forms of the resultative verbs. The negative marker for the actual resultative verb is 沒 méi. The sentence final particle 呢 may be added to denote continuing action.

 See L6–A4 for more on 呢.
See L9–A6, L15–A2.3, L18–A4 for more on resultative verb compounds.

B Usage of Common Phrases 詞組用法 cízǔ yòngfǎ

1. Compounds vs. noun phrases

Structure	Grammatical Category	Gloss
Monosyllabic Adj + N	Compound noun	Adj N
(Adv) + Adj + 的 + N	Noun phrase	The N that/which is Adj
Disyllabic Adj + 的 + N	Noun pharase	The N that/which is Adj
Polysyllabic Adj + 的 + N	Noun pharase	The N that/which are Adj

1. 舊 書   jiù shū
                                   used book

2. 新 字典   xīn zìdiǎn
                                   new dictionary

3. 舊的筆   jiù .de bǐ
                                   the pen that is old

4. 很好的錄音帶   hěn hǎo .de lùyīndài
                                   the audio tape that is very good

5. 便宜的電腦   pián.yí .de diànnǎo
                                   the computer that is cheap

6. 便宜一點兒的書   pián.yí yì.diǎnr .de shū
                                   books that are a bit cheaper

 In Chinese, a monosyllabic adjective may modify a noun and form a compound noun. But a disyllabic/polysyllabic adjectival phrase *must* combine with the subordinate particle 的 .de when it modifies a noun. When a noun phrase consists of this kind of obligatory use of the particle 的, it can be rendered as a relative clause (that, which, who) in English. But note that 的 is not a relative pronoun. There are no relative pronouns in Chinese.

2. The adverbial phrase 一點兒

Structure	Gloss
Adj 一點兒	a little bit Adj-er
有一點兒 SV	(is) a little bit too Adj

1. 哪兒有便宜一點兒的字典？

Nǎr yǒu pián.yí yì.diǎnr .de zìdiǎn?
Where (can I get) dictionaries that are a little cheaper?

他們書店有便宜一點兒的字典。

Tā.men shūdiàn yǒu pián.yí yì.diǎnr .de zìdiǎn.
Their bookstore has dictionaries that are a little cheaper.

2. 這個電腦貴不貴？

Zhèi .ge diànnǎo guì .buguì?
Is this computer expensive?

這個電腦有一點兒貴。

Zhèi .ge diànnǎo yǒu yì.diǎnr guì.
This computer is a little bit too expensive.

 In Chinese, adjectives do not have comparative or superlative forms. Various degrees of comparison are formed by adverbs. 一點兒 yìdiǎr is an adverb that can either precede a stative verb (an adjective in English) or follow an adjective.

3. 多少錢 expression

Question	Answer
N，一 M 多少錢？	(N)，一 M No. $

1. 漢英字典一本多少錢？

Hànyīng zìdiǎn yì běn duō.shǎo qián?
How much is the Chinese-English dictionary?

一本二十塊（錢）。

Yì běn èrshí kuài(qián).
Twenty dollars each.

2. 錄音帶一卷多少錢？

Lùyīndài yì juǎn duō.shǎo qián?
How much is the tape?

一卷一百塊（錢）。

Yì juǎn yìbǎi kuài(qián).
One hundred dollars each.

4. V 一 下 expression

Structure	Gloss
V(一)V	just VO
V 一 下	just VO

1. 你要買字典嗎？

   Nǐ yào mǎi zìdiǎn .ma?
   Do you want to buy dictionaries?

   不，我就看(一)看。

   Bù, wǒ jiù kàn(yí).kàn.
   No, I'm just taking a look.

2. 你累了嗎？

   Nǐ lèi .le .ma?
   Are you tired?

   我很累了，我得休息一下。

   Wǒ hěn lèi .le, wǒ děi xiū.xí.yíxià.
   I am very tired; I need to take a rest.

An action verb itself may be a measure serving as a cognate object with or without the numeral 一 yī, for example, 看(一)看 kàn(yí).kàn 'just take a look' and 問(一)問 wèn(yí).wèn 'just make an inquiry.' An action verb combined with 一 下 .yíxià 'once' may denote "just do... (a little)," for example, 喝一下 hē.yíxià 'just take a sip,' 查一下 chá.yíxià 'just look it up.'

5. The agreement particle 吧

Structure	Gloss
好吧！	O.K.!

1. 兩本十五塊，可以嗎？

   Liǎng běn shíwǔ kuài, kě.yǐ .ma?
   Two for $15.00; (is it) O.K.?

   好吧！

   Hǎo .ba!
   O.K.!

吧 is a sentence particle that has many functions. In the preceding example, it denotes agreement.

See L10–B1, L13–B2, L15–B2 for more on 吧.

Cultural Notes
文化點滴 wénhuà diǎndī

1. Chinese Monetary Units

Chinese monetary units follow the decimal system.

1,000,000	100,000	10,000	1,000	100	10	Dollar	Dime	Cent
百萬 (百万) bǎiwàn	十萬(十万) shíwàn	萬 (万) wàn	千 qiān	百 bǎi	十 shí	元/(塊/块) yuán/ kuài	角/毛 jiǎo/máo	分 fēn

In the Chinese language, different monetary words may be used to say the same thing in literary writing or colloquial speech.

Gloss	Literary	Colloquial
dollar	圓/圆/元 yuán	塊/块 kuài
dime	角 jiǎo	毛 máo

The 1997 rates for exchanging 美金/美元 měijīn/měiyuán 'U.S. dollar' with 人民幣 rénmínbì 'RMB—PRC's currency,' 台幣 táibì 'NT—New Taiwan's currency,' and 港幣 gǎngbì 'Hong Kong's currency' were as follows.

	RMB 人民幣	NT 台幣	HK 港幣
美金/美元 $1	8.32	27.5	7.72

2. For lunch at work or school, Chinese people take along a 飯盒 fànhé '[rice-box] box meal' or 便當 biàndāng '[convenient-should/equal] box lunch/meal' in the morning when they leave home. Nowadays in Taiwan, a lot of parents are working and can't find time to prepare lunch boxes for their children or for themselves, so many people go to a 小吃店 xiǎochīdiàn

'[small-eat-store] small restaurant' 自助餐廳 zìzhù cāntīng '[self-help-restaurant] cafeteria restaurant' to have a quick lunch instead.

3. When someone says 謝謝 xiè.xie 'thank you' to you, you must respond 不謝 búxiè 'no (need to) thank.' At home, when a family member does something for you, you don't have to say 謝謝 xiè.xie all the time. This doesn't mean that Chinese people are impolite; rather it means that among family members, you don't have to 客氣 kèqì 'be polite' or stick to the proprieties. Chinese always treat close friends as family members; thus they may also follow this behavior rule with their friends.

4. When you do shopping, you may use the phrase 請問 qǐngwèn, 'May I ask…, excuse me…' to initiate a conversation with a salesperson to show politeness, especially if the salesperson is a senior. It would be considered a bit rude by a stranger or older person if you didn't use 請問 when you asked for price or information.

5. Chinese highly value learning and the basic things that are used for learning. Thus 毛筆 máobǐ 'the writing brush,' 硯台 yàntái 'the inkstone,' 墨 mò 'the ink stick,' and 紙 zhǐ 'writing paper' are called 文房四寶 wénfáng sìbǎo 'the four treasures of study.' In the old days, people so respected learning that they would never throw paper with characters written on it into the wastebasket. Instead, they would burn the written paper in a burner called 惜字亭 xízìtíng 'cherishing-character-pavilion' or 敬字亭 jìngzìtíng 'respect-character-pavilion.'

第八課 你認識她嗎？

對話

〔小李和小高在學校遇到林美英，小李給小高介紹美英。〕

小李： 小高，你認識
她嗎？來，我
給你們介紹一
下。她叫林美
英，從東部來
的。他是高德
中，從西部來
的。

小林： 你好！我姓林，雙木林，美是美國的美，英是英國的英。
我媽媽是美國人，可是爸爸不是英國人，是中國人。

小高： 我是高德中，高矮的高，德國的德，中國的中。父母不是
德國人，也不是中國人，而是美國人。

小李： 有意思，你們兩個人走在一塊（兒）就成了「聯合國」
了。

小林： 聽說你（正）在學中文。中文難不難啊？明年我也想學。

小高： 難（倒）是不難，可是寫
漢字很花時間，因為要學
很多漢字。聲調雖然不
太容易，不過很好聽，像
唱歌一樣。你不是主修
音樂嗎？

小林：　對，我喜歡拉小提琴，也愛唱歌。聽你這麼說，（我）學
　　　　中文應該沒問題。 老師怎麼樣？

小高：　老師好極了！但是有點兒嚴，我們天天都得練習，還得上
　　　　語言實驗室聽錄音。

My questions:

对话

〔小李和小高在学校遇到林美英，小李给小高介绍美英。〕

小李： 小高，你认识她吗？来，我给你们介绍一下。她叫林美英，从东部来的。他是高德中，从西部来的。

小林： 你好！我姓林，双木林，美是美国的美，英是英国的英。我妈妈是美国人，可是爸爸不是英国人，是中国人。

小高： 我是高德中，高矮的高，德国的德，中国的中。父母不是德国人，也不是中国人，而是美国人。

小李： 有意思，你们两个人走在一块（儿）就成了「联合国」了。

小林： 听说你（正）在学中文。中文难不难啊？明年我也想学。

小高： 难（倒）是不难，可是写汉字很花时间，因为要学很多汉字。声调虽然不太容易，不过很好听，象唱歌一样。你不是主修音乐吗？

小林： 对，我喜欢拉小提琴，也爱唱歌。听你这么说，（我）学中文应该没问题。 老师怎么样？

小高： 老师好极了！但是有点儿严，我们天天都得练习，还得上语言实验室听录音。

Duìhuà

(Xiǎo Gāo hé Xiǎo Lǐ zài xuéxiào yù.dào Lín Měiyīng, Xiǎo Lǐ gěi Xiǎo
Gāo jiè.shào Měiyīng)

Xiǎo Lǐ: Xiǎo Gāo, nǐ rèn.shì tā .ma? Lái, wǒ gěi nǐ.men jiè.shào.yíxià. Tā
jiào Lín Měiyīng, cóng dōngbù lái .de. Tā shì Gāo Dézhōng, cóng
xībù lái .de.

Xiǎo Lín: Nǐ hǎo! Wǒ xìng Lín, shuāng mù lín, měi shì Měi.guó .de měi, yīng
shì Yīng.guó .de yīng. Wǒ mā.mā shì Měi.guórén, kě.shì bà.bà bú
shì Yīng.guórén, shì Zhōng.guórén.

Xiǎo Gāo: Wǒ shì Gāo Dézhōng, gāo'ǎi .de gāo, Dé.guó .de dé, Zhōng.guó .de
zhōng. Fùmǔ bú shì Dé.guórén, yě bú shì Zhōng.guórén, ér.shì
Měi.guórén.

Xiǎo Lǐ: Yǒuyì.si, nǐ.men liǎng .ge rén zǒu zài yíkuài(r) jiù chéng .le
"Liánhéguó" .le.

Xiǎo Lín: Tīngshuō nǐ (zhèng)zài xué Zhōngwén. Zhōngwén nán .bunán a?
Míng.nián wǒ yě xiǎng xué.

Xiǎo Gāo: Nán (dào).shì .bunán, kě.shì xiě hànzì hěn huā shíjiān, yīn.wèi yào
xué hěn duō hànzì. Shēngdiào suīrán bú tài róng.yì, bùguò hěn
hǎotīng, xiàng chànggē yíyàng. Nǐ búshì zhǔxiū yīnyuè .ma?

Xiǎo Lín: Duì, wǒ xǐhuān lā tíqín, yě ài chànggē. Tīng nǐ zhè.me shuō, (wǒ)
xué Zhōngwén yīnggāi méi wèntí. Lǎoshī zěn.meyàng?

Xiǎo Gāo: Lǎoshī hǎojí.le! Dàn.shì yǒu.diǎnr yán, wǒ.men tiāntiān dōu děi
liàn.xí, hái děi shàng yǔyán shíyànshì tīng lùyīn.

Dialogue

(Xiǎo Lǐ and Xiǎo Gāo run into Lín Měiyīng. Xiǎo Lǐ introduces Měiyīng to Xiǎo Gāo.)

Xiǎo Lǐ: Xiǎo Gāo, do you know her? Come over here; let me introduce
               you to each other. Her name is Lín Měiyīng. She is from the
               East Coast. He is Gāo Dézhōng, from the West Coast.

Xiǎo Lín: How are you? My last name is Lín, "double tree" Lín; Měi is
               the character Měi in "the U.S." and yīng is the character yīng in
               "England." My mother is an American, but my father is not an
               Englishman. He is Chinese.

Xiǎo Gāo: I am Gāo Dézhōng; Gāo is the character gāo in "tall or short," Dé is the
               character dé in "Germany," and zhōng is the character zhōng in "China." My
               parents are not Germans, nor are they Chinese. They are Americans.

Xiǎo Lǐ: It's interesting. You two together could form the "United Nations."

Xiǎo Lín: I have heard that you are studying Chinese. Is Chinese hard or not? I want to
               study it next year.

Xiǎo Gāo: It is not too hard, but writing characters takes a lot of time because we have to
               learn many characters. Although tones are not too easy, they sound nice. (It's)
               like (you're) singing! You major in music, don't you?

Xiǎo Lín: Yes, I do. I like to play the violin and love to sing. After hearing
               what you said, (I think) learning Chinese should be no problem.
               How are the teachers?

Xiǎo Gāo: They are great! But they are a bit strict. We have to practice every day and we
               also have to go to the language lab and listen to the tapes.

Mini-Dialogue
小對話 Xiǎoduìhuà

Introducing people to each other

1. A: 來，我給你們介紹一下。他是王新，她是李華。

Lái, wǒ gěi nǐ.men jiè.shào.yíxià. Tā shì Wáng Xīn, tā shì Lǐ Huá.

Come over here; let me introduce you to each other. This is Wang Xin. This is Li Hua.

B: 你好！

Nǐ hǎo!
Hi!

C: 你好！

Nǐ hǎo!
Hi!

Asking for and identifying a person's name

1. A: 你好！你貴姓啊？

Nǐ hǎo! Nǐ guìxìng a?
How are you? What's your last name?

B: 我姓張，弓長張，叫大明，大小的大，明天的明。你呢？

Wǒ xìng Zhāng, gōng cháng Zhāng, jiào Dàmíng, dàxiǎo .de dà, míng.tiān .de míng. Nǐ .ne?

My last name is Zhāng, "bow-long" Zhāng. I'm called Dàmíng. Dà is the character "big" in "size," Míng is the character míng in "tomorrow." How about you?

A: 我是陳國。耳東陳，國家的國。

Wǒ shì Chén Guó. Ěrdōng Chén, guójiā .de Guó.

I'm Chén Guó, "ear-east" Chén, and Guó is the character guó in "country."

Talking about one's place of origin and occupation

1. A: 你是從哪兒來的？

   Nǐ shì cóng nǎr lái .de?
   Where are you from?

   B: 我是從西部來的，現在是
       印大的學生。

   Wǒ shì cóng xībù lái .de, xiànzài shì
   Yìndà .de xué.shēng.
   I'm from the West Coast. Now I'm a
   student at IU.

   A: 我是從中西部來的，是這
       兒的老師。

   Wǒ shì cóng zhōngxībù lái .de, shì
   zhèr .de lǎoshī.
   I'm from the Midwest. I teach here.

 Asking about a person's opinion

1. A: 中文難不難啊？

   Zhōngwén nán .bunán .a?
   Is Chinese difficult or not?

   B: 不太難，可是很花時間。

   Bútài nán, kě.shì hěn huā shíjiān.
   Not too difficult, but it takes a lot of
   time.

2. A: 那位老師怎麼樣？

   Nà wèi lǎoshī zěn.meyàng?
   How is that instructor?

   B: 非常嚴，每天都給我們很
       多功課。

   Fēicháng yán, měitiān dōu gěi
   wǒ.men hěn duō gōngkè.
   Very strict. S/he gives us a lot of
   homework every day.

Vocabulary
生詞 Shēngcí

◎ **By Order of Appearance**

認識	认识	rèn.shí/rèn.shì	V	[recognize-recognize] to know (a person or a character/word)
介紹	介绍	jiè.shào	V	[introduce-introduce] to introduce
叫		jiào	EV	to call, to be called
從...來/去	从...来/去	cóng...lái/qù	V	[from...come/go] to come/go from (a place)
東部		dōngbù	N	[east-part] eastern (America)
西部		xībù	N	[west-part] western (America)
* 部		bù	N	a section, a part
姓		xìng	V	to be surnamed
* 名字		míng.zi	N	[name-character] name
雙	双	shuāng	M/N	double, measure word for a pair (of things)
木		mù	N	tree (=樹木)
林		Lín	N	forest (= 樹林), surname
美國	美国	Měi.guó	N	[beautiful-country] America
英國	英国	Yīng.guó	N	[outstanding-country] England
媽媽	妈妈	mā.mā	N	mother
* 母親	母亲	mǔ.qīn	N	[mother-relative] mother (formal)
人		rén	N	person, people
爸爸		bà.bà	N	father
* 父親	父亲	fù.qīn	N	[father-relative] father (formal)
中國	中国	Zhōng.guó	N	[middle-country] China
德國	德国	Dé.guó	N	[virtue-country] Germany
矮		ǎi	Adj	short
父母		fùmǔ	N	[father-mother] parents
而是		ér.shì	Conj	but (preceded by 不是)
有意思		yǒuyì.si	Adj	interesting
走		zǒu	V	to walk, to leave (a place)
一塊兒	一块儿	yíkuàir	Adv	[one-lump-Suf] together
成		chéng	V	to constitute
聯合國	联合国	Liánhéguó	N	[unite-close-country] United Nations
聽說	听说	tīngshuō	V	[hear-say] to hear someone say
* 聽	听	tīng	V	to hear
(正)在		(zhèng)zài	Prog Asp	[in the midst of] V-ing
難	难	nán	SV/Adv	(to be) difficult, hard
啊		.a	Part	particle for question
想		xiǎng	Aux V	would like to; to think (=覺得)

倒是		dào.shì	Adv	[upside down-to be] on the contrary
寫	写	xiě	V	to write
漢字	汉字	hànzì	N	[Han-character] Chinese character (M: 個)
花時間	花时间	huā shíjiān	SV	[spend-time] (to be) time-consuming
因為	因为	yīn.wèi	Conj	[reason-for] because
* 為什麼	为什么	wèishén.me	QW	[for-what] why
聲調	声调	shēngdiào	N	[sound-tone] tone
雖然	虽然	suīrán/suírán	Conj	[although-although] although
容易		róng.yì	SV/Adv	[to allow-easy] (to be) easy
不過	不过	búguò	Conj	and yet
好聽	好听	hǎotīng	SV	[good-to hear] (to be) delightful to listen to
像…一樣	象…一样	xiàng…yíyàng	VP	[like...one-style] (it) seems the same as ...
* 像	象	xiàng	V	to resemble
* 一樣	一样	yíyàng	SV	(to be) the same
唱歌		chànggē	VO	[sing-song] to sing
音樂	音乐	yīnyuè	N	music
拉		lā	V	to play (violin, viola), to pull
小提琴		xiǎotíqín	N	[small-carry-organ] violin
愛	爱	ài	V	to love
這麼	这么	zhè.me	Adv	[this-Suf] this way (as…), so (as this)
應該	应该	yīnggāi	Aux V	[should-should] should, ought to, must (=得)
老師	老师	lǎoshī	N	[old-teacher] teacher (M: 位 wèi)
好極了	好极了	hǎojí.le	IE	[good-extreme-Part] wonderful, bravo
但是		dàn.shì	Conj	but (= 可是)
嚴	严	yán	SV	(to be) strict, stern
練習	练习	liàn.xí	V	[exercise-learn] to practice
語言	语言	yǔyán	N	[language-language] language (M: 種 zhǒng 'kind')
實驗室	实验室	shíyànshì	N	[actual-experiment-room] laboratory (M: 間 jiān)
錄音	录音	lùyīn	N	[record-sound] recording

◎ By Grammatical Categories

Nouns/Pronouns

木		mù	N	tree (=樹木)
林		Lín	N	forest (= 樹林), surname
人		rén	N	person, people
* 部		bù	N	a section, a part
東部		dōngbù	N	[east-part] eastern (America)
西部		xībù	N	[west-part] western (America)
美國	美国	Měi.guó	N	[beautiful-country] America
英國	英国	Yīng.guó	N	[outstanding-country] England
中國	中国	Zhōng.guó	N	[middle-country] China
德國	德国	Dé.guó	N	[virtue-country] Germany
聯合國	联合国	Liánhéguó	N	[unite-close-country] United Nations
媽媽	妈妈	mā.mā	N	mother
* 母親	母亲	mǔ.qīn	N	[mother-relative] mother (formal)
爸爸		bà.bà	N	father
* 父親	父亲	fù.qīn	N	[father-relative] father (formal)
父母		fùmǔ	N	[father-mother] parents
* 名字		míng.zi	N	[name-character] name
漢字	汉字	hànzì	N	[Han-character] Chinese character (M: 個)
聲調	声调	shēngdiào	N	[sound-tone] tone
音樂	音乐	yīnyuè	N	music
小提琴		xiǎotíqín	N	[small-carry-organ] violin
老師	老师	lǎoshī	N	[old-teacher] teacher (M: 位 wèi)
語言	语言	yǔyán	N	[language-language] language (M: 種 zhǒng 'kind')
實驗室	实验室	shíyànshì	N	[actual-experiment-room] laboratory (M: 間 jiān)
錄音	录音	lùyīn	N	[record-sound] recording

Measure Words

雙	双	shuāng	M/N	double, measure word for a pair (of things)

Auxiliary Verbs

想		xiǎng	Aux V	would like to; to think (=覺得)
應該	应该	yīnggāi	Aux V	[should-should] should, ought to, must (=得)

Verbs/Stative Verbs/Adjectives

認識	认识	rèn.shí/rèn.shì	V	[recognize-recognize] to know (a person or a character/word)
介紹	介绍	jiè.shào	V	[introduce-introduce] to introduce
叫		jiào	EV	to call, to be called
姓		xìng	V	to be surnamed
從...來/去	从...来/去	cóng...lái/qù	V	[from...come/go] to come/go from (a place)
走		zǒu	V	to walk, to leave (a place)
成		chéng	V	to constitute
聽說	听说	tīngshuō	V	[hear-say] to hear someone say
* 聽	听	tīng	V	to hear
寫	写	xiě	V	to write
愛	爱	ài	V	to love
拉		lā	V	to play (violin, viola), to pull
唱歌		chànggē	VO	[sing-song] to sing
花時間	花时间	huā shíjiān	SV	[spend-time] (to be) time-consuming
練習	练习	liàn.xí	V	[exercise-learn] to practice
像...一樣	象...一样	xiàng...yíyàng	VP	[like...one-style] (it) seems the same as ...
* 像	象	xiàng	V	to resemble
* 一樣	一样	yíyàng	SV	(to be) the same
雙	双	shuāng	Adj/M	double; pair
有意思		yǒuyì.si	Adj	interesting
矮		ǎi	Adj	short
難	难	nán	SV/Adv	(to be) difficult, hard
容易		róng.yì	SV/Adv	[to allow-easy] (to be) easy
嚴	严	yán	SV	(to be) strict, stern
好聽	好听	hǎotīng	SV	[good-to hear] (to be) delightful to listen to
(正)在		(zhèng)zài	ProgAsp	[in the midst of] V-ing

Adverbs

一塊兒	一块儿	yíkuàir	Adv	[one-lump-Suf] together
倒是		dào.shì	Adv	[upside down-to be] on the contrary
這麼	这么	zhè.me	Adv	[this-Suf] this way (as...), so (as this)

Conjunctions

而是		ér.shì	Conj	but (preceded by 不是)
但是		dàn.shì	Conj	but (= 可是)
因為	因为	yīn.wèi	Conj	[reason-for] because
雖然	虽然	suīrán/suírán	Conj	[although-although] although
不過	不过	búguò	Conj	and yet

Question Words

   * 爲什麼   为什么   wèishén.me   QW   [for-what] why

Particles

   啊   .a   Part   particle for question

Idiomatic Expressions

   好極了   好极了   hǎojí.le   IE   [good-extreme-Part] wonderful, bravo

✛ Supplementary Vocabulary

1. Odds and Ends

南部		nánbù	N	[south-part] the southern part
北部		běibù	N	[north-part] the northern part
英文字母		Yīngwén zìmǔ	N	[English-character-mother] English alphabet
彈	弹	tán	V	to play (a piano, organ, guitar)
鋼琴	钢琴	gāngqín	N	[still-organ] piano
吉他		jítā	N	[lucky-he] guitar
大提琴		dàtíqín	N	cello
中提琴		zhōngtíqín	N	viola
小喇叭		xiǎolǎbā	N	trumpet

2. Antonyms

美	měi	beautiful	醜/丑	chǒu	ugly
好	hǎo	good	壞/坏	huài	bad
高	gāo	high	低	dī	low
高	gāo	tall	矮	ǎi	short
老	lǎo	old (age)	小	xiǎo	young (age)
嚴/严	yán	strict	鬆/松	sōng	relaxed, lenient
難/难	nán	difficult	容易	róng.yì	easy
難吃/难吃	nánchī	unpalatable	好吃	hǎochī	delicious
難喝/难喝	nánhē	hard to drink	好喝	hǎohē	delicious to drink
難聽/难听	nántīng	hard to listen to	好聽/好听	hǎotīng	pleasant to listen to
難學/难学	nánxué	hard to learn	容易學/容易学	róng.yìxué	easy to learn
難唱/难唱	nánchàng	hard to sing	容易唱	róng.yì chàng	easy to sing
難寫/难写	nánxiě	hard to write	容易寫/容易写	róng.yì xiě	easy to write
有意思	yǒuyì.si	interesting	沒意思	méiyì.si	dull, boring

Characters
漢字 Hànzì

老	師	姓	高
名	字	叫	美
想	走	過	來
正	從	因	爲
但	而	怎	樣

老

lǎo
old, elderly,
prefix　老
6　　(old)

老師	lǎoshī	teacher
*老人	lǎorén	old people
*老朋友	lǎopéng.yǒu	old friend
*老家	lǎojiā	hometown

A: **老師**今天上課說了什麼？
B: 她說我們得多學習。

師

shī
teacher　巾
10　　(a towel)

*師生　　shīshēng　　teacher and student

A: 那個**老師**好不好？
B: 好是好，可是她要我們看很多書。

姓

xìng
surname　女
8　　(female)

*貴姓　　guìxìng　　honorable surname

A: 請問，你**貴姓**？
B: 我**姓**高，高小朋。你呢？

高

gāo
to be tall, high
surname　高
10　　(tall)

*高矮　　gāo'ǎi　　height (tall and short)

A: 你這麼**高**，是像爸爸還是像媽媽？
B: 我像爸爸。

繁簡對照：	其他漢字：	✎ **My notes:**
師 师	*介 SC11 *紹 SC12 *矮 SC13	

名

míng
name   口
6   (mouth)

*名字   míng.zi   given name; full name
*有名   yǒumíng   famous

A: 你叫什麼**名字**？
B: 我叫林美文。

字

zì
a word,
character   宀
6

漢字   hànzì   Chinese characters

A: 她說的中國話很好聽。
B: 她寫的**漢字**也很好看。

叫

jiào
to call, be
named   口
5   (mouth)

*大叫   dàjiào   to yell

A: 小朋友，你**叫**什麼名字？
B: 我**叫**小美。

美

měi
beautiful   羊
9   (sheep/goat)

美國   Měi.guó   the United States
*美人   měirén   beauty

A: 他是不是**美國人**？
B: 不是，他是英國人。

繁簡對照：	其他漢字：	✎ **My notes:**
	*英 SC14 *漢 SC15	

想 V　　　　　xiǎng V　　　　　to want to V

想
xiǎng
to think, to want
心
13　(heart)

A: 他**想學**日文嗎？
B: **我 想**他**不想學**日文，他**想學**中文。

*走路　　　　zǒulù　　　　　to walk

走
zǒu
to walk, to leave
走
7　(to walk)

A: 不早了，我得**走**了。
B: 再坐一下吧！喝杯咖啡**再走**。

過
guò
to pass, go by
辶
13

不過　　　búguò　　　but
*過來　　　guò.lái　　to come over
*過去　　　guò.qù　　to go over

A: 你下午有課嗎？
B: 沒有，**不過**我得去打工。

來
lái
to come　人
8　(person)

從...來　　cóng...lái　　to come from

A: 你是**從**哪兒**來**的？
B: 我是**從**東部**來**的。

繁簡對照：	其他漢字：	✎ **My notes:**
過 过 來 来	*跑 SC16 *跳 SC17 去 L6	

正

正在   zhèngzài   (in the midst of) V-ing
*正要   zhèngyào   to be about to
*正好   zhènghǎo   exactly right (at the right
                                             moment or amount)

A: 他在做什麼呢？
B: 他**正在**吃飯呢。

zhèng
just, …ing, just
in the process of
            止
5   (to stop)

從

從…去   cóng…qù   to go from…
*從來不   cónglái bù   never
*從來沒   cónglái méi   never

A: 他是**從**哪兒**去**中國的？
B: 他是**從**日本**去**中國的。

cóng
from   彳
11

因

因為   yīn.wèi   because

A: 你為什麼不做功課？
B: **因為**我沒有書。

yīn
a reason   口
6

為

*為什麼   wèishén.me   why
*以為   yǐwéi   to take (something) to be

A: 你**為什麼**不學中文呢？
B: **因為**漢字太多、太難了。

wèi, wéi
because   灬
9   (fire)

繁簡對照：	其他漢字：	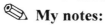 **My notes:**
從 从 爲 为		

但 　但是　　　　dàn.shì　　　but

dàn
but
7　亻(person)

A: 聽說寫漢字很難。
B: **雖然**寫漢字很難，**但是**說漢語不太難。

而

不是A而是B　bú.shì A ér.shì B　not A but B
*而且.　　　　érqiě　　　　moreover

ér
and, also, but
　　而
6　(and yet)

A: 他是從東部來的嗎？
B: 他**不是**從東部來的，**而**是從西部來的。

怎

怎麼樣　　　zěn.meyàng　　how is it?
*怎麼　　　　zěn.me　　　　how come, why

zěn
how, why　心
9　(heart)

A: 這本書**怎麼樣**？
B: 很好，但是貴了一點兒。

樣

像…一樣　　　xiàng…yíyàng　　seems the same as
*一樣　　　　yíyàng　　　　the same
*不一樣　　　bù yíyàng　　　different

yàng
kind, sort　木
15　(tree)

A: 他學中文，我也學中文。
B: 你們兩個都學中文。老師**一樣不一樣**？

繁簡對照：	其他漢字：	✎ **My notes:**
樣样		

Grammar
語法 yǔfǎ

🅐 Major Sentence Patterns 主要句型 zhǔyào jùxíng

1. 是... 的 construction

Structure	Gloss
S （是）Prep Phrase V O 的	It is/was Prep Phrase that S V O
S （是）從 Place₁ (到 Place₂) 來的	It was from Place₁ that S came to Place₂
S （是）Time When (從 Place₁) (到 Place₂) 來的	It was Time When that S came (from Place₁ to Place₂)

   1. 你是從什麼地方來的？

       Nǐ shì cóng shén.me dì.fāng lái .de?
       Where are you from? (lit. It was from where that you came?)

      我是從中國來的。

       Wǒ shì cóng Zhōng.guó lái .de.
       I am from China. (lit. It was from China that I came.)

   2. 他是什麼時候到美國來的？

       Tā shì shén.me shí.hòu dào Měi.guó lái .de?
       When did he come to America? (lit. It was when that he came to America?)

      他是去年到美國來的。

       Tā shì qù.nián dào Měi.guó lái .de.
       He came to America last year. (lit. It was last year that he came to America.)

A sentence with 是... 的 structure emphasizes the grammatical unit (a prepositional phrase or a time expression) that follows 是. In this structure, 是 is optional, while 的 is obligatory.

2. A 不是 X, 也不是 Y, 而是 Z

Structure	Gloss
A 不是 X, 也不是 Y, 而是 Z	A is not X, nor is (it) Y; (it) is Z

   1. 小林是韓國人還是日本人？

       Xiǎo Lín shì Hán.guórén hái.shì Rìběnrén?
       Is Xiao Lin Korean or Japanese?

      小林不是韓國人，也不是日本人，而是中國人。

       Xiǎo Lín bú shì Hán.guórén, yě bú shì Rìběnrén, ér.shì Zhōng.guórén.
       Xiao Lin is not Korean, nor is she Japanese; she is Chinese.

2.	他姓李還是姓高？	Tā xìng Lǐ hái.shì xìng Gāo? Is she surnamed Li or Gao?
	他不是姓李，也不是姓高，而是姓林。	Tā bú shì xìng Lǐ, yě bú shì xìng Gāo, ér.shì xìng Lín. She is not surnamed Li or Gao; she is surnamed Lin.

 The conjunctions 不是 X, 而是 Z connect two clauses in a fixed order. 不是 denotes the negation of the first clause, while 而是 denotes the affirmation of the second clause.

3. Adj 倒是(不) Adj, 可是...

Structure		Gloss
X,	Adj 倒是(不) Adj, 可是 ...	As for X, it's (not) Adj, but ...
Topic	Comment	

1.	中文難不難啊？	Zhōngwén nán .bunán .a? Is the Chinese language difficult?
	中文，難倒是不難，可是得學很多漢字。	Zhōngwén, nán dào.shì .bunán, kě.shì děi xué hěn duō hànzì. As for Chinese language, it's not difficult, but (one) has to learn a lot of Chinese characters.
2.	你們學校怎麼樣？/ 好不好？	Nǐ.men xuéxiào zěn.meyàng/hǎo .buhǎo? How is your school?/Is your school (very) good?
	我們學校，好倒是好，可是學生太多。	Wǒ.men xuéxiào, hǎo dào.shì hǎo, kě.shì xué.shēng tài duō. Our school is very good, but there are too many students.

From Topic to Comment Principle: Chinese is known for the prominence of the topic-comment usage. Chinese speakers commonly place whatever they would like to talk about at the beginning of a sentence, then present the comment on the topic.

4. The progressive aspect marker 在

Structure	Gloss
S (正) 在 VO (呢)	S is (in the midst of) Ving O

1.   小高在學什麼呢？

Xiǎo Gāo zài xué shén.me .ne?
What is Xiao Gao studying?

小高在學中文呢。

Xiǎo Gāo zài xué Zhōngwén .ne.
Xiao Gao is studying Chinese.

2.   他 在做什麼呢？

Tā zài zuò shén.me .ne?
What is he doing?

他正在聽錄音帶呢。

Tā zhèngzài tīng lùyīndài .ne.
He is listening to the tape.

Chinese is not an inflectional language: verbs don't have inflections when they change tenses or aspects. To express the progressive aspect, however, one can use aspect marker 在 with or without 正 as an intensifier. And sentence particle 呢 may be added to the end of a question or answer that consists of the progressive aspect marker 在 to denote the continuance of the action.

See L7–A1, L9–A3, L11–B2 for more on 在.
See L4–B1, L6–A1.4, A5 for more on 呢.
See L10–A5, L21–A1 for more on progressive aspect.

5. 雖然 ..., 可是/不過/但是 ... construction

Structure	Gloss
S 雖然 ..., 可是/不過/但是 (S) ...	Although S... , but...
雖然 S ..., 可是/不過/但是 (S)...	

1.   他說中文嗎？

Tā shuō Zhōngwén .ma?
Does he speak Chinese?

他雖然是中國人，可是他不說中文。

Tā suīrán shì Zhōng.guórén, kě.shì tā bù shuō Zhōngwén.
Even though he is Chinese, he does not speak Chinese.

2.   漢字難不難寫？

Hànzì nán .bùnán xiě?
Are Chinese characters very difficult to write?

雖然漢字很難寫，不過很有意思。

Suīrán hànzì hěn nán xiě, búguò hěn yǒuyì.si.
Even though Chinese characters are very difficult to write, (they) are very interesting.

3. 他買貴的東西嗎？

   Tā mǎi guì .de dōng.xī .ma?
   Does he buy expensive things?

   他雖然很有錢，但是不買貴的東西。

   Tā suīrán hěn yǒuqián, dàn.shì tā bù mǎi guì .de dōng.xī.
   Even though he is rich, he doesn't buy expensive things.

4. 你選了中文課嗎？

   Nǐ xuǎn .le Zhōngwén kè .ma?
   Did you take the Chinese course?

   沒有，雖然我很喜歡中文，但是我不能選中文課。

   Méi.yǒu, suīrán wǒ hěn xǐ.huān Zhōngwén, dàn.shì wǒ bù néng xuǎn Zhōngwén kè.
   No. Even though I like Chinese very much, I can't take the Chinese course.

 The conjunction 雖然 is movable; it may precede or follow the subject. But the conjunctions 可是/不過/但是 are not movable; they must occur in front of the subject if the subject is present in the second clause.

6. The movable adverb 為什麼

Structure	Gloss
S 為什麼 V O ?	Why do(es)/did S V O ?
為什麼 S V O ?	

1. 小林為什麼要學中文？

   Xiǎo Lín wèishén.me yào xué Zhōngwén?
   Why does Xiao Lin want to learn Chinese?

   因為小林的爸爸是中國人。

   Yīn.wèi Xiǎo Lín .de bà.bà shì Zhōng.guórén.
   Because Xiao Lin's father is Chinese.

2. 她為什麼學音樂？

   Tā wèishén.me xué yīnyuè?
   Why does she study music?

   因為她喜歡唱歌。

   Yīn.wèi tā xǐ.huān chànggē.
   Because she likes singing.

The question word 為什麼 wèishén.me 'why' and the adverb 因為 yīn.wèi 'because' are movable; they can either precede or follow the subjcet.

See L17–C1 for more on 為什麼 and 因為.

7. The auxiliary verb 想

Structure	Gloss
S (不) 想 VO	S (doesn't/don't) want(s) to VO
S 想 [A 不/沒 VO]	S doesn't/didn't think that A VO

1. 你跟他都想主修國貿嗎？
    Nǐ gēn tā dōu xiǎng zhǔxiū guómào .ma?
    Do you both want to major in international business?

    我想主修國貿，他不想主修國貿。
    Wǒ xiǎng zhǔxiū guómào, tā bù xiǎng zhǔxiū guómào.
    I want to major in international business; he doesn't want to major in international business.

2. 你想他喜不喜歡音樂？
    Nǐ xiǎng tā xǐ .buxǐ.huān yīnyuè?
    Do you think he likes music or not?

    我想他不喜歡音樂。
    Wǒ xiǎng tā bù xǐ.huān yīnyuè.
    I don't think he likes music. (lit. I think he doesn't like music.)

3. 你想小張喜不喜歡吃三明治？
    Nǐ xiǎng Xiǎo Zhāng xǐ .buxǐ.huān chī sānmíngzhì?
    Do you think Xiao Zhang likes to eat sandwiches or not?

    我想小張不喜歡吃三明治。
    Wǒ xiǎng Xiǎo Zhāng bù xǐ.huān chī sānmíngzhì.
    I don't think Xiao Zhang likes to eat sandwiches.

4. 你想他有沒有錢？
    Nǐ xiǎng tā yǒu méi.yǒu qián?
    Do you think he has money?

    我想他沒有錢。
    Wǒ xiǎng tā méi.yǒu qián.
    I don't think he has money.

The auxiliary verb 想 xiǎng 'think, want' may be negated by 不 or 沒, as in the answer to the question in example 1. When the negation is in the object clause of 想 xiǎng, the negative marker 不 or 沒 *must precede* the verb in the object clause, as in the answers in examples 2-4.

✗ Even though you can translate this kind of sentence into English as "I don't think he likes ... ," in Chinese it is ungrammatical to say 小張不想我喜歡吃三明治 / 我不想他有錢.

8. 不是...嗎？ **expression**

Structure	Gloss
S 不是 V O 嗎？ 不是 S V O 嗎？	Isn't it true that S V O ?

1. 你不是主修中文嗎？

   Nǐ búshì zhǔxiū Zhōngwén .ma?
   You major in Chinese, don't you?

   對，我主修中文。

   Duì, wǒ zhǔxiū Zhōngwén.
   Yes, I major in Chinese.

   不，我不是主修中文。

   Bù, wǒ búshì zhǔxiū Zhōngwén.
   No, I don't major in Chinese.

2. 你不是喜歡拉小提琴嗎？

   Nǐ búshì xǐ.huan lā xiǎotíqín .ma?
   You like to play the violin, don't you?

   對，我喜歡拉小提琴。

   Duì, wǒ xǐ.huan lā xiǎotíqín.
   Yes, I like to play the violin.

   不，我不喜歡拉小提琴。

   Bù, wǒ bù xǐ.huan lā xiǎotíqín.
   No, I don't like to play the violin.

不是...嗎？ affirms a piece of known information that the speaker has learned in the past. The element that follows 不是 is the focus of the sentence.

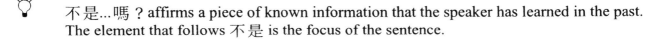
B Usage of Common Phrases 詞組用法 cízǔ yòngfǎ

1. The verbs 姓、叫

Question	Answer
您貴姓？/ S 姓什麼？	S 姓 X
S 姓 / 叫 (EV) 什麼名字？	S 叫 X
S 姓 / 叫 X 嗎？	S 姓 / 叫 X 不，S 不(是)姓 / 叫 X

1. 請問，您貴姓？

   Qǐngwèn, nín guìxìng?
   May I ask, what is your surname (lit. honorable surname)?

   我姓林。

   Wǒ xìng Lín.
   My surname is Lin.

2. 你叫什麼名字？

   Nǐ jiào shén.me míng.zi?
   What is your name?

我 叫 林美英 /我 叫 美英 。	Wǒ jiào Lín Měiyīng/ Wǒ jiào Měiyīng. My name is Lin Meiying/Meiying.

3.   他 姓 李 嗎 ?

Tā xìng Lǐ .ma?
Is his surname Li?

他 不(是) 姓 李 ， 他 姓 高 。

Tā bú (shì) xìng Lǐ, tā xìng Gāo.
His surname is not Li; he is surnamed Gao.

 您貴姓 ? 'What is your honorable surname?' is used only with people who are senior to the speaker or are strangers. In speaking to juniors or people of the same generation, one may use the expression 你叫什麼名字 ? 'What is your name?'

姓 xìng 'is surnamed' and 叫 jiào 'is called/named' are equational verbs. They can be negated directly by 不. However, 不是 may be used to stress that someone "*is not* surnamed/called..."

 Note: In reply, use 姓 'surname is,' *not* 貴姓 'honorable surname is.'

2.   The optional possessive marker 的

Structure	Gloss
Pron + (的) + kinship term	Possessive Pron + kinship term
Pron + (的) + 家/學校/宿舍	Possessive Pron + home/school/dormitory

1.   他爸爸/ 她男朋友

Tā bà.bà/ Tā nánpéng.yǒu
His father/ Her boyfriend

2.   我們學校

Wǒ.men xuéxiào
Our school

 When a possessive pronoun precedes a kinship term or a noun that is closely related to people, such as home, school, dormitory, or girl/boyfriend, the particle 的 .de is optional, whereas when the possessive pronoun modifies other nouns, the possessive particle 的 is obligatory.

3. 像...一樣 expression

Structure	Gloss
[S V (O)], 像 X 一樣	[S V (O)]; (It) seems/sounds/looks like X

1.   聲調很好聽，像唱歌一樣 。

Shēngdiào hěn hǎotīng, xiàng chànggē yíyàng.
Speaking with tones sounds nice; (it's) like singing.

2. 寫漢字很有意思，像畫畫兒一樣。

Xiě hànzì hěn yǒuyì.si, xiàng huà huàr yíyàng.
Writing Chinese characters is very interesting; (it's) like drawing a picture.

3. 他家有很多書，像圖書館一樣。

Tā jiā yǒu hěn duō shū, xiàng túshūguǎn yíyàng.
There are a lot of books in his house; (it) looks like a library.

像 X 一樣 is an idiomatic expression which refers to the situation of the preceding sentence as it seems/sounds/looks like the situation of X.

4. Verb-object construction

Structure	Gloss
[VO]$_N$ + Adv + SV	[Ving O] is Adv Adj

1. 寫漢字很花時間嗎？

Xiě hànzì hěn huā shíjiān .ma?
Is writing Chinese characters very time-consuming?

對，寫漢字很花時間。

Duì, xiě hànzì hěn huā shíjiān.
Yes, writing Chinese characters is very time-consuming.

2. 學日文容不容易？

Xué Rìwén róng .buróng.yì?
Is learning Japanese easy?

學日文不太容易。

Xué Rìwén bútài róng.yì.
Learning Japanese is not easy.

3. 說中文容不容易？

Shuō Zhōngwén róng .buróng.yì?
Is speaking Chinese easy?

說中文很容易，寫漢字不容易。

Shuō Zhōngwén hěn róngyì, xiě hànzì bù róng.yì.
To speak Chinese is easy; to write Chinese characters is not easy.

Since Chinese verbs don't have inflections, a verbal expression consisting of a [verb + object] may mean "to VO" or "V-ing O," thus functioning as an infinitive or a gerund.

5. The question particle 啊

Structure	Gloss
S V-not-V 啊 ？	Does S V O ？
QW question 啊 ？	QW question ？

1. 寫漢字難不難啊 ？

    寫漢字很難。

          Xiě hànzì nán .bunán .a?
          Is writing Chinese characters difficult?

          Xiě hànzì hěn nán.
          Writing Chinese characters is very difficult.

2. 你喜歡做什麼 啊 ？

    我 喜歡 拉小提琴。

          Nǐ xǐ.huān zuò shén.me .a?
          What do you like to do?

          Wǒ xǐ.huān lā xiǎotíqín.
          I like to play the violin.

    The sentence particle 啊 has many functions. In the preceding examples, 啊 functions as a question particle that softens the intonation of a question.

Cultural Notes
文化點滴 wénhuà diǎndī

1. A Chinese personal name generally consists of two to four characters, of which the first one or two constitute the surname and the last one or two the given name. Since every Chinese character has its own lexical meaning, a combination of any two characters usually represents the sum of the two lexical meanings or signifies a new derived meaning. Starting in the Zhou dynasty (1122?-256 BC), the custom called 避諱 bìhuì 'avoidance' required everyone to avoid using orally or in writing any characters from the name of the emperor, one's ancestors, or one's seniors, including grandparents, parents, uncles, aunts, and sometimes even senior in-laws. This practice was considered respectful of those whose names were avoided. Thus the common Western kin-name custom (naming after a relative) is not found in China (Sung 1981).

2. At school in China and Taiwan, teachers address a student by his or her full name; so do students in their peer groups. But students are required to address their teachers by "Surname + 老師 Lǎoshī" to show proper respect. Professional women in China use their maiden names even if they are married.   Thus female teachers are addressed by their maiden names.

3. Since Mandarin is the instructional language at schools in China and Taiwan, native speakers of non-Mandarin dialects are bilingual from the time they start their elementary education. Students in middle schools and high schools are required to take English as a foreign language. Literate Chinese thus are either bilingual or multilingual.

第九課 請問你打幾號？

對話

〔小高想約林美英出去吃飯、看電影兒。他給林美英打電話。〕

小高： 喂！請問林美英在嗎？

ＸＸ： 什麼 " 林 " ？請問你打幾號？

小高： 八一二、七六五四。

ＸＸ： 這兒是八一二、七六四五。

小高： 對不起，我打錯了。（重撥）

小高： 喂！請問林美英在
　　　　嗎？

小王： 在，請等一下，我
　　　　去叫她。請問你是
　　　　……？

小高： 我是高德中。

小林： 喂！高德中嗎？有
　　　　什麼事兒？

小高： 沒什麼事兒，你這
　　　　星期五有空兒嗎？
　　　　我想找你和小李一
　　　　塊兒去吃飯、看電
　　　　影兒。

小林　：　我星期五下午還有一堂英文作文，老師很嚴，不能不上
　　　　　（課）。四點半以後才有時間。出去吃飯挺貴的。我看咱
　　　　　們自己做飯好了。你喜歡吃什麼菜？

小高　：　自己做飯太麻煩了。還是出去吃吧！而且有小李一塊兒去
　　　　　，可以吃一頓地道的中國飯。

小林　：　也好，我雖然喜歡吃中國飯，可是飯做得不好。以後再請
　　　　　你吧！咱們五點半在校門口見。

小高　：　好，星期五見！

My questions:

对话

〔小高想约林美英出去吃饭、看电影儿。他给林美英打电话。〕

小高： 喂！请问林美英在吗？

ＸＸ： 什么"林"？请问你打几号？

小高： 八一二、七六五四。

ＸＸ： 这儿是八一二、七六四五。

小高： 对不起，我打错了。（重拨）

小高： 喂！请问林美英在吗？

小王： 在，请等一下，我去叫她。请问你是……？

小高： 我是高德中。

小林： 喂！高德中吗？有什么事儿？

小高： 没什么事儿，你这星期五有空儿吗？我想找你和小李一块儿去吃饭、看电影儿。

小林： 我星期五下午还有一堂英文作文，老师很严，不能不上（课）。四点半以后才有时间。出去吃饭挺贵的。我看咱们自己做饭好了。你喜欢吃什么菜？

小高： 自己做饭太麻烦了。还是出去吃吧！而且有小李一块儿去，可以吃一顿地道的中国饭。

小林： 也好，我虽然喜欢吃中国饭，可是饭做得不好。以后再请你吧！咱们五点半在校门口见。

小高： 好，星期五见！

Duìhuà

(Xiǎo Gāo xiǎng yuē Lín Měiyīng chū.qù chīfàn, kàn diànyǐngr. Tā gěi Lín Měiyīng
  dǎ diànhuà.)

Xiǎo Gāo:	Wéi? Qǐngwèn Lín Měiyīng zài .ma?
X X:	Shén.me "Lín"? Qǐngwèn nǐ dǎ jǐ hào?
Xiǎo Gāo:	Bā yī èr-qī liù wǔ sì.
X X:	Zhèr shì bā yī èr-qī liù sì wǔ.
Xiǎo Gāo:	Duì.buqǐ, wǒ dǎcuò .le. (Chóng bō)

Xiǎo Gāo:	Wéi? Qǐngwèn Lín Měiyīng zài .ma?
Xiǎo Wáng:	Zài, qǐng děng.yíxià. Wǒ qù jiào tā, qǐngwèn nǐ shì...?
Xiǎo Gāo:	Wǒ shì Gāo Dézhōng.

Xiǎo Lín:	Wéi? Gāo Dézhōng .ma? Yǒu shén.me shìr?
Xiǎo Gāo:	Méi shén.me shìr, nǐ zhè xīngqīwǔ yǒu kòngr .ma? Wǒ xiǎng zhǎo nǐ hé Xiǎo Lǐ yíkuàir qù chīfàn, kàn diànyǐngr.
Xiǎo Lín:	Wǒ xīngqīwǔ xià.wǔ hái yǒu yì táng Yīngwén Zuòwén. Lǎoshī hěn yán, bù néng bú shàng (kè). Sì diǎn bàn yǐhòu cái yǒu shíjiān. Chū.qù chīfàn tǐng guì .de. Wǒ kàn zán.men zìjǐ zuòfàn hǎo.le. Nǐ xǐ.huān chī shén.me cài?
Xiǎo Gāo:	Zìjǐ zuòfàn tài má.fán .le. Hái.shì chū.qù chī .ba! Érqiě yǒu Xiǎo Lǐ yíkuàir qù, kě.yǐ chī yí dùn dì.dào .de Zhōng.guó fàn.
Xiǎo Lín:	Yě hǎo, wǒ suīrán xǐ.huān chī Zhōng.guó fàn, kě.shì fàn zuò.de bù hǎo. Yǐhòu zài qǐng nǐ .ba! Zán.men wǔ diǎn bàn zài xiào ménkǒu jiàn.
Xiǎo Gāo:	Hǎo, xīngqīwǔ jiàn!

Dialogue

(Xiǎo Gāo wants to go out with Lín Měiyīng for dinner and a movie. He calls Lín Měiyīng.)

Xiǎo Gāo: Hello! Is Lín Měiyīng in?

X X: What "Lín"? May I ask what number you are calling?

Xiǎo Gāo: Eight one two, seven six five four.

X X: This is eight one two, seven six four five.

Xiǎo Gāo: I'm sorry. I dialed the wrong number. (Dialing again...)

Xiǎo Gāo: Hello! Is Lín Měiyīng in?

Xiǎo Wáng: Yes, please hold on a minute. I'll call her. May I ask who you are?

Xiǎo Gāo: This is Gāo Dézhōng.

Xiǎo Lín: Hello, Gāo Dézhōng, what's up?

Xiǎo Gāo: Nothing. Are you free this Friday? I want to invite you and Xiǎo Lǐ for dinner and a movie.

Xiǎo Lín: This Friday afternoon I have a class, English Composition. The teacher is very strict; I have to attend that class. I won't be free till four thirty. It's quite expensive to eat out. I think we can cook for ourselves. What do you like to eat?

Xiǎo Gāo: Cooking is too much trouble. (I still think) it's better to go out. Besides, with the company of Xiǎo Lǐ, we can have a real Chinese meal.

Xiǎo Lín: That's O.K. I'd like to eat Chinese food, but I can't cook very well. I'll treat you later. Let's meet at the entrance of the school at five thirty.

Xiǎo Gāo: All right, see you on Friday.

Mini-Dialogue
小對話 Xiǎoduìhuà

Asking for someone on the phone

1. A: 喂，請問高朋在嗎？

   Wéi, qǐngwèn Gāo Péng zài .ma?
   Hello! Is Gao Peng in?

   B: 我就是。

   Wǒ jiù shì.
   This is he.

2. A: 喂，請問王華在嗎？

   Wéi, qǐngwèn Wáng Huá zài .ma?
   Hello! Is Wang Hua in?

   B: 她不在。她還在學校上課呢！

   Tā bú zài. Tā hái zài xuéxiào shàngkè .ne!

   She is not in. She is still at school attending classes.

   A: 我等會兒再打來。

   Wǒ děng huǐr zài dǎ lái.
   I'll call back later.

3. A: 喂，李明在家嗎？

   Wéi, Lǐ Míng zài jiā .ma?
   Hello! Is Li Ming in?

   B: 在，請等一下，我去叫他。李明！你的電話。

   Zài, qǐng děng.yíxià. Wǒ qù jiào tā.
   Lǐ Míng, nǐ .de diànhuà.

   Yes, please hold on a minute. I'll call her. Li Ming! It's for you.

   C: 我馬上來。

   Wǒ mǎshàng lái.
   I'll come right away.

Making and responding to suggestions

1. A: 你這星期六下午有空兒嗎？咱們去看電影兒，怎麼樣？

   Nǐ zhè xīngqīliù xià.wǔ yǒu kòngr .ma? Zán.men qù kàn diànyǐngr, zěn.meyàng?

			Are you free this Saturday afternoon? Let's go see a movie. How about it?
	B:	對不起，星期六我得學習。下星期我有三個考試。	Duì.buqǐ, xīngqīliù wǒ děi xué.xí. Xià xīngqī wǒ yǒu sān .ge kǎoshì. Sorry, I have to study on Saturday. Next week I have three tests.
	A:	那等你考完再說吧！	Nà děng nǐ kǎowán zài shuō .ba! Then let's wait till you finish your test.
2.	A:	咱們一塊兒去吃晚飯，怎麼樣？	Zán.men yíkuàir qù chī wǎnfàn, zěn.meyàng? Let's go together to have dinner. How about it?
	B:	好啊！幾點？	Hǎo ā! Jǐ diǎn? Good! What time?
	A:	五點半吧！在宿舍門口見。	Wǔ diǎn bàn .ba! Zài sùshè ménkǒu jiàn. Five-thirty. Let's meet in front of the dormitory.

Vocabulary
生詞 Shēngcí

◎ **By Order of Appearance**

打(電話)	打(电话)	dǎ (diànhuà)	V(O)	[strike-electric-language] to make a telephone call
* 電話	电话	diànhuà	N	[electric-language] telephone (M: 個)
喂		wéi	Inter	hello
打錯	打错	dǎcuò	RV	[strike-wrong] to dial a wrong number
王		Wáng	N	[king] surname
等		děng	V	to wait
事		shì	N	matters, affairs, undertaking (M: 件 jiàn)
有空兒	有空儿	yǒu kòngr	SV	[have-empty] to have free time
* 空兒	空儿	kòngr	N	unoccupied time or space, leisure
* 有功夫		yǒu gōng.fū	SV	[have-merit-husband] to have free time
* 功夫/工夫	工夫	gōng.fū	N	time, leisure (=空兒); skill, work
找		zhǎo	V	to look for, to seek
看		kàn	V	to see, to think (when expressing one's opinion)
電影兒	电影儿	diànyǐngr	N	[electric-shadow] movie (M: 個/ 部 bù)
作文		zuòwén	N	[do-language] composition (M: 篇 piān)
能		néng	AuxV	can
* 會	会	huì	AuxV	will, can, to know how to
半		bàn	N	half
才		cái	Adv	not until, only then
時間	时间	shíjiān	N	[time-interval] time (=功夫)
出去		chū.qù	V	[go out-go] to go out
挺		tǐng	Adv	very, quite (=很)
咱們	咱们	zán.men	Pron	we, us (including the person addressed)
自己		zìjǐ	Pron	oneself
菜		cài	N	dishes, vegetables (M: 盤 pán 'dish'; 道 dào 'course')
麻煩	麻烦	má.fán	SV/N	(to be) troublesome, trouble, hassle
還是	还是	hái.shì	Adv	had better
而且		érqiě	Conj	[and yet-moreover] furthermore, besides
地道		dì.dào	Adj	[earth-road] authentic, genuine
* 道地		dào.dì	Adj	[earth-road] authentic, genuine (=地道)

以後	以后	yǐhòu	Conj/ Adv	[by means of-back] after (a given time), later
* 以前		yǐqián	Conj/ Adv	[by means of-front] before (a given time), previously
請	请	qǐng	V	to invite, treat
門口	门口	ménkǒu	N	[door-mouth] entrance

◎ By Grammatical Categories

Nouns/Pronouns

電影兒	电影儿	diànyǐngr	N	[electric-shadow] movie (M: 個/ 部 bù)
* 電話	电话	diànhuà	N	[electric-language] telephone (M: 個)
王		Wáng	N	[king] surname
事		shì	N	matters, affairs, undertaking (M: 件 jiàn)
作文		zuòwén	N	[do-language] composition (M: 篇 piān)
時間	时间	shíjiān	N	[time-interval] time (=功夫)
* 空兒	空儿	kòngr	N	unoccupied time or space, leisure
* 功夫	工夫	gōng.fū	N	time, leisure (=空兒); skill, work
菜		cài	N	dishes, vegetables (M: 盤 pán 'dish'; 道 dào 'course')
半		bàn	N	half
門口	门口	ménkǒu	N	[door-mouth] entrance
咱們	咱们	zán.men	Pron	we, us (including the person addressed)
自己		zìjǐ	Pron	oneself

Auxiliary Verbs

| 能 | | néng | AuxV | can |
| * 會 | 会 | huì | AuxV | will, can, to know how to |

Verbs/Stative Verbs/Adjectives

找		zhǎo	V	to look for, to seek
看		kàn	V	to see, to think (when expressing one's opinion)
等		děng	V	to wait
請	请	qǐng	V	to invite, treat
出去		chū.qù	V	[go out-go] to go out

打(電話)	打(电话)	dǎ (diànhuà)	V(O)	[strike-electric-language] to make a telephone call
打錯	打错	dǎcuò	RV	[strike-wrong] to dial a wrong number
有空兒	有空儿	yǒu kòngr	SV	[have-empty] to have free time
* 有功夫		yǒu gōng.fū	SV	[have-merit-husband] to have free time
麻煩	麻烦	má.fán	SV/N	(to be) troublesome, trouble, hassle
地道		dì.dào	Adj	[earth-road] authentic, genuine
* 道地		dào.dì	Adj	[earth-road] authentic, genuine (= 地道)

Adverbs

挺		tǐng	Adv	very, quite (=很)
還是	还是	hái.shì	Adv	had better
才		cái	Adv	not until, only then

Conjunctions

* 以前		yǐqián	Conj/Adv	[by means of-front] before (a given time), previously
以後	以后	yǐhòu	Conj/Adv	[by means of-back] after (a given time), later
而且		érqiě	Conj	[and yet-moreover] furthermore, besides

Others

喂		wéi	Inter	Hello

✚ Supplementary Vocabulary

1. Odds and Ends

躺		tǎng	V	to lie down
約	约	yuē	V	to date, to make an appointment
請客	请客	qǐngkè	VO	[invite-guest] to invite guests, to give a party
請吃飯	请吃饭	qǐng chīfàn	VO	[invite-eat-meal] to invite guests, to give a party
中餐		zhōngcān	N	[Chinese-meal] Chinese food
西餐		xīcān	N	[Western-meal] Western food
女朋友		nǚpéng.yǒu	N	[female-friend] girlfriend

男朋友		nánpéng.yǒu	N	[male-friend] boyfriend
接電話	接电话	jiē diànhuà	VO	[receive-telephone] to answer the phone
線忙	线忙	xiànmáng	SV	[thread-busy] the line is busy
電傳	电传	diànchuán	N	[electric-transmit] fax
電子信	电子信	diànzǐxìn	N	[electronic-letter] e-mail

2. Rooms and Places

書房	书房	shūfáng	N	[book-room] a study (M: 間 jiān)
客廳	客厅	kètīng	N	[guest-room] living room (M: 間)
臥房	卧房	wòfáng	N	[lie down-room] bedroom (M: 間)
廚房	厨房	chúfáng	N	[kitchen-room] kitchen (M: 間)
桌子		zhuō.zi	N	[table-Suf] table, desk (M: 張 zhāng)
書桌	书桌	shūzhuō	N	[book-table] desk (M: 張)
椅子		yǐ.zi	N	[chair-Suf] chair (M: 把 bǎ)
沙發	沙发	shāfā	N	[sand-issue] sofa (M: 個)
床		chuáng	N	bed (M: 張)
地毯		dì.tǎn	N	[earth-blanket] carpet (floor)
草地		cǎodì	N	[grass-earth] lawn (M: 塊 kuài, 片 piàn)

Characters
漢字 Hànzì

打	工	電	話
找	出	時	間
咱	們	作	事
前	後	能	見
半	和	對	起

打

dǎ
to beat, strike,
hit   扌
5   (hand)

打電話	dǎ diànhuà	to call (by telephone)
*打字	dǎzì	to type
*打針	dǎzhēn	to have a shot
*打球	dǎqiú	to play ball

A: 她在做什麼？
B: 她在給男朋友**打電話**呢。

工

gōng
work, job 工
3   (labor)

| 打工 | dǎgōng | to work (for a temporary job) |
| *工作 | gōngzuò | to work; work |

A: 你這麼忙，有時間**打工**嗎？
B: 有，我一、三、五下課以後有時間。

電

diàn
electricity 雨
13   (rain)

電話	diànhuà	telephone
電影兒	diànyǐngr	movie (electric image)
*電燈	diàndēng	electric light
*電視	diànshì	television

A: 你昨天給他**打電話**了沒有？
B: 沒有，我今天打。

話

huà
words, speech,
language 言
13   (speech)

中國話	Zhōng.guóhuà	Chinese language
日本話	Rìběnhuà	Japanese language
*說話	shuōhuà	to say, talk

A: 他這個人好像不喜歡**說話**。
B: 哪裏，他的**話**很多。

繁簡對照：	其他漢字：	✎ **My notes:**
電 电 話 话	*功 SC18	

找

zhǎo
to look for, to
find
7　扌 (hand)

*找人　　　zhǎo rén　　　to look for people
*找工作　　zhǎo gōngzuò　　to look for a job

A: 你有什麼事？
B: 我想**找你**去吃飯。

出

chū
to go out, to
come out　凵
5

出去　　　chū.qù　　　to go out
*出來　　　chū.lái　　　to come out

A: 你今天下午**出去不出去**？
B: 我**不出去**，得在家學中文。

時

shí
time, a period
日
10　　 (sun)

時間　　　shíjiān　　　time
*時候　　　shí.hòu　　　time, when

A: 你這幾天怎麼樣？**有沒有時間**看書？
B: 沒有，我也不知道我在忙什麼。

間

jiān
M for room
門
12　　 (door)

*一間屋子　yì jiān wū.zi　　a room
*房間　　　fángjiān　　　room

A: **這間屋子**一個月要多少錢？
B: 一個月要五百。

繁簡對照：	其他漢字：	✎ **My notes:**
時 时 間 间	進 L15	

咱

咱們   zán.men   we, us (including the person addressed)

zá
I, me   口
9   (mouth)

A: **咱們**出去看電影兒，怎麼樣？
B: 好！等我做完今天的功課。

們

我們   wǒ.men   we, us
你們   nǐ.men   you (plural)
他們   tā.men   they, them

.men
plural ending
for pronouns 亻
10   (person)

A: 我想請**你們**過來吃飯。
B: 不必麻煩了。

作

作文   zuòwén   composition
*工作   gōngzuò   work

zuò
to do, make   亻
7   (person)

A: 你喜歡英文**作文**那門課嗎？
B: 喜歡，老師很好，像我們的朋友一樣。

事

有事   yǒu shì   to be busy/occupied
沒事   méi shì   to be free
*事情   shì.qíng   things

shì
job, business
                亅
8

A: 你星期五下午**有事**嗎？我們去吃中國飯
   怎麼樣？
B: 好啊！

繁簡對照：	其他漢字：	✎ **My notes:**
們 们	做 L5 空 L15	

前

qián
before, in front,
(time) ago
9　　(knife)

*以前	yǐqián	before (a given time)
*前邊兒	qián.biānr	front
*前面	qiánmiàn	front

A: **出門以前**你得寫完今天的漢字。
B: 我早就寫完了。

後

hòu
after, in back of
彳
9

| 以後 | yǐhòu | after (a given time); later |
| *後來 | hòulái | later (in the past) |

A: **下課以後**你想做什麼？
B: 我要回家。

能

néng
to be able to,
can　　月
10　　(flesh)

| 不能 | bù néng | cannot |

A: 你明天下午**能不能**出來？
B: 對不起，我有事，**不能**出來。

見

jiàn
to see, to
perceive　見
7　　(to see)

再見	zàijiàn	goodbye
*看見	kàn.jiàn	to see
*見面	jiànmiàn	to meet (with someone)

A: 你昨天**看見**小林了嗎？
B: 沒有，我想他昨天沒來上課。

繁簡對照：	其他漢字：	✎ **My notes:**
後后 見见	會 L11	

五點半	wǔ diǎn bàn	five-thirty
*一半兒	yíbànr	half
*多半兒	duōbànr	for the most part

bàn
half   十
5   (ten)

A: 請問，現在幾點？
B: **五點半**。

hé
and, with   口
8   (mouth)

A: **你和小李**都上日文課嗎？
B: 不，我們都上中文課。

對不起   duì.buqǐ   (I'm) sorry

duì
correct, right, to
face, a pair   寸
14 (a measure of
length, 1/10 foot)

A: 我們這兒是三四五・三三三八，不是三三八三。
B: **對不起**，我打錯電話了。

*起來   qǐ.lái   to get up

qǐ
to rise, to get up
走
10   (to walk)

A: 你每天早上幾點**起來**？
B: 六點半。

繁簡對照：	其他漢字：	✎ **My notes:**
對对	全 L14 錯 L10	

Grammar
語法 yǔfǎ

Ⓐ Major Sentence Patterns 主要句型 zhǔyào jùxíng

1. The co-verb 給

Structure	Grammatical Function	Gloss
A 沒/要 給 B V O A 　　給 B V 了 O	Co-verb	A didn't/will V O to B A did V O to B
A 沒/要 V O 　給 B A 　　V 了 O 給 B A 　　V 了 O 給 B 了	Marker of indirect object construction	A didn't/will V O to B A did V O to B A has V-ed O to B

1. 你今天上午給小林打了電話了嗎？ 　Nǐ jīn.tiān shàng.wǔ gěi Xiǎo Lín dǎ .le diànhuà .le .ma?
   Did you make a phone call to Xiao Lin this morning?

   我今天上午給小林打了電話了。 　Wǒ jīn.tiān shàng.wǔ gěi Xiǎo Lín dǎ .le diànhuà .le.
   This morning I made a phone call to Xiao Lin.

   我今天上午沒給小林打電話。
   我明天要給她打電話。 　Wǒ jīn.tiān shàng.wǔ méi gěi Xiǎo Lín dǎ diànhuà. Wǒ míng.tiān yào gěi tā dǎ diànhuà.
   This morning I didn't call Xiao Lin. Tomorrow I will call her.

2. 他要給誰打電話？ 　Tā yào gěi shéi dǎ diànhuà?
   To whom will he make the phone call?

   他要給他的朋友打電話。 　Tā yào gěi tā .de péng.yǒu dǎ diànhuà.
   He will make the phone call to his friend.

In Chinese, there is a class of verbs, called co-verbs (CV), which occur with a main verb in a sentence to form an idiomatic expression that functions as a prepositional phrase in English. In a sentence with a co-verb, the negation 不/(還) 沒 and future tense marker 要 must occur in front of the co-verb, while the aspect marker 了 follows the main verb.

In examples 1 and 2, 給 serves as a co-verb and functions as the marker of the indirect-object construction. 給 means "to (a person)." The negation 不/(還) 沒 and future tense marker 要 must occur in front of 給, while the aspect marker 了 follows the main verb.

3. 昨天晚上爸爸打了一個電話給
    你嗎？

    Zuó.tiān wǎn.shàng bà.bà dǎ .le yí .ge diànhuà gěi nǐ .ma?
    Did Father call you last night?

    昨天晚上爸爸打了一個電話給
    我(了)。

    Zuó.tiān wǎn.shàng bà.bà dǎ .le yí .ge diànhuà gěi wǒ (.le).
    Last night Father called me.

    昨天晚上爸爸沒打電話給我。
    明天晚上爸爸要打電話給我。

    Zuó.tiān wǎn.shàng bà.bà méi dǎ diànhuà gěi wǒ. Míng.tiān wǎn.shàng bà.bà yào dǎ diànhuà gěi wǒ.
    Last night Father didn't call me. He will call me tomorrow evening.

4. 今天晚上你得打電話給誰？

    Jīn.tiān wǎn.shàng nǐ děi dǎ diànhuà gěi shéi?
    Whom do you have to phone tonight?

    今天晚上我得打電話給我媽媽。

    Jīn.tiān wǎn.shàng wǒ děi dǎ diànhuà gěi wǒ mā.mā.
    Tonight I have to phone my mother.

When 給 occurs after the [main verb + O], as in examples 3 and 4, it again serves as the marker of the indirect-object construction and means "to (a person)." In this case, the negation 不/(還)沒 and future tense marker 要 must occur in front of the main verb, while the aspect marker 了 follows the main verb.

See L14–A3, L18–A3, L22–A1 for more on 給.

2. ... 以前/以後 expressions

Structure	Gloss
Time Expression ＋ 以前,... V O ＋ 以前,... (reference point)	Before Time Expression, ... Before Ving O, ...

Time Expression ＋ 以後,...
      V 了 O ＋ 以後,...
      V 完 O ＋ 以後,...
(reference point)
	After Time Expression, ...
	After finishing VingO, ...

1. 什麼時候小李沒事？

    Shén.me shí.hòu Xiǎo Lǐ méi shì?
    When will Xiao Li be free?

    十點鐘以前小李沒事。

    Shí diǎnzhōng yǐqián Xiǎo Lǐ méi shì.
    Xiao Li doesn't have anything to do before ten o'clock.

2. 什麼時候小高給小林打了(一)個
電話？

Shén.me shí.hòu Xiǎo Gāo gěi Xiǎo Lín
dǎ .le (yí) .ge diànhuà?
When did Xiao Gao make a phone call to
Xiao Lin?

吃飯以前小高給小林打了(一)個
電話。

Chīfàn yǐqián Xiǎo Gāo gěi Xiǎo Lín dǎ
.le (yí) .ge diànhuà.
Xiao Gao made a phone call to Xiao Lin
before the meal.

3. 圖書館什麼時候關門？

Túshūguǎn shén.me shí.hòu guānmén?
When will the library be closed?

五點鐘以後圖書館關門。

Wǔ diǎnzhōng yǐhòu túshūguǎn guānmén.
The library is closed after five o'clock.

4. 他什麼時候到圖書館去了？

Tā shén.me shí.hòu dào túshūguǎn qù .le?
When did he go to the library?

寫了字以後他到圖書館去了。

Xiě.le zì yǐhòu tā dào túshūguǎn qù .le.
After writing the characters, he went to
the library.

 It is a general rule in Chinese that whatever one would like to use as a reference point, be it a time or a space, the reference point must be presented first, followed by 以前/以後 'before/after (a given time).' The whole "…以前/以後" expression is a movable time adverb which may precede or follow the subject.

3. The preposition 在

	Structure	Gloss
在…V	S (Time When) 在 Place V(O)	S V (O) at Place (Time When)
V 在…	S (Time When) V 在 Place	S V at/on/in Place (Time When)

1. 咱們五點半在哪兒見？

Zá.men wǔ diǎn bàn zài nǎr jiàn?
Where should we meet at 5:30?

咱們五點半在校門口見吧。

Zá.men wǔ diǎn bàn zài xiào ménkǒu jiàn
.ba.
Let's meet at the school entrance at 5:30.

2. 你們每天都在什麼地方做功課？

Nǐ.men měitiān dōu zài shén.me dì.fāng
zuò gōngkè?
Where do you do homework every day?

我們每天都在小王家做功課。 | Wǒ.men měitiān dōu zài Xiǎo Wāng jiā zuò gōngkè.
We do homework at Xiao Wang's house every day.

3.   他坐在什麼地方？ | Tā zuò zài shén.me dì.fāng?
Where does he sit?

他坐在椅子上。 | Tā zuò zài yǐ.zi shàng
He sits on the chair.

4.   小高喜歡躺在哪兒？ | Xiǎo Gāo xǐ.huān tǎng zài nǎr?
Where does Xiao Gao like to lie down?

小高喜歡躺在草地上。 | Xiǎo Gāo xǐ.huān tǎng zài cǎodì shàng.
Xiao Gao likes to lie down on the lawn.

The preposition 在 can take a place as its object and form a prepositional phrase of place [在 Place]. When the prepositional phrase [在 Place] occurs in front of a verb, as in examples 1 and 2, it denotes the location where the action of the main verb takes place. In a sentence giving the "Time When" and the "Place" where the action occurs, the word order follows the Temporal Sequence Principle.

When the prepositional phrase [在 Place] follows a verb, as in examples 3 and 4, it denotes the goal of the action.

[在 N 上] means 'on the N.'

See L7–A2, L8–A4, L11–B2 for more on 在.

4. 從 ...到 ...來/去 construction

Structure	Gloss
S Time When 從 Place₁ 到 Place₂ 來 /去	S is/was coming/going from Place₁ to Place₂ at/on Time When

1.   小李去年從哪兒到美國來？ | Xiǎo Lǐ qù.nián cóng nǎr dào Měi.guó lái?
Where did Xiao Li come from to the United States last year?

小李去年從中國到美國來了。 | Xiǎo Lǐ qù.nián cóng Zhōng.guó dào Měi.guó lái .le.
Xiao Li came to the United States from China last year.

2. 你什麼時候要從這兒到日本去？

Nǐ shén.me shí.hòu yào cóng zhèr dào
Rìběn qù?
When are you going to Japan (from here)?

明年我要從這兒到日本去。

Míng.nián wǒ yào cóng zhèr dào Rìběn qù.
Next year I will go to Japan (from here).

In a sentence that denotes someone taking a trip, the word order of the grammatical units follows the Temporal Sequence Principle. The departure point must precede the destination, because in reality one has to start from Place₁ in order to go to Place₂.

See L8–A1 for more on 從 Place 到 Place 來/去.

5. The adverb 才

Structure	Gloss
S Time When 才 V (O)	S won't V (O) until Time When
S V₁ 了 O 才 V₂ (O)	S won't V₂ (O) until finishing doing V₁ O

1. 你們六點鐘吃飯嗎？

Nǐ.men liù diǎnzhōng chīfàn .ma?
Do you eat at six o'clock?

我們八點鐘才吃飯。

Wǒ.men bā diǎnzhōng cái chīfàn.
We won't eat until eight o'clock.

2. 他今年要到中國去嗎？

Tā jīn.nián yào dào Zhōng.guó qù .ma?
Is he going to China this year?

他明年才要到中國去。

Tā míng.nián cái yào dào Zhōng.guó qù.
He won't go to China until next year.

3. 小林現在要到圖書館去嗎？

Xiǎo Lín xiànzài yào dào túshūguǎn qù .ma?
Is Xiao Lin going to the library now?

小林吃了飯才要到圖書館去。

Xiǎo Lín chī .le fàn cái yào dào túshūguǎn qù.
Xiao Lin won't go to the library until she finishes eating.

See L7–A5, L23–A1 for more on actions in sequence.

See L17–A3, L23–A2 for more on 才.

6. Resultative verbs — potential form

Potential RV	Structure	Gloss
Question	V 得 RE 不 RE?	can ... V or not?
Affirmative form	V 得 RE	can V...
Negative form	V(得) 不 RE	cannot V...

1. 漢字你寫得好不好？
    中文你說得好不好？

    Hànzì nǐ xiě.de hǎo .buhǎo?
    Zhōngwén nǐ shuō.de hǎo .buhǎo?
    Can you write Chinese characters well?
    Can you speak Chinese well?

    漢字我寫得不好，可是中文我
    說得很好。

    Hànzì wǒ xiě.de bù hǎo, kě.shì
    Zhōngwén wǒ shuō.de hěn hǎo.
    As for Chinese characters, I cannot write
    very well, but as for Chinese language, I
    can speak very well.

2. 中國飯他做得好不好？

    Zhōng.guófàn tā zuò.de hǎo .buhǎo?
    Can he cook Chinese food well?

    中國飯他做得不太好，可是美國
    飯他做得很好。

    Zhōng.guófàn tā zuò.de bútài hǎo, kě.shì
    Měi.guófàn tā zuò.de hěn hǎo.
    He cannot cook Chinese food very well,
    but he can cook American food well.

The potential form of a resultative verb (RV) is formed by (1) inserting a complement marker 得 'attainable' between the action verb (V) and the resultative verb ending (RE) to denote the possibility of attaining the result of the action; or (2) inserting 不 'not (attainable)' between the action verb (V) and the resultative verb ending (RE) to denote the impossibility of attaining the result of the action.

See L7–A6, L15–A2.3, L18–A4 for more on resultative verb compounds.

See L10–A1, L11–A3, L14–A6, L15–A2.3, L18–A4, L23–C1.5 for more on complement marker 得.

7. Topicalization

Structure		Gloss
O,	S V/RV	As for O, S (can/cannot) V...
Topic,	comment	
S,	O V/RV	As for O, S (can/cannot) V...

1. 中國飯你們會做嗎？

   Zhōng.guófàn nǐ.men huì zuò .ma?
   Can you cook Chinese food?

   我不會做中國飯，他會做中國飯。

   Wǒ bú huì zuò Zhōng.guófàn. Tā huì zuò Zhōng.guófàn.
   I cannot cook Chinese food. He can cook Chinese food.

2. 漢字他寫得好嗎？

   Hànzì tā xiě.de hǎo .ma?
   Can he write Chinese characters well?

   漢字他寫得很好。

   Hànzì tā xiě.de hěn hǎo.
   He can write Chinese characters very well.

 As already noted, in Chinese, when people wish to talk about something, they present it as the topic and place it at the beginning of a sentence; the comment follows it. The topic can be either an actor, which serves as the subject of a sentence, or an object.

B Usage of Common Phrases 詞組用法 cízǔ yòngfǎ

1. The adverbial phrase 一塊兒

Structure	Grammatical Function	Gloss
A 跟 B V$_i$ 在一塊兒	as the complement of the verb	A and B V$_i$ together
A 跟 B 一塊兒 V (O)	as an adverb which modifies the verb	A and B V(O) together

1. 小高跟誰走在一塊兒？

   Xiǎo Gāo gēn shéi zǒu zài yíkuàir?
   Who is Xiao Gao with?

   小高跟小林走在一塊兒。

   Xiǎo Gāo gēn Xiǎo Lín zǒu zài yíkuàir.
   Xiao Gao is with Xiao Lin.

2. 你跟誰一塊兒做飯？

   Nǐ gēn shéi yíkuàir zuòfàn?
   Who do you cook with?

   我跟他一塊兒做飯。

   Wǒ gēn tā yíkuàir zuòfàn.
   He and I cook together.

2. 請 vs. 問

Structure	Gloss
A 請 B VO	A invites/asks B to VO
A 問 B X	A asks B about X

1. 你請誰吃飯？

   我請小林吃飯。

   Nǐ qǐng shéi chīfàn?
   Who did you invite for dinner?

   Wǒ qǐng Xiǎo Lín chīfàn.
   I invited Xiao Lin to have dinner.

2. 你請他做什麼？

   我請他唱中國歌兒。

   Nǐ qǐng tā zuò shén.me?
   What did you ask him to do?

   Wǒ qǐng tā chàng Zhōng.guógēr.
   I asked him to sing a Chinese song.

3. 你問他什麼？

   我問他要不要去看電影兒。

   Nǐ wèn tā shén.me?
   What did you ask him about?

   Wǒ wèn tā yào .buyào qù kàn diànyǐngr.
   I asked him whether he wanted to go to the movie or not.

問 wèn is used to ask for information about something, whereas 請 qǐng is used to invite/ask someone to do something.

3. The auxiliary verbs 可以、能、會

Structure	Gloss
S (不) 可以/能/會 V O	S may/can/will (not) V O
可以	may, to be permitted to, it is all right to; can
能	may, to be permitted to = 可以; can, is able to (in terms of capability)
會	can, to know how to; will, could possibly or would probably

1. 老師，我現在可以來看您嗎？

   現在不可以。我下午兩點以後
   才有空兒。

   Lǎoshī, wǒ xiànzài kě.yǐ lái kàn nín .ma?
   Teacher, may I come to see you now?

   Xiànzài bù kě.yǐ. Wǒ xià.wǔ liǎng diǎn
   yǐhòu cái yǒu kòngr.

No, you cannot. I won't be free until two o'clock this afternoon.

2. 我們剛考完試，可以休息一下。

Wǒ.men gāng kǎowánshì, kě.yǐ xiū.xí .yíxià.
We just finished the test; (we) can rest a little.

太好了！

Tài hǎo.le!
It's great.

3. 他可以不可以回家？

Tā kě.yǐ .bukě.yǐ huíjiā?
Can he go home?

他功課還沒做完，他的老師說他不可以回家。

Tā gōngkè hái méi zuòwán, tā .de lǎoshī shuō tā bù kě.yǐ huíjiā.
He hasn't finished doing his homework yet; his teacher said that he can't go home.

4. 學生能叫老師名字嗎？

Xué.shēng néng jiào lǎoshī míng.zi .ma?
Can students call teachers by their name?

學生不可以叫老師名字。

Xué.shēng bù kě.yǐ jiào lǎoshī míng.zi.
Students cannot call teachers by name.

5. 你今天能不能唱歌？

Nǐ jīn.tiān néng .bunéng chànggē?
Can you sing (songs) today?

我今天很累，不能唱歌。

Wǒ jīn.tiān hěn lèi, bù néng chànggē.
Today I am very tired; (I) can't sing (songs).

6. 去年小李回中國去了嗎？

Qù.nián Xiǎo Lǐ huí Zhōng.guó .qù .le .ma?
Did Xiao Li go back to China last year?

去年小李很忙，不能回中國去。

Qù.nián Xiǎo Lǐ hěn máng, bù néng huí Zhōng.guó .qù.
Last year Xiao Li was very busy; (he) couldn't go back to China.

7. 他會不會寫中國字？

Tā huì .buhuì xiě Zhōng.guózì?
Can he write Chinese characters?

他很會說中國話，可是不會寫中國字。

Tā hěn huì shuō Zhōng.guóhuà, kě.shì bú huì xiě Zhōng.guózì.
He can speak Chinese well but cannot write Chinese characters.

8. 你什麼時候來看我們？

Nǐ shén.me shí.hòu lái kàn wǒ.men?
When will you visit us?

明天我沒什麼事，我會來看你們。

Míng.tiān wǒ méi shén.me shì, wǒ huì lái kàn nǐ.men.
Tomorrow I don't have anything to do. I will come to see you.

9. 他會唱中國歌兒嗎？

Tā huì chàng Zhōng.guógēr .ma?
Can he sing Chinese songs?

上個月他還不會唱中國歌兒，現在他會唱兩首了。

Shàng .ge yuè tā hái bú huì chàng Zhōng.guógēr, xiànzài tā huì chàng liǎng shǒu .le.
Last month he still couldn't sing Chinese songs; now he can sing two (songs).

The negation for the three auxiliary verbs 可以 / 能 / 會 is 不 even when they occur in a past-tense sentence (see examples 3, 6 and 9). The major difference between auxiliary verbs and other kinds of verbs is that auxiliary verbs *cannot* be suffixed by aspect markers 了, 過 guò (experiential aspect marker, see L10), and 著 .zhe (progressive aspect marker, see L10).

4. 看 for expressing opinions

	Structure	Gloss
Q.	你 看 … 怎麼 樣 ？	How about …?
	你 看 … 嗎 ？ / …V-not-V…?	Do you think …?/ Will …or not ?
A.	我 看 X…	I think (in my opinion) X…

1. 你看出去吃飯怎麼樣？

Nǐ kàn chū.qù chīfàn zěn.meyàng?
How about eating out?

我看出去吃飯太貴了，咱們自己做吧！

Wǒ kàn chū.qù chīfàn tài guì .le, zá.men zìjǐ zuò .ba.
I think it's too expensive to eat out. Let's cook ourselves.

2. 你看明天他會打電話給我嗎？

Nǐ kàn míng.tiān tā huì dǎ diànhuà gěi wǒ .ma?
Do you think he will call me tomorrow?

我看明天他會打電話給你。

Wǒ kàn míng.tiān tā huì dǎ diànhuà gěi nǐ.
I think he will call you tomorrow.

3. 你看今天他會不會來上課？

Nǐ kàn jīn.tiān tā huì .buhuì lái shàngkè?
Do you think he will come to the class today?

我看今天他不會來上課。

Wǒ kàn jīn.tiān tā bú huì lái shàngkè.
I don't think he will come to the class today.

 看 means "to see, to look," but it also denotes "to think, to consider" when asking for someone's opinion or expressing one's opinion. In the latter case, 看 is interchangeable with 想 or 覺得.

5. The particle ...好了

Structure	Gloss
咱們 VO 好了	Let's just VO
你 VO 好了	Why don't you just VO

1. 你看咱們自己做飯怎麼樣？

Nǐ kàn zá.men zìjǐ zuòfàn zěn.meyàng?
How about cooking the food ourselves?

我看自己做飯太麻煩了，咱們出去吃好了。

Wǒ kàn zìjǐ zuòfàn tài má.fán .le, zá.men chū.qù chī hǎo.le.
I think it's too troublesome to cook ourselves. Let's eat out.

2. 咱們上圖書館去吧！

Zá.men shàng túshūguǎn qù .ba!
How about us going to the library?

不行，我沒空兒去，你自己去好了。

Bù xíng, wǒ méi kòngr qù, nǐ zìjǐ qù hǎo.le.
No, I don't have time (to go). Why don't you just go by yourself?

...好了 is a sentence final particle which denotes that the speaker proposes a mild suggestion.

Cultural Notes
文化點滴 wénhuà diǎndī

1. In a Chinese community, when you would like to eat out with a friend and you initiate the action, this indicates that you also will 請客 qǐngkè 'to invite the guests, to give a party.' As a general rule, you will be expected to pay for the meal. But it is also common to see friends fight to pay for the meal after eating at a restaurant. This is because Chinese people value the principle of 禮尚往來 lǐ shàng wǎng lái 'courtesy demands reciprocity.' Thus if you were invited to have a meal by a friend, then the next time you should treat him/her in return. When a group of relatives eat out, usually the most senior one is expected to pay for the meal.

2. When a Chinese person invites you to have dinner, if you are not very familiar with him/her, you should not accept the invitation immediately when it is extended. You must first 婉拒 wǎnjù 'to decline an invitation, a present, etc., with great gentleness and courtesy.' After the second invitation, you may accept. This kind of decline-accept act is considered proper.

3. When Chinese young people first start dating, a friend (or friends) may go out with the couple to make their acquaintance less "awkward." This go-between friend is called 電燈泡 '[light-bulb] a go-between for new dates.'

第十課　我們吃什麼好呢？

對話

〔小高五點二十到了校門口，一會兒小林、小李也從宿舍走來
了。他們一起搭小高的車去吃飯。〕

（在車上）

小高：　　「湖南」怎麼樣？還是「長城」？

小李：　　那兩家飯館兒都不錯。「湖南」南方菜做得好，口味比
　　　　　較重。「長城」的北方菜比較地道。餃子和烤鴨尤其好
　　　　　。味道比較淡。

小高：　　小林，你喜歡哪一家？吃不吃辣的？

小林：　　我吃過餃子，試試南方菜好了！

（在飯館兒）

服務員：請問幾位？

小李：　　三位。

服務員：抽煙嗎？

小李：　　不抽煙。

服務員：請跟我來。

（三個人坐下，看菜單）

小高：　　小李，我們吃點兒什麼好呢？

小李：　　我看一個人叫一道菜好了。這家給的菜很多，大家可以
　　　　　分著吃。我來一個酸辣湯。

小林：　　嗯，不要牛肉，不要雞。來點兒海鮮、糖醋魚怎麼樣？

小高：　　好啊！吃魚對身體好。你叫糖醋魚，我來一個酸甜肉吧！

服務員：　你們要不要「春捲」什麼的？

小李：　　不必了，先給我們來壺茶吧！（問小林、小高）你們要
　　　　　不要喝點兒別的？汽水兒還是啤酒？

小高：　　想喝啤酒，可是今天我開車，算了！

对话

〔小高五点二十到了校门口，一会儿小林、小李也从宿舍走来
　了。他们一起搭小高的车去吃饭。〕

（在车上）

小高：　　「湖南」怎么样？还是「长城」？

小李：　　那两家饭馆儿都不错。「湖南」南方菜做得好，口味比
　　　　　较重。「长城」的北方菜比较地道。饺子和烤鸭尤其好
　　　　　。味道比较淡。

小高：　　小林，你喜欢哪一家？吃不吃辣的？

小林：　　我吃过饺子，试试南方菜好了！

（在饭馆儿）

服务员：请问几位？

小李：　　三位。

服务员：抽烟吗？

小李：　　不抽烟。

服务员：请跟我来。

（三个人坐下，看菜单）

小高：　　小李，我们吃点儿什么好呢？

小李：　　我看一个人叫一道菜好了。这家给的菜很多，大家可以
　　　　　分着吃。我来一个酸辣汤。

小林：　　嗯，不要牛肉，不要鸡。来点儿海鲜、糖醋鱼怎么样？

小高：　　好啊！吃鱼对身体好。你叫糖醋鱼，我来一个酸甜肉吧！

服务员： 你们要不要「春捲」什么的？

小李 ： 不必了，先给我们来壶茶吧！（问小林、小高）你们要不要喝点儿别的？汽水儿还是啤酒？

小高 ： 想喝啤酒，可是今天我开车，算了！

My questions:

Duìhuà

(Xiǎo Gāo wǔ diǎn èrshí dào .le xiào ménkǒu, yǐhuǐr Xiǎo Lín, Xiǎo Lǐ yě cóng sùshè zǒu lái .le. Tā.men yìqǐ dā Xiǎo Gāo .de chē qù chīfàn.)

(Zài chē .shàng)

Xiǎo Gāo: Húnán zěn.meyàng? Hái.shì Chángchéng?

Xiǎo Lǐ: Nà liǎng jiā fànguǎnr dōu búcuò. Húnán nánfāngcài zuò.de hǎo, kǒuwèi bǐjiào zhòng. Chángchéng .de běifāngcài bǐjiào dì.dào. Jiǎo.zi hé kǎoyā yóuqí hǎo, wèidào bǐjiào dàn.

Xiǎo Gāo: Xiǎo Lín, nǐ xǐ.huān nǎ yì jiā? Chī .bu.chī là .de?

Xiǎo Lín: Wǒ chī.guò jiǎo.zi, shì.shì nánfāng cài hǎo.le.

(Zài fànguǎnr)

Fúwùyuán: Qǐngwèn jǐ wèi?

Xiǎo Lǐ: Sān wèi.

Fúwùyuán: Chōuyān .ma?

Xiǎo Lǐ: Bù chōuyān.

Fúwùyuán: Qǐng gēn wǒ lái.

(Sān .ge rén zuò.xià, kàn càidān.)

Xiǎo Gāo: Xiǎo Lǐ, wǒ.men chī .diǎnr shén.me hǎo .ne?

Xiǎo Lǐ: Wǒ kàn yí .ge rén jiào yí dào cài hǎo.le. Zhè jiā gěi .de cài hěn duō, dàjiā kě.yǐ fēn.zhe chī. Wǒ lái yí .ge suānlàtāng.

Xiǎo Lín: En, búyào niúròu, búyào jī. Lái .diǎnr hǎixiān, tángcùyú zěn.meyàng?

Xiǎo Gāo: Hǎo .a! Chī yú duì shēntǐ hǎo, nǐ jiào tángcùyú. Wǒ lái yí .ge suāntiánròu .ba!

Fúwùyuán: Nǐ.men yào .buyào "chūnjuǎn" shén.me .de?

Xiǎo Lǐ: Búbì .le. Xiān gěi wǒ.men lái hú chá .ba! (Wèn Xiǎo Lín, Xiǎo Gāo) Nǐ.men yào .buyào hē .diǎnr bié .de? Qìshuǐr hái.shì píjiǔ?

Xiǎo Gāo: Wǒ xiǎng hē píjiǔ, kě.shì jīn.tiān wǒ kāichē. Suàn.le.

Dialogue

(Xiǎo Gāo arrives at the school entrance at five twenty. After a while, Xiǎo Lín and Xiǎo Lǐ come walking from their dorms. They go to the restaurant in Xiǎo Gāo's car.)

(In the car)

Xiǎo Gāo: How about Hunan? Or Great Wall?

Xiǎo Lǐ: Those two restaurants are both fine. Hunan cooks good southern dishes and their food has a richer flavor. Great Wall's northern cuisine is more authentic. Their dumplings and roast duck are especially good. Their food is more bland.

Xiǎo Gāo: Xiǎo Lín, which one do you like? Do you like spicy food or not?

Xiǎo Lín: I had some dumplings before. Let's try southern food (this time).

(In the restaurant)

Waiter: May I ask how many altogether?

Xiǎo Lǐ: Three.

Waiter: Do you want smoking or nonsmoking?

Xiǎo Lǐ: Nonsmoking.

Waiter: Please come with me.

(The three sit down and look at the menu.)

Xiǎo Gāo: Xiǎo Lǐ, what should we order?

Xiǎo Lǐ: I think each of us can order a dish. Since this restaurant gives lots of food, we can all share. I'll have hot and sour soup.

Xiǎo Lín: Hmm, not beef, not chicken. I want some seafood. How about sweet and sour fish?

Xiǎo Gāo: Sure! Fish is good for your health. You order sweet and sour fish; I'll have sweet and sour pork.

Waiter: Do you want spring rolls or something?

Xiǎo Lǐ: No, it's O.K. Could you give us a pot of tea first? (Asking Xiǎo Lín and Xiǎo Gāo:) Do you want something else to drink? Soda or beer?

Xiǎo Gāo: I'd like beer, but (since) I'm driving today, I'll do without it.

Mini-Dialogue
小對話 Xiǎoduìhuà

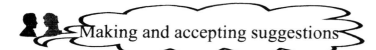
Making and accepting suggestions

1. A: 我餓死了。

    Wǒ èsǐ .le.
    I'm starving.

    B: 我也是。咱們去吃飯吧！

    Wǒ yě shì. Zán.men qù chīfàn .ba!
    Me too. Let's go and eat something!

    A: 好啊！「長城」怎麼樣？

    Hǎo .a! "Chángchéng" zěn.meyàng?
    O.K.! How about the Great Wall?

    B: 不錯！他們的菜很地道。

    Búcuò! Tā.men .de cài hěn dì.dào.
    Not bad! Their food is quite authentic.

Discussing what you want to eat

1. A: 小王，你想點什麼？

    Xiǎo Wáng, nǐ xiǎng diǎn shén.me?
    Xiao Wang, what do you want to
    order?

    B: 雞肉怎麼樣？

    Jīròu zěn.meyàng?
    How about chicken?

2. A: 好啊！喝什麼呢？

    Hǎo .a! Hē shén.me .ne?
    Fine! What should we have for drinks?

    B: 我們一人來一瓶汽水兒吧。

    Wǒ.men yì rén lái yì píng qìshuǐr .ba.
    Let's each have a bottle of soda.

Ordering food in a restaurant

1. A: 你們想吃點兒什麼？我們
        這兒的北京烤鴨很道地。

    Nǐ.men xiǎng chī .diǎnr shén.me?
    Wǒ.men zhèr .de Běijīng kǎoyā hěn dào.dì.
    What do you want to eat? Our Beijing duck is very authentic.

    B: 我來一個炸雞吧！

    Wǒ lái yí .ge zhájī .ba!
    I'll take fried chicken.

    C: 我要一個酸辣湯。

    Wǒ yào yí .ge suānlàtāng.
    I want a hot and sour soup.

Commenting on food

1. A: 這道菜看起來不錯，吃起
        來怎麼樣？

    Zhè dào cài kàn.qǐ.lái búcuò, chī.qǐ.lái zěn.meyàng?
    This dish looks good. How does it taste?

    B: 也不錯，辣了一點兒。

    Yě búcuò, là .le yì.diǎnr.
    Not bad. A little spicy.

2. A: 這條魚看起來很新鮮。

    Zhè tiáo yú kàn.qǐ.lái hěn xīnxiān.
    This fish looks very fresh.

    B: 味道淡了一點兒。

    Wèidào dàn .le yì.diǎnr.
    It tastes a little plain.

Vocabulary
生詞 Shēngcí

◎ **By Order of Appearance**

湖南		Húnán	N	[lake-south] Hunan—name of a province
長城	长城	Chángchéng	N	[long-city] the Great Wall
飯館兒	饭馆儿	fànguǎnr	N	[meal-hall] restaurant (M: 家 jiā)
南方		nánfāng	N	[south-direction] the south
口味兒	口味儿	kǒuwèir	N	[mouth-taste] taste, flavor
比較	比较	bǐjiào	Adv/N	[compare-compare] comparatively, comparison
* 比		bǐ	V	to compare
北方		běifāng	N	[north-direction] the north
餃子	饺子	jiǎo.zi	N	[dumpling-Suf] dumpling (M: 個)
烤鴨	烤鸭	kǎoyā	N	roast duck (M: 隻 zhī 'M for birds')
尤其		yóuqí	Adv	[especially-he/she/it] especially
味道		wèidào	N	[taste-way] taste , flavor (=口味兒), odor
淡		dàn	SV	(to be) light (taste, color), weak or thin (tea, coffee, etc.)
辣		là	SV	(to be) hot, spicy
過	过	.guò	Asp	[pass] experiential suffix to verbs
試(一)試	试(一)试	shì(.yí).shì	V	[try-try] to try, to give it a try
位		wèi	M	measure word for people (polite)
抽		chōu	V	to smoke (cigarettes, etc.), to inhale
* 吸		xī	V	to smoke (cigarettes, etc.) (= 抽), to inhale
煙	烟	yān	N	cigarette (M: 根 , 包), smoke
跟		gēn	CV/P	[heel] to follow; with (person)
叫		jiào	V	to order
道		dào	M	measure word for dishes
大家		dàjiā	N	[big-family] all, everybody
分		fēn	V	to divide
著	着	.zhe	Asp	durative aspect marker
酸		suān	SV	(to be) sour
湯	汤	tāng	N	soup (M: 碗 wǎn 'bowl')
牛肉		niúròu	N	[cow-meat] beef (M: 斤 jīn 'catty,' 磅 bàng 'pound')
雞	鸡	jī	N	chicken (M: 隻 zhī 'M for birds')
海鮮	海鲜	hǎixiān	N	[sea-fresh] seafood

糖		táng	N	sugar, candy
醋		cù	N	vinegar
魚	鱼	yú	N	fish (M: 條 tiáo 'stripe,' M for long and soft things)
對...好	对...好	duì...hǎo	PP	be nice to...
身體	身体	shēntǐ	N	[body-body] body, health
甜		tián	SV	(to be) sweet
春捲兒	春卷儿	chūnjuǎnr	N	[spring-roll] eggroll
什麼的	什么的	shén.me .de	N	[what-particle] and so forth
不必		búbì	Adv	not necessarily
壺	壶	hú	M/N	a pot (of tea)
茶		chá	N	tea (M: 杯 bēi 'cup')
汽水兒	汽水儿	qìshuǐr	N	[vapor-water] soft drink (M: 杯 bēi 'cup,' 罐 guàn 'can,' 瓶 píng 'bottle')
啤酒		píjiǔ	N	[beer-wine] beer (M: 杯 bēi 'cup,' 罐 guàn 'can,' 瓶 píng 'bottle')
* 牛奶		niúnǎi	N	milk
* 桔子水		jú.zishuǐ	N	orange juice
開	开	kāi	V	to drive (a vehicle), to open (a can, box, etc.)
車	车	chē	N	car, vehicle (M: 輛 liàng, 部 bù)
算了		suàn.le	IE	forget it

◎ By Grammatical Categories

Nouns/Pronouns

湖南		Húnán	N	[lake-south] Hunan—name of a province
長城	长城	Chángchéng	N	[long-city] the Great Wall
飯館兒	饭馆儿	fànguǎnr	N	[meal-hall] restaurant (M: 家 jiā)
南方		nánfāng	N	[south-direction] the south
北方		běifāng	N	[north-direction] the north
口味兒	口味儿	kǒuwèir	N	[mouth-taste] taste, flavor
味道		wèidào	N	[taste-way] taste, flavor (=口味兒), odor
餃子	饺子	jiǎo.zi	N	[dumpling-Suf] dumpling (M: 個)
烤鴨	烤鸭	kǎoyā	N	roast duck (M: 隻 zhī 'M for birds')
牛肉		niúròu	N	[cow-meat] beef (M: 斤 jīn 'catty,' 磅 bàng 'pound')
雞	鸡	jī	N	chicken (M: 隻 zhī 'M for birds')
海鮮	海鲜	hǎixiān	N	[sea-fresh] seafood

湯	汤	tāng	N	soup (M: 碗 wǎn 'bowl')
魚	鱼	yú	N	fish (M: 條 tiáo 'stripe,' M for long and soft things)
糖		táng	N	sugar, candy
醋		cù	N	vinegar
春捲兒	春卷儿	chūnjuǎnr	N	[spring-roll] eggroll
大家		dàjiā	N	[big-family] all, everybody
身體	身体	shēntǐ	N	[body-body] body, health
什麼的	什么的	shén.me .de	N	[what-particle] and so forth
煙	烟	yān	N	cigarette (M: 根 / 包), smoke
茶		chá	N	tea (M: 杯 bēi 'cup')
汽水兒	汽水儿	qìshuǐr	N	[vapor-water] soft drink (M: 杯 bēi 'cup,' 罐 guàn 'can,' 瓶 píng 'bottle')
啤酒		píjiǔ	N	[beer-wine] beer (M: 杯 bēi 'cup,' 罐 guàn 'can,' 瓶 píng 'bottle')
* 牛奶		niúnǎi	N	milk
* 桔子水		jú.zishuǐ	N	orange juice
車	车	chē	N	car, vehicle (M: 輛 liàng, 部 bù)

Measure Words

位		wèi	M	measure word for people (polite)
道		dào	M	measure word for dishes
壺	壶	hú	M/N	a pot (of tea)

Verbs/Stative Verbs/Adjectives

* 比		bǐ	V	to compare
試(一)試	试(一)试	shì(.yí).shì	V	[try-try] to try, to give it a try
抽		chōu	V	to smoke (cigarettes, etc.), to inhale
* 吸		xī	V	to smoke (cigarettes, etc.), to inhale (= 抽)
跟		gēn	CV/P	[heel] to follow; with (person)
叫		jiào	V	to order
分		fēn	V	to divide
開	开	kāi	V	to drive (a vehicle), to open (a can, box, etc.)
淡		dàn	SV	(to be) light (taste, color), weak or thin (tea, coffee, etc.)
辣		là	SV	(to be) hot, spicy
酸		suān	SV	(to be) sour
甜		tián	SV	(to be) sweet

對 ... 好	对 ... 好	duì...hǎo	PP	be nice to...

Adverbs

比較	比较	bǐjiào	Adv/ N	[compare-compare] comparatively, comparison
尤其		yóuqí	Adv	[especially-he/she/it] especially
不必		búbì	Adv	not necessarily

Particles

過	过	.guò	Asp	[pass] experiential suffix to verbs
著	着	.zhe	Asp	durative aspect marker

Idiomatic Expressions

算了		suàn.le	IE	forget it

✚ Supplementary Vocabulary

1. Chinese Tea

茶葉	茶叶	cháyè	N	[tea-leaf] tea
紅茶	红茶	hóngchá	N	[red-tea] black tea
綠茶	绿茶	lǜchá	N	green tea
烏龍茶	乌龙茶	wūlóngchá	N	[black-dragon] Oolong tea (a kind of black tea produced in Táiwān)
香片		xiāngpiàn	N	[fragrant-piece] jasmine tea
龍井茶	龙井	lóngjǐngchá	N	[dragon-well] Dragon Well tea (a kind of green tea produced at Hángzhōu, Zhèjiāng)
鐵觀音	铁观音	tiěguānyīn	N	[iron-Buddha] Goddess of Mercy tea (a kind of black tea produced at Ānxī, Fújiàn)
普洱茶		pǔ'ěrchá	N	Pu-er tea (a kind of tea brick produced at Pú'ěr, Yúnnán)

2. Major Terms Used on Chinese Menus

頭檯	头檯	tóutái	N	[head-table] appetizers
雞類	鸡类	jīlèi	N	[chicken-category] food made with chicken
鴨類	鸭类	yālèi	N	[duck-catogory] food made with duck
肉類	肉类	ròulèi	N	[meat-category] food made with meat

豬肉	猪肉	zhūròu	N	[pig-meat] pork
海鮮	海鲜	hǎixiān	N	[sea-fresh] seafood
蔬菜		shūcài	N	[vegetable-vegetable] vegetables
素菜		sùcài	N	[plain-vegetable] vegetarian dishes
葷菜	荤菜	hūncaì	N	[meat/fish-diet] dishes containing meat or fish
湯	汤	tāng	N	soup (M: 碗 wǎn 'bowl')
炒飯	炒饭	chǎofàn	N	[fry-rice] fried rice
麵	面	miàn	N	noodles, food made with flour
河粉		héfěn	N	[river-flour] food made with rice flour
飲料	饮料	yǐnliào	N	[drink-material] drinks
點心	点心	diǎnxīn	N	[dot-heart] refreshments (Cantonese dím sām)
甜點	甜点	tiándiǎn	N	[sweet-refreshment] desserts

3. American Drinks/Food

熱狗	热狗	règǒu	N	[hot-dog] hot dog
炸雞	炸鸡	zhájī	N	[fry-chicken] fried chicken
皮薩	皮萨	písà	N	[skin-a surname] pizza
可口可樂	可口可乐	kě kǒu kě lè	N	[may-mouth-may-happy] Coca-Cola
七喜		qīxǐ	N	[seven-happy] 7-Up
冰淇淋		bīngqílín	N	[ice-a river name-sprinkle] ice cream
養樂多	养乐多	yǎnglèduō	N	[raise-happy-much] yogurt

4. Fruits

蘋果	苹果	píngguǒ	N	[apple-fruit]apple
杏子		xì.zi	N	[apricot-Suf] apricot
香蕉		xiāngjiāo	N	[fragrant-banana] banana
藍莓	蓝莓	lánméi	N	[blue-berry] blueberry
櫻桃		yīngtáo	N	[cherry-peach] cherry
柚子		yòu.zi	N	[pomelo-Suf] Chinese pomelo
葡萄		pú.táo	N	grape
葡萄柚		pú.táoyòu	N	[grape-pomelo] grapefruit
蜜瓜		mìguā	N	[honey-melon] honeydew
荔枝		lìzhī	N	[lichee-branch] lichee
龍眼	龙眼	lóngyǎn	N	[dragon-eye] longan
芒果		mángguǒ	N	[mango-fruit] mango
柳丁		liǔdīng	N	[willow-male adult] orange
桃子		táo.zi	N	[peach-Suf] peach
梨		lí	N	pear
李子		lǐ.zi	N	[plum-Suf] plum
草莓		cǎoméi	N	[grass-berry] strawberry

橘子		jú.zi	N	[orange-Suf] tangerine
西瓜		xīguā	N	[west-melon] watermelon

5. Vegetables

豆芽		dòuyá	N	[bean-sprout] bean sprout
青菜花		qīngcàihuā	N	[green-vegetable-flower] broccoli
紅蘿蔔	红萝蔔	hóngluó.bo	N	[red-turnip] carrot
菜花		càihuā	N	[vegetable-flower] cauliflower
黃瓜	黃瓜	huángguā	N	[yellow-melon] cucumber
芹菜		qíncài	N	[celery-vegetable] celery
白菜		báicài	N	[white-vegetable] Chinese cabbage
韭菜		jiǔcài	N	[leek-vegetable] Chinese leek
白蘿蔔	白萝蔔	báiluó.bo	N	[white-turnip] Chinese turnip
茄子		qié.zi	N	[eggplant-Suf] eggplant
蒜		suàn	N	garlic
薑		jiāng	N	ginger
四季豆		sìjìdòu	N	[four-season-bean] green bean
蔥	葱	cōng	N	green onion
青辣椒		qīng làjiāo	N	[green-pepper] green pepper
辣椒		làjiāo	N	[hot-pepper] hot pepper
芥藍菜	芥蓝菜	jièláncài	N	[mustard-blue-vegetable] kale
蘑菇		mógū	N	[mushroom-mushroom] mushroom
芥菜		jiècài	N	[mustard-vegetable] mustard green
洋蔥	洋葱	yáng cōng	N	[ocean-onion] onion
豌豆		wāndòu	N	[pea-bean] peas
馬鈴薯	洋山芋	mǎlíngshǔ/ yángshānyù	N	[horse-bell-yam]/[foreign-mountain-taro] potato
青江菜		qīngjiāngcài	N	[green-river vegetable] Shanghai Pak Choi
雪豆		xuědòu	N	[snow-pea] snow pea
黃豆	黃豆	huángdòu	N	[yellow-bean] soy bean
菠菜		bōcài	N	[spinach-vegetable] spinach
蕃茄	西红柿	fānqié/ xīhóngshì	N	[barbarian-eggplant] tomato
空心菜		kōngxīncài	N	[empty-heart-vegetable] water spinach
蕃薯		fānshǔ	N	[barbarian-yam] yam

Characters
漢字 Hànzì

菜

cài
vegetable, dish
of food
12   艹 (grass)

| 中國菜 | Zhōng.guócài | Chinese food |
| *生菜 | shēngcài | lettuce |

A: 這家飯館的**菜**做得怎麼樣？
B: 做得很道地。

館

guǎn
a house   食
16   (to eat)

飯館兒	fànguǎnr	restaurant
*圖書館	túshūguǎn	library
*旅館	lǚguǎn	hotel

A: 這個大學的**圖書館**比那個大多了。
B: 可不是嗎！

喝

hē
to drink   口
12   (mouth)

*好喝	hǎohē	tasty (good to drink)
*喝茶	hē chá	to drink tea
*喝酒	hē jiǔ	to drink wine
*喝水	hē shuǐ	to drink water

A: 你**喝不喝茶**？
B: **不喝**，我**就喝水**。

著

.zhe
suffix for
progressive
action   艹
12   (grass)

A: 我們應該叫幾道菜？
B: 一人一道，大家**分著吃**好了。

繁簡對照：	其他漢字：	✎ **My notes:**
館 馆	吃 L7	
著＝着		

| 酸辣湯 | suānlàtāng | hot and sour soup |
| *雞湯 | jītāng | chicken soup |

tāng
soup
12　　　氵　(water)

A: 你要**湯**嗎？
B: 好啊！咱們來個**酸辣湯**吧。

| 汽水兒 | qìshuǐr | soda |
| *礦泉水 | kuàngquánshuǐ | mineral water |

shuǐ
water　　水
4　　　(water)

A: 你想喝什麼**汽水兒**？
B: 可口可樂。

| *金魚 | jīnyú | goldfish |
| *釣魚 | diàoyú | to fish |

yú
fish　　魚
11　　(fish)

A: 這家飯館做的**魚**味道好極了。
B: 是嗎？我没吃過。

牛肉	niúròu	beef
*豬肉	zhūròu	pork
*羊肉	yángròu	mutton

ròu
meat　　肉
6　　　(meat)

A: 你想吃菜還是**吃肉**？
B: **吃肉**，不過我不吃**紅肉**。

繁簡對照：	其他漢字：	✎ **My notes:**
湯　汤	*冰 SC19	
魚　鱼	*杯 SC20	

喜

xǐ
to rejoice 口
12 (mouth)

喜歡　　　　xǐ.huān　　　　to like

A: 你**喜歡**中文還是日文？
B: 我**喜歡**中文，不過中國字有點兒難。

歡

huān
joyous 欠
22 (to owe)

A: 你**喜歡**寫中國字嗎？
B: **喜歡**，不過我寫的字不好看。

茶

chá
tea ＋＋
10 (grass)

喝茶　　　　hē chá　　　　to drink tea
*紅茶　　　　hóngchá　　　　black tea
*綠茶　　　　lǜchá　　　　green tea
*清茶　　　　qīngchá　　　　green tea

A: 給我來杯熱**紅茶**吧！
B: 好，請等一下。

酒

jiǔ
wine 酉
10 (the tenth of
the 12 terrestrial
branches)

啤酒　　　　píjiǔ　　　　beer
*白酒　　　　báijiǔ　　　　white wine
*紅酒　　　　hóngjiǔ　　　　red wine
*酒店　　　　jiǔdiàn　　　　wineshop

A: 他每個星期五下午都去**酒店**喝**啤酒**。
B: 聽說他一個晚上可以喝一打**啤酒**。
A: 真是個**酒鬼**。

繁簡對照：	其他漢字：	✎ **My notes:**
歡 欢	*愛 SC21 *抽 SC22 *煙 SC23	

南

nán
south   十
9   (ten)

南方	nánfāng	south
*東南	dōngnán	southeast
*西南	xīnán	southwest

A: 你喜歡**南方菜**還是北方菜？
B: 都喜歡，做得好吃就好了。

北

běi
north   匕
5   (a ladle)

北方	běifāng	north
*西北	xīběi	northwest
*東北	dōngběi	northeast

A: 我們下星期一塊兒做飯吧！
B: 好啊！咱們包餃子吧！我喜歡吃**北方菜**。

方

fāng
square,
direction   方
4   (square)

南方	nánfāng	the south
*東方人	dōngfāngrén	Orientals
*西方人	xīfāngrén	Westerners
*地方	dì.fāng	place, space

A: 很多**西方人**喜歡吃中國菜。
B: 對，但是**西方**很多飯館的中國菜不地道。

比

bǐ
to compare 比
4 (to compare)

| 比較 | bǐjiào | comparatively |
| *比賽 | bǐsài | game, contest |

A: 這道菜**比較不辣**。吃太辣的對身體不好。
B: 可是味道太淡了，我比較喜歡那道菜。

繁簡對照：	其他漢字：	**My notes:**

開

kāi
to open, to turn
on 　　門
12 　　(door)

開車	kāichē	to drive
*開門	kāimén	to open a door
*開燈	kāidēng	to turn on a light
*開始	kāishǐ	to begin

A: 我想來杯啤酒。
B: 那今天我**開車**好了。

車

chē
vehicle 　車
7 　(vehicle)

*車子	chē.zi	car
*汽車	qìchē	automobile
*火車	huǒchē	train
*公車	gōngchē	bus

A: 她**開車**開得怎麼樣？
B: 不錯，快了一點兒。

錯

cuò
error 　金
16 　(metal)

| 不錯 | búcuò | not bad, quite good |
| *說錯 | shuōcuò | to say something incorrectly |

A: 她中文說得好嗎？
B: 還**不錯**，她才學了四個月。

重

zhòng, chóng
heavy, again
　　　里
9 　(a unit—
　　1/3 miles)

| *重要 | zhòngyào | important |

A: 我喜歡吃辣的，尤其是四川菜。
B: 你的**口味太重**了。

繁簡對照：	其他漢字：	✎ **My notes:**
開 开	*關 SC24	
車 车	*部 SC25	
錯 错	輕 L22	

Grammar
語法 yǔfǎ

Ⓐ Major Sentence Patterns 主要句型 zhǔyào jùxíng

1. V 得 Adj construction

Structure	Gloss
S V O V 得 (Adv) Adj S O V 得 (Adv) Adj	S V (very/quite) Adj O
S V O V 得 不 (Adv) Adj S O V 得 不 (Adv) Adj	S cannot V Adj O

1. 這家飯館兒北方菜做得怎麼樣？

   Zhè jiā fànguǎr běifāngcài zuò.de zěn.meyàng?
   How is this restaurant's northern cuisine?

   這家飯館兒北方菜做得很好。

   Zhè jiā fànguǎr běifāngcài zuò.de hěn hǎo.
   This restaurant makes very good northern cuisine.

   這家飯館兒北方菜做得不太好。

   Zhè jiā fànguǎr běifāngcài zuò.de bútài hǎo.
   This restaurant's northern cuisine is not very good.

2. 他糖醋魚做得怎麼樣？

   Tā tángcùyú zuò.de zěn.meyàng?
   How is his sweet and sour fish?

   他糖醋魚做得不錯。

   Tā tángcùyú zuò.de búcuò.
   He makes pretty good sweet and sour fish.

   他糖醋魚做得不行。

   Tā tángcùyú zuò.de bùxíng.
   His sweet and sour fish is not very good.

When a predicate of a sentence consists of [V 得 + descriptive complement], 得 is an infix, serving as a marker of the complement. The construction of the predicate then must consist of either a repeated V, in the form of [V O V 得/不 (Adv) Adj], or a preposed object, in the form of [O V 得/不 (Adv) Adj].

See L9–A6, L11–A3, L14–A6, L15–A2, L18–A4, L23–C1.5 for more on complement marker 得.

2. Comparative constructions

2.1 Explicit comparison

	Structure	Gloss
Question	A 比 B Adj 嗎？	Is A Adj-er than B
Answer	A 比 B Adj	A is Adj-er than B
	A 比 B Adj（得）多了	A is much more Adj-er than B
	A 比 B Adj 一點兒	A is a little bit Adj-er than B
	A 不比 B Adj	A is not as Adj as B

1. 南方菜比北方菜甜嗎？

   Nánfāngcài bǐ běifāngcài tián .ma?
   Is southern food sweeter than northern food?

   南方菜比北方菜甜得多了。

   Nánfāngcài bǐ běifāngcài tián .de duō .le.
   Southern food is much sweeter than northern food.

2. 你的中文比他的(中文)好嗎？

   Nǐ .de Zhōngwén bǐ tā .de (Zhōngwén) hǎo .ma?
   Is your Chinese better than his (Chinese)?

   我的中文比他的(中文)好一點兒。

   Wǒ .de Zhōngwén bǐ tā .de (Zhōngwén) hǎo yì.diǎnr.
   My Chinese is a little bit better than his (Chinese).

Comparison of two things can be made either explicitly or implicitly. The comparisons in examples 1 and 2 are explicit, because both parties of the comparisons are clearly stated.

The word order of a comparative sentence follows the *Temporal Sequence Principle*. You must compare two things first, then give result of the comparison.

To express "A is much more expensive than B" you should say A比B貴(得)多了, *not* A比B很貴.

3. 他比你高嗎？

   Tā bǐ nǐ gāo .ma?
   Is he taller than you?

   他不比我高。

   Tā bù bǐ wǒ gāo.
   He is not as tall as I (am).

4. 中文比日文難嗎？

   Zhōngwén bǐ Rìwén nán .ma?
   Is Chinese more difficult than Japanese?

中文不比日文難。

Zhōngwén bù bǐ Rìwén nán.
Chinese is not more difficult than Japanese.

 The A 比 B Adj construction denotes "A is more… than B." Therefore the positive form of the stative verb is always used. If you would like to express the contradictory of the comparison, you should put the negative adverb 不 before 比, as in examples 3 and 4.

2.2 Implicit comparison

	Structure	Gloss
Question	(A 跟 B), 哪 M (比較) Adj?	(As for A and B), which one is Adj-er?
Answer	A (比較) Adj A Adj (得) 多了 A Adj 一點兒	A is Adj-er A is much more Adj A is a little bit more Adj

1. (餃子跟包子), 哪個(比較) 好吃 ?

(Jiǎo.zi gēn bāo.zi), něi .ge (bǐjiào) hǎochī?
Which one is more delicious? Dumplings or steamed stuffed buns?

餃子(比較) 好吃。

Jiǎo.zi (bǐjiào) hǎochī.
Dumplings are more delicious.

2. (牛肉 跟雞), 哪個(比較) 貴 ?

(Niúròu gēn jī), něi .ge (bǐjiào) guì?
Which one is more expensive? Beef or chicken?

牛肉(比較) 貴。

Niúròu (bǐjiào) guì.
Beef is more expensive.

 The comparisons in these examples are implicit, because the ones being compared are omitted (as understood in the conversational context).

2.3 Equaling-degree comparison

	Structure	Gloss
Question	A 有沒有 B (這麼 / 那麼) Adj ?	Is A as Adj as B?
Answer	A 有 B (這麼 / 那麼) Adj A 沒有 B (這麼 / 那麼) Adj	A is as Adj as B A is not as Adj as B

1. 魚有沒有烤鴨那麼貴 ?

Yú yǒu .méi.yǒu kǎoyā nà.me guì?
Is the fish as expensive as the roast duck?

魚有烤鴨那麼貴。

Yú yǒu kǎoyā nà.me guì.
The fish is as expensive as the roast duck.

2. 雞有海鮮這麼好吃嗎？

Jī yǒu hǎixiān zhè.me hǎochī .ma?
Is chicken as delicious as seafood?

雞沒有海鮮這麼好吃。

Jī méi.yǒu hǎixiān zhè.me hǎochī.
Chicken is not as delicious as seafood.

In the equaling-degree construction A 有沒有 B (這麼/那麼) Adj?, A compares with B from below and equals it on the scale of Adj.

2.4 Equal-degree comparison

	Structure	Gloss
Question	A　跟 B　一樣 Adj 嗎？	Are A and B equally Adj ?
Answer	A　跟 B　一樣 Adj	A and B are equally Adj
	A　跟 B 不一樣 Adj	A and B are not equally Adj
	A不跟 B　一樣 Adj	A is not equally Adj with B

1. 湖南的菜跟長城的菜一樣貴嗎？

Húnán .de cài gēn Chángchéng .de cài yíyàng guì .ma?
Are Hunan's food and Changcheng's food equally expensive?

湖南的菜(不)跟長城的菜一樣貴。

Húnán .de cài (bù) gēn Chángchéng .de cài yíyàng guì.
Hunan's food and Changcheng's food are (not) equally expensive.

2. 烤雞跟烤鴨一樣好吃嗎？

Kǎojī gēn kǎoyā yīyàng hǎochī .ma?
Is the roast chicken as delicious as the roast duck?

烤雞跟烤鴨(不)一樣好吃。

Kǎojī gēn kǎoyā (bù) yíyàng hǎochī.
The roast chicken and the roast duck are (not) equally delicious.

In the equal-degree construction A 跟 B 一樣 Adj, the negative adverb 不 may precede 跟 as in example 1, or it may precede the adverb 一樣 yíyàng 'the same,' as in example 2.

See L12–C1, L19–A2, A3, L21–A5 for more on comparisons.

3. ... 的 N construction

Structure	Gloss
S V 的 O	The O that S V

1. 這家飯館兒做的魚怎麼樣？

    Zhè jiā fànguǎr zuò .de yú zěn.meyàng?
    How is the fish that this restaurant made?

    這家飯館兒做的魚味道好極了。

    Zhè jiā fànguǎr zuò .de yú wèidào hǎojí.le.
    The fish that this restaurant made is extremely delicious.

2. 他寫的中國字怎麼樣？

    Tā xiě .de Zhōng.guózì zěn.meyàng?
    How are the Chinese characters that he wrote?

    他寫的中國字真好看。

    Tā xiě .de Zhōng.guózì zhēn hǎokàn.
    The Chinese characters that he wrote are really good-looking.

3. 你喜歡吃誰做的菜？

    Nǐ xǐ.huān chī shéi zuò .de cài?
    Whose dishes do you like to eat?

    我喜歡吃我媽媽做的菜。

    Wǒ xǐ.huān chī wǒ mā.mā zuò .de cài.
    I like to eat the dishes that my mother made.

 Chinese *does not* have relative pronouns, such as *that* and *which* in English. Thus there are no relative clauses in Chinese. Instead, English-type relative clauses are expressed in terms of modifying clauses, which are constructed in the form of [S V 的 O]. Modifying clauses in Chinese are prenominal; that is, the modifier clause precedes the noun that is being modified in accordance with this basic rule: the modifier precedes that which is modified. Between the modifier clause and the noun, a modifier marker 的 is inserted. A clause in the form of [S V 的 O] can serve as a subject (see examples 1 and 2) or as an object (see example 3) of a complex sentence.

See L11–C1 for more on ... 的 N construction.

4. The experiential aspect marker 過

Q.	S V 過 O 嗎 ?	Has S ever done ...(before)?
	S 没 V 過 O 嗎 ?	Hasn't S done... (before)?
A.	V 過 /S V 過 O	S has done ... (before)
	還 没 V 過 /S 還 没 V 過 O	S hasn't done... yet

1.	你吃過北京烤鴨嗎？	Nǐ chī.guò Běijīng kǎoyā .ma? Have you ever eaten Beijing roast duck (before)?
	吃過/我吃過北京烤鴨。	Chī.guò/wǒ chī.guò Běijīng kǎoyā. (Yes, I) have/I have eaten Beijing roast duck (before).
	還沒吃過/我還沒吃過北京烤鴨。	Hái méi chī.guò/wǒ hái méi chī.guò Běijīng kǎoyā. Not yet/I have not eaten Beijing roast duck yet.
2.	你看過那本書了嗎？	Nǐ kàn.guò nèi běn shū .le .ma? Have you ever read that book (before)?
	看過/我看過那本書了。	Kàn.guò/wǒ kàn.guò nèi běn shū .le. (Yes, I) have/I have read that book (before).
	還沒看過/我還沒看過那本書。	Hái méi kàn.guò/wǒ hái méi kàn.guò nèi běn shū. Not yet/ I haven't read that book yet.

 A verb with the experiential aspect marker 過 denotes that someone has experienced the event at an indefinite time in the past. The negative form for 過 is (還) 沒 '(still) not... yet.'

 See L11–A2.2, L14–A5 for more on 過.

5. The progressive aspect marker 著

Structure	Gloss
S (正)V著 O (呢)	S is (in the midst of) Ving O
S V著(O) V (O)	S V (O) while Ving (O)

1.	他在做什麼？	Tā zài zuò shén.me? What is he doing?
	他正打著電話呢。	Tā zhèng dǎ.zhe diànhuà .ne. He is making a phone call.
2.	小林喜歡吃著飯做什麼？	Xiǎo Lín xǐ.huān chī.zhe fàn zuò shén.me? What does Xiao Lin like to do while eating?
	小林喜歡吃著飯看書。	Xiǎo Lín xǐ.huān chī.zhe fàn kànshū. Xiao Lin likes to read while eating.

3.   他們叫了一隻烤鴨，大家分著   Tā.men jiào .le yì zhī kǎoyā, dàjiā fēn.zhe
     吃。   chī.
                                                They ordered roast duck, and everyone
                                                shared it.

著 is the verb suffix for the progressive/durative aspect. When it is joined to an
action/activity verb, it may denote an action/activity or a state that is going on at the
moment of speech. It also may be used as an adverb to describe the manner of the action.

著 can also be used in commands with action verbs, e.g., 坐著! zuò.zhe 'Sit there!' 記著
! jì.zhe! 'Remember!'

See L4–A1, L6–A1.4, A5, L8–A4 for more on 呢.

B Usage of Common Phrases 詞組用法 cízǔ yòngfǎ

1. The suggestion particle 吧

Structure	Gloss
(S) 來 (一) M N (吧)	Let (S) have N!
(S) 來 (一)點 兒 N (吧)	How about having/ordering N?

1.   我們吃什麼好呢？   Wǒ.men chī shén.me hǎo .ne?
                                         What should we order?

     我們來一個糖醋魚吧！   Wǒ.men lái yí .ge tángcùyú .ba!
                                         How about sweet and sour fish?

2.   先生，你想吃點兒什麼？   Xiān.shēng, nǐ xiǎng chī .diǎr shén.me?
                                         Sir, what do you want to order?

     來三十個餃子吧！   Lái sānshí .ge jiǎo.zi .ba!
                                         Let me have thirty dumplings!

3.   你想喝點兒什麼？   Nǐ xiǎng hē .diǎr shén.me?
                                         What do you want to drink?

     來點兒烏龍茶吧！   Lái .diǎr Wūlóngchá .ba!
                                         Let me have some Oolong tea!

[來 (一) M N (吧)!] and [來 (一)點 兒 N (吧)!] are common expressions used by
customers or waiters/waitresses at restaurants when they are discussing or suggesting
what to order.

See L7–B5, L13–B2, L15–B2 for more on 吧.

2. A 對 B 好

Structure	Gloss
A　對 B　　(Adv) 好	A is (Adv) good/nice for/to B
VO 對 B　　(Adv) 好	Ving O is (Adv) good for/to B
A　對 B 不 (Adv) 好	A is not (Adv) good/nice for/to B
VO 對 B 不 (Adv) 好	Ving O is not (Adv) good for/to B

1.　小高對誰很好？

　　　　　　　　　　Xiǎo Gāo duì shéi hěn hǎo?
　　　　　　　　　　To whom is Xiao Gao very nice?

　　小高對小林很好。

　　　　　　　　　　Xiǎo Gāo duì Xiǎo Lín hěn hǎo.
　　　　　　　　　　Xiao Gao is very nice to Xiao Lin.

2.　什麼對身體很不好？

　　　　　　　　　　Shén.me duì shēntǐ hěn bù hǎo?
　　　　　　　　　　What is not very good for (one's) health?

　　抽煙對身體很不好。

　　　　　　　　　　Chōuyān duì shēntǐ hěn bù hǎo.
　　　　　　　　　　Smoking is not very good for (one's) health.

See L16–A1, L17–A4, L18–A2, L20–B4, L23–B4 for more on A 對 B...

Cultural Notes
文化點滴 wénhuà diǎndī

1. When Chinese people eat out together, they usually share the various dishes. But students who have limited allowances for their daily off-campus meals may order a single dish of food for themselves.

2. In China and Taiwan, at meals or banquets served in restaurants or at home, soup is served in the middle of the meal or as the last course. From the Chinese point of view, if guests have soup first, they won't have much room left for other good food. If the hostess served soup first, that would mean that she didn't want her guests to have more food. This hostess would be considered "not sincere in inviting guests."

3. At a Chinese banquet, fish is served as the last main course, followed by a sweet soup as dessert. Because Chinese feasts generally consist of ten to twelve courses, by the time the fish is served, the diners are usually full and find it hard to eat any more. Consequently, the fish is left over—which is considered a good omen because the phrase 吃剩有魚 chī shèng yǒu yú 'to have fish leftover after eating' is homophonic with 吃剩有餘 chī shèng yǒu yú 'to have surplus after eating—to have money saved.' The fish served at a banquet must be 全魚 quányú '[whole-fish] a fish with the head,' because 全 quán also means perfect, which is what Chinese want their lives to be.

年年有餘

第十一課　那部電影兒怎麼樣？

對話

〔吃飽了飯，小高、小李、小林三個人一起去看「喜福會」。〕

（在電影院裏）

小高：　小李，剛才你吃得真快，好像餓了一個禮拜似的。

小李：　可不是嗎？天天吃宿舍的飯，倒盡了胃口。不是生菜沙拉
　　　　就是牛油麵包。一星期（吃）一兩次還可以，（要是）吃
　　　　多了可就受不了。所以有人說「中國胃」是最麻煩的。

小林：　別說了，電影快開始了。

（看完電影，小林臉色不太好看。）

小高：　小林，你怎麼了？哭了嗎？別難過了。

小李：　我也挺難過的。中國電影多半兒都是悲劇。好（倒）是好
　　　　，可是看完了讓人心裏不舒服。下次咱們看個喜劇吧！

小林：　這個片子談到母親和女兒的關係，你們是不明白的。

小高：　我雖然自己沒有經驗，可是從這部片子，我也可以看得出來女人在中國社會上的地位。最近幾十年，婦女研究相當流行，我也看了一些這方面的書。

小李：　這些研究我一點兒也不懂。「喜福會」那本小說我也沒看過。可是我想這部電影誰看了都會感動的。那幾個演員都演得很好，很自然。我特別喜歡那個女主角。她長得真漂亮。

小林：　好了，好了！時間不早了。我們也該走了。下次再聽你的高見吧！

My questions:

对话

〔吃饱了饭，小高、小李、小林三个人一起去看「喜福会」。〕

（在电影院裏）

小高： 小李，刚才你吃得真快，好像饿了一个礼拜似的。

小李： 可不是吗？天天吃宿舍的饭，倒尽了胃口。不是生菜沙拉就是牛油面包。一星期（吃）一两次还可以，（要是）吃多了可就受不了。所以有人说「中国胃」是最麻烦的。

小林： 别说了，电影快开始了。

（看完电影，小林脸色不太好看。）

小高： 小林，你怎么了？哭了吗？别难过了。

小李： 我也挺难过的。中国电影多半儿都是悲剧。好（倒）是好，可是看完了让人心里不舒服。下次咱们看个喜剧吧！

小林： 这个片子谈到母亲和女儿的关系，你们是不明白的。

小高： 我虽然自己没有经验，可是从这部片子，我也可以看得出来女人在中国社会上的地位。最近几十年，妇女研究相当流行，我也看了　些这方面的书。

小李： 这些研究我一点儿也不懂。「喜福会」那本小说我也没看过。可是我想这部电影谁看了都会感动的。那几个演员都演得很好，很自然。我特别喜欢那个女主角。她长得真漂亮。

小林： 好了，好了！时间不早了。我们也该走了。下次再听你的高见吧！

Duìhuà

(Chībǎo .le fàn, Xiǎo Gāo, Xiǎo Lǐ, Xiǎo Lín sān .ge rén yìqǐ qù kàn *Xīfúhuì*.)

(Zài diànyǐng yuàn .lǐ)

Xiǎo Gāo: Xiǎo Lǐ, gāngcái nǐ chī.de zhēn kuài, hǎo.xiàng è .le yī .ge lǐbài .shì.de.

Xiǎo Lǐ: Kě bú.shì .ma? Tiāntiān chī sùshè .de fàn, dǎojìn .le wèikǒu. Bú.shì shēngcài shālā, jiù.shì niúyóu miànbāo. Yī xīngqī (chī) yī-liǎng cì hái kě.yǐ, (yào.shì) chī duō .le kě jiù shòu.buliǎo. Suǒ.yǐ yǒu rén shuō "Zhōng.guó wèi" shì zuì má.fán .de.

Xiǎo Lín: Bié shuō .le. Diànyǐng kuài kāishǐ .le!

(Kànwán diànyǐng, Xiǎo Lín liǎnsè bútài hǎokàn.)

Xiǎo Gāo: Xiǎo Lín, nǐ zěn.me .le? Kū .le .ma? Bié nánguò .le.

Xiǎo Lǐ: Wǒ yě tǐng nánguò .de. Zhōng.guó diànyǐng duōbànr dōu shì bēijù. Hǎo .shì hǎo, kě.shì kànwán .le ràng rén xīn.lǐ bù shū.fú. Xià.cì zán.men kàn .ge xǐjù .ba!

Xiǎo Lín: Zhè .ge piàn.zi tándào mǔ.qīn hé nǚr .de guān.xi. Nǐ.men shì bù míng.bái .de.

Xiǎo Gāo: Wǒ suīrán zìjǐ méi.yǒu jīngyàn, kě.shì cóng zhè bù piàn.zi, wǒ yě kě.yǐ kàn.dechū.lái nǚrén zài Zhōng.guó shèhuì .shàng .de dìwèi. Zuìjìn jǐ shí nián, fùnǚ yánjiū xiāngdāng liúxíng. Wǒ yě kàn .le yìxiē zhè fāngmiàn .de shū.

Xiǎo Lǐ: Zhè xiē yānjiū wǒ yì.diǎnr yě bù dǒng. *Xīfúhuì* nà běn xiǎoshuō wǒ yě méi kàn.guò. Kě.shì wǒ xiǎng zhè bù diànyǐng shéi kàn .le dōu huì gǎndòng .de. Nà jǐ .ge yǎnyuán dōu yǎn .de hěn hǎo, hěn zìrán. Wǒ tèbié xǐ.huān nà .ge nǚzhǔjiǎo. Tā zhǎng .de zhēn piào.liàng.

Xiǎo Lín: Hǎo.le, hǎo.le! Shíjiān bù zǎo .le. Wǒ.men yě gāi zǒu .le. Xià.cì zài tīng nǐ .de gāojiàn .ba!

Dialogue

(After dinner, Xiǎo Gāo, Xiǎo Lǐ, and Xiǎo Lín go together to see the movie *Joy Luck Club*.)

(In the movie theater)

Xiǎo Gāo: Xiǎo Lǐ, you ate so fast, it looked like you had been starving for a week.

Xiǎo Lǐ: Isn't it true? My appetite was all gone after eating dorm food every single day. If we are not eating lettuce salad, we are having bread and butter. Having that kind of food once or twice a week is O.K., but I can't stand it every day. So (that's why) some people say (having a) "Chinese stomach" is a pain.

Xiǎo Lín: Stop talking. The movie is about to start.

(After watching the film, Xiǎo Lín looks upset.)

Xiǎo Gāo: Xiǎo Lín, are you O.K.? Did you cry? Don't be sad.

Xiǎo Lǐ: I was quite sad, too. Most of the Chinese movies are tragedies. They are good, but they make people upset when they watch them. Next time we should watch a comedy.

Xiǎo Lín: This film talks about the relationship between mothers and daughters. You guys don't understand.

Xiǎo Gāo: Even though I don't have any experience myself, this movie shows the status of women in Chinese society. In recent years, Women's Studies is quite popular. I've read some books in this area, too.

Xiǎo Lǐ: I don't understand these studies at all and I have not read the novel *Joy Luck Club*. But I think no matter who watches this movie, they will be touched. These actresses performed really well. Their acting was natural. I especially liked the lead actress. She looked really beautiful.

Xiǎo Lín: All right, all right. It's getting late. We have to go. I'll listen to your view next time.

Mini-Dialogue
小對話 Xiǎoduìhuà

Asking for and giving an opinion

1.　A:　你喜歡這部電影兒嗎？

Nǐ xǐ.huān zhè bù diànyǐngr .ma?
Do you like this movie?

　　B:　還可以，可是讓人太難過了。

Hái kě.yǐ, kě.shì ràng rén tài nánguò .le.
Yes, but it makes people too sad.

2.　A:　那個節目怎麼樣？

Nà .ge jiémù zěn.meyàng?
How is that program?

　　B:　不錯，可是時間太晚了。

Búcuò, kě.shì shíjiān tài wǎn .le.
Not bad, but it's on too late.

Talking about experience and preferences

1.　A:　你看過中國電影兒嗎？

Nǐ kàn.guò Zhōng.guó diànyǐngr .ma?
Have you ever seen a Chinese movie?

　　B:　我看過一次。中國電影兒很有意思。

Wǒ kàn.guò yí cì. Zhōng.guó diànyǐngr hěn yǒuyì.si.

I have seen (a Chinese movie) once. Chinese movies are very interesting.

2.　A:　你喜歡看喜劇還是悲劇？

Nǐ xǐ.huān kàn xǐjù hái.shì bēijù?
Do you like to watch comedy or tragedy?

　　B:　我喜歡看喜劇。

Wǒ xǐ.huān kàn xǐjù.
I like to watch comedy.

Vocabulary
生詞 Shēngcí

◎ By Order of Appearance

部		bù	M	measure word for films, cars, etc.
喜福會	喜福会	Xǐfúhuì	N	[happy-bless-meeting] *Joy Luck Club*—title of a movie
剛才	刚才	gāngcái	MTA	just now, a moment ago
好像...似的	好象...似的	hǎo.xiàng....shì.de/.sì.de	IE	[seems-as if] it seems as if...
餓	饿	è	SV	(to be) hungry
* 飽	饱	bǎo	SV	to eat to the full, (to be) satisfied (stomach)
可不是嗎	可不是吗	kě bú.shì .ma	IE	isn't it true?
倒盡	倒尽	dǎojìn	V	[pour out-exert the utmost] to lose completely (one's appetite)
胃口		wèikǒu	N	[stomach-mouth] appetite
* 胃		wèi	N	stomach
生菜		shēngcài	N	[raw-vegetable] raw vegetables, lettuce
沙拉		shālā	N	[sand-pull] salad
牛油		niúyóu	N	[cow-oil] butter
麵包	面包	miànbāo	N	[flour-wrap] bread (M: 個/ 片 piàn 'slice')
次		cì	M	measure word for frequency
要是		yào.shì	Conj	if, suppose, in case
可		kě	Adv	emphatic marker
受不了		shòu.buliǎo	RV	[received-not-finish] cannot stand it
所以		suǒ.yǐ	Conj	[that-which-by means of] therefore
別		bié	Adv	don't
開始	开始	kāishǐ	V	[open-start] to begin, to start
怎麼	怎么	zěn.me	QW	how come?
哭		kū	V	to cry
* 笑		xiào	V	to laugh
難過	难过	nánguò	SV	[hard-to pass through] (to be) sad
* 高興	高兴	gāoxìng	SV	[high-happy] (to be) happy
多半兒	多半儿	duōbànr	Adv	[many-half-Suf] most of
悲劇	悲剧	bēijù	N	[sad-play] tragedy
讓	让	ràng	V	to make, let (causative)
心裏	心里	xīn.lǐ	N	in the heart, in mind
舒服		shū.fú	SV	(to be) comfortable

下次		xià.cì	N	next time
喜劇	喜剧	xǐjù	N	[happy-play] comedy
片子		piàn.zi	N	[piece-suffix] film (M: 部 bù)
談到	谈到	tándào	V	to talk about
女兒	女儿	nǚ'ér	N	[female-child] daughter (M: 個)
* 兒子	儿子	ér.zi	N	[child-child] son (M: 個)
關係	关系	guān.xì	N	[close-relationship] relationship
明白		míng.bái	SV	to understand
經驗	经验	jīngyàn	N	[pass through-experiment] experience
從	从	cóng	Prep	from
看出來	看出来	kàn.chū.lái	RV	[see-come out] to figure out
女		nǚ	N/Adj	female (for human beings)
* 男		nán	N/Adj	male (for human beings)
社會	社会	shèhuì	N	[society-meeting] society
地位		dìwèi	N	[earth-position] position (of a person), ranking, status
最近		zuìjìn	Adj/Adv	[the most-near] recently, lately
婦女	妇女	fùnǚ	N	[woman-female] woman, women (M: 個)
研究	研究	yánjiū/jiù	N/V	[investigate-investigate] research, to research
相當	相当	xiāngdāng	Adv	[mutual-ought] quite, rather (=挺)
流行		liúxíng	SV	(to be) in fashion, (to be) in vogue
方面		fāngmiàn	N	[direction-face] an aspect, (in this or that) respect
懂		dǒng	SV	to understand (=明白)
感動	感动	gǎndòng	SV	[feel-move] (to be) moved, (to be) touched
演員	演员	yǎnyuán	N	[act-personnel] actor (M: 個)
演		yǎn	V	to act
自然		zìrán	SV	[self-nature] (to be) natural
特別		tèbié	Adv	[special-other] especially, particularly
主角	主角	zhǔjué/jiǎo	N	[host-character] leading actor
長	长	zhǎng	V	to grow
眞	真	zhēn	Adv/Adj	really, real
漂亮		piào.liàng	SV	[to bleach-bright] (to be) pretty, (to be) beautiful
高見	高见	gāojiàn	N	[high-opinion] high opinion

◎ **By Grammatical Categories**

Nouns/Pronouns

喜福會	喜福会	Xǐfúhuì	N	[happy-bless-meeting] *Joy Luck Club* — title of a movie
* 胃		wèi	N	stomach
胃口		wèikǒu	N	[stomach-mouth] appetite
生菜		shēngcài	N	[raw-vegetable] raw vegetables, lettuce
沙拉		shālā	N	[sand-pull] salad
牛油		niúyóu	N	[cow-oil] butter
麵包	面包	miànbāo	N	[flour-wrap] bread (M: 個/片 piàn 'slice')
悲劇	悲剧	bēijù	N	[sad-play] tragedy
喜劇	喜剧	xǐjù	N	[happy-play] comedy
片子		piàn.zi	N	[piece-suffix] film (M: 部 bù)
女兒	女儿	nǚ'ér	N	[female-child] daughter (M: 個)
* 兒子	儿子	ér.zi	N	[child-child] son (M: 個)
關係	关系	guān.xì	N	[close-relationship] relationship
經驗	经验	jīngyàn	N	[pass through-experiment] experience
社會	社会	shèhuì	N	[society-meeting] society
地位		dìwèi	N	[earth-position] position (of a person), ranking, status
* 男		nán	N/Adj	male (for human beings)
女		nǚ	N/Adj	female (for human beings)
婦女	妇女	fùnǚ	N	[woman-female] woman, women (M: 個)
研究	研究	yánjiū/jiù	N/V	[investigate-investigate] research, to research
方面		fāngmiàn	N	[direction-face] an aspect, (in this or that) respect
演員	演员	yǎnyuán	N	[act-personnel] actor (M: 個)
主角	主角	zhǔjué/jiǎo	N	[host-character] leading actor
高見	高见	gāojiàn	N	[high-opinion] high opinion
心裏	心里	xīn.lǐ	N	in the heart, in mind
下次		xià.cì	N	next time

Measure Words

次		cì	M	measure word for frequency
部		bù	M	measure word for films, cars, etc.

Verbs/Stative Verbs/Adjectives

開始	开始	kāishǐ	V	[open-start] to begin, to start

倒盡	倒尽	dǎojìn	V	[pour out-exert the utmost] to lose completely (one's appetite)
哭		kū	V	to cry
* 笑		xiào	V	to laugh
談到	谈到	tándào	V	to talk about
演		yǎn	V	to act
長	长	zhǎng	V	to grow
讓	让	ràng	V	to make, let (causative)
受不了		shòu.buliǎo	RV	[received-not-finish] cannot stand it
看出來	看出来	kàn.chū.lái	RV	[see-come out] to figure out
明白		míng.bái	SV	to understand
懂		dǒng	SV	to understand (=明白)
感動	感动	gǎndòng	SV	[feel-move] (to be) moved, (to be) touched
餓	饿	è	SV	(to be) hungry
* 飽	饱	bǎo	SV	to eat to the full, (to be) satisfied (stomach)
難過	难过	nánguò	SV	[hard-to pass through] (to be) sad
* 高興	高兴	gāoxìng	SV	[high-happy] (to be) happy
舒服		shū.fú	SV	(to be) comfortable
流行		liúxíng	SV	(to be) in fashion, (to be) in vogue
自然		zìrán	SV	[self-nature] (to be) natural
漂亮		piào.liàng	SV	[to bleach-bright] (to be) pretty/beautiful
最近		zuìjìn	Adj/Adv	[the most-near] recently, lately
從	从	cóng	Prep	from

Adverbs

別		bié	Adv	don't
多半兒	多半儿	duōbànr	Adv	[many-half-Suf] most of
相當	相当	xiāngdāng	Adv	[mutual-ought] quite, rather (=挺)
特別		tèbié	Adv	[special-other] especially, particularly
剛才	刚才	gāngcái	MTA	just now, a moment ago
眞	真	zhēn	Adv/Adj	really
可		kě	Adv	emphatic marker

Conjunctions

要是		yào.shì	Conj	if, suppose, in case
所以		suǒ.yǐ	Conj	[that-which-by means of] therefore

Question Words

怎麼	怎么	zěn.me	QW	how come?

Idiomatic Expressions

好像...	好象...	hǎo.xiàng...	IE	[seems-as if] it seems as if...
似的	似的	.shì.de/.sì.de		
可不是	可不是	kě bú.shì .ma	IE	isn't it true?
嗎	吗			

✚ Supplementary Vocabulary

1. Films and Plays

電影院	电影院	diànyǐngyuàn	N	[electric-shadow-yard] cinema, movie theater
劇院	剧院	jùyuàn	N	[play-yard] theater
劇場	剧场	jùchǎng	N	[play-field] theater
歌劇	歌剧	gējù	N	[song-play] opera
導演	导演	dǎoyǎn	N	[guide-act] director
配角		pèijiǎo	N	[match-character] supporting actor/actress
明星		míngxīng	N	[bright-star] movie star
歌星		gēxīng	N	[song-star] singing star
臉色	脸色	liǎnsè	N	[face-color] facial expression

2. Chinese Kinship Terms

祖父		zǔfù	N	[ancestor-father] grandfather (paternal)
爺爺	爷爷	yé.ye	N	[father-father] grandfather (paternal)
祖母		zǔmǔ	N	[ancestor-mother] grandmother (paternal)
奶奶		nǎi.nai	N	[milk-milk] grandmother (paternal)
外祖父		wàizǔfù	N	[outside-ancestor-father] grandfather (maternal)
外公		wàigōng	N	[outside-grandfather] grandfather (maternal)
外祖母		wàizǔmǔ	N	[outside-ancestor-mother] grandmother (maternal)
外婆		wàipó	N	[outside-grandmother] grandmother (maternal)
伯父		pófù	N	[uncle-father] father's older brother, uncle
伯母		pómǔ	N	[uncle-mother] father's older brother's wife, aunt
叔叔		shū.shū	N	[uncle-uncle] father's younger brother, uncle
嬸嬸		shěn.shěn	N	[aunt-aunt] father's younger brother's wife, aunt
舅舅/舅父		jiù.jiù/jiùfù	N	[uncle-uncle/father] mother's brother, uncle
舅母		jiùmǔ	N	[aunt-mother] mother's brother's wife, aunt
姨父		yífù	N	[aunt-father] mother's sister's husband, uncle
姨母		yímǔ	N	[aunt-mother] mother's sister, aunt
哥哥		gē.gē	N	[brother-brother] older brother
弟弟		dì.dì	N	[brother-brother] younger brother
姐姐		jiě.jiě	N	[sister-sister] older sister
妹妹		mèi.mèi	N	[sister-sister] younger sister

Characters
漢字 Hànzì

牛	油	包	子
別	餓	男	女
自	己	會	懂
所	談	真	像
每	次	最	近

牛

niú
ox, cow   牛
4   (cow)

| 牛肉 | niúròu | beef |
| 牛油 | niúyóu | butter |

A: 宿舍的飯怎麼樣？
B: 難吃極了，不是**牛油**麵包就是生菜沙拉。

油

yóu
oil   氵
8   (water)

| *汽油 | qìyóu | gas |
| *石油 | shíyóu | petroleum |

A: 汽車的**油**快沒了。
B: 我等會兒就去加。

包

bāo
wrap, a bundle
            勹
5

| *皮包 | píbāo | wallet |
| *書包 | shūbāo | schoolbag |

A: 你每天都背個大**書包**來學校，重不重？
B: 重啊！沒辦法，誰叫我這學期選了五門課。

子

zǐ
son, child,
suffix   子
3   (child)

*兒子	ér.zi	son
*孩子	hái.zi	child, children
*桌子	zhuō.zi	desk

A: 他有**孩子**嗎？
B: 有，三個女的一個男的。

繁簡對照：	其他漢字：	✎ **My notes:**
	*汽 SC26 麵 L12	

別
bié
part, other,
don't
7　　(knife)

*別的　　　bié.de　　　other
*別人　　　biérén　　　other people

A: 明天我有四個考試。
B: **別叫了**，吃完飯快開始學習吧。

餓
è
to be hungry 食
15　　(to eat)

*餓死　　　èsǐ　　　starving

A: 我**餓死了**，可以吃下四十個水餃。
B: 你幾天沒吃飯了？

男
nán
male
7　　田 (field)

*男人　　　nánrén　　　man
*男朋友　　nánpéng.yǒu　boyfriend

A: 聽說她的**男朋友**是個演員。
B: 他都演些什麼？演得怎麼樣？

女
nǚ
female　女
3　　(female)

女兒　　　nǚ'ér　　　daughter
婦女　　　fùnǚ　　　woman
*女生　　　nǚshēng　　girl/woman student
*女士　　　nǚshì　　　lady, madam

A: 他做什麼研究？
B: 他研究的是現代**婦女**文學。

繁簡對照：	其他漢字：	✎ **My notes:**
餓饿	*飽 SC27	

自

zì
self, personal,
private 自
6 (self)

自己   zìjǐ   self

A: 要是你不懂，你爲什麼不問老師？
B: 老師要**我們自己**先想想再問他。

己

jǐ
self, oneself 己
3 (self)

A: 你跟我一塊兒去看電影兒，怎麼樣？
B: **你自己**去吧！我不喜歡看悲劇。

會

huì
to know how to;
to meet 人
13 (person)

A: 你**會說**中國話嗎？
B: **會說**一點兒，可是我說得不好。

懂

dǒng
to understand 忄
16 (heart)

*看不懂   kàn.budǒng   can't understand (by reading)
*懂事   dǒngshì   sensible, thoughtful

A: 那本小說好看嗎？
B: 我不知道，我一點兒都**看不懂**。

繁簡對照：	其他漢字：	✎ **My notes:**
會 会	能 L9	

所
suǒ
M for houses
戶
8　(a door)

所以　　suǒ.yǐ　　therefore

A: 我要是吃多了牛油麵包，肚子就不舒服。

B: **所以**我說你這個人太麻煩了。

談
tán
to talk, to chat
言
15　(speech)

談到　　tándào　　to talk about
*談話　　tánhuà　　conversation, talk
*談天　　tántiān　　to chat, make conversation

A: 他的中國話是怎麼學的？說得那麼好？
B: 他每天都用中文跟中國同學**談話**。

真
zhēn
true, genuine,
really
目
10　(eyes)

真好　　zhēn hǎo　　really nice

A: 他這個人**真好**，你有事兒找他，他一定會來。
B: 所以我說他是個「大好人」。

像
xiàng
image, resemble
亻
14　(person)

像…一樣　xiàng…yíyàng　(it) seems the same as…
*好像　　　hǎo.xiàng　　it seems

A: 中文**像**日文**一樣**難嗎？
B: 不，日文難多了。

繁簡對照：	其他漢字：	✎ **My notes:**
談 谈 真 =真 像 象	說 L7	

měi
each, every 母
7   (don't)

每天	měitiān	every day
*每次	měi.cì	each time
*每個人	měi .ge rén	everyone

A: 我們的功課很多。**每天**不是寫漢字就
是學生字。
B: 所以你們學得這麼好。

cì
a time, M for
verbs   欠
6   (to owe)

| 下次 | xià.cì | next time |
| *上次 | shàng.cì | last time |

A: 那家飯館的菜做得好吃不好吃？
B: 我不知道，我們**下次**去試試。

zuì
the most,
marker of
superlative 曰
12   (to say)

| 最近 | zuìjìn | recently |
| *最好 | zuìhǎo | the best |

A: 你**最近**看了電影沒有？
B: 沒有。我就上個月看了一次 。

jìn
close to, near

             辶
8

| *附近 | fùjìn | vicinity, nearby |

A: 他**最近**好像很忙似的？
B: 沒錯，我聽說他每個星期打三次工，
一次五個小時。

繁簡對照：	其他漢字： 遠 L21	✎ **My notes:**

Grammar
語法 yǔfǎ

A Major Sentence Patterns 主要句型 zhǔyào jùxíng

1. 不是..., 就是 ... construction

Structure	Gloss
不是 A, 就是 B	If it is not A, then it is B (It must be either A or B)

1. 宿舍的飯怎麼樣？

   Sùshè .de fàn zěn.meyàng?
   How is the food (served) in the dormitory?

   宿舍的飯不太好，不是沙拉，就是漢堡。

   Sùshè .de fàn bútài hǎo, bú.shì shālā, jiù.shì hànbǎo.
   The food (served) in the dormitory is not very good. It's either salad or hamburger.

2. 小高打電話給誰？

   Xiǎo Gāo dǎ diànhuà gěi shéi?
   To whom does Xiao Gao make phone calls?

   小高不是打電話給我，就是打電話給小李。

   Xiǎo Gāo bú.shì dǎ diànhuà gěi wǒ, jiù.shì dǎ diànhuà gěi Xiǎo Lǐ.
   Xiao Gao makes phone calls either to Xiao Li or to me.

3. 週末他做什麼？

   Zhōumò tā zuò shen.me?
   What does he do on weekends?

   週末他不是看電視，就是看電影兒。

   Tā zhōumò bú.shì kàn diànshì, jiù.shì kàn diànyǐngr.
   On weekends, he either watches TV or goes to the movies.

 A sentence with the conjunctions 不是..., 就是... denotes "it must be either A or B." The conjuctions connect two grammatical units, which can be noun phrases, verb phrases, or clauses. They signify an alternative relation between the two units. The order of these two conjunctions is fixed: the unit with conjunction 不是 always comes before the unit with conjuction 就是.

2. Frequency expressions

2.1 Do something no. of times per day/week/month/year

Structure	Gloss
S 一/每 + 天/年 VO 幾次？ S 一/每 + 天/年 V 幾次 O？ S 每 + No. + 天/年 VO 幾次？ S 每 + No. + 天/年 V 幾次 O？	How many times does SVO a day/year? How many times does SVO per no. of days/years?
S 每 + (一)個 + 星期/月 VO 幾次？ S 每 + (一)個 + 星期/月 V 幾次 O？ S (每) + No. M N VO 幾次？ S (每) + No. M N V 幾次 O？	How many times does SVO a week/month? How many times does SVO per no. of weeks/months/years?

1. 小李一天上圖書館幾次？/ 幾次
圖書館？

   Xiǎo Lǐ yì tiān shàng túshūguǎn jǐ .cì?/ jǐ .cì túshūguǎn?
How many times a day does Xiao Li go to the library?

   小李一天上圖書館兩次 / 兩次圖
書館。

   Xiǎo Lǐ yì tiān shàng túshūguǎn liǎng .cì/ liǎng .cì túshūguǎn.
Xiao Li goes to the library twice a day.

2. 你們一個星期去看電影兒幾次？
/ 幾次電影兒？

   Nǐ.men yí .ge xīngqī qù kàn diànyǐngr jǐ .cì?/ jǐ .cì diànyǐngr?
How many times a week do you go to see movies?

   我們一個星期去看電影兒一次 /
一次電影兒。

   Wǒ.men yí .ge xīngqī qù kàn diànyǐngr yí .cì./ yí .cì diànyǐngr.
We go to see a movie once a week.

3. 他每三年回中國幾次？/ 幾次中
國？

   Tā měi sān nián huí Zhōng.guó jǐ .cì?/ jǐ .cì Zhōng.guó?
Over a three year period, how often does he go back to China?

   他每三年回中國兩次。/ 兩次中
國。

   Tā měi sān nián huí Zhōng.guó liǎng .cì./ liǎng .cì Zhōng.guó.
He goes back to China twice every three years.

The frequency expression in Chinese is a post-verbal adverb, which counts the times of the actual action that the subject has completed. Thus the word order of a sentence with frequency expression follows the Temporal Sequence Principle. In this pattern, the object may either precede or follow the frequency adverb.

2.2 Did/have done something no. of times in the past/up to now

Structure	Gloss
S V過　幾 次　O ? O , S V過　幾 次　?	How many times did S V O (in the past)? As for O, how many times did S V it (in the past)?
S V過　　幾次 O 了 ? S V過 O 幾次　　了 ? O , S V過幾次　　了 ?	How many times has S done V O (up to this moment)? As for O, how many times has S done V (up to this moment)?

1. 他上個月去過中國幾次？/ 幾
   次中國？

   他上個月去過中國兩次 / 兩次中
   國。

   Tā shàng .ge yuè qù.guò Zhōng.guó jǐ
   .cì?/ jǐ .cì Zhōng.guó?
   How many times did he go to China last
   month (sometime in last month)?

   Tā shàng .ge yuè qù.guò Zhōng.guó liǎng
   .cì./ liǎng .cì Zhōng.guó.
   He went to China twice last month
   (sometime in last month).

2. 中國飯，小高吃過幾次？

   中國飯，小高吃過很多次。

   Zhōng.guófàn, Xiǎo Gāo chī.guò jǐ .cì?
   How many times has Xiao Gao eaten
   Chinese food (sometime in the past)?

   Zhōng.guófàn, Xiǎo Gāo chī.guò hěn duō cì.
   Xiao Gao has eaten Chinese food many
   times (sometime in the past).

3. 你媽媽來過美國幾次了？

   我媽媽來過美國五次了。

   Nǐ mā.mā lái.guò Měi.guó jǐ .cì .le?
   How many times has your mother been to
   America (up to now)?

   Wǒ mā.mā lái.guò Měi.guó wǔ cì .le.
   My mother has been to America five
   times (up to now).

4. 日本飯，他吃過幾次了？

   日本飯，他吃過很多次了。

   Rìběnfàn, tā chī.guò jǐ .cì .le?
   As for Japanese food, how many times
   has he eaten it (up to now)?

   Rìběnfàn, tā chī.guò hěn duō cì .le.
   As for Japanese food, he has eaten it
   many times (up to now).

In this pattern, 過 is a verb suffix that serves as an indefinite past aspect marker. When a
sentence doesn't end with 了, it denotes how many times the actions *had been*

compeleted in the indefinite past, whereas when a sentence does end with 了, it denotes how many times the actions *have been completed* up to now.

 In this pattern, the object of the sentence may either precede or follow the frequency adverb. If one would like to stress the object, then the object may be placed at the beginning of the sentence to serve as the topic.

 See L10–A4 for more on 過.

2.3 Have never done X before

Structure	Gloss
S O 一次 也/都 沒V過	S has never done V O even once
O, S 一次 也/都 沒V過	As for O, S has never done V O even once

1. 他法國去過幾次？

    Tā Fà.guó qù.guò jǐ cì?
    How many times has he been to France?

    他法國一次都沒去過。

    Tā Fà.guó yí cì dōu méi qù.guò.
    He hasn't been to France even once.

2. 中國電影，小高看過幾次？

    Zhōng.guó diànyǐng, Xiǎo Gāo kàn.guò jǐ cì?
    How many times has Xiao Gao seen Chinese movies?

    中國電影，小高一次也沒看過。

    Zhōng.guó diànyǐng, Xiǎo Gāo yí cì yě méi kàn.guò.
    As for Chinese movies, Xiao Gao has never seen (them) once.

 To express that someone hasn't done something even once before the speech time, the word order follows the Temporal Sequence Principle. Since the action has never been done, the frequency adverb 一次" *must precede* the negative verb.

3. Manner or degree complements

	Structure	Gloss
Question	S (O) V 得 SV 不 SV ?	Does S V (O) Adv or not?
	S (O) V 得 怎麼樣 ?	How does S V O?
Affir. Ans.	S (VO) V 得 Adv SV	S V (O) Adv Adj
Neg. Ans.	S (VO) V 得 不 SV	S V (O) not (Adv) Adj

1. 那個男主角(演戲)演得好不好？　　　Nèi .ge nánzhǔjiǎo (yǎnxì) yǎn.de hǎo
   那個男主角(演戲)演得怎麼樣？　　　.bùhǎo?/ Nèi .ge nánzhǔjiǎo(yǎnxì) yǎn
   　　　　　　　　　　　　　　　　　.de zěn.meyàng?
   　　　　　　　　　　　　　　　　　Does the actor act well (or not well)?/
   　　　　　　　　　　　　　　　　　How does he act?

   那個男主角(演戲)演得很好。　　　　Nèi .ge nánzhǔjiǎo (yǎnxì) yǎn.de hěn hǎo.
   　　　　　　　　　　　　　　　　　The actor acts very well.

   那個男主角(演戲)演得很不好。　　　Nèi .ge nánzhǔjiǎo (yǎnxì) yǎn.de hěn bù
   　　　　　　　　　　　　　　　　　hǎo.
   　　　　　　　　　　　　　　　　　The actor acts very poorly.

2. 他的女朋友長得漂亮不漂亮？/　　　Tā .de nǚpéng.yǒu zhǎng.de piào.liàng
   他的女朋友長得怎麼樣？　　　　　　.bupiaò.liàng? / Tā .de nǚpéng.yǒu
   　　　　　　　　　　　　　　　　　zhǎng.de zěn.meyàng?
   　　　　　　　　　　　　　　　　　Is his girlfriend pretty (or not pretty)? /
   　　　　　　　　　　　　　　　　　How does his girlfriend look?

   他的女朋友長得非常漂亮。　　　　　Tā .de nǚpéng.yǒu zhǎng.de fēicháng
   　　　　　　　　　　　　　　　　　piào.liàng.
   　　　　　　　　　　　　　　　　　His girlfriend is very (unusually) pretty.

   他的女朋友長得不太漂亮。　　　　　Tā .de nǚpéng.yǒu zhǎng.de bútài
   　　　　　　　　　　　　　　　　　piào.liàng.
   　　　　　　　　　　　　　　　　　His girlfriend is not very pretty.

 In the predicate of a sentence, the word (or words) that illustrates the manner or degree of an action/a verb is called a descriptive complement. A verb must combine with the particle 得 in order to be followed and modified by the complement. If a question seeks information about the manner or degree of an action or a verb, the information is the focus of the sentence. Thus such a question will have the choice type (A-not-A) structure.

See L9–A6, L10–A1, L14–A6, L15–A2, L18–A4, L23–C1.5 for more on complement marker 得.

4. 要是..., 就... construction

Structure	Gloss
S (要是)...,(S) 就... (MA)	If S..., (then) S...

1. 小李要是沙拉吃多了，就怎麼　　　　Xiǎo Lǐ yào.shì shālā chī duō .le, jiù
   了？　　　　　　　　　　　　　　　zěn.me .le?

	If Xiao Li ate too much salad, then what will happen to him?
小李要是沙拉吃多了，就受不了。	Xiǎo Lǐ yào.shì shālā chī duō .le, jiù shòu.buliǎo. If Xiao Li ate too much salad, then he can't stand (it).
2. 要是你有很多錢，你就要做什麼？	Yào.shì nǐ yǒu hěn duō qián, nǐ jiù yào zuò shén.me? If you have a lot of money, what are you going to do?
要是我有很多錢，我就要到中國去念書。	Yào.shì wǒ yǒu hěn duō qián, wǒ jiù yào dào Zhōng.guó qù niànshū. If I have a lot of money, (then) I will go to China to study.

   In Chinese, if the subject has appeared once in a conversational context or within a paragraph, it is common practice not to repeat it in the next clause (if the subject is the same person). This is very different from English, where the subject is obligatory in every clause. When you are studying Chinese, build up the habit of referring to the previous context to understand the meaning of the deleted element.

In Chinese, when a complex sentence consists of 要是 ..., (S) 就... 'If..., then...' which denotes supposition, the conjunction 要是 'if' is optional, while 就 'then' is obligatory. This is contrary to English, where "if" is obligatory and "then" is optional.

5. 一點兒也/都 不 **construction**

Structure	Gloss
S 一點兒也/都 不 AuxV (VO)	S doesn't AuxV (VO) at all
O, S 一點兒也/都 不 AuxV	As for O, S doesn't AuxV at all

1. 你喜歡看悲劇嗎？	Nǐ xǐ.huān kàn bēijù .ma? Do you like to see tragedies?
我一點兒也不喜歡看悲劇。	Wǒ yì.diǎnr yě bù xǐ.huān kàn bēijù. I don't like to see tragedies at all.
2. 那些研究他都懂嗎？	Nèixiē yánjiù tā dōu dǒng .ma? Can he understand all of those studies?
那些研究他一點兒都不懂。	Nèixiē yánjiù tā yì.diǎnr dōu bù dǒng. As for those studies, he can't understand (them) at all.

一點兒也/都不 'not ... at all' is an adverbial phrase which *precedes* and modifies an auxiliary verb or a verb.

6. Question word 都(不)...construction

Structure	Gloss
誰 ... 都(不)...	Everyone (No one)...
哪個人... 都(不)...	Everyone (No one)...

1. 誰要學中文？

   Shéi yào xué Zhōngwén?
   Who would like to learn Chinese?

   誰都要學中文。

   Shéi dōu yào xué Zhōngwén.
   Everyone would like to learn Chinese.

2. 誰喜歡看那部小說？

   Shéi xǐ.huān kàn nèi bù xiǎoshuō?
   Who would like to read that novel?

   誰都喜歡看那部小說。

   Shéi dōu xǐ.huān kàn nèi bù xiǎoshuō.
   Everyone would like to read that novel.

 In Chinese, question words can be used as indefinite pronouns to denote inclusiveness or exclusiveness, depending on whether they occur in an affirmative or a negative sentence.

See L14–A2, L17–A1 for more on question words used for inclusiveness and exclusiveness.

Ⓑ Usage of Common Phrases 詞組用法 cízǔ yòngfǎ

1. 上/這/下(一)次

Gloss	Structure
which time?	哪(一)次？
last time	上(一)次
this/that time	這(一)次/ 那(一)次
next time	下(一)次

1. 你上(一)次到日本去是什麼時候？

   Nǐ shàng(yí)cì dào Rìběn qù shì shén.me shí.hòu?

   When was the last time that you went to Japan?

我 上(一)次 到日本 去是一九九   Wǒ shàng(yí)cì dào Rìběn qù shì yījiǔjiǔ
四年 五月。   sì nián wǔyuè.
                                  The last time that I went to Japan was
                                  May 1994.

2.   你下(一)次要看什麼電影兒？   Nǐ xià(yí)cì yào kàn shén.me diànyǐngr?
                                  Which movie would you like to go see
                                  next time?

我 下(一)次要看「飲食男女」。   Wǒ xià(yí)cì yào kàn *Yǐn Shí Nán Nǚ.*
                                  Next time I would like to go see *Eat,
                                  Drink, Men, Women.*

The concept of above-below to denote the past and the future holds in the expressions
"last time, this time, next time," similar to the expressions "last month/week, this
month/week, last month/week."

See L6–B2 for related usage.

2. The prepositional phrase 在 ... 上

Structure	Gloss
在 N/NP 上	In (the aspect of) ..., in terms of...

1.   在中國研究上這本書怎麼樣？   Zài Zhōng.guó yánjiù shàng, zhèi běn
                                  shū zěn.meyàng?
                                  In terms of Chinese studies, how is this
                                  book?

在中國研究上這本書最好。   Zài Zhōng.guó yánjiù shàng, zhèi běn
                                  shū zuì hǎo.
                                  In terms of Chinese studies, this book is
                                  the best.

2.   在這個社會上，婦女的地位怎麼   Zài zhèi .ge shèhuì shàng, fùnǚ .de dìwèi
樣？   zěn.meyàng?
                                  In this society, how is women's status?

在這個社會上，婦女的地位很   Zài zhèi .ge shèhuì shàng, fùnǚ .de dìwèi
低。   hěn dī.
                                  In this society, women have low status.

In the prepositional phrase , the noun or head noun of the NP must be an abstract noun.

See L4–B1, L6–A1.4, A5, L8–A4, L9–A3 for more on 在.

3. The superlative marker 最

			Comparative	Superlative
Structure	Adj	很 Adj	更 Adj	最 Adj
Gloss	Adj	very Adj	even Adj-er	the most Adj/Adj-est

1. 好 'good'   很好 'very good'   更好 'even better'   最好 'the best'

2. 高 'high/tall'   很高 'very high/tall'   更高 'even higher/ taller'   最高 'the highest/ tallest'

3. 近 'close'   很近 ' very close'   更近 'even closer'   最近 'closest'

In Chinese, there are no inflections in adjectives. Instead, adverbs are used in front of the adjectives to denote the comparative degrees. Some adjectives may also be used as adverbs; for example, 最近 is used as an adjective when it precedes a noun/noun phrase and as an adverb when it precedes a verb.

1. 最近幾十年什麼很流行？

Zuìjìn jǐ shí nián shén.me hěn liúxíng?
What has become fashionable over the last several decades?

最近幾十年婦女研究很流行。

Zuìjìn jǐ shí nián fùnǚ yánjiù hěn liúxíng.
Over the last several decades, Womens' Studies has become fashionable.

2. 最近的電影兒是喜劇還是悲劇？

Zuìjìn .de diànyǐngr shì xǐjù hái.shì bēijù?
Are the recent movies comedies or tragedies?

最近的電影兒多半兒是喜劇。

Zuìjìn .de diànyǐngr duōbànr shì xǐjù.
Most of the recent movies are comedies.

3. 他最近看了什麼電影兒？

Tā zuìjìn kàn .le shén.me diànyǐngr?
What movie did he see recently?

他最近看了一部中國電影兒。

Tā zuìjìn kàn .le yí bù Zhōng.guó diànyǐngr.
Recently he saw a Chinese movie.

4. 你最近寫了什麼？

Nǐ zuìjìn xiě .le shén.me?
What did you write recently?

我最近寫了一本小說。

Wǒ zuìjìn xiě .le yì běn xiǎoshuō.
Recently I wrote a novel.

When 最近 modifies a phrase consisting of [no. + time word], as in example 1, 最近 means "over the last..." or "recently."

4. 好像 ... 似的 expression

Structure	Gloss
S 好像...似的	It seems that S...

1. 她怎麼了？

   她好像要哭似的。

   Tā zěn.me .le?
   What's wrong with her?

   Tā hǎo.xiàng yào kū .shì.de.
   It seems that she is going to cry.

2. 小林怎麼了？

   小林好像很難過似的。

   Xiǎo Lin zěn.me .le?
   What's wrong with Xiao Lin?

   Xiǎo Lin hǎo.xiàng hěn nánguò .shì.de.
   It seems that Xiao Lin is very upset.

 In this pattern, the subject must precede the idiomatic expression 好像...似的.

C Reentry 複習 fùxí

1. More on ...的 N construction

Structure	Gloss
[S₂ V₂ 的 N] SV₁ 　　　　　　S₁	[The N which S₂ V₂] to be Adj₁ 　　　　　　S₁
S₁ (AuxV) V₁ [S₂ V₂ 的 N] 　　　　　　　　O	S₁ (AuxV) V₁ [The N which S₂ V₂] 　　　　　　　　O

1. [什麼人在中國社會上的地位] 很低？

   [女人在中國社會上的地位] 很低。

   Shén.me rén zài Zhōng.guó shèhuì shàng .de dìwèi hěn dī?
   What people in Chinese society have a very low position?

   Nǔrén zài Zhōng.guó shèhuì shàng .de dìwèi hěn dī.
   The position of Chinese women in society is very low.

2.　[他寫的小說]怎麼樣？

Tā xiě .de xiǎoshuō zěn.meyàng?
How are the novels that he wrote?

　　[他寫的小說]都很有意思。

Tā xiě .de xiǎoshuō dōu hěn yǒuyì.si.
The novels that he wrote are all very interesting.

3.　你喜歡[誰演的電影兒]？

Nǐ xǐ.huān shéi yǎn .de diànyǐngr?
Whose movies do you like?

　　我很喜歡[他演的電影兒]。

Wǒ hěn xǐ.huān tā yǎn .de diànyǐngr.
I like the movies that he acts in.

4.　小李想看[誰寫的新書]？

Xiǎo Lǐ xiǎng kàn shéi xiě .de xīnshū?
Whose new book would Xiao Li like to read?

　　小李想看[我寫的新書]。

Xiǎo Lǐ xiǎng kàn wǒ xiě .de xīnshū.
Xiao Li would like to read the new book that I wrote.

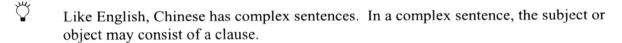 Like English, Chinese has complex sentences. In a complex sentence, the subject or object may consist of a clause.

See L10–A3 for more on Chinese clauses.

Cultural Notes
文化點滴 wénhuà diǎndī

1. With only a few exceptions, such as cucumbers, carrots, and turnips, Chinese eat no raw vegetables. Traditional Chinese consider eating uncooked vegetables as "barbarian/uncivilized behavior." Therefore it is quite difficult for a "Chinese stomach" to get used to eating American vegetable salads.

2. Most Chinese eat three meals a day. For breakfast, people in the south usually eat rice gruel with such complements as pickled vegetables, tofu, and roast ground pork (since rice grows in the south), while people in the north eat noodles, flour cakes, steamed bread, and food made of flour or corn (wheat grows in the north). Some people eat bread, toast, and milk if they are Westernized and cannot find time to prepare a Chinese meal. For lunch and dinner, people eat steamed rice or steamed bread with meat or vegetable dishes.

3. Chinese parent-child relationships are dominant-submissive, but typical Chinese parents are 嚴父 yán fù 'stern father,' 慈母 cí mǔ 'loving/fond mother.' When a child is punished by the father, it is common for the mother to "rescue" or protect the child. Therefore children usually are much closer to their mother than their father.

第十二課　這件大衣怎麼樣？

對話

（天氣越來越冷了，林美英跟王華一起出去買衣服。）

小林： 嘿！王華，別看電視了。除了籃球（以外），還是籃球，
　　　 咱們出去逛逛街吧！你看，去「大學商場」怎麼樣？

小王： 商場有什麼好逛的？一群人在裏頭走來走去，真沒意思。
　　　 而且那幾家百貨公司我都去過了，東西貴極了！

小林： 那兒最近在冬季大拍賣。聽說很多東西都打了折（扣），
　　　 有的還打對折，咱們去看看吧！

小王： 好吧！天氣越來越冷了。我也得加件外套了。

（林美英跟王華坐公車到了大學商場）

小林： 這件藍色的大衣怎麼樣？你不是喜歡藍色的嗎？

小王：顏色還可以，可是樣子太老了。

小林：這件咖啡的怎麼樣？長度挺合適的。

小王：我穿穿看。（穿上大衣）嗯，小了一點兒，有點兒緊。裏邊兒穿毛衣肯定穿著緊。你幫我看看有沒有九號的。

小林：没有九號的，有十二號的。

小王：十二號又太大了。你看這件是不是比那件大一點兒？（拿另一件，比衣服的大小）

小林：這件的顏色沒有原來那件好看。我看你就買黑色的好了。黑色有九號的。大小、長短都很合適。價錢也不貴。而且你不是有黑色的靴子、圍巾兒和手套嗎？可以配成一套。要不要再買件黑色的襯衫和裙褲？最近挺流行穿裙褲的。

小王：是不是還要頂黑帽子？真是的，我可不想做個「黑衣女郎」，過個「黑色的冬季」呀！

My questions:

对话

〔天气越来越冷了，林美英跟王华一起出去买衣服。〕

小林：嘿！王华，别看电视了。除了篮球（以外），还是篮球，
　　　咱们出去逛逛街吧！你看，去「大学商场」怎么样？

小王：商场有什么好逛的？一群人在里头走来走去，真没意思。
　　　而且那几家百货公司我都去过了，东西贵极了！

小林：那儿最近在冬季大拍卖。听说很多东西都打了折（扣），
　　　有的还打对折，咱们去看看吧！

小王：好吧！天气越来越冷了。我也得加件外套了。

（林美英跟王华坐公车到了大学商场）

小林：这件蓝色的大衣怎么样？你不是喜欢蓝色的吗？

小王：颜色还可以，可是样子太老了。

小林：这件咖啡的怎么样？长度挺合适的。

小王：我穿穿看。（穿上大衣）嗯，小了一点儿，有点儿紧。里
　　　边儿穿毛衣肯定穿着紧。你帮我看看有没有九号的。

小林：没有九号的，有十二号的。

小王：十二号又太大了。你看这件是不是比那件大一点儿？（拿
　　　另一件，比衣服的大小）

小林：这件的颜色没有原来那件好看。我看你就买黑色的好了。
　　　黑色有九号的。大小、长短都很合适。价钱也不贵。而且
　　　你不是有黑色的靴子、围巾儿和手套吗？可以配成一套。
　　　要不要再买件黑色的衬衫和裙裤？最近挺流行穿裙裤的。

小王：是不是还要顶黑帽子？真是的，我可不想做个「黑衣女郎
　　　」，过个「黑色的冬季」呀！

Duìhuà

(Tiān.qì yuè lái yuè lěng .le, Lín Měiyīng gēn Wáng Huá yìqǐ chū.qù mǎi yī.fú.)

Xiǎo Lín: Hèi! Wáng Huá, bié kàn diànshì .le. Chú.le lánqiú (yǐwài), hái.shì lánqiú, zán.men chū.qù guàng.guàngjiē .ba! Nǐ kàn, qù "Dàxué Shāngchǎng" zěn.meyàng?

Xiǎo Wáng: Shāngchǎng yǒu shén.me hǎo guàng .de? Yì qún rén zài lǐ.tóu zǒu lái zǒu qù, zhēn méiyì.si. Érqiě nà jǐ jiā bǎihuò gōngsī wǒ dōu qù.guò .le, dōng.xi guì jí .le!

Xiǎo Lín: Nàr zuìjìn zài dōngjì dàpāimài. Tīngshuō hěn duō dōng.xi dōu dǎ .le zhé(kòu). Yǒu .de hái dǎ duìzhé, zán.men qù kàn.kàn .ba!

Xiǎo Wáng: Hǎo .ba! Tiān.qì yuè lái yuè lěng .le, wǒ yě děi jiā jiàn wàitào .le.

(Lín Měiyīng gēn Wáng Huá zuò gōngchē dào .le Dàxué Shāngchǎng.)

Xiǎo Lín: Zhè jiàn lánsè.de dàyī zěn.meyàng? Nǐ bú.shì xǐ.huān lánsè.de .ma?

Xiǎo Wáng: Yánsè hái kě.yǐ, kě.shì yàng.zi tài lǎo .le.

Xiǎo Lín: Zhè jiàn kāfēi.de zěn.meyàng? Chángdù tǐng héshì .de!

Xiǎo Wáng: Wǒ chuān.chuān.kàn. (Chuān.shàng dàyī) Ēn, xiǎo .le yì.diǎnr, yǒu .diǎnr jǐn, lǐ.biānr chuān máoyī kěndìng chuān.zhe jǐn. Nǐ bāng wǒ kàn.kàn yǒu méi.yǒu jiǔhào.de.

Xiǎo Lín: Méi.yǒu jiǔhào.de, yǒu shí'èrhào.de.

Xiǎo Wáng: Shí'èrhào yòu tài dà .le. Nǐ kàn zhè jiàn shì .bú.shì bǐ nà jiàn dà yì.diǎnr? (Ná lìng yí jiàn, bǐ yī.fú .de dàxiǎo.)

Xiǎo Lín: Zhè jiàn .de yánsè méi.yǒu yuánlái nà jiàn hǎokàn. Wǒ kàn nǐ jiù mǎi hēisè.de hǎo.le. Hēisè yǒu jiǔhào.de. Dàxiǎo, chángduǎn dōu hěn héshì. Jià.qián yě bú guì. Érqiě nǐ bú.shì yǒu hēisè.de xuē.zi, wéijīnr hé shǒutào .ma? Kě.yǐ pèi chéng yí tào. Yào .bu.yào zài mǎi jiàn hēisè.de chènshān hé qúnkù? Zuìjìn tǐng liúxíng chuān qúnkù .de.

Xiǎo Wáng: Shì .bú.shì háiyào dǐng hēi mào.zi? Zhēn.shì.de, wǒ kě bù xiǎng zuò .ge "hēiyī nǚláng," guò .ge "hēisè .de dōngjì" .ya.

Dialogue

(The weather is getting colder and colder. Lín Měiyīng and Wáng Huá go out together to buy clothes.)

Xiǎo Lín: Hi! Wáng Huá, don't watch TV. There's nothing on except basketball games. Let's go out and shop. What do you think of going to College Mall?

Xiǎo Wáng: What's good about the mall? Groups of people walking back and forth inside; it's really boring. Besides, I've been to those department stores. The things they sell are so expensive.

Xiǎo Lín: Recently they've been having winter sales. I've heard that many things have been discounted. Some of them are 50% off. Let's go and take a look.

Xiǎo Wáng: All right! The weather is getting colder and colder. I need an overcoat too.

                   (Lín Měiyīng and Wáng Huá go to College Mall by bus.)
Xiǎo Lín: How about this blue coat? Don't you like blue?

Xiǎo Wáng: The color is fine, but it looks old-fashioned.

Xiǎo Lín: How about this brown one? The length suits you pretty well.

Xiǎo Wáng: Let me try. (Puts on the coat.) Hmm, it's a little too small, a little tight. I am sure having a sweater inside will definitely be too tight. Could you help me see if they have size nine?

Xiǎo Lín: There is no size nine.   There is a size twelve.

Xiǎo Wáng: Size twelve is too big. Do you think this one is a little bigger than that one? (Taking another one, and comparing the size of the clothes.)

Xiǎo Lín: The color of this one doesn't look as good as the first one. I think you should buy a black coat. There is a size nine in black. The size and length both fit, and it is inexpensive. Besides, you have black boots, scarf, and gloves, don't you? They match. Do you want to get a black skort? It's now pretty popular to wear skorts.

Xiǎo Wáng: (Do you think) I should get a black hat too? Give me a break!/That's a little too much. I don't want to be a "woman dressed in black" spending a "dark winter."

Mini-Dialogue
小對話 Xiǎoduìhuà

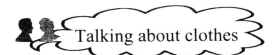

Talking about the seasons and the weather

1. A: 最近天氣越來越冷了。

Zuìjìn tiān.qì yuè lái yuè lěng .le.
The weather is getting colder and colder these days.

B: 可不是嗎？已經十一月了！

Kě bú.shì .ma? Yǐ.jīng shíyīyuè .le!
Isn't it true? It's already November!

Expressing likes and dislikes

1. A: 這件大衣怎麼樣？

Zhè jiàn dàyī zěn.meyàng?
How is this overcoat?

B: 我不喜歡，樣子太老了。

Wǒ bù xǐ.huān, yàng.zi tài lǎo .le.
I don't like it. It looks old-fashioned.

A: 那件呢？

Nà jiàn .ne?
How's that one?

B: 太大了。

Tài dà .le.
It's too big.

Talking about clothes

1. A: 那條裙子怎麼樣？長度很
合適。

Nà tiáo qún.zi zěn.meyàng? Chángdù
hěn héshì.
How's that skirt? The length fits
nicely.

B: 我穿穿看 。

Wǒ chuān.chuān.kàn.
Let me try it on.

Talking about colors

1. A. 你喜歡什麼顏色的褲子？   Nǐ xǐ.huān shén.me yánsè .de kù.zi?
                                        What color of pants do you like?

    B. 藍色、咖啡色的都可以。   Lánsè, kāfēisè .de dōu kě.yǐ.
                                        Both blue and brown are fine.

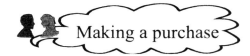

Making a purchase

1. A. 你想買什麼？   Nǐ xiǎng mǎi shén.me?
                                        What would you like to buy?

    B. 短大衣。   Duǎn dàyī.
                                        A short overcoat.

    A. 幾號的？   Jǐ hào .de?
                                        What size?

    B. 八號。   Bā hào.
                                        Size eight.

    A. 這件怎麼樣？   Zhè jiàn zěn.meyàng?
                                        How's this one?

    B. 不錯，我就要這件吧。   Búcuò. Wǒ jiù yào zhè jiàn .ba.
                                        Not bad. Let me have this one.

Vocabulary
生詞 Shēngcí

◎ **By Order of Appearance**

*	衣服		yī.fú	N	clothes (M: 件, V: 穿)
	件		jiàn	M	measure word for upper garments and coats, affairs
	大衣		dàyī	N	[big-clothes] an overcoat (M: 件, V: 穿)
	華	华	huá	N/Adj	China (=中華), splendid, gorgeous (=華麗)
	電視	电视	diànshì	N	[electric-watch] TV
	除了…以外		chú.le… yǐwài	PP	[to rid of-Part…by means of-outside] besides, except for
	籃球	篮球	lánqiú	N	[basket-ball] basketball (M: 個)
	逛街		guàngjiē	V	[stroll-street] to do window shopping
	大學	大学	dàxué	N	[big-school] university, college (M: 個/間)
	商場	商场	shāngchǎng	N	[business-field] mall (M: 個)
	有什麼好逛的	有什么好逛的	yǒu shén.me hǎo guàng .de	IE	what is there to see window shopping?
	群		qún	M	measure word for a group of people or animals
	裏頭	里头	lǐ.tóu	Loc	[inside-Suf] inside
*	外頭	外头	wài.tóu	Loc	[outside-Suf] outside
	百貨公司	百货公司	bǎihuò gōngsī	N	[hundred-goods company] department store (M: 家)
*	百貨大樓	百货大楼	bǎihuò dàlóu	N	[hundred-goods big building] department store (M: 家) (China)
*	百貨	百货	bǎihuò	N	[hundred-goods] goods, commodities
*	公司		gōngsī	N	[public-have charge of] company (M: 家)
	冬季		dōngjì	N	[winter-season] winter (season)
	拍賣	拍卖	pāimài	N	[clap-sell] a sale, an auction
*	減價	减价	jiǎnjià	N	[reduce-price] price reduction
	打折		dǎzhé	V/VO	[hit-fold] to give a discount
	對折	对折	duìzhé	N	[a pair-fold] a 50% discount
	天氣	天气	tiān.qì	N	[sky-air] weather
	越來越…	越来越…	yuè lái yuè …	Adv	[go beyond-come-go beyond] (it's becoming) more/much Adj-er
	冷		lěng	SV	(to be) cold
*	熱	热	rè	SV	(to be) hot (temperature)
	外套		wàitào	N	[outside-case] an overcoat (M: 件, V: 穿) (=大衣)
	藍色	蓝色	lánsè	N	[blue-color] blue

顏色	颜色	yánsè	N	[color-color] color
樣子	样子	yàng.zi	N	[style-Suf] style
咖啡		kāfēi	N	brown (color)
長度	长度	chángdù	N	[long-degree] length
合適	合适	héshì	SV	(to be) suitable
穿穿看		chuān.chuān.kàn	V	[wear-wear-see] to try (garments) on
* 穿		chuān	V	to wear (garments and shoes)
* 戴		dài	V	to wear (glasses, gloves, jewelry)
* 圍	围	wéi	V	to wear (scarf), to surround
緊	紧	jǐn	SV	(to be) tight
* 寬		kuān	SV	(to be) loose
毛衣		máoyī	N	[wool-clothes] sweater (M: 件, V: 穿)
肯定		kěndìng	Adv	[promise-certain] certainly
幫	帮	bāng	V	to help, to assist
又		yòu	Adv	again, moreover
* 更		gèng	Adv	even
原來	原来	yuánlái	Adv	[original-come] originally
黑色		hēisè	N	[black-color] black
大小		dàxiǎo	N	[big-small] size
長短	长短	chángduǎn	N	[long-short] length
價錢	价钱	jià.qián	N	[price-money] price
靴子		xuē.zi	N	[boot-Suf] boots (M: 雙, V: 穿)
圍巾兒	围巾儿	wéijīnr	N	[surround-handkerchief] scarf (M: 條, V: 圍)
圍脖兒	围脖儿	wéibór	N	[surround-neck] scarf (M: 條, V: 圍) (=圍巾兒)
手套		shǒutào	N	[hand-case] gloves (M: 雙/付 fù, V: 戴)
配成		pèichéng	V	[match-become] to match and form
套		tào	N/M	a set
襯衫	衬衫	chènshān	N	[inner garment-shirt] shirt (M: 件, V: 穿)
裙褲	裙裤	qúnkù	N	[skirt-pants] skort (M: 條, V: 穿)
* 褲子	裤子	kù.zi	N	[pants-Suf] pants (M: 條, V: 穿)
* 裙子		qún.zi	N	[skirt- Suf] skirt (M: 條, V: 穿)
帽子		mào.zi	N	[hat-Suf] hat, cap (M: 頂 dǐng, V: 戴)
真是的	真是的	zhēn.shì.de	IE	[real-to be-Part] give me a break!; (someone is) impossible; (something is) a little too much
女郎		nǚláng	N	[female-man] woman (derogatory)
呀		.ya	Part	sentence particle–a variant of 啊 when the preceding vowel ending is /i/

◎ By Grammatical Categories

Nouns/Pronouns

華	华	huá	N/Adj	China (=中華), splendid, gorgeous (=華麗)
* 衣服		yī.fú	N	clothes (M: 件, V: 穿)
電視	电视	diànshì	N	[electric-watch] TV
籃球	篮球	lánqiú	N	[basket-ball] basketball (M: 個)
大學	大学	dàxué	N	[big-school] university, college (M: 個/間)
商場	商场	shāngchǎng	N	[business-field] mall (M: 個)
百貨公司	百货公司	bǎihuò gōngsī	N	[hundred-goods company] department store (M: 家)
* 百貨大樓	百货大楼	bǎihuò dàlóu	N	[hundred-goods big building] department store (M: 家) (China)
* 百貨	百货	bǎihuò	N	[hundred-goods] goods, commodities
* 公司		gōngsī	N	[public-have charge of] company (M: 家)
冬季		dōngjì	N	[winter-season] winter (season)
拍賣	拍卖	pāimài	N	[clap-sell] a sale, an auction
價錢	价钱	jià.qián	N	[price-money] price
* 減價	减价	jiǎnjià	N	[reduce-price] price reduction
對折	对折	duìzhé	N	[a pair-fold] a 50% discount
天氣	天气	tiān.qì	N	[sky-air] weather
大衣		dàyī	N	[big-clothes] an overcoat (M: 件, V: 穿)
外套		wàitào	N	[outside-case] an overcoat (M: 件, V: 穿) (=大衣)
顏色	颜色	yánsè	N	[color-color] color
藍色	蓝色	lánsè	N	[blue-color] blue
黑色		hēisè	N	[black-color] black
咖啡		kāfēi	N	brown (color)
樣子	样子	yàng.zi	N	[style-Suf] style
長度	长度	chángdù	N	[long-degree] length
長短	长短	chángduǎn	N	[long-short] length
大小		dàxiǎo	N	[big-small] size
毛衣		máoyī	N	[wool-clothes] sweater (M: 件, V: 穿)
靴子		xuē.zi	N	[boot-Suf] boots (M: 雙, V: 穿)
圍巾兒	围巾儿	wéijīnr	N	[surround-handkerchief] scarf (M: 條, V: 圍)
圍脖兒	围脖儿	wéibór	N	[surround-neck] scarf (M: 條, V: 圍) (=圍巾兒)
手套		shǒutào	N	[hand-case] gloves (M: 雙/付 fù, V: 戴)
套		tào	N/M	a set
襯衫	衬衫	chènshān	N	[inner garment-shirt] shirt (M: 件, V: 穿)
裙褲	裙裤	qúnkù	N	[skirt-pants] skort (M: 條, V: 穿)
* 褲子	裤子	kù.zi	N	[pants-Suf] pants (M: 條, V: 穿)

*	裙子		qún.zi	N	[skirt-Suf] skirt (M: 條, V: 穿)
	帽子		mào.zi	N	[hat-Suf] hat, cap (M: 頂 dǐng, V: 戴)
	女郎		nǚláng	N	[female-man] woman (derogatory)

Measure Words

	群		qún	M	measure word for a group of people or animals
	件		jiàn	M	measure word for upper garments and coats, affairs

Verbs/Stative Verbs/Adjectives

	除了...以外		chú.le... yǐwài	PP	[to rid of-Part...by means of-outside] besides, except for
	逛街		guàngjiē	V	[stroll-street] to do window shopping
	打折		dǎzhé	V/VO	[hit-fold] to give a discount
	配成		pèichéng	V	[match-become] to match and form
*	穿		chuān	V	to wear (garments and shoes)
	穿穿看		chuān.chuān.kàn	V	[wear-wear-see] to try (garments) on
*	戴		dài	V	to wear (glasses, gloves, jewelry)
*	圍	围	wéi	V	to wear (scarf), to surround
	幫	帮	bāng	V	to help, to assist
	冷		lěng	SV	(to be) cold
*	熱	热	rè	SV	(to be) hot (temperature)
	緊	紧	jǐn	SV	(to be) tight
*	寬		kuān	SV	(to be) loose
	合適	合适	héshì	SV	(to be) suitable

Adverbs

	越來越...	越来越...	yuè lái yuè...	Adv	[go beyond-come-go beyond] (it's becoming) more/much Adj-er
	肯定		kěndìng	Adv	[promise-certain] certainly
	原來	原来	yuánlái	Adv	[original-come] originally
	又		yòu	Adv	again, moreover
*	更		gèng	Adv	even

Particles

	呀		.ya	Part	sentence particle–a variant of 啊 when the preceding vowel ending is /i/

Localizers

裏頭	里头	lǐ.tóu	Loc	[inside-Suf] inside
* 外頭	外头	wài.tóu	Loc	[outside-Suf] outside

Idiomatic Expressions

有什麼 好逛的	有什么 好逛的	yǒu shén.me hǎo guàng .de	IE	what is there to see window shopping?
眞是的	真是的	zhēn.shì.de	IE	[real-to be-Part] give me a break!; (someone is) impossible; (something is) a little too much

✛ Supplementary Vocabulary

1. Clothes and Accessories

牛仔夾克		niúzǎijiākè	N	[cow-child-jacket] jeans jacket (M: 件, V: 穿)
牛仔褲	牛仔裤	niúzǎikù	N	[cow-child-pants] jeans (M: 條, V: 穿)
運動褲	运动裤	yùndòngkù	N	[exercise-pants] sports pants (M: 條, V: 穿)
運動衣	运动衣	yùndòngyī	N	[exercise-clothes] sports clothes (M: 件, V: 穿)
內衣		nèiyī	N	[inside-clothes] undershirt (M: 件, V: 穿)
內褲	内裤	nèikù	N	[inside-pants] underwear (M: 條, V: 穿)
襪子	袜子	wà.zi	N	[socks-Suf] socks, stockings (M: 雙/隻, V: 穿)
鞋子		xié.zi	N	[shoes-Suf] shoes (M: 雙 pair/ 隻 one, V: 穿)
運動鞋	运动鞋	yùndòngxié	N	[exercise-shoes] sneakers (M: 雙/隻 ,V: 穿)
領帶兒	领带儿	lǐngdàir	N	[collar-belt] necktie (M:條, V:打)
眼鏡	眼镜	yǎnjìng	N	[eye-mirror] eyeglasses (M: 付, V: 戴)
太陽眼鏡	太阳眼镜	tàiyáng yǎnjìng	N	[sun-eye-mirror] sunglasses (M: 付, V: 戴)
耳環	耳环	ěrhuán	N	[ear-ring] earrings (M: 付, V: 戴)
項鏈	项链	xiàngliàn	N	[nape-chain] necklace (M: 條, V: 戴)
戒指		jièzhǐ	N	[guard against-finger] ring (M: 隻, V: 戴)

2. Season and Weather

天氣預報	天气预报	tiānqì yùbào	N	[sky-air-advance-tell] weather forecast
氣象 報告	气象 报告	qìxiàng bàogào	N	[air-phenomenon-report-tell] weather report
四季		sìjì	N	[four-season] four seasons
春天		chūntiān	N	[spring-day] springtime
夏天		xiàtiān	N	[summer-day] summertime
秋天		qiūtiān	N	[autumn-day] autumn
冬天		dōngtiān	N	[winter-day] wintertime
氣候	气候	qì.hòu	N	[air-situation] climate

溫度	温度	wēndù	N	[warm-degree] temperature
氣溫	气温	qìwēn	N	[weather-temperature] temperature
攝氏	摄氏	shèshì	N	[absorb-surname] Celsius (thermometer)
華氏	华氏	huáshì	N	[China-surname] Fahrenheit (thermometer)
最高		zuì gāo	Adj	[the most-high] the highest
最低		zuì dī	Adj	[the most-low] the lowest
零下		língxià	Adj	[zero-below] subzero
度		dù	N	degree
冷		lěng	SV	(to be) cold
冷死了		lěng.sǐ .le	IE	[cold-die-Asp] cold to death
凍	冻	dòng	SV	(to be) icy, to freeze
涼快	凉快	liángkuài	SV	[cool-fast] (to be) cool
暖和		nuǎn.huó	SV	[warm-peace] (to be) warm
熱	热	rè	SV	(to be) hot
悶(熱)	闷(热)	mēnrè	SV	[stuffy-hot] humid and hot, muggy
晴(朗)		qíng(lǎng)	SV	[clear-bright] (to be) clear, sunny
晴天		qíngtiān	N	[clear-sky] a fine day, sunny day
出太陽了	出太阳了	chū tàiyáng .le	IE	[out-sun-Asp] the sun came out
陰	阴	yīn	SV	(to be) cloudy
陰天	阴天	yīntiān	N	[cloudy-sky] cloudy day
多雲	多云	duōyún	SV	[much-cloud] cloudy
下雨		xiàyǔ	V	[down-rain] to rain
大/小雨		dà/xiǎoyǔ	N	[big/small-rain] heavy/light rain
毛毛雨		máomáoyǔ	N	[feather-feather-rain] drizzle
偶陣雨	偶阵雨	ǒuzhènyǔ	IE	[occasional-spell of time-rain] shower occasionally
閃電	闪电	shǎndiàn	N	[lightning-electricity] flash lightning
打雷		dǎléi	V	[hit-thunder] to thunder
有霧	有雾	yǒuwù	SV	[have-fog] (to be) foggy
下霜		xiàshuāng	VO	[down-frost] to have frost
下雪		xiàxuě	VO	[down-snow] to snow
颳風	刮风	guāfēng	VO	[blow-wind] wind blowing
暴風雨	暴风雨	bàofēngyǔ	N	[fierce-wind-rain] storm
暴風雪	暴风雪	bàofēngxuě	N	[fierce-wind-snow] blizzard
颶風	飓风	jùfēng	N	[hurricane-wind] hurricane
龍捲風	龙捲风	lóngjuǎnfēng	N	[dragon-curl-wind] tornado
颱風	台风	táifēng	N	[typhoon-wind] typhoon
地震	地震	dìzhèn	N/V	[earth-shake] earthquakes, to have earthquakes
級	级	jí	N	grade, scale (of earthquake or typhoon)

Characters
漢字 Hànzì

長　短　貴　冷

且　穿　毛　衣

球　麵　塊　錢

裏　頭　除　外

還　聽　寫　號

長
cháng, zhǎng
to be long, to
grow   長
8   (long)

長度	chángdù	length
長短	chángduǎn	length (long-short)
*長途	chángtú	long distance

A: 這件衣服怎麼樣？
B: **長度**挺合適的。

短
duǎn
to be short   矢
12   (a dart)

| *短褲 | duǎnkù | shorts |

A: 那條裙子太**短**了！
B: 今年流行**短裙**嘛！

貴
guì
to be noble
to be honorable
expensive   貝
12   (shells)

| *貴姓 | guìxìng | honorable surname |

A: 你要不要這件外套，我們可以給你八折。
B: 八折也太**貴**了。

冷
lěng
to be cold   冫
7

| *冷水 | lěngshuǐ | cold water |

A: 天氣越來越**冷**了。
B: 可不是嗎！，我得去買件大衣了。

繁簡對照：	其他漢字：	✎ **My notes:**
長 长 貴 贵	*便 SC28 *宜 SC29	

且

而且　　　　érqiě　　　　　moreover

qiě
moreover,
further　　　一
5　　　　(one)

A: 你為什麼要學中文呢？
B: 我是中國人，**而且**我的專業是中國文
　學。

穿

*穿上　　　　chuān.shàng　　　to put on

chuān
to wear　　　穴
9　　　　(cave)

A: 這件衣服看起來有點兒小。
B: 我**穿穿看**。

毛

毛衣　　　máoyī　　　sweater
*毛巾　　　máojīn　　　towel

máo
hair, fur, feather
　　　毛
4　　(hair, fur)

A: 我想買件**毛衣**。
B: 你是給自己買還是給別人買？

衣

大衣　　　dàyī　　　overcoat
衣服　　　yī.fú　　　clothes

yī
clothing, dress
　　　衣
6　　(clothing)

A: 這家店賣的**衣服**真貴！
B: 他們還打了折呢！

繁簡對照：	其他漢字：	✎ **My notes:**
	*戴 SC30 *件 SC31	

球

qiú
ball, sphere,
globe   玉
11   (jade)

籃球	lánqiú	basketball
*足球	zúqiú	football
*棒球	bàngqiú	baseball
*球鞋	qiúxié	sneakers

A: 他**球**打得怎麼樣？
B: 打得不好，可是還是喜歡打。

麵

miàn
flour   麥
20   (wheat)

| 麵包 | miànbāo | bread |
| *牛肉麵 | niúròumiàn | beef noodle |

A: 你早飯吃了什麼？
B: 就吃了一點兒**麵包**。

塊

kuài
M, lump, piece
土
13   (soil)

| 一塊兒 | yíkuàir | together |
| *一塊錢 | yí kuài qián | one dollar |

A: 你們兩個整天在**一塊兒**，不是出去玩兒
就是在家看電視。
B: 那裏，我們也學習。

錢

qián
money   金
16   (metal)

*有錢	yǒuqián	with money, rich
*沒錢	méiqián	no money
*有錢人	yǒuqiánrén	rich people

A: 你說你**沒有錢**，可是你買了這麼多東
西。
B: 我的朋友**有錢**。

繁簡對照：	其他漢字：	✎ **My notes:**
麵 面 塊 块 錢 钱	*碗 SC32	

裏

lǐ
inside   衣
13   (clothing)

裏頭	lǐ.tóu	inside
*裏面	lǐmiàn	inside
*這裏	zhè.lǐ	here
那裏	nà.lǐ	there

A: **這**裏看來看去，没什麼好東西。
B: 就是，越看越没意思。

頭

tóu
head, noun
suffix   頁
16   (head)

裏頭	lǐ.tóu	inside
*外頭	wài.tóu	outside
*前頭	qián.tóu	front

A: 這件大衣太緊了，裏**頭**穿毛衣肯定穿
   不下。
B: 你幫我找一件大一點兒的。

除

chú
aside from;
except   阝
10   (a mound)

除了…以外   chú.le…yǐwài   besides; except for

A: **除了**外套**以外**，你還要買點兒什麼？
B: 我**除了**外套**以外**，還要買一雙手套。

外

wài
outside, foreign
夕
5   (evening)

外套	wàitào	an overcoat
*外頭	wài.tóu	outside
*外邊兒	wài.biānr	outside
*外國	wàiguó	foreign country

A: **外邊**冷不冷？
B: 還好，不過你最好穿件**外套**。

繁簡對照：	其他漢字：	✎ **My notes:**
裏里 頭头	腦 L14	

還

hái
still, yet   辶
17

還有   hái yǒu   still have
還是   hái.shì   or

A: 你今天上午上中文課還是日文課？
B: 我上中文課。

聽

tīng
to listen   耳
22   (ear)

聽說   tīngshuō   to hear of
*好聽   hǎotīng   pleasant to hear
*聽寫   tīngxiě   dictation
*聽話   tīnghuà   to be obedient

A: 聽說你在學中文？
B: 對，中文是我的專業。

寫

xiě
to write   宀
15

寫字   xiězì   to write (words)
*寫信   xiěxìn   to write letters

A: 你一天得寫多少個中國字？
B: 一天得寫二十個。

號

hào
AN for ordinal
numbers   虍
13

八號   bā hào   size eight
大號   dàhào   large size
中號   zhōnghào   medium size
小號   xiǎohào   small size

A: 你穿幾號的衣服？
B: 八號。大一點兒的也可以。

繁簡對照：	其他漢字：	✎ My notes:
還 还 聽 听 寫 写 號 号	*公 SC33 *司 SC34	

Grammar
語法 yǔfǎ

Ⓐ Major Sentence Patterns 主要句型 zhǔyào jùxíng

1. 除了... (以外) construction

Structure	Gloss
(1) S 除了 N/VP (以外), 還/也 VO	Besides N/Ving O, S VO
(2) 除了 N/VP (以外), S 還/也 VO	
(3) 除了 A (以外), B 也 VO	Besides A, B VO

1. 小林除了大衣 (以外), 還買了什麼？

   Xiǎo Lín chú.le dàyī (yǐwài), hái mǎi .le shén.me?
   What did Xiao Lin buy besides an overcoat?

   小林除了大衣 (以外), 還買了一雙手套。

   Xiǎo Lín chú.le dàyī (yǐwài), hái mǎi .le yì shuāng shǒutào.
   Besides an overcoat, Xiao Lin bought a pair of gloves.

2. 除了買靴子 (以外), 小王也要做什麼？

   Chú.le mǎi xuē.zi (yǐwài), Xiǎo Wáng yě yào zuò shén.me?
   What does Xiao Wang want to do besides buying boots?

   除了買靴子 (以外), 小王也要買一件襯衫。

   Chú.le mǎi xuē.zi (yǐwài), Xiǎo Wáng yě yào mǎi yí jiàn chènshān.
   Besides buying boots, Xiao Wang wants to buy a shirt.

3. 除了小高以外, 誰也買了一條牛仔褲？

   Chú.le Xiǎo Gāo yǐwài, shéi yě mǎi .le yì tiáo niúzǎikù?
   Who bought a pair of jeans besides Xiao Gao?

   除了小高以外, 小李也買了一條牛仔褲。

   Chú.le Xiǎo Gāo yǐwài, Xiǎo Lǐ yě mǎi .le yì tiáo niúzǎikù.
   Besides Xiao Gao, Xiao Li bought a pair of jeans.

 除了 N/VP (以外), is a movable prepositional phrase. It can occur either in front of or right after the subject of the sentence. In pattern (3), when A and B are different subjects (see example 3), you can only use the adverb 也 before the VO.

2. 越 ... 越 ... **construction**

Structure	Gloss
S (O) 越 V 越 Adj	The more S V (O), the more Adj he/she becomes
S 越 來 越 Adj	S becomes more/much Adj-er
S₁ 越 V(O), S₂ 越 Adj	The more S₁ V (O), the more S₂ becomes Adj

1. 小高中文怎麼樣？

    小高中文越說越好了。

    Xiǎo Gāo Zhōngwén zěn.meyàng?
    How is Xiao Gao's spoken Chinese?

    Xiǎo Gāo Zhōngwén yuè shuō yuè hǎo .le.
    Xiao Gao's spoken Chinese is getting better
    and better.

2. 他的女兒怎麼樣？

    他的女兒越長越漂亮了。

    Tā .de nǚ'ér zěn.meyàng?
    How is his daughter?

    Tā .de nǚ'ér yuè zhǎng yuè piào.liàng .le.
    His daughter is becoming prettier and prettier.

3. 最近天氣怎麼樣？

    天氣越來越冷了。

    Zuìjìn tiān.qì zěn.meyàng?
    How's the weather lately?

    Tiān.qì yuè lái yuè lěng .le.
    The weather is getting colder and colder.

4. 他這麼說，你覺得怎麼樣？

    他越說，我越高興。

    Tā zhè.me shuō, nǐ jué.de zěn.meyàng?
    How do you feel when he (keeps) saying this?

    Tā yuè shuō, wǒ yuè gāoxìng.
    The more he says, the happier I am.

In a sentence with only one subject , the correlative adverbs 越 ... 越 ... correlate two
verbs. The first verb is an action verb, while the second one must be a stative verb/
adjective of degree. If no specific action is ascribed to the first verb, then a dummy verb
來 must be used. In a complex sentence with two different subjects, each 越 goes with
one verb in each clause.

B Usage of Common Phrases 詞組用法 cízǔ yòngfǎ

1. V 來 V 去 expression

Structure	Gloss
S （在 Place） V 來 V 去	S keeps on Ving back and forth (at a place)

1.　人們在商場裏頭做什麼？

Rén.men zài shāngchǎng .lǐ.tóu zuò shén.me?
What are people doing at the shopping center?

人們在商場裏頭走來走去。

Rén.men zài shāngchǎng .lǐ.tóu zǒu lái zǒu qù.
People are walking back and forth at the shopping center.

2.　她最後買了什麼？

Tā zuìhòu mǎi .le shén.me?
What did she finally buy?

她看來看去還是買了那件大衣。

Tā kàn lái kàn qù hái.shì mǎi .le nèi jiàn dàyī.
She kept looking back and forth and (finally) bought that overcoat.

💡 V 來 V 去 is a verbal phrase that describes someone doing an action back and forth or over and over again.

2. Other usages of 的
2.1 The nominalizer 的

Structure	Gloss
X 的 N → 　 X 的	X one
V (O) 的 N → V (O) 的	the one that V(O)

1.　藍的衣服 → 藍的。

Lán.de yí.fú → lán.de.
Blue clothes → blue one.

他喜歡藍的，我喜歡紅的。

Tā xǐ.huān lán.de, wǒ xǐ.huān hóng.de.
He likes the blue one; I like the red one.

2.　有的東西 → 有的。

Yǒu.de dōng.xī → yǒu.de.
Some things → some.

有的打對折，有的打八折。

Yǒu.de dǎ duìzhé, yǒu.de dǎ bāzhé.
Some are 50% off; some are 20% off.

3.　我做的襯衫 → 我做的。

Wǒ zuò.de chènshān → wǒ zuò.de.
The shirt that I made → the one that I made.

這件襯衫是我做的，不是買的。

Zhèi jiàn chènshān shì wǒ zuò.de, bú shì mǎi.de.

This shirt is the one that I made, not the one that (I) bought.

4. 做衣服的人→ 做衣服的   zuò yī.fú.de rén → zuò yī.fú.de
    做飯的人→ 做飯的   zuòfàn.de rén → zuòfàn.de.
                                     the one that makes clothes→ a tailor
                                     the one that makes food→ a cook

    他是做衣服的,不是做飯的。   Tā shì zuò yī.fú.de, bú shì zuòfàn.de.
                                     He is a tailor, not a cook.

Besides serving as the subordinative particle, 的 has other functions. In a construction that consists of X 的 N or V(O) 的 N, if the head N is understood within the conversational context, then the N is omittable. In this case, 的 functions as a pronoun, "one."

2.2 The situational 的

Structure	Gloss
Clause 的	Such is the case or this is the kind of situation

1. 這件大衣怎麼樣 ?   Zhèi jiàn dàyī zěn.meyàng?
                                     How is this overcoat?

    這件大衣,長度挺合適的 。   Zhèi jiàn dàyī, chángdù tǐng héshì .de.
                                     (As for) this overcoat, the length fits quite well.

2. 最近流行穿什麼 ?   Zuìjìn liúxíng chuān shén.me?
                                     What's been popular to wear lately?

    最近挺流行穿長裙子的 。   Zuìjìn tǐng liúxíng chuān cháng qún.zi .de.
                                     Lately it's been very popular to wear long skirts.

The situational 的 refers to the whole situation with the meaning of "such is the case" or "this is the kind of situation."

See L23–C1.1, C1.2, C1.3 for more on 的.

3. 打幾折 expression

Structure	Gloss
打幾折 ?	How much is the discount?
打九折	(charge 90%) take 10% off
打八折	(charge 80%) take 20% off

打五/對折	(charge 50%) take 50% off
打四折	(charge 40%) take 60% off

1. 那件毛衣打幾折？

   Nèi jiàn máoyī dǎ jǐ zhé?
   How much off is that sweater?

   那件毛衣打對折。

   Nèi jiàn máoyī dǎ duìzhé.
   That sweater is 50% off.

2. 這些東西都打幾折？

   Zhèi xiē dōng.xi dōu dǎ jǐ zhé?
   How much off are all of these (things)?

   這些東西都打四折。

   Zhèi xiē dōng.xi dōu dǎ sì zhé.
   All of these (things) are 60% off.

Literally 折 means "to fold, to tear into halves." In terms of discount, 折 means "10% off the original price." 打九折 means "charge 90% of the original price —10% discount," and so forth.

4. Antonym compounds

Antonym		Gloss
大小	dàxiǎo	size
長短	chángduǎn	length
寬窄	kuānzhǎi	width
冷熱	lěngrè	temperature

1. 你看這件襯衫的大小怎麼樣？

   Nǐ kàn zhèi jiàn chènshān dàxiǎo zěn.meyàng?
   What do you think about the size of this shirt?

   我覺得大小挺合適，可是長短不合適。

   Wǒ jué.de dàxiǎo tǐng héshì, kě.shì chángduǎn bù héshì.
   I think the size is just right, but the length is not right.

2. 你看這條褲子的長度怎麼樣？

   Nǐ kàn zhèi tiáo kù.zi .de chángdù zěn.meyàng?
   What do you think about the length of this pair of pants?

   我覺得長短還可以，可是有一點兒緊。

   Wǒ jué.de chángduǎn hái kě.yǐ, kě.shì yǒu yì.diǎnr jǐn.
   I think the length is O.K., but they're a little bit tight.

Compounds of antonyms are formed with two adjectives of opposite qualities in coordination. These compounds are translated into single words in English. But their usages are limited. They may be used only in questions such as "What do you think about the size/length/width of X?" or in expressions such as "I think the size/length/width of X is ..."

 Don't use these compounds in the following sentence structures:

那件大衣的大小很大。

這條褲子的長短很長。

5. 號 as "size"

Structure	Gloss
特大號	extra-large size
大/中/小 號	large/medium/small size
no. 號	size no.

1.   你穿幾號的襯衫？

Nǐ chuān jǐ hào .de chènshān?
What size shirt do you wear?

在中國我是穿大號的，在美國
有時候得買小號的。

Zài Zhōng.guó wǒ shì chuān dàhào.de,
zài Měi.guó yǒushí.hòu děi mǎi
xiǎohào.de.
In China I wear large size, (but) in
America, sometimes I have to buy the
small one.

2.   這條三十號的褲子合適嗎？

Zhèi tiáo sānshíhào.de kù.zi héshì .ma?
Do these size 30 pants fit (you)?

三十號的有一點兒緊，請你給
我一條三十一號的吧！

Sānshíhào.de yǒu yì.diǎnr jǐn, qǐng nǐ gěi
wǒ yì tiáo sānshíyīhào.de .ba!
Size 30 is a little bit too tight; please give
me a size 31.

 The lexical meaning of 號 is "number," but for clothes and things that involve size, 號 denotes "size."

6. 有什麼好V的

Structure	Gloss
X 有什麼好V的	What's the point of Ving X!

1. 我買那件襯衫怎麼樣？ | Wo mǎi nèi jiàn chènshān zěn.meyàng?
How about me buying that shirt?

那件襯衫有什麼好買的！ | Nèi jiàn chènshān yǒu shén.me hǎo mǎi .de!
What's the point of buying that shirt!

2. 咱們去看籃球吧！ | Zán.men qù kàn lánqiú .ba!
Let's go watch a basketball game!

籃球有什麼好看的！ | Lánqiú yǒu shén.me hǎo kàn .de!
What's the point of watching a basketball game!

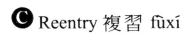 Reentry 複習 fùxí

1. More on comparative construction

1.1 Explicit comparison

	Structure	Gloss
Question	A　比　B　Adj 嗎？	Is A Adj-er than B?
Answer	A　比　B　Adj	A is Adj-er than B
	A　比　B　Adj（得)多了	A is much more Adj-er than B
	A　比　B　Adj　一點兒	A is a little bit Adj-er than B
	A 不比　B　Adj	A is not as Adj as B

1. 這件大衣比那件(大衣)好看嗎？ | Zhèi jiàn dàyī bǐ nèi jiàn (dàyī) hǎokàn .ma?
Is this overcoat better looking than that one?

這件大衣比那件好看多了。 | Zhèi jiàn dàyī bǐ nèijiàn hǎokàn duō .le.
This overcoat is much better looking than that one.

2. 那條褲子比這條長嗎？ | Nèi tiáo kù.zi bǐ zhèi tiáo cháng .ma?
Is that pair of pants longer than this one?

那條褲子不比這條長。 | Nèi tiáo kù.zi bù bǐ zhèi tiáo cháng.
That pair of pants is not as long as this one.

 As already noted, comparison of two things can be made either explicitly or implicitly. The comparisons in examples 1 and 2 are explicit, because both parties of the comparisons are clearly stated. The word order of a comparative sentence follows the Temporal Sequence Principle because you must compare two things first, then the result of the comparison follows.

To express "A is much longer than B," you should say A 比 B 長(得)多了, *not* A 比 B 很長.

3.   這件襯衫比那件好看嗎？

   Zhèi jiàn chènshān bǐ nèi jiàn hǎokàn .ma?
   Is this shirt prettier than that one?

   這件襯衫不比那件好看。

   Zhèi jiàn chènshān bù bǐ nèi jiàn hǎokàn.
   This shirt is not prettier than that one.

4.   這條裙子比那條長嗎？

   Zhèi tiáo qún.zi bǐ nèi tiáo cháng .ma?
   Is this skirt longer than that one?

   這條裙子不比那條長。

   Zhèi tiáo qún.zi bù bǐ nèi tiáo cháng.
   This skirt is not longer than that one.

 Because the A 比 B Adj construction denotes "A is more… than B," the positive form of stative verb is always used. If you would like to express the contradictory of the comparison, you should put the negative adverb 不 before 比, as in examples 3 and 4.

2.2 Implicit comparison

	Structure	Gloss
Question	(A 跟 B), 哪 M (比較) Adj?	(As for A and B), which one is Adj-er?
Answer	A (比較) Adj A Adj(得)多了 A Adj 一點兒	A is Adj-er A is much more Adj A is a little bit more Adj

1.   (藍的跟紅的)，哪個(比較)好看？

   (Lán.de gēn hóng.de), něi .ge (bǐjiào) hǎokàn?
   Which one is better looking? The blue one or the red one?

   紅的(比較)好看。

   Hóng.de (bǐjiào) hǎokàn.
   The red one is prettier.

2.   (長褲跟短褲)，哪個(比較)合適？

   (Chángkù gēn duǎnkù), něi .ge (bǐjiào) héshì?
   Which one fits better? The long pants or the shorts?

   短褲(比較)合適。

   Duǎnkù (bǐjiào) héshì.
   The shorts fit better.

 The comparisons in these examples are implicit, since the ones being compared are omitted (as understood in the conversational context).

2.3 Equaling-degree comparison

	Structure	Gloss
Question	A 有沒有 B (這麼 / 那麼) Adj？	Is A as Adj as B?
Answer	A　　　有 B (這麼 / 那麼) Adj	A is as Adj as B
	A　　沒有 B (這麼 / 那麼) Adj	A is not as Adj as B

1. 毛衣有沒有大衣那麼貴？

   Máoyī yǒu méi.yǒu dàyī nà.me guì?
   Is the sweater more expensive than the overcoat?

   毛衣沒有大衣那麼貴。

   Máoyī méi.yǒu dàyī nà.me guì.
   The sweater is not as expensive as the overcoat.

2. 大號的有沒有中號的那麼合適？

   Dàhào.de yǒu méi.yǒu zhōnghào.de nà.me héshì?
   Does the large size fit better than the medium one?

   大號的有中號的那麼合適。

   Dàhào.de yǒu zhōnghào.de nà.me héshì.
   The large size fits as well as the medium one.

In the A 有沒有 B (這麼 / 那麼) Adj construction, A compares with B from below and equals it on the scale of Adj.

2.4 Equal-degree comparison

	Structure	Gloss
Question	A　　跟 B　　一樣 Adj 嗎？	Are A and B equally Adj？
Answer	A　　跟 B　　一樣 Adj	A and B are equally Adj
	A　　跟 B 不 一樣 Adj	A and B are not equally Adj
	A 不跟 B　　一樣 Adj	A is not equally Adj with B

1. 藍的襯衫跟紅的一樣大嗎？

   Lán.de chènshān gēn hóng.de yíyàng dà .ma?
   Is the blue shirt as big as the red one?

   藍的襯衫(不)跟紅的一樣大。

   Lán.de chènshān (bù)gēn hóng.de yíyàng dà.
   The blue shirt is (not) as big as the red one.

2. 白的毛衣跟黑的一樣貴嗎？

   Bái.de máoyī gēn hēi.de yíyàng guì .ma?
   Is the white sweater as expensive as the black one?

白的毛衣跟黑的(不) 一樣貴。   Bái.de máoyī gēn hēi.de bù yíyàng guì.
                                                  The white sweater and the black one are
                                                  (not) equally expensive.

💡   In the equal-degree construction A 跟 B 一樣 Adj, the negative adverb 不 may precede
       跟 as in example 1 or it may precede the adverb 一樣 yíyàng 'the same' as in example 2.

🔄   See L10–A2, L19–A2, A3, L21–A5 for more on comparisons.

Cultural Notes
文化點滴 wénhuà diǎndī

1. In China, traditional formal clothes for men are 長袍馬掛
    chángpáo mǎguà 'long gown and short jacket' or 中山裝
    zhōngshānzhuāng 'a military uniform-like dress with closed
    collar.' The clothes for women are 旗袍 qípáo 'long gown with
    Mandarin collar introduced by the Manchus.' But nowadays,
    Western suits for men and dresses for women have also been
    accepted as formal wear.

2. The printed patterns and colors on Chinese clothes have social
    significance. Ordinarily, older people wear things with plain or
    simpler designs and darker colors (which are considered more
    steady and calm or dignified), while young people wear fancier
    designs and lighter/brighter colors. Natural color (unbleached
    white) clothing, which American people like, is taboo in China,
    because some types of mourning dress for funerals are made of
    unbleached white cloth.

3. In Chinese there are three verbs, 穿 chuān, 戴 dài and 圍 wéi, which mean "to wear" in
    English. But in Chinese, 穿 chuān, which also means "to go through," can only be used in
    cases where the piece of clothing has a "big hole" in it (e.g., sleeves, pants, socks) so that part
    of your body has to "go through" the hole when you wear it. 戴 dài can only be used in
    cases where you have to put the clothes (e.g., hat, gloves) or jewelry (e.g., glasses, earrings,
    rings, etc.) "on or above" your body part. 圍 wéi, which also means "to surround or to
    encircle," can only be used to signify something that encircles your body (e.g., scarf, apron).

4. Commodities in department stores in the PRC (state owned) and Taiwan all have a set price. You cannot haggle over the price. But when you shop at the 自由市場 zìyóu shìchǎng 'free market' in the PRC or at the 夜市 yèshì 'night market' in Taiwan, you can bargain for the price.

第十三課 感恩節過得好嗎？

對話

（感恩節過後，小林在校園裏踫到小李、小高。）

小高：嘿！小林，怎麼樣？
感恩節還好嗎？回家
了沒有？

小林：回家了。正好星期五
沒課，可以早一天走
。在家裏真好，比宿
舍舒服多了。我媽媽
做的火雞特別好吃，
是中國式的。

小高：你真有口福！是坐飛機回去的嗎？怎麼不告訴我？我可以
送你去機場。

小林：那怎麼好意思。而且是上午的飛機，所以一早就得走。我
在校門口搭了部去機場的小巴，很方便。從這兒去機場只
要四十多分鐘。你回家了嗎？

小高：沒有，期末要交幾個報告，正好利用上個禮拜做做研究。
不過我也吃了火雞和南瓜派，是在超級市場買的。

小林：小李，你呢？是不是也一肚子的火雞？

小李：可不是嗎？我那些美國朋友真好客，都要請我去他們家吃
飯。下午一頓，晚上又一頓，你們看！（拍拍自己的肚
子）我的肚子是不是越來越大了？

小高： 還好，還好，只要少
喝點兒汽水兒就行了
。看起來只有「兩個
月大」。（笑）

小李： （打小高）別開玩笑
了，說真的，放假的
時候大吃大喝，放假
以後就得努力工作了—減肥。

小林： 可不是嗎？我也重了好幾磅，可別變成了「火雞」才好。
咱們快去運動場或（者）健身房鍛練一下吧！

My questions:

对话

（感恩节过后，小林在校园裏碰到小李、小高。）

小高：嘿！小林，怎么样？感恩节还好吗？回家了没有？

小林：回家了。正好星期五没课，可以早一天走。在家里真好，
比宿舍舒服多了　我妈妈做的火鸡特别好吃，是中国式的。

小高：你真有口福！是坐飞机回去的吗？怎么不告诉我？我可以
送你去机场。

小林：那怎么好意思。而且是上午的飞机，所以一早就得走。我
在校门口搭了部去机场的小巴，很方便。从这儿去机场只
要四十多分钟。　你回家了吗？

小高：没有，期末要交几个报告，正好利用上个礼拜做做研究。
不过我也吃了火鸡和南瓜派，是在超级市场买的。

小林：小李，你呢？是不是也一肚子的火鸡？

小李：可不是吗？我那些美国朋友真好客，都要请我去他们家吃
饭。下午一顿，晚上又一顿，你们看！（拍拍自己的肚
子）我的肚子是不是越来越大了？

小高：还好，还好，只要少喝点儿汽水儿就行了。看起来只有「
两个月大」。（笑）

小李：（打小高）别开玩笑了，说真的，放假的时候大吃大喝，
放假以后就得努力工作了—减肥。

小林：可不是吗？我也重了好几磅，可别变成了「火鸡」才好。
咱们快去运动场或（者）健身房锻练一下吧！

Duìhuà

(Gǎn'ēnjié guò hòu, Xiǎo Lín zài xiàoyuán .lǐ pèng.dào Xiǎo Lǐ hé Xiǎo Gāo.)

Xiǎo Gāo: Hèi! Xiǎo Lín, zěn.meyàng? Gǎn'ēnjié hái hǎo .ma? Huíjiā .le méi.yǒu?

Xiǎo Lín: Huíjiā .le. Zhènghǎo xīngqīwǔ méi kè, kě.yǐ zǎo yī tiān zǒu. Zài jiā .lǐ zhēn hǎo, bǐ sùshè shū.fú duō .le. Wǒ mā.mā zuò.de huǒjī tèbié hǎochī, shì Zhōng.guóshì .de.

Xiǎo Gāo: Nǐ zhēn yǒu kǒufú! Shì zuò fēijī huíqù .de .ma? Zěn.me bú gào.sù wǒ? Wǒ kě.yǐ sòng nǐ qù jīchǎng.

Xiǎo Lín: Nà zěn.me hǎoyì.si. Érqiě shì shàng.wǔ .de fēijī, suǒ.yǐ yìzǎo jiù děi zǒu. Wǒ zài xiào ménkǒu dā .le bù qù jīchǎng .de xiǎobā, hěn fāngbiàn. Cóng zhèr qù jīchǎng zhǐ yào sìshí duō fēnzhōng. Nǐ huíjiā .le .ma?

Xiǎo Gāo: Méi.yǒu. Qīmò yào jiāo jǐ .ge bàogào, zhènghǎo lìyòng shàng .ge lǐbài zuò.zuò yánjiū, búguò wǒ yě chī .le huǒjī hé nánguāpài, shì zài chāojí shìchǎng mǎi .de.

Xiǎo Lín: Xiǎo Lǐ, nǐ .ne? Shì .bú.shì yě yí dù.zi .de huǒjī?

Xiǎo Lǐ: Kě bú.shì .ma? Wǒ nèi xiē Měi.guó péng.yǒu zhēn hàokè, dōu yào qǐng wǒ qù tā.men jiā chīfàn. Xià.wǔ yí dùn, wǎn.shàng yòu yí dùn, nǐ.men kàn! (Pāi.pāi zìjǐ .de dù.zi) Wǒ.de dù.zi shì .bu.shì yuè lái yuè dà .le?

Xiǎo Gāo: Hái hǎo, hái hǎo, zhǐyào shǎo hē .diǎnr qìshuǐr jiù xíng .le. Kàn.qǐ.lái zhǐ yǒu "liǎng .ge yuè" dà.

Xiǎo Lǐ: (Dǎ Xiǎo Gāo) Bié kāiwánxiào .le. Shuō zhēn.de, fàngjià .de shí.hòu dà chī dà hē, fàngjià yǐhòu jiù děi nǔlì gōngzuò .le — jiǎnféi.

Xiǎo Lín: Kě bú.shì .ma? Wǒ yě zhòng .le hǎo jǐ bàng, kě bié biànchéng .le "huǒjī" cái hǎo. Zán.men kuài qù yùndòngchǎng huò(.zhě) jiànshēnfáng duàn.liàn.yíxià .ba!

Dialogue

(After Thanksgiving, Xiǎo Lín runs into Xiǎo Lǐ and Xiǎo Gāo on campus.)

Xiǎo Gāo: Hey! Xiǎo Lín, how is everything going? Did you have a nice Thanksgiving? Did you go home?

Xiǎo Lín: Yes, I did. Because I didn't have classes on Friday, I could leave a day early. It was really nice to be home, much more comfortable than my dorm. The turkey my mother made was especially delicious. It was (cooked in) Chinese style.

Xiǎo Gāo: You are really lucky. Did you go home by plane? Why didn't you tell me? I could have given you a ride to the airport.

Xiǎo Lín: That would have been too much trouble. Besides, it was a morning flight, so I had to leave very early. I took a mini-bus that went to the airport from the entrance of the school. It was very convenient. It took only a little over forty minutes from here to the airport. Did you go home?

Xiǎo Gāo: No. I have to hand in several papers at the end of the semester. I made good use of last week to do some research, but I also had turkey and pumpkin pie. I bought them in the supermaket.

Xiǎo Lín: Xiǎo Lǐ, how about you? Did you have a stomach full of turkey, too?

Xiǎo Lǐ: Isn't that what we (always) do? My American friends were really hospitable. They all wanted to invite me to have dinner at their places. One meal in the afternoon, another meal in the evening. See! (Patting his stomach.) Isn't it true that my stomach is getting bigger and bigger?

Xiǎo Gāo: It's O.K. as long as you drink less soda. (It) only looks like "two months (pregnant)" to me. (Laughing.)

Xiǎo Lǐ: (Hitting Xiǎo Gāo.) Quit joking. Be serious; we eat and drink a lot on the holidays, so we have to work hard after the break— (we) go on a diet.

Xiǎo Lín: Isn't that true? I have also gained several pounds. But I won't let myself become a "turkey." Let's go to the athletic field or gym to work out!

Mini-Dialogue
小對話 Xiǎoduìhuà

Talking about the holidays

1. A: 你感恩節回家了沒有？

   Nǐ Gǎn'ēnjié huíjiā .le méi.yǒu?
   Did you go home for Thanksgiving?

   B: 沒有。我留在這兒寫報告。

   Méi.yǒu. Wǒ liú zài zhèr xiě bàogào.
   No. I stayed here and wrote papers.

2. A: 你感恩節過得怎麼樣？

   Nǐ Gǎn'ēnjié guò.de zěn.meyàng?
   How was your Thanksgiving?

   B: 不錯，吃了一頓又一頓。

   Búcuò, chī .le yí dùn yòu yí dùn.
   Not bad! I had one meal after another.

Talking about transportation

1. A: 你感恩節回家了嗎？是怎麼走的？

   Nǐ Gǎn'ēnjié huíjiā .le .ma? Shì zěn.me zǒu .de?
   Did you go home for Thanksgiving? How did you go?

   B: 我是坐飛機回去的。

   Wǒ shì zuò fēijī huí.qù .de.
   I went back by plane.

2. A: 你每天怎麼來學校？是開車來的嗎？

   Nǐ měitiān zěn.me lái xuéxiào? Shì kāichē lái .de .ma?
   How do you come to school every day? Do you drive to school?

   B: 不，是走路來的。我住得離學校不遠，十分鐘就到了。

   Bù, shì zǒulù lái .de. Wǒ zhù.de lí xuéxiào bù yuǎn, shí fēnzhōng jiù dào .le.
   No. I walk. I live close to the school. It takes only ten minutes.

Vocabulary
生詞 Shēngcí

◎ **By Order of Appearance**

感恩節	感恩节	Gǎn'ēnjié	N	[feel-gratitude-festival] Thanksgiving
正好		zhènghǎo	Adv	[right-good] exactly right (at the moment), exactly right (amount)
火雞	火鸡	huǒjī	N	[fire-chicken] turkey(M: 隻)
式		shì	N	style (Suf)
口福		kǒufú	N	[mouth-blessing] enjoyment of the palate
坐		zuò	V/CV	to go by (bus, airplane, ship)
飛機	飞机	fēijī	N	[fly-machine] airplane (M: 架 jià)
告訴	告诉	gào.sù	V	[tell-tell] to tell
送		sòng	V	to take (someone to some place); to see (a person) off
* 接		jiē	V	to pick someone up
(飛)機場	(飞)机场	(fēi)jīchǎng	N	[fly-machine-field] airport (M: 個)
怎麼好意思	怎么好意思	zěn.me hǎo yì.si	IE	[how-good-meaning] how can (one) let someone do...?
* 不好意思		bù hǎo yì.si	IE	[not-good-meaning] (to be) ashamed, (to be) embarrassed, feel shy
一早		yìzǎo	N/MTA	[one-early] early morning
搭		dā	V	to take (a vehicle, an airplane, a ship)
小巴		xiǎobā	N	[small-bus] van, mini-bus (M: 部/輛)
* 公車	公车	gōngchē	N	[public-car] bus (M: 部/輛)
* 公共汽車	公共汽车	gōnggòng qìchē	N	[public-car] bus (M: 部/輛)
方便		fāngbiàn	SV	[direction-convenient] (to be) convenient
只要		zhǐ yào	Adv/Conj	[only-want] only (if/takes)
期末		qīmò	N	[period-end] end of a semester
交		jiāo	V	to turn in (homework), to pay (a fee)
報告	报告	bàogào	N/V	[report-tell] report, (term) paper (M: 篇/個)
* 作業	作业	zuòyè	N	[do-profession] homework (= 功課)

利用		lìyòng	V	[profit-use] to utilize, to use (time/tool/chance)
南瓜派		nánguāpài	N	[south-melon-pie] pumpkin pie
超級市場	超级市场	chāojí shìchǎng	N	[surpass-grade-city-field] supermarket (M: 個)
肚子		dù.zi	N	[stomach-Suf] stomach (belly)
好客		hàokè	SV	[to like-guest] (to be) hospitable
頓	顿	dùn	M	measure word for meals
行		xíng	SV	(to be) all right, can do, O.K.
看起來	看起来	kàn.qǐ.lái	V	(it) looks, (it) seems
開玩笑	开玩笑	kāiwánxiào	V	[open-play-laugh] to crack a joke, to joke
說眞的	说真的	shuō zhēn.de	IE	be serious!; quit kidding/joking!
放假		fàngjià	V	[release-holiday] to have a holiday/vacation
大吃大喝		dà chī dà hē	IE	[big-eat-big-drink] to eat and drink a lot
努力		nǔlì	SV	[exert-strength] (to be) hard-working
減肥		jiǎnféi	V	[reduce-fat] to go on a diet
* 節食	节食	jiéshí	V	[restrain-eat] to go on a diet (=減肥)
重		zhòng	V	to gain weight
好幾-	好几-	hǎojǐ-	Adj	[good-several] several
磅		bàng	N	pound
變成	变成	biànchéng	V	[change-accomplish] to become
運動場	运动场	yùndòngchǎng	N	[move-move-field] athletic field
或(者)		huò(.zhě)	Conj	or
健身房		jiànshēnfáng	N	[health-body-room] gym
鍛練	锻练	duàn.liàn	V	[forge-refine] to do physical training

◎ By Grammatical Categories

Nouns/Pronouns

感恩節	感恩节	Gǎn'ēnjié	N	[feel-gratitude-festival] Thanksgiving
一早		yìzǎo	N/MTA	[one-early] early morning
火雞	火鸡	huǒjī	N	[fire-chicken] turkey (M: 隻)
式		shì	N	style (Suf)
口福		kǒufú	N	[mouth-blessing] enjoyment of the palate
飛機	飞机	fēijī	N	[fly-machine] airplane (M: 架 jià)
(飛)機場	(飞)机场	(fēi)jīchǎng	N	[fly-machine-field] airport (M: 個)
小巴		xiǎobā	N	[small-bus] van, mini-bus (M: 部/輛)
* 公車	公车	gōngchē	N	[public-car] bus (M: 部/輛)
* 公共汽車	公共汽车	gōnggòng qìchē	N	[public-car] bus (M: 部/輛)
期末		qīmò	N	[period-end] end of a semester
報告	报告	bàogào	N/V	[report-tell] report, (term) paper (M: 篇/個)
* 作業	作业	zuòyè	N	[do-profession] homework (=功課)
南瓜派		nánguāpài	N	[south-melon-pie] pumpkin pie
超級市場	超级市场	chāojí shìchǎng	N	[surpass-grade-city-field] supermarket (M: 個)
肚子		dù.zi	N	[stomach-Suf] stomach (belly)
磅		bàng	N	pound
運動場	运动场	yùndòngchǎng	N	[move-move-field] athletic field
健身房		jiànshēnfáng	N	[health-body-room] gym

Measure Words

頓	顿	dùn	M	measure word for meals

Verbs/Stative Verbs/Adjectives

坐	zuò	V/CV	to go by (bus, airplane, ship)
搭	dā	V	to take (a vehicle, an airplane, a ship)
送	sòng	V	to take (someone to some place); to see (a person) off
* 接	jiē	V	to pick someone up
交	jiāo	V	to turn in (homework), to pay (a fee)
告訴	告诉	gào.sù	V	[tell-tell] to tell

利用		lìyòng	V	[profit-use] to utilize, to use (time/tool/chance)
看起來	看起来	kàn.qǐ.lái	V	(it) looks, (it) seems
開玩笑	开玩笑	kāiwánxiào	V	[open-play-laugh] to crack a joke, to joke
放假		fàngjià	V	[release-holiday] to have a holiday/vacation
減肥		jiǎnféi	V	[reduce-fat] to go on a diet
* 節食	节食	jiéshí	V	[restrain-eat] to go on a diet (=減肥)
鍛練	锻练	duàn.liàn	V	[forge-refine] to do physical training
變成	变成	biànchéng	V	[change-accomplish] to become
方便		fāngbiàn	SV	[direction-convenient] (to be) convenient
好客		hàokè	SV	[to like-guest] (to be) hospitable
努力		nǔlì	SV	[exert-strength] (to be) hard-working
行		xíng	SV	(to be) all right, can do, O.K.
重		zhòng	V	to gain weight
好幾-	好几-	hǎojǐ-	Adj	[good-several] several

Adverbs

正好		zhènghǎo	Adv	[right-good] exactly right (at the moment), exactly right (amount)
只要		zhǐ yào	Adv/ Conj	[only-want] only (if/takes)

Conjunctions

或(者)		huò(.zhě)	Conj	or

Idiomatic Expressions

怎麼好意思	怎么好意思	zěn.me hǎo yì.si	IE	[how-good-meaning] how can (one) let someone do...?
* 不好意思		bù hǎo yì.si	IE	[not-good-meaning] (to be) ashamed, (to be) embarrassed, feel shy
說眞的	说真的	shuō zhēn.de	IE	be serious!; quit kidding/joking!
大吃大喝		dà chī dà hē	IE	[big-eat-big-drink] to eat and drink a lot

✚ **Supplementary Vocabulary**

1. Odds and Ends

校園	校园	xiàoyuán	N	[school-garden] campus
節日	节日	jiérì	N	[festival-day] holiday, festival
過節	过节	guòjié	N	[pass-festival] to observe a holiday, to celebrate a festival
身高		shēngāo	N	[body-high] body height
體重	体重	tǐzhòng	N	[body-heavy] body weight
胖了		pàng .le	V	[fat-Asp] to gain weight
瘦了		shòu .le	V	[skinny-Asp] to lose weight
輕了	轻了	qīng .le	V	[light-Asp] to lose weight

2. Measurement

盎斯	àngsī	N	ounce
英尺	yīngchǐ	N	[English-foot] British foot
英寸	yīngcùn	N	[English-inch] British inch
公斤	gōngjīn	N	[public-catty] kilogram
公克	gōngkè	N	[public-gram] gram
公尺	gōngchǐ	N	[public-foot] meter
公分	gōngfēn	N	[public-divide] centimeter

3. Vehicle and Action

汽車	汽车	qìchē	N	[vapor-car] car, automobile
校車	校车	xiàochē	N	[school-car] school bus
計程車	计程车	jìchéngchē	N	[calculate-distance-car] taxi
出租汽車	出租汽车	chūzū qìchē	N	[out-rent-car] taxi
火車	火车	huǒchē	N	[fire-car] train
自行車	自行车	zìxíngchē	N	[self-walk-car] bicycle
腳踏車	脚踏车	jiǎotàchē	N	[foot-tread-car] bicycle
機車	机车	jīchē	N	[machine-car] motorcycle
摩托車	摩托车	mótuōchē	N	[motor-car] motorcycle
船		chuán	N	boat, ship
騎	骑	qí	V	to ride (a bicycle, a motorcycle, a horse)
開車	开车	kāichē	V	[open-car] to drive (a car)
走路		zǒulù	V	[walk-road] to walk, to go on foot

Characters
漢字 Hànzì

送	行	門	口
回	家	宿	舍
放	假	星	期
玩	笑	火	雞
鐘	節	市	只

送

sòng
to send, deliver,
give (a gift) 辶
10

*送行   sòngxíng   to see somebody off
*送客   sòngkè   to see a visitor out

A: 你明天上午可以**送**我到機場去嗎？
B: 可以，我正好上午沒課。

行

xíng
be fine, will do
行
6   (to walk)

*不行   bùxíng   won't do, won't go

A: 我明天給他寫信，**行不行**？
B: **不行**，你得立刻給他打電話。

門

mén
door   門
8   (door)

門口   ménkǒu   entrance, doorway

A: 我們不是說好了下課以後在**校門口**見嗎？
B: 沒錯，我等了三十分鐘，你沒來，我就走了。

口

kǒu
mouth; opening;
gate   口
3   (mouth)

口福   kǒufú   enjoyment of the palate

A: 今天的菜裏酸辣湯最好，可是你正好不能吃辣的。
B: 我就是**沒有口福**。

繁簡對照：	其他漢字：	✎ **My notes:**
門门	*接 SC35 *校 SC36	

回

huí
to return, to
reply　　口
6

回家　　huíjiā　　to go home
回去　　huí.qù　　to go back

A: 期末交完報告以後，你要上哪兒去？
B: 我要**回家**去。

家

jiā
family, home
　　宀
10

*家人　　jiārén　　family (members)
*家庭　　jiātíng　　family

A: 你**家**在哪兒？
B: 我**家**在大學那兒。

宿

sù
to stay
overnight　宀
11

*宿舍　　sùshè　　dormitory

A: 咱們快回**宿舍**去吧！
B: 好，咱們要走路回去還是開車回去？

舍

shè
a house; an inn
　　　舌
8　　(tongue)

*旅舍　　lǚshè　　an inn

A: 放假以後你還會在**宿舍**嗎？
B: 會，我不回家。

繁簡對照：	其他漢字：	✎ **My notes:**

放假　　　fàngjià　　　to have a day off, to have holidays

*放下　　　fàng.xià　　　to put down

放
fàng
to put, place,
let go　　攵
8

A: 我們什麼時候**放假**？
B: 快了，再過兩個星期就**放假**了。

*請假　　　qǐngjià　　　to ask for leave
*事假　　　shìjià　　　leave of absence (to attend to private affairs)

*假日　　　jiàrì　　　day off, holiday
*假期　　　jiàqī　　　vacation

假
jià
holiday, leave
of absence　亻
11　　(person)

A: 明天我得去機場，不能去上課。
B: 你得先跟老師**請假**。

星期　　　xīngqī　　　week (days of the week)

星
xīng
star; planet　日
9　　(sun)

A: **這星期**我得交兩個報告。你別來找我。
B: 誰要來找你？你還是少說話多做事吧！

期末　　　qīmò　　　end of a semester
學期　　　xuéqī　　　semester
*假期　　　jiàqī　　　holiday, vacation

期
qī
period, time　月
12　　(moon)

A: 我想利用**這個星期**寫完**期末報告**。
B: 你不是開玩笑吧！

繁簡對照：	其他漢字：	✎ **My notes:**

| 開玩笑 | kāiwánxiào | to crack a joke |
| *好玩 | hǎowán | (to be) amusing, interesting |

玩
wán
to play　玉
8　　(jade)

A: 他這個人就是喜歡**開玩笑**，你別放在心上。
B: 沒事兒。

開玩笑	kāiwánxiào	to crack a joke
*好笑	hǎoxiào	(to be) funny
*笑話	xiào.huà	joke
*鬧笑話	nàoxiào.huà	to make a fool of oneself

笑
xiào
to laugh, smile
竹
10　(bamboo)

A: 那不是個喜劇片嗎？
B: 可是一點兒也不**好笑**。

火雞	huǒjī	turkey
*火車	huǒchē	train
*一肚子火	yí dù.zi huǒ	full of anger (lit. a belly of fire)

火
huǒ
fire, flames　火
4　　(fire)

A: 別生氣了，咱們快走吧！我請你去看電影。
B: 我**一肚子火**，看電影也沒用。

| *雞肉 | jīròu | chicken (as food) |
| *雞蛋 | jīdàn | (hen's) egg |

雞
jī
chicken　隹
18　(short-tailed birds)

A: 他喜歡吃**雞蛋**，每天早上都吃好幾個。
B: 他不知道吃太多**雞蛋**對身體不好嗎？

| 繁簡對照： | 其他漢字： | ✎ **My notes:** |
| 雞鸡 | *哭 SC37
*鴨 SC38 | |

鐘

zhōng
clock, bell 金
20   (metal)

no. 分鐘   no. fēnzhōng   no. of minutes
*鐘頭   zhōngtóu   hour
*…點鐘   …diǎnzhōng   …o'clock

A: 從這兒到機場要多長時間 ？
B: 四十多**分鐘** 。

節

jié
joint, holiday,
M for classes
            竹
15   (bamboo)

感恩節   Gǎn'ēnjié   Thanksgiving
*耶誕節   Yēdànjié   Christmas
*節日   jiérì   holiday
*一節課   yì jié kè   one session/class

A: 中國人過不過**耶誕節** ？
B: 現在也過了 。

市

shì
market, city 巾
5   (towel)

超級市場   chāojí shìchǎng   supermarket
市場   shìchǎng   market
*城市   chéngshì   city

A: 你一個月到**市場**買幾次菜 ？
B: 四次 。

只

zhǐ
merely   口
5   (mouth)

只好   zhǐhǎo   the only alternative is…
只要   zhǐ yào   only want; only (takes)
*只有   zhǐ yǒu   only have

A: 到學校去的公車方便嗎 ？
B: 很方便，每十五分鐘有一班車，**只要**八
   分鐘就到學校了 。

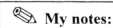

繁簡對照：	其他漢字：	✎ **My notes:**
鐘 钟 節 节	*式 SC39 *越 SC40	

Grammar
語法 yǔfǎ

A Major Sentence Patterns 主要句型 zhǔyào jùxíng

1. 坐 …到/回 …來/去 construction

Structure	Gloss
S (要) 坐 Conveyance 到/回 Place 來/去 VO	S come/go to Place to VO by Conveyance

1. 小林坐什麼回家去過感恩節？

   Xiǎo Lín zuò shén.me huíjiā qù guò Gǎn'ēnjié?
   How did Xiao Lin get home to celebrate Thanksgiving?

   小林坐飛機回家去過感恩節。

   Xiǎo Lín zuò fēijī huíjiā qù guò Gǎn'ēnjié.
   Xiao Lin went home by airplane to celebrate Thanksgiving.

2. 你們要怎麼到學校去上課？

   Nǐ.men yào zěn.me dào xuéxiào qù shàngkè?
   How will you get to school (to attend class)?

   我要騎自行車到學校去上課，他要走路去。

   Wǒ yào qí zìxíngchē dào xuéxiào qù shàngkè, tā yào zǒulù qù.
   I will ride a bicycle to school to attend class; he will walk (to school).

3. 你的朋友要怎麼到美國來？

   Nǐ.de péng.yǒu yào zěn.me dào Měi.guó lái?
   How will your friend come to America?

   他要坐船來。

   Tā yào zuò chuán lái.
   He will come by boat.

4. 王老師要怎麼來上課？

   Wáng lǎoshī yào zěn.me lái shàngkè?
   How will Teacher Wang get to the class?

   王老師要開車來。

   Wáng lǎoshī yào kāichē lái.
   Teacher Wang will drive (to the class).

 The word order of this pattern follows the Temporal Sequence Principle. The subject must first take a conveyance in order to go to school to attend class. Thus you would say 我坐飛機回家, *not* 我回家坐飛機. When the conveyance provides seats, you use the co-verb/preposition 坐 zuò 'to go by or to ride,' e.g., 坐汽車 zuò qìchē 'to go by car,' 坐船 zuò chuán 'to go by ship.' If you must straddle the conveyance in order to "ride" on it, then you use the verb 騎 qí 'to ride,' e.g., 騎自行車 qí zìxíngchē 'to ride a bicycle.' If you drive somewhere, then you use the verb 開 kāi 'to drive or to operate,' e.g., 開車 kāi chē 'to drive a car.' If you go someplace on foot, then you use the verb 走路 zǒulù '[walk-road] to walk.'

2. 是 坐 ...到/回 ...來/去 的 **construction**

Structure	Gloss
S 是 坐 Conveyance 到 Place 來/去 的 嗎 ?	Is it by Conveyance that S come/go to Place? Did S come/go to Place by Conveyance?

1. 你是坐飛機到美國來的嗎？

    Nǐ shì zuò fēijī dào Měi.guó lái .de .ma?
    Did you come to America by airplane ?

    對，我 是 坐飛機到美國來的。

    Duì, wǒ shì zuò fēijī dào Měi.guó lái .de.
    Yes, I came to America by airplane.

    不 ，我 不 是 坐飛機來的，(我)是 坐船 來的。

    Bù, wǒ bú shì zuò fēijī lái .de, (wǒ) shì zuò chuán lái .de.
    No, I didn't come by airplane; (I) came by ship.

2. 小林是坐小巴到圖書館去的嗎？

    Xiǎo Lín shì zuò xiǎobā dào túshūguǎn qù .de .ma?
    Did Xiao Lin go to the library by mini-bus?

    對，小林是坐小巴到圖書館去 的 。

    Duì, Xiǎo Lín shì zuò xiǎobā dào túshūguǎn qù .de.
    Yes, Xiao Lin went to the library by mini-bus.

    不 ，小林不是坐小巴去的，他 是坐公車去的 。

    Bù, Xiǎo Lín bú shì zuò xiǎobā qù .de, tā shì zuò gōngchē qù .de.
    No, Xiao Lin didn't go by mini-bus; he went by public bus.

In this pattern, since the emphasis is on the conveyance, the emphatic marker 是 or 不是 must precede the conveyance.

3. 從 ...坐 ...到 ...來/去 **construction**

Structure	Gloss
S (MTA) (要) 從 Place₁ 坐 Conveyance 到 Place₂ 來/去 S (MTA) (要) 坐 Conveyance 從 Place₁ 到 Place₂ 來/去	(Time) S (will) come/go from Place₁ to Place₂ by Conveyance

1. 你要從什麼地方坐飛 到中國去？

Nǐ yào cóng shén.me dì.fāng zuò fēijī dào Zhōng.guó qù?
From where will you fly to China?

我要從印地坐飛機到中國去。

Wǒ yào cóng Yìndì zuò fēijī dào Zhōng.guó qù.
I will fly from Indianapolis to China.

2. 你要坐什麼從印地到中國去？

Nǐ yào zuò shén.me cóng Yìndì dào Zhōng.guó qù?
How will you get from Indianapolis to China?

我要坐飛機從印地到中國去。

Wǒ yào zuò fēijī cóng Yìndì dào Zhōng.guó qù.
I will take an airplane from Indianapolis to China.

 When an expression involves both the departing point and the conveyance, the word order of these two components follows the Principle of Simultaneous Existence, because, in reality, when you are departing from a place the conveyance is also *at* that place. In a question, you may inquire about either the departure point, as in example 1, or the conveyance, as in example 2.

See L 5–A2.2 for more on the Principle of Simultaneous Existence.

4. Pivotal construction

Structure	Gloss
S_1 V_1 [O_1/S_2 V_2 O_2]	S_1 V_1O_1 to V_2O_2

1. 你請誰來你家過感恩節？

Nǐ qǐng shéi lái nǐ jiā guò Gǎn'ēnjié?
Whom did you invite to come to your home to celebrate Thanksgiving?

我請他來我家過感恩節。

Wǒ qǐng tā lái wǒ jiā guò Gǎn'ēnjié.
I invited him to come to my home to celebrate Thanksgiving.

2. 小高叫誰別看電視？

Xiǎo Gāo jiào shéi bié kàn diànshì?
Whom did Xiao Gao tell not to watch TV?

小高叫小李別看電視。

Xiǎo Gāo jiào Xiǎo Lǐ bié kàn diànshì.
Xiao Gao told Xiao Lǐ not to watch TV.

A pivotal construction/sentence (兼語句 jiānyǔjù), consists of a verb V₁ followed by a nominal expression serving as the object of V₁ and at the same time serving as the subject of V₂. Verbs such as 請 qǐng 'requests, invites, asks,' 叫 jiào 'causes, tells,' 讓 ràng 'lets,' and 要 yào 'wants,' which belong to the "cause" type and take clauses as their objects, can occur in a pivotal construction.

5. 只要… 就… construction

Structure	Gloss
S 只要 Adv VO 就… 只要 S Adv VO 就… 只要 VO S 就…	So (As) long as S VO…/Only if S VO…then…
只要 No M N 就…	(It) takes only No M…

1. 我的肚子越來越大了，怎麼辦？

   Wǒ.de dù.zi yuè lái yuè dà .le, zěn.me bàn?
   My stomach is getting bigger and bigger, what should I do?

   你只要少喝一點兒汽水兒就行了。

   Nǐ zhǐyào shǎo hē yìdiǎnr qìshuǐr jiù xíng .le
   It will be fine as long as you you drink less soda.

2. 我的聲調老說不對，怎麼辦？

   Wǒ .de shēngdiào lǎo shuō bú duì, zěn.me bàn?
   I always pronounce the tones wrong, what should I do?

   只要你多練習就行了。

   Zhǐyào nǐ duō liàn.xí jiù xíng .le.
   So long as you do more practice it will be fine.

3. 坐公共汽車到學校去要多久？

   Zuò gōnggòng qìchē dào xuéxiào qù yào duójiǔ?
   How long will it take to get to school by bus?

   只要十分鐘就到了。

   Zhǐyào shí fēn zhōng jiù dào .le.
   (It) takes only ten minutes to get there.

4. 坐飛機到紐約去要多久？

   Zuò fēijī dào Niǔyuē qù yào duójiǔ?
   How long will it take to get to New York by airplane?

   只要兩個小時就到了。

   Zhǐyào liǎng .ge xiǎoshí jiù dào .le.
   (It) takes only two hours to get there.

In examples 1 and 2, 只要...就 functions as conjunctions to form a conditional sentence. 只要 is a movable adverb, thus it may precede the subject (S) or follows the subject. In examples 3 and 4, 只要 functions as an adverb which modifies a noun phrase which consists of a number (No), a measure (M) and a noun.

B Usage of Common Phrases 詞組用法 cízǔ yòngfǎ

1. 多/少 V 一點兒 O expressions

Structure	Gloss
多/少 V 一點兒 O	V a little bit more/less of O

1. 我應該多做一點兒什麼？少看一點兒什麼？

   Wo yīnggāi duō zuò yì.diǎnr shén.me? shǎo kàn yì.diǎnr shén.me?
   What should I do a little bit more? (What should I) do a little bit less?

   你應該多做一點兒運動，少看一點兒電視。

   Nǐ yīnggāi duō zuò yì.diǎnr yùndòng, shǎo kàn yì.diǎnr diànshì.
   You should do a little bit more exercise, watch a little bit less TV.

2. 多吃一點兒什麼，少吃一點兒什麼才行呢？

   Duō chī yì.diǎnr shén.me? shǎo chī yì.diǎnr shén.me cái xíng .ne?
   It's not O.K. until (I) eat a little bit more of what? (and) eat a little bit less of what?

   多吃一點兒生菜，少吃一點兒肉就行了。

   Duō chī yì.diǎnr shēngcài, shǎo chī yì.diǎnr ròu jiù xíng .le.
   (It) will be fine if (you) eat a little bit more raw vegetables and eat a little bit less meat.

 In this pattern, 多 duō 'more' and 少 shǎo 'less' are adverbs that modify the verb 吃 chī 'eat,' whereas the adverb 一點兒 yì.diǎnr 'a little' serves as a complement to the verb. This pattern usually is used in giving suggestions or in persuading.

2. ...的時候 expression

Structure	Gloss
S [Adj/VO 的時候], ... (movable)	When S is/was/are/were Adj/Ving...,
NP 的時候, ...	At the time of NP,...

1. 放假的時候你做什麼了？   Fàngjià .de shí.hòu nǐ zuò shén.me .le?
                                                            What did you do on the holidays?

    放假的時候我大吃大喝，現在   Fàngjià .de shí.hòu wǒ dà chī dà hē,
    得努力減肥了。   xiànzài děi nǔlì jiǎnféi .le.
                                                            I ate and drank a lot on the holidays; now
                                                            (I) have to work hard to lose weight.

2. 你開車的時候不可以做什麼？   Nǐ kāichē .de shí.hòu bù kě.yǐ zuò shén.me?
                                                            What are you not allowed to do while you
                                                            are driving?

    我開車的時候不可以喝酒。   Wǒ kāichē .de shí.hòu bù kě.yǐ hē jiǔ.
                                                            While I am driving I am not allowed to drink.

 ... 的時候 '...time when' can be preceded by an adjective, a V-O expression, or a noun
(phrase) to form a time expression that may occur at the beginning of a sentence or follow
the subject.

3. The suggestion and command particle 吧

Structure	Gloss
S 快VO 吧！	Let's (hurry and) go to VO!
(S)快V(O)！	(S) hurry and go to VO!

1. 咱們快去坐小巴到飛機場吧！   Zá.men kuài qù zuò xiǎobā dào fēijīchǎng .ba!
                                                    Let's hurry and catch the mini-bus to the
                                                    airport!

2. (你們)快來運動！   Nǐ.men kuài lái yùndòng!
                                                    (You people) come to do exercise quickly!

 When adverb 快 kuài 'quickly or hurry' precedes a verb, it denotes doing something
quickly. In a sentence ending with 吧 .ba, it is a suggestion and its sentence intonation is
in a softer and slightly higher key. In a sentence without 吧 .ba, it is a command; its
intonation is stronger and there is a slight accelerated tempo toward the end of the
sentence.

4. Better not VO expression

Structure	Gloss
可別 VO 才好！	(X) better not VO!

1. 你每天喝牛奶，可別變成乳牛才好！

Nǐ měitiān hē niúnǎi, kě bié biànchéng rǔniú cái hǎo.
You drink milk every day; (you'd) better not become a cow!

2. 我天天大吃大喝，可別變成大南瓜才好！

Wǒ tiān.tiān dà chī dà hē, kě bié biànchéng dà'nánguā cái hǎo.
I eat and drink a lot every day; (I'd) better not become a big pumpkin!

5. 再 vs. 又

Structure	Gloss
S MTA 又（要） VO （了）	S (will) VO again
S MTA 又 VO （了）	S did VO again
S MTA （要）再 VO	S will VO again

1. 你昨天又喝了牛奶了嗎？

Nǐ zuó.tiān yòu hē .le niúnǎi .le ma?
Did you drink milk again yesterday?

對了，我昨天又喝了牛奶了。

Duì.le, wǒ zuó.tiān yòu hē.le niúnǎi .le.
Yes, I drank milk again yesterday.

2. 小林明年又要到臺灣去嗎？

Xiǎo Lín míng.nián yòu yào dào Táiwān qù .ma?
Is Xiao Lin going to Taiwan again next year?

對了，小林明年又要到臺灣去。

Duì.le, Xiǎo Lín míng.nián yòu yào dào Táiwān qù.
Yes, Xiao Lin is going to Taiwan again next year.

3. 你今天到圖書館去了嗎？

Nǐ jīn.tiān dào túshūguǎn qù .le .ma?
Did you go to the library today?

對了，我今天上午到圖書館去了，下午還要再去。

Duì.le, wǒ jīn.tiān shàng.wǔ dào túshūguǎn qù .le, xià.wǔ hái yào zài qù.
Yes, I went to the library this morning; (I) will go again this afternoon.

4. 別再看電視！

Bié zài kàn diànshì!
Don't watch TV again!

又 and 再 both mean "again." But 又 may be applied in the action that occured in the past or will occur in the future when *followed* by 要, while 再 may be applied only in the future action when it is *preceded* by 要 or in a command.

See L16–A2 for more on 又.

6. Subject omission

Structure	Gloss
S₁ VP₁, VP₂, VP₃...	S₁ VP₁, S₁VP₂, S₁VP₃...

1. 小林：(我)回家了。正好星期五
   沒課，可以早一天走。

   Xiǎo Lín: (Wǒ) huíjiā .le. Zhènghǎo
   xīngqīwǔ méi kè, kě.yǐ zǎo yì tiān zǒu.
   Xiao Lin: (I) went home. Because (I)
   didn't have classes on Friday, (I) could
   leave a day early.

In Chinese, within a conversational context or discourse, if the subject or actor has appeared/been mentioned in a previous sentence, then in the following sentence(s), the same subject need not be mentioned again.

ⓒ Reentry 複習 fùxí
1. More on ...的 N construction

Structure	Gloss
到 Place 去/來 的 N	The N that goes/comes to Place

1. 到中國去的飛機多不多？

   Dào Zhōng.guó qù .de fēijī duō .bùduō?
   Are there many airplanes that go to China?

   到中國去的飛機很多。

   Dào Zhōng.guó qù .de fēijī hěn duō.
   There are many airplanes that go to China.

2. 坐到學校來的公車方便嗎？

   Zuò dào xuéxiào lái .de gōngchē fāng.biàn
   .ma?
   Is it convenient to take the bus to school?

   坐到學校來的公車很方便。

   Zuò dào xuéxiào lái .de gōngchē hěn
   fāng.biàn.
   Taking the bus to school is very convenient.

Remember that in Chinese a subordinate clause that modifies a noun always *precedes* the noun, while in English the head noun is modified and *followed* by a clause that is always introduced by a relative pronoun (that, which, who).

Cultural Notes
文化點滴 wénhuà diǎndī

1. Chinese people consider anyone who has plenty of good things to eat as having 口福 kǒufú 'luck in having good food.' 福 fú stands for 福氣 fúqì 'good luck.' 有福氣 yǒufúqì means "to be lucky."

2. 中國人很好客 Zhōng.guórén hěn hàokè 'Chinese people are very hospitable.' They always serve the best food to their friends or strangers who visit them. In China, people are always welcome to drop by anytime and join the host family's meal, even uninvited.

3. Owing to long-term poverty and a low-fat diet (Chinese people eat lots of vegetables), Chinese usually don't 減肥 jiǎnféi '[to reduce-fat] to go on a diet' or 節食 jiéshí '[to restrain-eat] to go on a diet.' 瘦 shòu '(to be) skinny' is considered "poor and without food to eat," while 胖 pàng '(to be) fat' is considered 福相 fúxiàng '[good luck-image] a countenance of good luck.'

4. When someone gives you a gift or does you a favor, you should say (眞) 不好意思 (zhēn) bù hǎo yì.sì '(I really) feel embarrassed,' which means that you feel embarrassed to let her spend so much money buying the gift for you or so much time doing you a favor.

5. In China and Taiwan, buses are the most important form of mass transportation. It is common to see buses crowded with students and working people during rush hours. Chinese use the expression 公車擠得像沙丁魚 gōngchē jǐ.de xiàng shādīngyú 'The people on the bus were packed in like sardines' to describe the crowded situation.

Appendixes

Appendix 1. Review of Lessons 4-8

Check ☑ the box in front of the sentence patterns and usages that you have forgotten or do not understand. Review them with your teachers and classmates.

A. Asking Questions

☐ 1. With sentence-final particles 嗎, 呢 (L4, L5, L6)

1	S 是 O 嗎 ?	是/對了, S　是 O 不/不是 , S 不是 O
2	S MTA 有 O 嗎 ?	對(了), S MTA 有　　　O 不,　　　S MTA 沒(有) O
3	S MTA (也)(都)有 O 嗎 ?	對(了), S MTA　　　(也)(都)有　　　O 不,　　　S Time When(也)(都) 沒(有) O
4	S MTA 得 V O 嗎 ?	對, S　MTA 得　　V O 不, S　MTA 不必 V O 不, S　MTA 不用 V O
5	S (MTA) 要 上/到 Place 來/去 嗎 ? S (MTA) 上/到 Place 來/去 了 嗎 ?	S (MTA) (不)要 上/到 Place 來/去 S (MTA)　　　上/到 Place 來/去 了 S (MTA)　　　沒 上/到 Place 來/去
6	S₁ 是 X, S₂ 呢 ? S₁ Time When V O, S₂ 呢 ?	S₁ is X, how about S₂? S₁ Time When V O, how about S₂?

☐ 2. With choice-type/yes-no questions (L4, L5)

S　是不是　O ?	是/對了, S　是 O 不/不是, S 不是 O
S (MTA) 有沒有 O ? S (MTA) 有 O 沒有 ?	有,　S　(MTA)　　　有 O 沒有 , S　(MTA) 沒(有)O

☐ 3. With 還是 (coordinate construction) (L6)

S (AuxV) VO₁ 還是 VO₂ (呢) ? S (AuxV) VA　還是 B　　(呢) ?	S (AuxV) V (O) S (AuxV) VA/ S (AuxV) VB

❏ 4. With question words 幾, 甚麼, 哪兒, 誰, 誰的, 爲什麼, 多少 (L4, L5, L6, L7, L8)

When	S 是 星期幾 ? S 是 幾月幾號 ? S 哪一天 V O ? S 幾點鐘 V (O) ? S 什麼時候 V (O) ?	S 是 星期 no. S 是 no. 月 no. 號 S Time When V O S Time When V (O)
What	S MTA 有什麼 N ? S MTA 上什麼課 ? S MTA 做什麼 ?	S MTA 有 N/NP S MTA 上 X 課 S MTA VO
Where	S (MTA) (要)上 / 到哪兒來/去 ? 什麼地方	S (MTA)(要)上 / 到 Place 來/去 S (MTA) 上 / 到 Place 來/去了
Who	S 是 誰 ?	S 是 X
Whose	# 月 # 號是誰的生日 ?	no. 月 no. 號 是 X 的生日
Why	S 爲什麼 V O ? 爲什麼 S V O ?	Why do(es)/did S V O?
How much	N, 一 M 多少錢 ?	(N), 一 M No. $

B. Expressing identification

❏ 5. With verb 是 (L4)

S +	Equative Verb +	O
(N/NP)	(EV)	(N/NP)
S (也)	是	O
S (也) 不是	O	
S (不)是 A, 也(不)是 B		
S 不是 A, 也不是 B, 而是 C		

❏ 6. With verb 姓/叫 (L8)

您貴姓 ? / S 姓什麼 ?	S 姓 X
S 姓 / 叫 什麼名字 ?	S 叫 X
S 姓 / 叫 X 嗎 ?	S 姓 / 叫 X 不，S 不(是)姓 / 叫 X

C. *Indicating Existence*

❑ 7. With verb 有 (L7)

Place 有沒有 X？	Is there X at Place?
Place 有 X	There is X at Place
Place 沒有 X	There is no X at Place

D. *Indicating Action*

❑ 8. In progress (L8)

S (正) 在 V O (呢)	S is (in the midst of) Ving O

❑ 9. In sequence (L7)

S 先 $V_1 O_1$，再 $V_2 O_2$	S will $V_1 O_1$ first, (and) then $V_2 O_2$

❑ 10. Completed/Changed (L6, L7)

S V 了 O 嗎？	Did S V O?
S V 了 O 沒有？	Has S V-ed O?
S V 了 O 了	S did V O
S 還沒 V O 呢！	S hasn't V-ed O yet
S (已經) V (O) 了 嗎？	Has S already V-ed O?
S V (O) 了沒有？	
S (已經/早就) V (O) 了	S has already V-ed (O)
O, S 已經 V＋RE 完＋了	S has finished Ving O

❑ 11. Imminent (L6)

S (快要) V (O) 了 嗎？	Is S about to V (O)?
S V 了 (O) 沒有？	
S (快要) V (O) 了	S is about to V (O)
S 還沒 V (O) 呢！	S has not yet V-ed (O)
O, S (還) 沒 V＋RE 完 (呢)！	S (still) hasn't finished Ving O (yet)

E. Expressing Time

☐ 12. By the clock (L6)

Gloss	O'clock		Quarter	Minute	Second
	點(鐘)		刻	分	秒
6:15	六點(鐘)		一刻		
4:15:7	四點			十五分	七秒
8:06	八點	(零)		六分	
10:03	十點	過		三分	
8:58	九點	差		兩分	

☐ 13. With the notion of "this," "last," and "next" (L6)

Gloss	Year	Month	Week	Weekend	Day
last	去年	上個月	上個星期	上個週末	昨天
this	今年	這個月	這個星期	這個週末	今天
next	明年	下個月	下個星期	下個週末	明天

☐ 14. With movable time adverb (MTA) (L5)

> MTA S (AuxV) VO
> S MTA (AuxV) VO

F. Indicating Location

☐ 15. With verb 在 (L7)

S (MTA) 在 哪兒 /甚麼地方 ?	S (MTA)　在 Place
S (MTA) 在不在 Place ?	S (MTA)不 在 Place
S (MTA) 在 Place 嗎 ?	

☐ 16. With place words (L7)

> Pron/N ＋ localizer

☐ 17. With the usage of 就 (L7)

X 就在 Place	X is right over at Place

G. *Expressing Movement*

☐ 18. Of going to some place to do something (L6)

S (MTA) (要) 上 / 到 Place 來/去 VO 嗎 ?
S (MTA) (不) (要) 上 / 到 Place 來/去 VO
S (MTA) (没) 上 / 到 Place 來/去 VO

H. *Expressing Emphasis*

☐ 19. With 是 ... 的 construction (L8)

S (是) Prep Phrase VO 的	It is/was Prep Phrase that S VO
S (是) 從 Place₁ (到 Place₂) 來 的	It was from Place₁ that S came to Place₂
S (是) Time When (從 Place₁) (到 Place₂) 來 的	It was Time When that S came (from Place₁ to Place₂)

☐ 20. With 才 ... 就要 construction (L7)

才 No. M 就要 No. 塊(錢)	(It's) only No. M and (it) costs No. dollars

☐ 21. With 不 是 ...嗎 expression (L8)

S 不 是 VO 嗎 ?	Isn't it true that S V O?
不 是 S VO 嗎 ?	

I. *Expressing Opinions/Comments*

☐ 22. With conjunctions 雖然 ..., 可是/不過... (L8)

S 雖然 ..., 可是/不過 (S) ...	Although S ..., but ...
雖然 S ..., 可是/不過 (S)...	

☐ 23. With Adj 倒是 (不) Adj, 可是/不過... (L8)

X,	Adj 倒是(不)Adj, 可是 ...	As for X, it's (not) Adj, but ...
Topic	Comment	

☐ 24. With the auxiliary verb 想 (L8)

S (不) 想 VO	S (doesn't/don't) want(s) to VO
S 想 [A 不/沒 VO]	S doesn't/didn't think that A VO

☐ 25. With the adverbial phrase 一點兒 (L7)

Adj 一點兒	a little bit Adj-er
有一點兒 SV	(is) a little bit too Adj

J. Others

☐ 26. 也、跟、和 (L5)

S (MTA) (Neg) V O, 也   (Neg) V O
S (MTA) (Neg) V₁ O₂ 跟/和 (Neg) V₂ O₂
A 跟/和 B (Time When) 都   (Neg) V O

☐ 27. Disyllabic Adj + 的 + N (L7)

Disyllabic Adj + 的 + N	The N that/which is Adj
Polysyllabic Adj + 的 + N	

Review of Lessons 9-13

Check ☑ the box in front of the sentence patterns and usages that you have forgotten or do not understand. Review them with your teachers and classmates.

A. *Indicating Action*

☐ 1. With potential result (L9)

V 得 RE 不 RE ?	can...V or not?
V 得 RE	can V...
V (得)不 RE	cannot V...

☐ 2. With descriptive complement (L10)

S V O V 得 (Adv) Adj S O V 得 (Adv) Adj	S V (very/quite) Adj O
S V O V 得 不 (Adv) Adj S O V 得 不 (Adv) Adj	S cannot V Adj O

☐ 3. With manner/degree complement (L11)

S (O) V 得 SV 不 SV ? S (O) V 得 怎麼樣 ?	Does S V (O) Adv or not? How does S V O?
S (VO) V 得 Adv SV S (VO) V 得 不 SV	S V (O) Adv Adj S V (O) not (Adv) Adj

☐ 4. With experiential aspect marker 過 (L10)

S V 過 O 嗎 ? S 沒 V 過 O 嗎 ?	Has S ever done ...(before)? Hasn't S done...(before)?
V 過 /S V 過 O 還沒 V 過 /S 還沒 V 過 O	S has done ... (before) S hasn't done... yet

☐ 5. In progress (L10)

S (正)V 著 O (呢) S V 著 (O) V (O)	S is (in the midst of) Ving O S V (O) while Ving (O)

❑ 6. Repeated (L12)

S（在 Place）V 來 V 去	S keeps on Ving back and forth (at a place)

❑ 7. Together (L9)

A 跟 B V$_i$ 在一塊兒	A and B V$_i$ together
A 跟 B 一塊兒 V (O)	A and B V(O) together

❑ 8. To another person (L9)

A 沒/要 給 B V　O A　　　給 B V 了 O	Co-verb	A didn't/will VO to B A did VO to B
A 沒/要 V O 給 B A　　　V 了 O 給 B A　　　V 了 O 給 B 了	Marker of indirect object construction	A didn't/will VO to B A did V　O to B A has V-ed O to B

❑ 9. Toward a person/thing (L10)

A　對 B　　（Adv）好 VO 對 B　　（Adv）好	A is (Adv) good/nice for/to B Ving O is (Adv) good for/to B
A　對 B 不（Adv）好 VO 對 B 不（Adv）好	A is not (Adv) good/nice for/to B Ving O is not (Adv) good for/to B

B. Expressing Movement

❑ 10. Of going/coming from one place to another (L9)

S Time When 從 Place$_1$ 到 Place$_2$ 來 /去	S is/was coming/going from Place$_1$ to Place$_2$ at/on Time When

❑ 11. Of going/coming to a place by conveyance (L13)

S（要）坐 conveyance 到/回 Place 來 /去 VO	S come/go to Place to VO by conveyace

❑ 12. Of going/coming from one place to another by conveyance (L13)

S (MTA)（要）從 Place$_1$ 坐 Conveyance 到 Place$_2$ 來/去 S (MTA)（要）坐 Conveyance 從 Place$_1$ 到 Place$_2$ 來/去	(Time) S (will) come/go from Place$_1$ to Place$_2$ by Conveyance.

C. *Expressing Comparison*

☐ 13. Explicitly (L10, L12)

A　比　B　Adj 嗎 ?	Is A Adj-er than B?
A　比　B　Adj	A is Adj-er than B
A　比　B　Adj (得) 多了	A is much more Adj-er than B
A　比　B　Adj 一點兒	A is a little bit Adj-er than B
A 不比　B　Adj	A is not as Adj as B

☐ 14. Implicitly (L10, L12)

(A 跟 B), 哪 M (比較) Adj ?	(As for A and B), which one is Adj-er?
A （比較） Adj	A is Adj-er
A Adj (得) 多了	A is much more Adj
A Adj 一點兒	A is a little bit more Adj

☐ 15. Of equaling-degree (L10, L12)

A 有沒有 B (這麼 / 那麼) Adj ?	Is A as Adj as B?
A　　有 B (這麼 / 那麼) Adj	A is as Adj as B
A　沒有 B (這麼 / 那麼) Adj	A is not as Adj as B

☐ 16. Of equal-degree (L10, L12)

A　跟 B　　一樣 Adj 嗎 ?	Are A and B equally Adj ?
A　跟 B　　一樣 Adj	A and B are equally Adj
A　跟 B 不一樣 Adj	A and B are not equally Adj
A 不跟 B　　一樣 Adj	A is not equally Adj with B

D. *Expressing Frequency*

☐ 17. Of how many times per day/month/year (L11)

S　一/每 ＋　天/年　VO 幾次 ?	How many times does S V O a day/ year?
S　一/每 ＋　天/年　V 幾次 O ?	
S 每 ＋ No. ＋ 天/年　VO 幾次 ?	How many times does S V O per no. of days/years?
S 每 ＋ No. ＋ 天/年　V 幾次 O ?	
S 每 ＋ (一) 個 ＋ 星期 / 月VO 幾次 ?	How many times does S V O a week/ month?
S 每 ＋ (一) 個 ＋ 星期 / 月V 幾次 O ?	
S (每) ＋ No. M N　　　VO 幾次 ?	How many times does S V O per no. of weeks/months/years?
S (每) ＋ No. M N　　　V 幾次 O ?	

❑ 18. Of how many times in the past/up to now (L11)

S V過 幾 次 O ? O, S V過 幾 次 ?	How many times did S V O (in the past)? As for O, how many times did S V it (in the past)?
S V過　　幾次 O 了？ S V過 O 幾次　　了？ O , S V過幾次　　了？	How many times has S done VO (up to this moment)? As for O, how many times has S done V (up to this moment)?

❑ 19. Of not even once (L11)

S O 一次 也/都 没V過 O, S 一次 也/都 没V過	S has never done V O even once As for O, S has never done V O even once

E. Expressing Condition

❑ 20. With the adverb 才 (L9)

S Time When 才 V (O)	S won't V (O) until Time When
S V₁ 了 O 　　才 V₂ (O)	S won't V₂ (O) until finishing doing V₁ O

❑ 21. With the conjunction 要是..., 就... (L11)

S (要是) ..., (S) 就 ... (MA)	If S. ..., (then) S....

❑ 22. With 只要... 就... construction (L13)

S 只要 Adv VO 就... 只要 S Adv VO 就... 只要 VO 　　S 就...	So (As) long as S VO.../Only if S VO...then...
只要 No M N 就...	(It) takes only No M...

❑ 23. With the adverb 越... 越 ... (L12)

S (O) 越 V越 Adj	The more S V (O), the more Adj he/she becomes
S 　　越來越 Adj	S becomes more/much Adj-er
S₁ 越 V(O), S₂ 越 Adj	The more S₁ V (O), the more S₂ becomes Adj

F. *Expressing Exclusiveness/Inclusiveness*

☐ 24. With question words (L11)

誰 ... 都(不)...	Everyone (No one)...
哪個人... 都(不)...	Everyone (No one)...

☐ 25. With prepositional phrase 除了... (以外) (L12)

(1) S 除了 N/VP (以外), 還/也 VO (2) 除了 N/VP (以外), S 還/也 VO	Besides N/Ving O, S V O
(3) 除了 A (以外), B 也 VO	Besides A, B V O

☐ 26. With correlative conjunctions 不是..., 就是... (L11)

不是 A, 就是 B	If it is not A, then it is B (It must be either A or B)

☐ 27. With the adverbial phrase 一點兒也/都 不 (L11)

S 一點兒也/都 不 AuxV (VO) O, S 一點兒也/都不 AuxV	S doesn't AuxV (VO) at all As for O, S doesn't AuxV at all

G. *Expressing Time*

☐ 28. With relative time expressions 以前/ 以後 (L9)

Time Expression+ 以前,... V O + 以前,... (reference point)	Before Time Expression, ... Before Ving O, ...

Time Expression   + 以後,...
          V 了 O + 以後,...
          V 完 O + 以後,...
(reference point)
	After Time Expression, ...
	After finishing VingO, ...

☐ 29. With 的時候 (L13)

S [Adj/VO 的時候], ... (movable)	When S is/was/are/were Adj/Ving...,
NP 的時候, ...	At the time of NP,...

☐ 30. With the word 次 (L11)

which time?	哪(一)次?
last time	上(一)次
this/that time	這(一)次/ 那(一)次
next time	下(一)次

H. Indicating Location

☐ 31. With preposition 在 (L9)

| 在...V | S (Time When) 在 Place V(O) | S V (O) at Place (Time When) |
| V 在... | S (Time When) V 在 Place | S V at/on/in Place (Time When) |

☐ 32. With prepositional phrase 在 ... 上 (L11)

| 在 N/NP 上 | In (the aspect of)..., in terms of... |

I. Expressing Emphasis

☐ 33. On conveyance (L13)

| S 是 坐 Conveyance 到 Place 來/去的嗎? | Is it by conveyance that S come/go to Place? Did S come/go to Place by conveyance ? |

☐ 34. Through topicalization (L9)

| O, S V/RV Topic, comment | As for O, S (can/cannot) V... |
| S, O V/RV | As for O, S (can/cannot) V... |

J. Expressing Opinions / Suggestions

☐ 35. With 看 (L9)

| 你看...怎麼樣? 你看...嗎?/...V-not-V...? | How about ...? Do you think ...?/ Will ...or not ? |
| 我看 X... | I think (in my opinion) X... |

❏ 36. With 多/少 expression (L13)

多/少 V一點兒 O	V a little bit more/ less of O

❏ 37. With 有什麼好V的 (L12)

X 有什麼好V的	What's the point of Ving X!

❏ 38. With 可別 VO 才好 (L13)

可別 VO 才好	(X) better not VO!

❏ 39. With 好像...似的 (L11)

S 好像...似的	It seems that S...

❏ 40. With the particle...好了 (L9)

咱們 V O 好了 你　 V O 好了	Let's just VO Why don't you just VO

❏ 41. With the particle 吧 (L10, L13)

(S) 來 (一) M N (吧)！ (S) 來 (一)點兒 N (吧)！	Let (S) have N! How about having/ordering N?
S 快VO吧！ (S) 快V(O)！	Let's (hurry and) go to VO! (S) hurry and go to VO!

K. Others

❏ 42. The auxiliary verbs 可以、能、會 (L9)

S (不) 可以/能/會 VO	S may/can/will (not) VO
可以	may, to be permitted to, it is all right to; can
能	may, to be permitted to = 可以; can, is able to (in terms of capability)
會	can, to know how to; will, could possibly or would probably

❑ 43. 請 vs. 問 (L9)

A 請 B VO	A invites/asks B to VO
A 問 B X	A asks B about X

❑ 44. 再 vs. 又 (L13)

S MTA 又 (要) 　 VO (了)	S (will) VO again
S MTA 又 　　 VO (了)	S did VO again
S MTA 　 (要) 再 VO	S will VO again

❑ 45. … + 的 + N (Chinese clause/complex sentences) (L10, L11, L13)

S V 的 O	The O that S V
[S$_2$ V$_2$ 的 N] SV$_1$ S$_1$	[The N which S$_2$ V$_2$] to be Adj$_1$ S$_1$
S$_1$ (AuxV) V$_1$ [S$_2$ V$_2$ 的 N] O	S$_1$ (AuxV) V$_1$ [The N which S$_2$ V$_2$] O

❑ 46. 的 as nominalizer (L12)

X 的 N → 　 X 的	X one
V(O) 的 N → V(O) 的	the one that V(O)

Appendix 2. Supplementary Characters 1-40

SC 1-8

1
您

nín
you (polite
form) 心
11 (heart)

2
人

rén
person, human
being 人
2 (person)

3
她

tā
she, her 女
6 (female)

4
它

tā
it 宀
5

5
畫

huà
to paint or draw
田
12 (field)

6
筆

bǐ
writing
instrument 竹
12 (bamboo)

7
紙

zhǐ
paper 糸
10

8
壞

huài
bad 土
19 (soil)

繁簡對照：

畫　画　　紙　纸
筆　笔　　壞　坏

SC 9-16

9 賣
mài
to sell   貝
15   (shell)

13 矮
ǎi
short; low 矢
13   (dart)

10 頓
dùn
M for meals
頁
13   (head)

14 英
yīng
flower,
outstanding 艹
9   (grass)

11 介
jiè
to lie between
人
4   (person)

15 漢
hàn
Chinese
language   氵
14   (water)

12 紹
shào
to connect 糸
11

16 跑
pǎo
to run   足
12   (foot)

繁簡對照：

賣 卖 試 试   漢 汉
頓 顿

SC 17-24

17
跳
tiào
to jump　足
13　　(foot)

21
愛
ài
to love　心
13　　(heart)

18
功
gōng
effort;
achievement
　　　力
5　　(strength)

22
抽
chōu
to take out (from
in between)　扌
8　　(hand)

19
冰
bīng
ice　　冫
6

23
煙
yān
smoke　火
13　　(fire)

20
杯
bēi
cup　　木
8　　(wood)

24
關
guān
to close　門
19　　(door)

繁簡對照：

愛爱　關关
煙烟

SC 25-32

25 部

bù
M for car;
section   阝
11   (city)

29 宜

yí
right; fitting
             宀
8

26 汽

qì
vapor, steam
             氵
7   (water)

30 戴

dài
to wear   戈
18   (weapon)

27 飽

bǎo
to be full   食
13   (to eat)

31 件

jiàn
M for things
             亻
6   (person)

28 便

pián, biàn
             亻
9   (person)

32 碗

wǎn
bowl   石
13   (stone)

繁簡對照：

飽饱

SC 33-40

33
公

gōng
public, open to
all　　八
4　　(eight)

34
司

sī
to have charge of
　　口
5　　(mouth)

35
接

jiē
to pick up, catch,
receive　　扌
11　　(hand)

36
校

xiào
school　　木
10　　(tree)

37
哭

kū
to cry　　口
10　　(mouth)

38
鴨

yā
duck　　鳥
16　　(bird)

39
式

shì
style, type, form
　　弋
6　　(to catch)

40
越

yuè
even more, the
more　　走
12　　(to walk)

繁簡對照：

鴨 鸭

Appendix 3. Radicals (Arranged by Number of Strokes)

In the following table you will find the 213 standard radicals (R) which are included in *A New Practical Chinese-English Dictionary*, edited by Liang Shih-chiu (Taipei). They are listed according to the number of strokes (S No.) used to write them. The spoken form in Pinyin romanization and an English meaning are also given; note that some radicals have no meaning.[1] The last column shows you the order in which to write the strokes.

Of the 213 standard radicals, only 35 have been simplified in the PRC. For easier recognition, we list the simplifications along with their standard counterparts. We list the rest of the radicals, which are used in both traditional (or complicated) and simplified characters, only under the "Radical" column. The only simplified radical that has no standard counterpart is 业 yè, which is the simplified version of the traditional character 業 yè 'profession.' Traditionally, the character 業 yè belongs to the radical 木 mù 'tree or wood.' When you are familiar with the table, you will find that it is quite easy to convert from the traditional radicals to their simplified counterparts. Characters/graphs in parentheses under the radical column are variants of their corresponding radicals.

Since most of the Chinese characters (both the traditional and simplified) are made of one or more of these radicals, grasping them early on is the quickest way to learn Chinese characters well in a limited amount of time.

S No.	R No.	Radical/ Simplified	Pinyin/ English	Example	Stroke Order
1	1	一	yī one	丁不	
	2	丨	shù	中串	
	3	丶	diǎn dot	丸主	
	4	丿	piě	久乒	
	5	乙 乙 (乛 乛乚)	yǐ a Celestial Stem	九也	
	6	亅	jué	了事	

---

[1] Radical 26 doesn't have sound or meaning.

2	7	二	èr two	云五	一	二	
	8	亠	tóu	京交	丶	亠	
	9	人（亻） 人（亻入）	rén man	位們	丿	人	
	10	儿	rén	元先	丿	儿	
	11	入	rù enter	内全	丿	入	
	12	八 八（丷）	bā eight	公六	丿	八	
	13	冂	jiōng	再册	丨	冂	
	14	冖	mì	冠冤	丶	冖	
	15	冫	bīng	冬冰	丶	冫	
	16	几 几（𠘧）	jǐ a small table	凡凳	丿	几	
	17	凵	qū	出函	凵	凵	
	18	刀（刂） 刀（刂⺈）	dāo knife	切刻	𠃌	刀	
	19	力	lì power	功勤	𠃌	力	
	20	勹	bāo	包勿	丿	勹	
	21	匕	bǐ a ladle	化匙	丿	匕	

	22	匚	fāng power	匡匠	一	匚	
	23	匸	xì	匹區	一	匸	
	24	十	shí ten	千午	一	十	
	25	卜 卜（⼘）	bǔ to divine	卦卡	丨	卜	
	26	卩（巳） 卩（巳）		印即	ㄱ	卩	
	27	厂	hǎn	原厚	一	厂	
	28	厶	sǐ	去參	ㄥ	厶	
	29	又	yòu again	友受	フ	又	
3	30	口	kǒu mouth	叫可	丶	冂	口
	31	囗	wéi	回國	丨	冂	口
	32	土	tǔ soil	坐地	一	十	土
	33	士	shì a scholar	壬壯	一	十	士
	34	夊	suī ten	夏夔	丿	夂	夊
	35	夕	xì evening	多夢	丿	夕	夕
	36	大	dà big	天太	一	𠂇	大

3	37	女	nǔ female	好姓	ㄑ	ㄣ	女	
	38	子	zǐ child, son	學孩	ㄱ	了	子	
	39	宀	mián	安客	丶	宀	宀	
	40	寸	cùn Chinese inch	對封	一	寸	寸	
	41	小 小 (⺌)	xiǎo small	少尖	亅	小	小	
	42	尢 (尣兀)	wāng	就尤	一	尢	尢	
	43	尸	shī a corpse	屋尺	ㄱ	ㄹ	尸	
	44	屮	chè	屯	ㄴ	ㄩ	屮	
	45	山	shān mountain	島岸	丨	山	山	
	46	巛	chuān a river	州巢	ㄑ	巜	巛	
	47	工	gōng labor	左差	一	工	工	
	48	己 己 (巳)	jǐ self	已巷	ㄱ	ㄹ	己	
	49	巾	jīn towel	布師	丨	冂	巾	
	50	干	gān a Celestial Stem	年平	一	二	干	
	51	幺	yāo one	幼幾	ㄥ	幺	幺	

	52	广	yǎn	店座	、	宀	广	
	53	廴	yǐn ten	建延	㇇	乛	廴	
	54	卄	gǒng	弄弊	一	𠂇	廾	
	55	弋	yì to catch	式	一	弋	弋	
	56	弓	gōng a bow	弟張	㇕	弓	弓	
	57	彐 (彑彐)	jì	彗彙	㇕	彐	彐	
	58	彡	shān	形影	ノ	彡	彡	
	59	彳	chì	很得	ノ	彳	彳	
4	60	心 (忄,⺗)	xīn heart	念忙	丶	心	心	心
	61	戈	gē a spear	我戰	一	弋	戈	戈
	62	戶	hù a door	房所	㇒	厂	戶	戶
	63	手 (扌)	shǒu hand	打抱	㇗	二	三	手
	64	支	zhī to pay, support	支	一	十	攴	支
	65	攴 (攵)	pū a spear	放改	丨	卜	攴	攴
	66	文	wén literature	斑斌	、	亠	宀	文

4	67	斗	dǒu Chinese peck	料斜	丶	二	三	斗	
	68	斤	jīn catty	新斯	ノ	┌	斤	斤	
	69	方	fāng square	旁旅	丶	一	亠	方	
	70	无	wú not, no	旣	一	二	无	无	
	71	日	rì sun	早明	∣	冂	日	日	
	72	曰	yuē to say	書最	∣	冂	曰	曰	
	73	月	yuè moon	有朋	ノ	月	月	月	
	74	木	mù tree, wood	李東	一	十	才	木	
	75	欠	qiàn to owe	次歌	ノ	𠂉	勹	欠	
	76	止	zhǐ to stop	正步	∣	卜	止	止	
	77	歹 (歺)	dǎi bad	死殖	一	丆	歹	歹	
	78	殳	shū a weapon	段殺	ノ	几	殳	殳	
	79	毋 (母)	wù don't	每毒	㇄	口	毋	毋	
	80	比	bǐ to compare	毖毗	㇉	比	比	比	
	81	毛	máo hair	毯毽	一	二	三	毛	

	82	氏	shì family, clan	民氓	ノ	﹁	𫝀	氏	
	83	气	qì air	氣氧	ノ	﹁	𠂉	气	
	84	水 (氵氺)	shuǐ water	江洋	亅	刁	𣄼	水	
	85	火 (灬)	huǒ fire	炒煮	丶	⸂	少	火	
	86	爪 (爫)	zhuǎ claw	爬爭	ノ	厂	爪	爪	
	87	父	fù father	爸爹	ノ	八	分	父	
	88	爻	yáo line (of a divination diagram)	爽爾	ノ	乂	爻	爻	
	89	爿	qiáng	牆	ᅩ	丬	爿	爿	
	90	片	piàn a piece	牌版	ノ	丿	广	片	
	91	牙	yá tooth	牙	一	𠃋	牙	牙	
	92	牛 (牜)	niú cow	物特	ノ	𠂉	𠂉	牛	
	93	犬 (犭)	quǎn dog	狗狼	一	大	大	犬	
5	94	玄	xuán far and obscure	率	丶	亠	玄	玄	玄
	95	玉 (王)	yù jade	玩理	一	二	千	王	玉
	96	瓜	guā melon	瓢瓣	ノ	厂	瓜	瓜	瓜

5	97	瓦	wǎ a tile	瓶瓷	一	丁	工	瓦	瓦
	98	甘	gān sweet	甜甚	一	十	廿	甘	甘
	99	生	shēng born, to live	產甥	丿	亇	牜	牛	生
	100	用	yòng use	甫甬	丿	冂	月	月	用
	101	田	tián field	男當	丨	冂	冃	田	田
	102	疋(疋疋)	yǎ/pǐ	疑疏	乛	了	下	疋	疋
	103	疒	chuáng	病癌	丶	亠	疒	疒	疒
	104	癶	bō	發登	丿	癶	癶	癶	癶
	105	白	bái white	的百	丿	亻	白	白	白
	106	皮	pí skin, leather	皺	乛	十	产	皮	皮
	107	皿	mǐn saucer	盡盆	丨	冂	皿	皿	皿
	108	目(罒)	mù eye	看睏	丨	冂	月	目	目
	109	矛	máo a spear	矜	乛	乛	予	予	矛
	110	矢	shǐ a dart	知短	丿	亇	牜	矢	矢
	111	石	shí stone	砂研	一	丆	石	石	石

	112	示 (礻)	shì to show	祝神	一	二	亍	亓	示	
	113	内	róu	禹禽	丨	冂	冂	内	内	
	114	禾	hé rice plant	種科	丿	二	千	禾	禾	
	115	穴	xuè a cave	穿空	丶	八	宀	宀	穴	
	116	立	lì to stand	站章	丶	二	亠	立	立	
		业	yè profession	业邺	丨	刂	业	业	业	
6	117	竹 (𥫗)	zhú bamboo	筆第	丿	𠂉	𠂆	𠂆	𥫗	竹
	118	米	mǐ rice	精粥	丶	丷	丷	半	米	米
	119	糸 (糹) 幺	mì	紅級	乚	纟	幺	糸	糸	糸
	120	缶	fǒu a crock	缺罐	丿	𠂉	上	午	缶	缶
	121	网	wǎng	罷罰	丨	冂	冂	网	网	网
	122	羊 (䒑) 羊 (𦍌)	yáng a sheep, a goat	美義	丶	丷	丷	兰	兰	羊
	123	羽	yǔ feather	習翁	乛	习	刃	羽	羽	羽
	124	老	lǎo old	考者	一	十	土	耂	老	老
	125	而	ér and yet	耐耍	一	丆	广	而	而	而

6	126	耒	lěi handle of a plough	耕耙	ノ	二	三	丰	丰	耒
	127	耳	ěr ear	聲聞	一	丁	耳	耳	耳	耳
	128	聿 聿(⺕聿)	yù pen, brush	肆肅	㇆	㇇	圭	圭	圭	聿
	129	肉（月）	ròu flesh, meat	肌肚	l	冂	内	内	肉	肉
	130	臣	chén a minister	臥臨	一	匚	匸	臣	臣	臣
	131	自	zì self	臭臬	ノ	亻	冇	自	自	自
	132	至	zhì to arrive at	致臺	一	厶	至	至	至	至
	133	臼(⺽)	jiù a mortar	舊興	ノ	亻	乍	臼	臼	臼
	134	舌	shé tongue	舍舒	ノ	二	千	千	舌	舌
	135	舛	chuǎn chaotic	舞舜	ノ	ク	夕	夕	舛	舛
	136	舟	zhōu boat	船航	ノ	亻	冂	舟	舟	舟
	137	艮 艮(⻗)	gèn name of a divination diagram	良艱	㇆	㇈	㇈	艮	艮	艮
	138	色	sè color	艶	ノ	ク	⺈	名	多	色
	139	屮屮(⺾) ⺾	cǎo grass	花草	㇄	凵	屮	艹	艹	艸
	140	虍	hū rice	號虎	㇑	⺊	㇒	广	卢	虍

	141	虫	chóng worm	蛋蛇	丨	口	口	虫	虫	虫	
	142	血	xuè/ xiě blood	衆	丿	亇	血	血	血	血	
	143	行	xíng to walk	街衛	丿	彳	彳	彳	行	行	
	144	衣 (衤)	yī clothing	裏褲	丶	亠	㐅	衣	衣	衣	
	145	襾 (襾) 西 (襾)	yà	要覆	一	冂	冂	襾	襾	西	
7	146	見 见	jiàn to see	視覺	丨	冂	冃	月	目	見	見
	147	角 角	jiǎo angle	解觸	丿	夕	夕	角	角	角	角
	148	言 言 (讠)	yán speech	說記	亠	二	言	言	言	言	言
	149	谷	gǔ a valley	谷	丿	八	公	父	谷	谷	谷
	150	豆	dòu bean	豇豌	一	冂	冃	豆	豆	豆	豆
	151	豕	shǐ hog	豬象	一	丆	丆	豕	豕	豕	豕
	152	豸	zhì reptiles without feet	貌豹	丿	豸	豸	豸	豸	豸	豸
	153	貝 贝	bèi shell	買貴	丨	冂	冃	月	目	貝	貝
	154	赤	chì red	赫赦	一	十	土	丰	赤	赤	赤
	155	走	zǒu to walk	起趕	一	十	土	丰	走	走	走

	156	足（足）	zú foot	跟跌	丨	口	口	早	呈	足	足	
	157	身	shēn body	躺躬	ノ	亻	竹	阜	自	身	身	
	158	車 车	chē vehicle	輪輛	一	厂	厂	巨	白	車	車	
	159	辛	xīn a Celestial Stem	辣辦	丶	一	六	立	立	立	辛	
	160	辰	chén a Terrestrial Branch	農辱	一	厂	戸	戸	辰	辰	辰	
	161	辵（辶/辶） 辶	chuò 進近	進近	ノ	刁	彡	彳	辛	弃	辵	
	162	邑（right 阝）	yì a city	那都	丨	口	口	吕	吊	吊	邑	
	163	酉	yǒu a Terrestrial Branch	酒酷	一	厂	厄	丙	酉	酉	酉	
	164	釆（采） 采	biàn/ cǎi to gather	釋釉	ノ	亻	彡	立	平	采	采	
	165	里	lǐ Chinese mile	重量	丨	冂	曰	日	旦	里	里	
8	166	金 金（釒）	jīn gold, metal	錢銀	ノ	人	人	合	全	全	金	金
	167	長（镸） 长	cháng long	長	一	丁	F	F	巨	長	長	長
	168	門 门	mén door	開關	丨	冂	月	月	門	門	門	門
	169	阜（left 阝）	fù a mound	阿陳	ノ	亻	阝	卩	阜	自	自	阜
	170	隸	tài long	隸	⺧	一	⺕	聿	聿	隶	隶	隶

	171	隹	zhuī short-tail birds	隻雛	ノ 亻 亻 亻 住 隹 隹 隹
	172	雨（雨）	yǔ rain	雪雲	一 厂 雨 雨 雨 雨 雨 雨
	173	青	qīng green	靜靖	一 二 丰 圭 青 青 青 青
	174	非	fēi not, un-	靠靡	ノ 丿 非 非 非 非 非 非
9	175	面	miàn face	面	一 丁 兀 丏 丏 面 面 面
	176	革	gé reform, leather	鞋靴	一 十 廿 廿 苔 苔 革 革
	177	韋 韦	wěi tanned leather	韓韞	フ 艹 五 圭 音 音 章 韋
	178	韭	jiǔ leeks	韭	丨 十 非 非 非 非 非 韭
	179	音	yīn sound	響韻	丶 亠 立 立 音 音 音
	180	頁 页	yè a page	題預	一 丆 冂 冃 百 百 頁 頁
	181	風 风	fēng wind	颱颭	丿 几 凡 凡 凨 凬 風 風
	182	飛 飞	fēi to fly	飛	乀 乁 飞 飞 飛 飛 飛 飛
	183	食 食（饣）	shí to eat	飯餓	ノ 人 人 今 今 食 食 食
	184	首	shǒu head	首	丶 丷 艹 艹 产 首 首 首
	185	香	xiāng fragrant	馥馨	ノ 二 千 禾 禾 禾 香 香
10	186	馬 马	mǎ horse	騎駛	一 厂 厂 馬 馬 馬 馬 馬 馬

	No.	部首	拼音/義	例字	筆順
	187	骨 骨	gǔ / bone	體	丨 冂 冎 冎 冎 咼 骨 骨 骨 / 骨
	188	高	gāo / high, tall	高	丶 亠 亠 亨 亨 亯 高 高 高 / 高
	189	髟	biāo	髮 鬍	一 丆 丆 丆 县 镸 镸 镸 髟 / 髟
	190	鬥 斗	dòu / to struggle	鬧	丨 丨 丨 丨 鬥 鬥 鬥 鬥 鬥 / 鬥
	191	鬯	chàng / sacrificial spirits	鬱	ㄩ ㄩ 凵 凶 凶 凶 凶 鬯 / 鬯
	192	鬲	gé / name of an ancient state	鬹	一 冖 鬲 鬲 鬲 鬲 鬲 鬲 / 鬲
	193	鬼	guǐ / ghost	魅 魔	丿 丿 白 白 申 申 鬼 鬼 / 鬼
11	194	魚 鱼	yú / fish	鮭 鮮	丿 ク ク 乃 乃 角 魚 魚 魚 / 魚 鱼
	195	鳥 鸟	niǎo / bird	鳳 鴨	丿 冂 白 白 自 鳥 鳥 鳥 / 鳥 鸟
	196	鹵 卤	lǔ / alkaline	鹹 鹽	丨 卜 卣 卤 鹵 鹵 鹵 鹵 / 鹵 卤
	197	鹿	lù / deer	麋 麒	丶 广 广 庐 庐 庐 鹿 鹿 鹿 / 鹿 鹿
	198	麥 麦	mài / wheat	麵 麴	一 丆 𡿨 以 来 夾 夾 麥 麥 / 麥 麦
	199	麻	má / hemp	麼	丶 广 广 庁 庁 床 床 麻 / 麻 麻
12	200	黃 黄	huáng / yellow	黃	一 十 卅 苫 苗 苗 苗 黃 黃 黃 / 黃 黃 黄
	201	黍	shǔ / millet	黍	丿 千 千 禾 禾 禾 黍 黍 黍 / 黍 黍
	202	黑	hēi / black	點 黛	丶 冂 罒 四 四 里 黑 黑 黑 / 黑 黑 黑

	203	黹 zhǐ embroidery	黹	丨	丬	丬	坐	쓰	㳀	쓰	将
				紫	黹	黹					
13	204	黽 黾 mǐn to strive	黽	丶	冂	冂	冋	它	它	它	它	電
				電	電	電	黽				
	205	鼎 dǐng tripod	鼎	丨	冂	冃	目	目	归	鼡	鼡
				鼡	鼎	鼎	鼎				
	206	鼓 gǔ drum	鼓	一	十	士	吉	吉	吉	吉	壴
				壴	壴	鼓	鼓				
	207	鼠 shǔ mouse	鼬	丨	仁	乍	臼	臼	臼	臼	臼
				鼠	鼠	鼠	鼠				
14	208	鼻 bí nose	鼾	丨	冂	白	自	自	鼻	鼻
				鼻	鼻	鼻	鼻	鼻			
	209	齊 齐 qí equal, uniform	齋	丶	亠	亠	亠	亣	齐	齐	齐
				齊	齊	齊	齊	齊			
15	210	齒 齿 chǐ tooth	齡	丨	上	止	止	此	齿	齿
				崗	崗	崗	齒	齒	齒		
16	211	龍 龙 lóng dragon	龔	丶	亠	宀	立	产	音	音
				龍	龍	龍	龍	龍	龍	龍	
	212	龜 龟 guī turtle	龜	丿	𠂊	龟	龟	龟	龟	龟	龟
				龜	龜	龜	龜	龜	龜	龜	
17	213	龠 yuè a kind of flute	龠	丿	人	合	合	合	侖	命	命
				命	侖	侖	侖	龠	龠	龠	龠

Appendix 4. Characters with Two or More Readings

Character	Reading	Example			
長　长	cháng zhǎng	長短 長得很漂 亮	长短 长得很漂 亮	chángduǎn zhǎng .de hěn piào.liàng	length to look really pretty
待	dāi dài	待在家裏 招待	待在家里	dāi zài jiā .lǐ zhāodài	to stay at home to entertain
得	dé děi .de	得到 得上課 看得懂	 得上课	dédào děi shàngkè kàn.dedǒng	to succeed in obtaining to have to attend the class can understand by reading
法	fǎ/fà fǎ	法國 法子	法国	Fǎ.guó/Fà.guó fǎ.zi	France method
好	hǎo hào	很好 好動 喜好	 好动	hěn hǎo hàodòng xǐhào	very good to be active to like
教	jiāo jiào	教書 教室	教书	jiāoshū jiàoshì	to teach classroom
覺　觉	jué jiào	覺得 睡覺	觉得 睡觉	jué.de shuìjiào	to feel to sleep
空	kōng kòng	空氣 有空兒	空气 有空儿	kōngqì yǒukòngr	air to have free time
樂　乐	lè yuè	快樂 音樂	快乐 音乐	kuàilè yīnyuè	(to be) happy music
了	.le liǎo	來了 吃不了	来了	lái .le chī.bùliǎo	came cannot finish eating
爲　为	wèi wéi	因爲 以爲	因为 以为	yīnwèi yǐwéi	because to think incorrectly
行	xíng háng	不行 銀行	 银行	bùxíng yínháng	won't do bank
要	yào yāo	要買 要求	要买	yào mǎi yāo.qiú	to want to buy to request
著　着	.zhe zháo	看著電視 睡著	看着电视	kàn.zhe diànshì shuìzháo	watching at TV to have fallen asleep
重	zhòng chóng	很重 重寫 重做	 重写	hěn zhòng chóng xiě chóng zuò	very heavy to rewrite to redo

Appendix 5. Bibliography

Chang, Kuang-yuan (張光遠)
 1995   "Shang Dynasty Bronze Inscriptions and Their Historical Significance: Bronze
         Inscriptions as Standard Script and Oracle Bone Inscriptions as Simplified Script."
         In National Palace Museum, *A Catalogue of Shang Dynasty Bronze Inscriptions :
         Ancient Chinese Script from the 1st Millenium BC* (商代金文圖錄—三千年前中
         國文字特展), 1-27.

Chao, Yuen Ren (趙元任)
 1930   "A System of Tone Letters." *Le Ma î tre phonétique,* troisième série, 30: 24-7.
         Reprinted in *Fangyan* (方言)1980, 2: 81-83.
 1968   *A Grammar of Spoken Chinese.* Berkeley: University of California Press.

Gao, Shufan (高樹藩), ed.
 1984   *Zhengzhong Xing Yin Yi Zonghe Da Zidian* (正中形音義綜合大字典). Rev. 5th
         ed. Taibei: Zhengzhong Shuju.

*Lianhebao*聯合報, January 6, 1992.

Liang, Shih-chiu (梁實秋)
 1971   *A New Practical Chinese-English Dictionary* (最新實用漢英字典). Taipei: Far
         East Book Co. Ltd.

National Palace Museum (國立故宮博物院)
 1995   *A Catalogue of Shang Dynasty Bronze Inscriptions : Ancient Chinese Script from the
         1st Millenium BC* (商代金文圖錄—三千年前中國文字特展). Taipei: National
         Palace Museum.

Norman, Jerry
 1988   *Chinese.* Cambridge: Cambridge University Press.

Ramsey, S. Robert
 1987   *The Languages of China.* Princeton: Princeton University Press.

Sung, Margaret M. Yan (嚴 棉)
 1979   "Chinese Language and Culture: A Study of Homonyms, Lucky Words and
         Taboos." *Journal of Chinese Linguistics* 7.1: 15-28.
 1981   "Chinese Personal Naming." *Journal of the Chinese Language Teachers
         Association* 16.2: 67-90.

Tai, James H-Y. (戴浩一)
    1985   "Temporal Sequence and Chinese Word Order." In *Iconicity in Syntax*, ed. John Haiman. Amsterdam: Benjamins.
    1987   "Temporal Sequence and Chinese Word Order." In *Wang Li Memorial Volumes, English Volume*, ed. the Chinese Language Society of Hong Kong, 377-404.
    1989   "Toward a Cognition-Based Functional Grammar of Chinese." In *Functionalism and Chinese Grammar*, ed. Tai and Hsueh, 187-226.

Tai, James H-Y. (戴浩一), and Frank F. S. Hsueh (薛鳳生), eds.
    1989   *Functionalism and Chinese Grammar* (功能學說與中文文法). Chinese Language Teachers Association Monograph Series No.1, Ohio State University, Columbus.

Wang, William S-Y. (王士元), ed.
    1991   *Languages and Dialects of China*. Monograph Series No. 3, Journal of Chinese Linguistics, University of California, Berkeley.

Wang, Yun-wu (王雲五)
    1967   *Zijiao Haoma Jianzifa* (四角號碼檢字法). Taipei: Taiwan Shangwu Yinshuguan (臺灣商務印書館).

Yan, Margaret Mian (嚴棉)
    1993   "Active Chinese—A Multimedia Beginning Chinese Text for College Students" (with computer technical assistance of I-feng Jeng). Paper presented at the Annual Meeting of the American Council on the Teaching of Foreign Languages, November 20-22, San Antonio.

Yin, Binyong (尹斌庸), and Mary Felley (傅曼麗)
    1990   *Chinese Romanization: Pronunciation and Orthography* (漢語拼音和正詞法). Beijing: Sinolingua.

Zhongguo Da Baike Quanshu Chubanshe Bianjibu (中國大百科全書出版社編輯部編), eds.
    1988   *Zhongguo Da Baike Quanshu: Yuyan Wenzi* (中國大百科全書：語言文字). Beijing: Zhongguo Da Baike Quanshu Chubanshe.

Indexes

Index 1. Vocabulary

◎ **By Pinyin**

	Pinyin	Character		English	L
A					
	.a	啊		particle for question	8
	ǎi	矮		short	8
	ài	愛	爱	to love	8
B					
	.ba	吧		particle for agreement	7
	bā	八		eight	4
	bà.bà	爸爸		father	8
	bǎi	百		hundred	7
*	bǎihuò	百貨	百货	goods, commodities	12
*	bǎihuò dàlóu	百貨大樓	百货大楼	department store (M: 家) (China)	12
	bǎihuò gōngsī	百貨公司	百货公司	department store (M: 家)	12
	bàn	半		half	9
	bāng	幫	帮	to help, to assist	12
	bàng	磅		pound	13
*	bǎo	飽		to eat to the full, (to be) satisfied (stomach)	11
	bàogào	報告	报告	report, (term) paper (M: 篇/個)	13
	bēi	杯		measure word for tea, wine, coffee; cup	7
	bēijù	悲劇	悲剧	tragedy	11
	běifāng	北方		the north	10
	běn	本		measure word for books, notebooks	6
	běn.zi	本子		notebook (M: 本/個)	7
	bǐ	筆	笔	pen (M: 枝 zhī)	7
*	bǐ	比		to compare	10
	bǐjiào	比較	比较	comparatively, comparison	10
	biànchéng	變成	变成	to become	13
	bié	別		don't	11
	bié.de	別的		other	7
	bù	不		no, not	4
*	búbì	不必		doesn't have to, need not (=不用)	5
	búbì	不必		not necessarily	10
	búcuò	不錯	不错	(to be) not bad, quite good	6
	búguò	不過	不过	and yet	8
	bútài	不太		not quite, not very	6

*	búxiè	不謝	不谢	you're welcome	7
*	búyòng	不用		doesn't have to, need not (=不必)	5
*	bù hǎo yì.si	不好意思		(to be) ashamed, (to be) embarrassed, feel shy	13
*	bù	部		a section, a part	8
	bù	部		measure word for films, cars, etc.	11
C					
	cái	才		only	7
	cái	才		not until, only then	9
	cài	菜		dishes, vegetables (M: 盤 pán 'dish'; 道 dào 'course')	9
	chá	查		to check	7
	chá	茶		tea (M: 杯 bēi 'cup')	10
*	chà	差		to be short of, lack	6
	Chángchéng	長城	长城	the Great Wall	10
	chángdù	長度	长度	length	12
	chángduǎn	長短	长短	length	12
	chànggē	唱歌		to sing	8
	chāojí shìchǎng	超級市場	超级市场	supermarket (M: 個)	13
	chē	車	车	car, vehicle (M: 輛 liàng, 部 bù)	10
	chènshān	襯衫	衬衫	shirt (M: 件, V: 穿)	12
	chéng	成		to constitute	8
	chī	吃		to eat	7
	chū.qù	出去		to go out	9
	chú.le... yǐwài	除了...以外		besides, except for	12
	chūnjuǎnr	春捲兒	春卷儿	eggroll	10
	chōu	抽		to smoke (cigarettes, etc.) (=吸) , to inhale	10
*	chuān	穿		to wear (garments and shoes)	12
	chuān.chuān.kàn	穿穿看		to try (garments) on	12
	cídài	磁帶	磁带	audio tape (M: 盤 pán) (China)	7
	cì	次		measure word for frequency	11
	cóng	從	从	from	11
	cóng...lái/qù	從...來/去	从...来/去	to come /go from (a place)	8
	cù	醋		vinegar	10
D					
	dā	搭		to take (a vehicle, an airplane, a ship)	13
	dǎcuò	打錯	打错	to dial a wrong number	9
	dǎ (diànhuà)	打(電話)	打(电话)	to make a telephone call	9
	dǎgōng	打工		to work (for a temporary job)	5

	dǎzhé	打折		to give a discount	12
	dà	大		(to be) big, large, old (age)	4
	dà chī dà hē	大吃大喝		to eat and drink a lot	13
	dàjiā	大家		all, everybody	10
	dàxiǎo	大小		size	12
	dàxué	大學	大学	university, college (M: 個/間)	12
	dàyī	大衣		an overcoat (M: 件, V: 穿)	12
*	dài	戴		to wear (glasses, gloves, jewelry)	12
	dàn	淡		(to be) light (taste, color), weak or thin (tea, coffee, etc.)	10
	dàn.shì	但是		but	8
	dǎojìn	倒盡	倒尽	to lose completely (one's appetite)	11
	dào	道		measure word for dishes	10
*	dào.dì	道地		authentic, genuine (=地道)	9
	dào...qù/lái	到...去/來	到...去/来	to go there / come here	6
	dào.shì	倒是		on the contrary	8
	.de	的		possessive marker	4
	Dé.guó	德國	德国	Germany	8
	děi	得		must, to have to	5
	děng	等		to wait	9
*	dì	第		an ordinalizing prefix	4
*	dì yī	第一		the first	4
	dì.dào	地道		authentic, genuine	9
	dìwèi	地位		position (of a person), ranking, status	11
	diǎn(zhōng)	點(鐘)	点(钟)	o'clock	6
*	diànhuà	電話	电话	telephone (M: 個)	9
	diànnǎo	電腦	电脑	computer (M: 個 .ge)	7
	diànshì	電視	电视	TV	12
	diànyǐngr	電影兒	电影儿	movie (M: 個/部 bù)	9
	dōngbù	東部		eastern (America)	8
	dōng.xī	東西	东西	thing	7
	dōngjì	冬季		winter (season)	12
	dǒng	懂		to understand (=明白)	11
	dōu	都		all, both	5
	dù.zi	肚子		stomach (belly)	13
	duàn.liàn	鍛練	锻练	to do physical training	13
*	duì	對	对	(to be) right, to face	4
*	duì.buqǐ	對不起	对不起	(I am) sorry	6

duì...hǎo	對... 好	对... 好	be nice to...	10
duìzhé	對折	对折	a 50% discount	12
dùn	頓	顿	measure word for meals	13
duō	多		(to be) much; many	6
duōbànr	多半兒	多半儿	most of	11
duō.shǎo	多少		how much, how many?	7
E				
érqiě	而且		furthermore, besides	9
ér.shì	而是		but (preceded by 不是)	8
* ér.zi	兒子	儿子	son (M: 個)	11
è	餓	饿	(to be) hungry	11
èr	二		two	4
F				
fàn	飯	饭	rice, meal (M: 頓 dùn)	7
fànguǎnr	飯館兒	饭馆儿	restaurant (M: 家 jiā)	10
fāng.biàn	方便		(to be) convenient	13
fāngmiàn	方面		an aspect, (in this or that) respect	11
fàngjià	放假		to have a holiday/vacation	13
* fēicháng	非常		unusually, extraordinarily	6
fēijī	飛機	飞机	airplane (M: 架 jià)	13
(fēi)jīchǎng	(飛)機場	(飞)机场	airport (M: 個)	13
* fēn	分		minute	6
fēn	分		to divide	10
* fēn (qián)	分(錢)	分(钱)	cent	7
fùmǔ	父母		parents	8
* fù.qīn	父親	父亲	father (formal)	8
fùnǚ	婦女	妇女	woman, women (M: 個)	11
fùxiū	副修		minor, to minor in	6
G				
gǎndòng	感動	感动	(to be) moved, (to be) touched	11
Gǎn'ēnjié	感恩節	感恩节	Thanksgiving	13
gāngcái	剛才	刚才	just now, a moment ago (MTA)	11
Gāo	高		surname, high, tall	4
gāojiàn	高見	高见	high opinion	11
gāoxìng	高興	高兴	(to be) happy	11
gào.sù	告訴	告诉	to tell	13
* .ge	個	个	measure word for persons and things	5
gěi	給	给	to give	7
gēn	跟		and	5

	gēn	跟		to follow; with (person)	10
*	gèng	更		even	12
*	gōngchē	公車	公车	bus (M: 部/輛)	13
*	gōnggòng qìchē	公共汽車	公共汽车	bus (M: 部/輛)	13
*	gōngsī	公司		company (M: 家)	12
*	gōng.fū	功夫/工夫	工夫	time, leisure (=空兒), skill, work	9
	gōngkè	功課	功课	homework	5
*	gōngzuò	工作		to work	5
	guānmén	關門	关门	to close the door	6
	guān.xì	關係	关系	relationship	11
	guāngdié	光碟		CD (compact disc)	7
	guàngjiē	逛街		to do window shopping	12
	guì	貴	贵	(to be) expensive	7
	guómào	國貿	国贸	international business	6
	.guò	過	过	experiential suffix to verbs	10
*	guò	過	过	to pass	6
H					
	hái	還	还	still	6
	hái.shì	還是	还是	or	6
	hái.shì	還是	还是	had better	9
	hǎixiān	海鮮	海鲜	seafood	10
*	hàn	和		and	5
	hànbǎo(bāo)	漢堡	汉堡包	hamburger (M: 個)	7
	hànzì	漢字	汉字	Chinese character (M: 個)	8
	hǎo	好		(to be) good	6
	hǎojǐ-	好幾-	好几-	several	13
	hǎojí .le	好極了	好极了	wonderful, bravo	8
	hǎotīng	好聽	好听	(to be) delightful to listen to	8
	hǎo.xiàng... shì.de/sì.de	好像...似的	好象...似的	it seems as if...	11
	hàokè	好客		(to be) hospitable	13
	hào	號	号	number, day of the month (colloquial), size (clothing only)	4
	hē	喝		to drink	7
*	hé	和		and	5
	héshì	合適	合适	(to be) suitable	12
	hēisè	黑色		black	12
	hèi	嘿		an interjection	4
	hěn	很		very	6

	hú	壺	壶	pot	10
	Húnán	湖南		Hunan—name of a province	10
	hòu.tiān	後天	后天	the day after tomorrow	4
	huā shíjiān	花時間	花时间	(to be) time-consuming	8
	huá	華	华	China (=中華), splendid, gorgeous (=華麗)	12
*	huán	還	还	to return (something)	6
*	huí	回		to return (to a place; from a trip; to original state), go back	6
*	huì	會	会	will, can, to know how to	9
	huǒjī	火雞	火鸡	turkey (M: 隻)	13
	huò(.zhě)	或(者)		or	13

J

	jī	雞	鸡	chicken (M: 隻 zhī 'M for birds')	10
	jǐ	幾	几	how many, how much	4
	jǐ	幾	几	few, some (+M+N) (indefinite)	6
*	jǐ diǎn zhōng	幾點鐘	几点钟	what time?	6
*	jiā	家		measure word for stores, restaurants, cinema; home	6
	jiā	加	加	to add	6
	jià.qián	價錢	价钱	price	12
	jiǎnféi	減肥		to go on a diet	13
*	jiǎnjià	減價	减价	price reduction	12
	jiàn	件		measure word for upper garments and coats, affairs	12
	jiànshēnfáng	健身房		gym	13
	jiāo	交		to turn in (homework), to pay (a fee)	13
*	jiāo	教		to teach	5
*	jiǎo	角	角	dime (as printed on real money)	7
	jiǎo.zi	餃子	饺子	dumpling (M: 個)	10
	jiào	叫		to call, be called	8
	jiào	叫		to order	10
*	jiē	接		to pick someone up	13
*	jié	節	节	measure word for classes	5
*	jiéshí	節食	节食	to go on a diet (=減肥)	13
	jiè	借		to borrow	6
	jiè.shào	介紹	介绍	to introduce	8
*	jīn.nián	今年		this year	5
	jīn.tiān	今天		today	4
	jǐn	緊	紧	(to be) tight	12

	jīngyàn	經驗	经验	experience	11
	jiǔ	九		nine	4
	jiù	就		just, precisely, then	7
	jiù	舊	旧	old (for things), used	7
*	jú.zishuǐ	桔子水		orange juice	10
	jué.de	覺得	觉得	to feel, think	7
	juédìng	決定	决定	to decide	6
K					
	kāfēi	咖啡		coffee	7
	kāfēi	咖啡		brown (color)	12
	kāi	開	开	to drive (a vehicle), to open (a can, box, etc.)	10
*	kāimén	開門	开门	to open the door	6
	kāishǐ	開始	开始	to begin, to start	11
	kāiwánxiào	開玩笑	开玩笑	to crack a joke, to joke	13
	kāixué	開學	开学	to start school/classes	4
	kàn	看		to see, to think (when expressing one's opinion)	9
	kàn.chū.lái	看出來	看出来	to figure out	11
	…kàn.kàn	(VO) 看看		just VO and see what happens	7
	kàn.qǐ.lái	看起來	看起来	(it) looks, (it) seems	13
	kǎoyā	烤鴨	烤鸭	roast duck	10
	kě	可		emphatic marker	11
	kě bú.shì .ma	可不是嗎	可不是吗	isn't it true?	11
	kě.shì	可是		but	6
	kě.yǐ	可以		may	7
*	kè	課	课	lesson, course	4
*	kè	刻		quarter; to engrave	6
	kěndìng	肯定		certainly	12
*	kòngr	空兒	空儿	unoccupied time or space, leisure	9
	kǒufú	口福		enjoyment of the palate	13
	kǒuwèir	口味兒	口味儿	taste, flavor	10
	kū	哭		to cry	11
*	kù.zi	褲子	裤子	pants (M: 條, V: 穿)	12
	kuàilè	快樂	快乐	happiness; happy	4
	kuài(yào)	快(要)		soon, before long	6
	kuài (qián)	塊(錢)	块钱	dollar (colloquial)	7
*	kuān	寬		(to be) loose	12

L

lā	拉		to play (violin, viola), to pull	8
là	辣		(to be) hot, spicy	10
* lái	來	来	to come	6
lánqiú	籃球	篮球	basketball (M: 個)	12
lánsè	藍色	蓝色	blue	12
lǎoshī	老師	老师	teacher (M: 位 wèi)	8
.le	了		aspect marker for completed action	6
lèi	累		(to be) tired	6
lěng	冷		(to be) cold	12
Lǐ	李		surname	4
* lǐbài	禮拜	礼拜	(colloquial) week	4
lǐ.tóu	裏頭	里头	inside	12
lìyòng	利用		to utilize, to use (time/tool/chance)	13
Liánhéguó	聯合國	联合国	United Nations	8
liàn.xí	練習	练习	to practice	8
liǎng	兩	两	two (occurs only before a measure word)	5
Lín	林		surname, forest (= 樹林)	8
* líng	零		zero	4
liúxíng	流行		(to be) in fashion, (to be) in vogue	11
liù	六		six	4
lùyīn	錄音	录音	recording	8
lùyīndài	錄音帶	录音带	audio tape (M: 卷juǎn)	7

M

.ma	嗎	吗	particle for yes-or-no question	4
mā.ma	媽媽	妈妈	mother	8
má.fán	麻煩	麻烦	(to be) troublesome, trouble, hassle	9
mǎi	買	买	to buy	6
* mài	賣	卖	to sell	6
màiwán	賣完	卖完	sold out	7
* máng	忙		(to be) busy	6
máo (qián)	毛(錢)	毛(钱)	dime (colloquial)	7
máoyī	毛衣		sweater (M: 件, V: 穿)	12
mào.zi	帽子		hat, cap (M: 頂 dǐng, V: 戴)	12
méi cuò	沒錯	没错	(you are) right	7
méi(.yǒu)	沒(有)		to not have	5
Měi.guó	美國	美国	America	8
měitiān	每天		every day	5
mén	門	门	measure word for courses	6

ménkǒu	門口	门口	entrance	9
miànbāo	麵包	面包	bread (M: 個/片 piàn 'slice')	11
* miǎo	秒		second	6
míng.bái	明白		to understand	11
* míng.nián	明年		next year	5
míng.tiān	明天		tomorrow	4
* míng.zi	名字		name	8
* mǔ.qīn	母親	母亲	mother (formal)	8
mù	木		tree (=樹木)	8

N

* nǎ	哪		which	4
nǎr	哪兒	哪儿	where?	6
nǎ yì tiān	哪一天		which day?	4
nà	那		that	6
nàr	那兒	那儿	there	7
* nán	男		male (for human beings)	11
nán	難	难	(to be) difficult, hard	8
nánguò	難過	难过	(to be) sad	11
nánfāng	南方		the south	10
nánguāpài	南瓜派		pumpkin pie	13
.ne	呢		particle for interest in additional information; how about...?	4
* něi	哪		which	4
něi yì tiān	哪一天		which day?	4
nèi	那		that	6
* nèixiē	那些		those	7
néng	能		can	9
nǐ	你		you (sing.)	4
nǐ .de	你的		your	4
* nǐ.men	你們	你们	you (pl.)	4
* nián	年		year	4
niàn	念		to study (a subject)	6
* niúnǎi	牛奶		milk	10
niúròu	牛肉		beef (M: 斤 jīn 'catty,' 磅 bàng 'pound')	10
niúyóu	牛油		butter	11
nǚ	女		female (for human beings)	11
nǚ'ér	女兒	女儿	daughter (M: 個)	11
nǚláng	女郎		woman (derogatory)	12
nǔlì	努力		(to be) hard-working	13

P

pāimài	拍賣	拍卖	a sale, an auction	12
pàotāng	泡湯	泡汤	to be gone, finish	7
pèichéng	配成		to match and form	12
* péng.yǒu	朋友		friend	5
píjiǔ	啤酒		beer (M: 杯 bēi 'cup,' 罐 guàn 'can,' 瓶 píng 'bottle')	10
pián.yí	便宜		(to be) cheap	7
piàn.zi	片子		film (M: 部 bù)	11
piào.liàng	漂亮		(to be) pretty, (to be) beautiful	11

Q

qī	七		seven	4
qīmò	期末		end of a semester	13
qìshuǐr	汽水兒	汽水儿	soft drink (M: 杯 bēi 'cup,' 罐 guàn 'can,' 瓶 píng 'bottle')	10
qián	錢	钱	money	7
qián.tiān	前天		the day before yesterday	4
* qīng	輕	轻	(to be) light (course load, weight)	6
* qǐng	請	请	please, to request	7
qǐng	請	请	to invite, treat	9
qǐngwèn	請問	请问	may I ask?	7
* qù	去		to go	6
* qù.nián	去年		last year	5
qún	群		measure word for a group of people or animals	12
qúnkù	裙褲	裙裤	skort (M: 條, V: 穿)	12
* qún.zi	裙子		skirt (M: 條, V: 穿)	12

R

ràng	讓	让	to make, let (causative)	11
* rè	熱	热	(to be) hot (temperature)	12
rén	人		person, people	8
rèn.shí/rèn.shì	認識	认识	to know (a person or a character/word)	8
* rì	日		day of the month (written form)	4
Rìwén	日文		Japanese language	5
róng.yì	容易		(to be) easy	8

S

sān	三		three	4
sānmíngzhì	三明治		sandwich (M: 個)	7
shālā	沙拉		salad	11
shāngchǎng	商場	商场	mall (M: 個)	12

*	shàng	上		to ascend; to go to (street/school/class/work)	4
	shàng...qù/lái	上...去/來	上...去/来	to go there /come here	6
	shàngkè	上課	上课	to go to class; to attend class	4
	shàng.wǔ	上午		morning, forenoon	5
*	shǎo	少		(to be) little (quantity), few	6
	shèhuì	社會	社会	society	11
*	shéi	誰	谁	who, whoever, whom, whomever	4
*	shéi .de	誰的	谁的	whose	4
	shēn.shàng	身上		on one's body, with one's self	7
	shēntǐ	身體	身体	body, health	10
	shén.me	什麼/甚麼	什么	what?	5
	shén.me .de	什麼的	什么的	and so forth	10
*	shén.me dì.fāng	什麼地方	什么地方	what place? where?	6
*	shén.me shí.hòu	什麼時候	什么时候	what time? when?	6
	shēngcài	生菜		raw vegetables, lettuce	11
	shēng.rì	生日		birthday	4
	shēngdiào	聲調	声调	tone	8
	shí	十		ten	4
*	shí.hòu	時候	时候	time	6
	shíjiān	時間	时间	time	9
	shíyànshì	實驗室	实验室	laboratory (M: 間 jiān)	8
	shì	是		to be (is, was, are, were)	4
	shì	事		matters, affairs, undertaking (M: 件 jiàn)	9
	shì	式		style (Suf)	13
	shì(.yí)shì	試(一)試	试(一)试	to try, to give it a try	10
	shū.fú	舒服		(to be) comfortable	11
	shū	書	书	book	6
	shūdiàn	書店	书店	bookstore (M: 家 jiā)	6
	shǒutào	手套		gloves (M: 雙 /付 fù, V: 戴)	12
	shòu.bùliǎo	受不了		cannot stand it	11
	shuāng	雙	双	double, measure word for a pair (of things)	8
	shuō	說	说	to say	7
	shuō zhēn .de	說真的	说真的	be serious!; quit kidding/joking!	13
	sì	四		four	4
	sòng	送		to take (someone to some place); to see (a person) off	13
	sùshè	宿舍		dormitory (M: 棟 dòng, 間 jiān)	7
	suān	酸		(to be) sour	10

	suàn.le	算了		forget it	10
	suīrán/suírán	雖然	虽然	although	8
	suíshēntīng	隨身聽	随身听	portable stereo, Walkman (M: 個 .ge)	7
	suǒ.yǐ	所以		therefore	11
T					
*	tā	他		he, she, him, her	4
*	tā	它		it	4
*	tā	她		she, her	4
*	tā .de	他的		his/her	4
	tā.men	他們	他们	they, them	4
	tándào	談到	谈到	to talk about	11
	tāng	湯	汤	soup (M: 碗 wǎn 'bowl')	10
	táng	糖		sugar, candy (M: 塊/ 盒 hé 'box')	10
	táng	堂		measure word for classes	5
	tào	套		a set	12
	tèbié	特別		especially, particularly	11
*	tiān	天		day, sky	4
	tiān.qì	天氣	天气	weather	12
	tiān.tiān	天天		every day	5
	tián	甜		(to be) sweet	10
*	tīng	聽	听	to hear	8
	tīngshuō	聽說	听说	to hear someone say	8
	tǐng	挺		very, quite (=很)	9
	túshūguǎn	圖書館	图书馆	library (M: 個 .ge)	6
	tuì	退		to drop (a course), to withdraw (from school), to return (something to the store)	6
W					
	wàitào	外套		an overcoat (M: 件, V: 穿) (=大衣)	12
*	wài.tóu	外頭	外头	outside	12
*	wán	完		to finish	7
*	wǎn.shàng	晚上		evening, night	5
	Wáng	王		surname	9
	wéi	喂		hello	9
*	wéi	圍	围	to wear (scarf), to surround	12
	wéibór	圍脖兒	围脖儿	scarf (M: 條, V: 圍)	12
	wéijīnr	圍巾兒	围巾儿	scarf (M: 條, V: 圍) (=圍巾兒)	12
	wèi	位		measure word for people (polite)	10
*	wèi	胃		stomach	11
	wèikǒu	胃口		appetite	11

	wèidào	味道		taste, flavor (=口味兒), odor	10
*	wèishén.me	爲什麼	为什么	why	8
*	wèn	問	问	to ask	7
	wǒ	我		I, me	4
	wǒ.de	我的		my	4
*	wǒ.men	我們	我们	we, us	4
	wǔ	五		five	4

X

*	xī	吸		to smoke (cigarettes, etc.) (= 抽), to inhale	10
	xībù	西部		western (America)	8
	Xǐfúhuì	喜福會	喜福会	*Joy Luck Club*—title of a movie	11
	xǐ.huān	喜歡	喜欢	to like	6
	xǐjù	喜劇	喜剧	comedy	11
*	xià	下		to descend, to go down; to get off (class/work)	4
	xià.cì	下次		next time	11
*	xiàkè	下課	下课	class dismissed	4
	xià.wǔ	下午		afternoon	5
	xiān	先		first	7
*	xiànzài	現在	现在	now	6
	xiāngdāng	相當	相当	quite, rather (=挺)	11
	xiǎng	想		would like to; to think (=覺得)	8
*	xiàng	像	象	to resemble	8
	xiàng...yíyàng	像... 一樣	象...一样	(it) seems the same as...	8
*	xiǎo	小		(to be) small, little (size), young (age)	4
	xiǎobā	小巴		van, mini-bus (M: 部/ 輛)	13
	xiǎoshuō	小說	小说	novel, fiction (M: 本běn)	7
	xiǎotíqín	小提琴		violin	8
*	xiào	笑		to laugh	11
	xiē	些		measure word for plural nouns; some (of plural N)	7
	xiě	寫	写	to write	8
	xiè.xie	謝謝	谢谢	thank (you)	7
	xīn.lǐ	心裏	心里	in the heart, in mind	11
*	xīn	新		new	7
	xīngqī	星期		(literary) week	4
	xíng	行		(to be) all right, can do, O.K.	13
	xìng	姓		to be surnamed	8
	xiū.xí	休息		to take a rest, to rest from work	5

xuǎn	選	选	to take (a course) , to elect	6
xuē.zi	靴子		boots (M: 雙, V: 穿)	12
* xué	學	学	to learn, to study (=學習)	5
xuéfēn	學分	学分	credits (M: 個 .ge)	6
xuéqī	學期	学期	semester (M: 個 .ge)	6
* xué.shēng	學生	学生	student	4
* xuéxí	學習	学习	to learn, to study (=學)	5
* xuéxiào	學校	学校	school	4
Y				
.ya	呀		sentence particle–a variant of 啊	12
yān	煙	烟	cigarette, smoke	10
yán	嚴	严	(to be) strict, stern	8
yánjiū/yánjiù	研究	研究	to research	11
yánsè	顏色	颜色	color	12
yǎn	演		to act	11
yǎnyuán	演員	演员	actor (M: 個)	11
yàng.zi	樣子	样子	style	12
yào	要		to want, will (=會), shall	6
yào.shì	要是		if, suppose, in case	11
yě	也		also, too	4
yè	頁	页	page	7
* yī.fú	衣服		clothes (M: 件, V: 穿)	12
yī	一		one	4
yígòng	一共		altogether	7
yíkuàir	一塊兒	一块儿	together	8
…yíxià	V 一下		just V…	7
* yíyàng	一樣	一样	(to be) the same	8
yì.diǎnr	一點兒	一点儿	a little bit	7
yìzǎo	一早		early morning	13
yǐhòu	以後	以后	after (a given time), later	9
* yǐqián	以前		before (a given time), previously	9
yǐ.jīng	已經	已经	already	6
yīn.wèi	因為	因为	because	8
yīnyuè	音樂	音乐	music	8
Yīng.guó	英國	英国	England	8
Yīngwén	英文		English	5
yīnggāi	應該	应该	should, ought to, must (=得)	8
* yònggōng	用功		(to be) diligent	6

	yóuqí	尤其		especially	10
	yǒu	有		to have	5
*	yǒu .de	有的		some (+N)	7
*	yǒu gōng.fū	有功夫		to have free time	9
	yǒu kòngr	有空兒	有空儿	to have free time	9
	yǒu shén.me hǎo guàng .de?	有什麼好逛的	有什么好逛的	what is there to see window shopping?	12
	yǒuyì.si	有意思		interesting	8
	yòu	又		again, moreover	12
	yú	魚	鱼	fish (M: 條 tiáo 'stripe,' M for long and soft things)	10
	yǔyán	語言	语言	language (M: 種 zhǒng 'kind')	8
	yù.bèi	預備	预备	to prepare	5
*	yuán	元		dollar (written form)	7
*	yuán	圓	圆	dollar (as printed on real money)	7
	yuánlái	原來	原来	originally	12
	yuè	月		month	4
	yuè lái yuè…	越來越…	越来越…	(it's becoming) more/much Adj-er	12
	yùndòngchǎng	運動場	运动场	athletic field	13
Z					
	zài	在		(be) located at, in, on	7
	zài	再		then	7
	zàijiàn	再見	再见	goodbye	6
	zán.men	咱們	咱们	we, us (including the person addressed)	9
	zǎojiù	早就		to have already…	7
*	zǎo.shàng	早上		morning, forenoon (= 上午)	5
	zěn.me?	怎麼	怎么	how come?	11
	zěn.me hǎo yì.si	怎麼好意思	怎么好意思	how can (one) let someone do…	13
	zěn.meyàng?	怎麼樣	怎么样	how is it?	6
*	zhàn	站		to stand	7
	zhǎng	長	长	to grow	11
	zhǎo	找		to look for, to seek	9
	.zhe	著	着	durative aspect marker	10
*	zhè/zhèi	這	这	this	6
	zhè.me	這麼	这么	this way (as…), so (as this)	8
	zhèr	這兒	这儿	here	7
	zhèixiē	這些	这些	these	7
	zhēn	眞	真	really, real	11

	zhēn.shì.de	眞是的	真是的	give me a break!; (someone is) impossible; (something is) a little too much	12
	zhènghǎo	正好		exactly right (at the moment/amount)	13
	(zhèng)zài	(正) 在		V-ing	8
	zhǐhǎo	只好		the only alternative is ...	7
	zhǐ yào	只要		only (if/takes)	13
	Zhōng.guó	中國	中国	China	8
	Zhōngwén	中文		Chinese	5
*	zhōng.wǔ	中午		noon	5
	zhòng	重		(to be) heavy (course load, taste, weight)	6
	zhòng	重		to gain weight	13
	zhōumò	週末	周末	weekend	5
	zhǔjué/jiǎo	主角	主角	leading actor	11
	zhǔxiū	主修		major, to major in	6
*	zhù	祝		to wish	4
	zhùcè	註冊	注册	to register (at school)	4
*	zhuānyè	專業	专业	specialty, major	6
	zìdiǎn	字典		dictionary (M: 本)	7
	zìjǐ	自己		oneself	9
	zìrán	自然		(to be) natural	11
	zǒu	走		to walk, to leave (a place) (intrans. V)	8
	zuìjìn	最近		recently, lately	11
*	zuó.tiān	昨天		yesterday	4
	zuò	坐		to sit	7
	zuò	坐		to go by (bus, airplane, ship)	13
	zuò	做		to do, to make	5
	zuòwén	作文		composition (M: 篇 piān)	9
*	zuòyè	作業	作业	homework (= 功課)	13

◎ By English

	English	Pinyin	Character		L
A					
	act, to	yǎn	演		11
	actor	yǎnyuán	演員	演员	11
	add, to	jiā	加	加	6
	affairs	shì	事		9
	after (a given time)	yǐhòu	以後	以后	9
	afternoon	xià.wǔ	下午		5
	again	yòu	又		12
	airplane	fēijī	飛機	飞机	13
	airport	(fēi)jīchǎng	(飛)機場	(飞)机场	13
	all (Adv)	dōu	都		5
	all (N)	dàjiā	大家		10
	all right, (to be)	xíng	行		13
	already	yǐ.jīng	已經	已经	6
	also	yě	也		4
	although	suīrán/suírán	雖然	虽然	8
	altogether	yígòng	一共		7
	America	Měi.guó	美國	美国	8
	and	gēn	跟		5
*	and (= 和)	hé/hàn	和		5
	and so forth	shén.me .de	什麼的	什么的	10
	and yet	búguò	不過	不过	8
	appetite	wèikǒu	胃口		11
*	ascend, to	shàng	上		4
*	ashamed, (to be)	bù hǎo yì.si	不好意思		13
*	ask, to	wèn	問	问	7
	aspect marker for completed action	.le	了		6
	aspect marker, durative	.zhe	著	着	10
	aspect, an	fāngmiàn	方面		11
	assist, to	bāng	幫	帮	12
	athletic field	yùndòngchǎng	運動場	运动场	13
	attend class, to	shàngkè	上課	上课	4
	auction, an	pāimài	拍賣	拍卖	12
	audio tape	lùyīndài	錄音帶	录音带	7
	audio tape (China)	cídài	磁帶	磁带	7

authentic	dì.dào	地道		9
* authentic (= 地道)	dào.dì	道地		9
B				
basketball	lánqiú	籃球	篮球	12
be nice to...	duì...hǎo	對... 好	对... 好	10
be serious!	shuō zhēn .de	說眞的	说真的	13
be, to	shì	是		4
beautiful, (to be)	piào.liàng	漂亮		11
because	yīn.wèi	因爲	因为	8
become, to	biànchéng	變成	变成	13
beef	niúròu	牛肉		10
beer	píjiǔ	啤酒		10
* before (a given time)	yǐqián	以前		9
before long	kuài(yào)	快(要)		6
begin, to	kāishǐ	開始	开始	11
besides (Conj)	chú.le... yǐwài	除了...以外		12
besides (Conj)	érqiě	而且		9
big, (to be)	dà	大		4
birthday	shēng.rì	生日		4
black	hēisè	黑色		12
blue (colloquial)	lánsè	藍色	蓝色	12
body	shēntǐ	身體	身体	10
book	shū	書	书	6
bookstore	shūdiàn	書店	书店	6
boots	xuē.zi	靴子		12
borrow, to	jiè	借		6
both	dōu	都		5
bravo	hǎojí.le	好極了	好极了	8
bread	miànbāo	麵包	面包	11
brown (color)	kāfēi	咖啡		12
* bus	gōnggòng qìchē	公共汽車	公共汽车	13
* bus (= 公共汽車)	gōngchē	公車	公车	13
* busy, (to be)	máng	忙		6
but	kě.shì	可是		6
but (= 可是)	dàn.shì	但是		8
but (preceded by 不是)	ér.shì	而是		8
butter	niúyóu	牛油		11
buy, to	mǎi	買	买	6

C

	English	Pinyin	Traditional	Simplified	Lesson
	call, to	jiào	叫		8
	called, to be	jiào	叫		8
	can	néng	能		9
*	can (to know how to)	huì	會	会	9
	can do	xíng	行		13
	candy	táng	糖		10
	cannot stand it	shòu.bùliǎo	受不了		11
	cap	mào.zi	帽子		12
	car	chē	車	车	10
	CD (compact disc)	guāngdié	光碟		7
*	cent	fēn (qián)	分(錢)	分(钱)	7
	certainly	kěndìng	肯定		12
	cheap, (to be)	pián.yí	便宜		7
	check, to	chá	查		7
	chicken	jī	雞	鸡	10
	China	Zhōng.guó	中國	中国	8
	China (=中華)	huá	華	华	12
	Chinese	Zhōngwén	中文		5
	Chinese character	hànzì	漢字	汉字	8
	cigarette	yān	煙	烟	10
*	class dismissed	xiàkè	下課	下课	4
	close the door, to	guānmén	關門	关门	6
*	clothes	yī.fú	衣服		12
	coffee	kāfēi	咖啡		7
	cold, (to be)	lěng	冷		12
	college	dàxué	大學	大学	12
	color	yánsè	顏色	颜色	12
	come /go from (a place), to	cóng...lái/qù	從...來/去	从...来/去	8
*	come, to	lái	來	来	6
	comedy	xǐjù	喜劇	喜剧	11
	comfortable, (to be)	shū.fú	舒服		11
*	commodities	bǎihuò	百貨	百货	12
*	company	gōngsī	公司		12
	comparatively	bǐjiào	比較	比较	10
*	compare, to	bǐ	比		10
	comparison	bǐjiào	比較	比较	10
	composition	zuòwén	作文		9

	computer	diànnǎo	電腦	电脑	7
	constitute, to	chéng	成		8
	convenient, (to be)	fāng.biàn	方便		13
*	course	kè	課	课	4
	crack a joke, to	kāiwánxiào	開玩笑	开玩笑	13
	credits	xuéfēn	學分	学分	6
	cry, to	kū	哭		11
	cup	bēi	杯		7

D

	daughter	nǚ'ér	女兒	女儿	11
*	day	tiān	天		4
	day after tomorrow, the	hòu.tiān	後天	后天	4
	day before yesterday, the	qián.tiān	前天		4
	day of the month (colloquial)	hào	號	号	4
*	day of the month (written)	rì	日		4
	decide, to	juédìng	決定	决定	6
	delightful to listen to, (to be)	hǎotīng	好聽	好听	8
	department store	bǎihuò gōngsī	百貨公司	百货公司	12
*	department store (China)	bǎihuò dàlóu	百貨大樓	百货大楼	12
*	descend, to	xià	下		4
	dial a wrong number, to	dǎcuò	打錯	打错	9
	dictionary	zìdiǎn	字典		7
	difficult, (to be)	nán	難	难	8
*	diligent, (to be)	yònggōng	用功		6
	dime (colloquial)	máo (qián)	毛(錢)	毛(钱)	7
*	dime (as printed on real money)	jiǎo	角	角	7
	dishes	cài	菜		9
	divide, to	fēn	分		10
	do physical training, to	duàn.liàn	鍛練	锻练	13
	do window shopping, to	guàngjiē	逛街		12
	do, to	zuò	做		5
*	doesn't have to	búyòng	不用		5
*	doesn't have to (=不必)	búbì	不必		5
	dollar (colloquial)	kuài (qián)	塊 (錢)	块钱	7
*	dollar (written form)	yuán	元		7
*	dollar (as printed on real money)	yuán	圓	圆	7
	don't	bié	別		11
	dormitory	sùshè	宿舍		7

	double	shuāng	雙	双	8
	drink, to	hē	喝		7
	drive (a vehicle), to	kāi	開	开	10
	drop (a course), to	tuì	退		6
	dumpling	jiǎo.zi	餃子	饺子	10
E					
	early morning	yìzǎo	一早		13
	eastern (America)	dōngbù	東部		8
	easy, (to be)	róng.yì	容易		8
	eat and drink a lot, to	dà chī dà hē	大吃大喝		13
*	eat to the full, to	bǎo	飽	饱	11
	eat, to	chī	吃		7
	eggroll	chūnjuǎnr	春捲兒	春卷儿	10
	eight	bā	八		4
	elect, to	xuǎn	選	选	6
*	embarrassed, (to be)	bù hǎo yì.si	不好意思		13
	emphatic marker	kě	可		11
	end of a semester	qīmò	期末		13
	England	Yīng.guó	英國	英国	8
	English	Yīngwén	英文		5
	enjoyment of the palate	kǒufú	口福		13
	entrance	ménkǒu	門口	门口	9
	especially	tèbié	特別		11
	especially	yóuqí	尤其		10
*	even (Adv)	gèng	更		12
*	evening (MTA)	wǎn.shàng	晚上		5
	everybody	dàjiā	大家		10
	every day	měitiān	每天		5
	every day (=每天)	tiān.tiān	天天		5
	exactly right (at the moment/amount)	zhènghǎo	正好		13
	except for	chú.le...yǐwài	除了...以外		12
	expensive, (to be)	guì	貴	贵	7
	experience	jīngyàn	經驗	经验	11
*	extraordinarily	fēicháng	非常		6
F					
*	face, to	duì	對	对	4
	father	bà.bà	爸爸		8
*	father (formal)	fù.qīn	父親	父亲	8

* feel shy, to	bù hǎo yì.si	不好意思		13
feel, to	jué.de	覺得	觉得	7
female (for human beings)	nǚ	女		11
few (indefinite)	jǐ	幾	几	6
* few, (to be)	shǎo	少		6
fiction	xiǎoshuō	小說	小说	7
fifty percent discount, a	duìzhé	對折	对折	12
figure out, to	kàn.chū.lái	看出來	看出来	11
film	piàn.zi	片子		11
finish	pàotāng	泡湯	泡汤	7
* finish, to	wán	完		7
first	xiān	先		7
* first, the	dìyī	第一		4
fish	yú	魚	鱼	10
five	wǔ	五		4
flavor	kǒuwèir	口味兒	口味儿	10
flavor (=口味兒)	wèidào	味道		10
follow, to	gēn	跟		10
forenoon	shàng.wǔ	上午		5
* forenoon (=上午)	zǎo.shàng	早上		5
forest (= 樹林)	lín	林		8
forget it	suàn.le	算了		10
four	sì	四		4
* friend	péng.yǒu	朋友		5
from	cóng	從	从	11
furthermore	érqiě	而且		9
G				
gain weight, to	zhòng	重		13
genuine	dì.dào	地道		9
* genuine (=地道)	dào.dì	道地		9
Germany	Dé.guó	德國	德国	8
* get off (class, work), to	xià	下		4
give a discount, to	dǎzhé	打折		12
give it a try, to	shì(.yí)shì	試(一)試	试(一)试	10
give me a break!	zhēn.shì.de	眞是的	真是的	12
give, to	gěi	給	给	7
gloves	shǒutào	手套		12
* go back, to	huí	回		6

*	hear, to	tīng	聽	听	8
	heavy (course load, taste, weight), (to be)	zhòng	重		6
	hello	wéi	喂		9
	help, to	bāng	幫	帮	12
*	her	tā	她		4
	here	zhèr	這兒	这儿	7
	high	gāo	高		4
	high opinion	gāojiàn	高見	高见	11
*	him	tā	他		4
*	his/her	tā .de	他的		4
	home	jiā	家		6
	homework	gōngkè	功課	功课	5
*	homework (= 功課)	zuòyè	作業	作业	13
	hospitable, (to be)	hàokè	好客		13
*	hot (temperature), (to be)	rè	熱	热	12
	hot, (to be)	là	辣		10
	how about...?	.ne	呢		4
	how can (one) let someone do…	zěn.me hǎo yì.si	怎麼好意思	怎么好意思	13
	how come?	zěn.me?	怎麼	怎么	11
	how is it?	zěn.meyàng?	怎麼樣	怎么样	6
	how many, how much	jǐ	幾	几	4
	how many	duō.shǎo	多少		7
	how much	duō.shǎo	多少		7
	Hunan—name of a province	Húnán	湖南		10
	hundred	bǎi	百		7
	hungry, (to be)	è	餓	饿	11
I					
	I	wǒ	我		4
	if	yào.shì	要是		11
	impossible, (someone is)	zhēnshì.de	眞是的	真是的	12
	in case	yào.shì	要是		11
	in fashion, (to be)	liúxíng	流行		11
	in mind	xīn.lǐ	心裏	心里	11
	in the heart	xīn.lǐ	心裏	心里	11
	in vogue, (to be)	liúxíng	流行		11
	inhale, to	chōu	抽		10
*	inhale, to (= 抽)	xī	吸		10
	inside	lǐ.tóu	裏頭	里头	12

interesting	yǒuyì.si	有意思		8
interjection, an	hèi	嘿		4
international business	guómào	國貿	国贸	6
introduce, to	jiè.shào	介紹	介绍	8
invite, to	qǐng	請	请	9
isn't it true?	kě bú.shì .ma?	可不是嗎	可不是吗	11
* it	tā	它		4
it seems as if...	hǎo.xiàng... shì.de/ sì.de	好像...似的		11
it seems...	kàn.qǐ.lái...	看起來	看起来	13

J

Japanese language	Rìwén	日文		5
joke, to	kāiwánxiào	開玩笑	开玩笑	13
Joy Luck Club—title of a movie	Xǐfúhuì	喜福會	喜福会	11
just	jiù	就		7
just (V...)	....yíxià	V一下		7
just now (MTA)	gāngcái	剛才	刚才	11

K

know (a person or a character/ word), to	rèn.shí/rèn.shì	認識	认识	8
* know how to, to	huì	會	会	9

L

laboratory	shíyànshì	實驗室	实验室	8
* lack, to	chà	差		6
language	yǔyán	語言	语言	8
large, (to be)	dà	大		4
* last year	qù.nián	去年		5
lately	zuìjìn	最近		11
later	yǐhòu	以後	以后	9
* laugh, to	xiào	笑		11
leading actor	zhǔjué/jiǎo	主角	主角	11
* learn, to	xuéxí	學習	学习	5
* learn, to (=學習)	xué	學	学	5
leave (a place), to (intrans. V)	zǒu	走		8
* leisure	kòngr	空兒	空儿	9
leisure (=空兒)	gōng.fū	功夫／工夫	工夫	9
length	chángduǎn	長短	长短	12
length	chángdù	長度	长度	12
* lesson	kè	課	课	4
let, to	ràng	讓	让	11

	lettuce	shēngcài	生菜		11
	library	túshūguǎn	圖書館	图书馆	6
*	light (course load, weight), (to be)	qīng	輕	轻	6
	light (taste, color), (to be)	dàn	淡		10
	like, to	xǐ.huān	喜歡	喜欢	6
*	little (quantity), (to be)	shǎo	少		6
*	little (size, age), (to be)	xiǎo	小		4
	little bit, a	yì.diǎnr	一點兒	一点儿	7
	located at/in/on, (be)	zài	在		7
	look for, to	zhǎo	找		9
	looks…, (it)	kàn.qǐ.lái	看起來	看起来	13
*	loose, (to be)	kuān	寬		12
	lose completely (one's appetite), to	dǎojìn	倒盡	倒尽	11
	love, to	ài	愛	爱	8

M

*	major	zhuānyè	專業	专业	6
	major, to/a	zhǔxiū	主修		6
	make a telephone call, to	dǎ (diànhuà)	打(電話)	打(电话)	9
	make, to	zuò	做		5
	make, to (causative)	ràng	讓	让	11
*	male (for human beings)	nán	男		11
	mall	shāngchǎng	商場	商场	12
	many, (to be)	duō	多		6
	match and form, to	pèichéng	配成		12
	matters	shì	事		9
	may	kě.yǐ	可以		7
	may I ask?	qǐngwèn	請問	请问	7
	me	wǒ	我		4
	meal	fàn	飯	饭	7
	measure word for a group of people or animals	qún	群		12
	measure word for a pair (of things)	shuāng	雙	双	8
	measure word for books, notebooks	běn	本		6
*	measure word for classes	jié	節	节	5
	measure word for classes	táng	堂		5
	measure word for courses	mén	門	门	6
	measure word for dishes	dào	道		10
	measure word for films, cars, etc.	bù	部		11

	measure word for frequency	cì	次		11
	measure word for meals	dùn	頓	顿	13
	measure word for people (polite)	wèi	位		10
*	measure word for persons and things	.ge	個	个	5
	measure word for plural nouns	xiē	些		7
*	measure word for stores, restaurants, cinema; home	jiā	家		6
	measure word for tea, wine, coffee	bēi	杯		7
	measure word for upper garments and coats, affairs	jiàn	件		12
*	milk	niúnǎi	牛奶		10
	mini-bus	xiǎobā	小巴		13
	minor, a/to	fùxiū	副修		6
*	minute	fēn	分		6
	moment ago, a	gāngcái	剛才	刚才	11
	money	qián	錢	钱	7
	month	yuè	月		4
	more/much Adj-er, (it's becoming)	yuè lái yuè…	越來越…	越来越…	12
	moreover	yòu	又		12
	morning	shàng.wǔ	上午		5
*	morning (=上午)	zǎo.shàng	早上		5
	most of	duōbànr	多半兒	多半儿	11
	mother	mā.ma	媽媽	妈妈	8
*	mother (formal)	mǔ.qīn	母親	母亲	8
	moved, (to be)	gǎndòng	感動	感动	11
	movie	diànyǐngr	電影兒	电影儿	9
	much, (to be)	duō	多		6
	music	yīnyuè	音樂	音乐	8
	must	děi	得		5
	must (=得)	yīnggāi	應該	应该	8
	my	wǒ .de	我的		4
N					
*	name	míng.zi	名字		8
	natural, (to be)	zìrán	自然		11
*	need not	búyòng	不用		5
*	need not (=不用)	búbì	不必		5
*	new	xīn	新		7
	next time	xià.cì	下次		11

* next year	míng.nián	明年		5
* night (MTA)	wǎn.shàng	晚上		5
nine	jiǔ	九		4
no	bù	不		4
* noon	zhōng.wǔ	中午		5
north, the	běifāng	北方		10
not	bù	不		4
not bad, (to be)	búcuò	不錯	不错	6
not have, to	méi(.yǒu)	没(有)		5
not necessarily	búbì	不必		10
not quite	bútài	不太		6
not until	cái	才		9
not very	bútài	不太		6
notebook	běn.zi	本子		7
novel	xiǎoshuō	小說	小说	7
* now	xiànzài	現在	现在	6
number	hào	號	号	4
O				
o'clock	diǎn(zhōng)	點(鐘)	点(钟)	6
odor	wèidào	味道		10
O.K.	xíng	行		13
old (age), (to be)	dà	大		4
old (things), (to be)	jiù	舊	旧	7
on one's body	shēn.shàng	身上		7
on the contrary	dào.shì	倒是		8
one	yī	一		4
oneself	zìjǐ	自己		9
only	cái	才		7
only (if/takes)	zhǐ yào	只要		13
only alternative is ... , the	zhǐhǎo	只好		7
only then	cái	才		9
open (a can, box, etc.), to	kāi	開	开	10
* open the door, to	kāimén	開門	开门	6
or	hái.shì	還是	还是	6
or	huò(.zhě)	或 (者)		13
* orange juice	jú.zishuǐ	桔子水		10
order, to	jiào	叫		10
originally	yuánlái	原來	原来	12

	other	bié .de	別的		7
	ought to	yīnggāi	應該	应该	8
*	outside	wài.tóu	外頭	外头	12
	overcoat, an	dàyī	大衣		12
	overcoat, an (=大衣)	wàitào	外套		12

P

	page	yè	頁	页	7
*	pants	kù.zi	褲子	裤子	12
	paper (term)	bàogào	報告	报告	13
	parents	fùmǔ	父母		8
*	part, a	bù	部		8
	particle for agreement	.ba	吧		7
	particle for interest in additional information	.ne	呢		4
	particle for question	.a	啊		8
	particle for yes-or-no question	.ma	嗎	吗	4
	particle–a variant of 啊	.ya	呀		12
	particularly	tèbié	特別		11
*	pass, to	guò	過	过	6
	pay (a fee) , to	jiāo	交		13
	pen	bǐ	筆	笔	7
	people	rén	人		8
	person	rén	人		8
*	pick someone up, to	jiē	接		13
	play (violin, viola), to	lā	拉		8
*	please	qǐng	請	请	7
	portable stereo	suíshēntīng	隨身聽	随身听	7
	position (of a person)	dìwèi	地位		11
	possessive marker	.de	的		4
	pot	hú	壺	壶	10
	pound	bàng	磅		13
	practice, to	liàn.xí	練習	练习	8
	precisely	jiù	就		7
*	prefix, an ordinalizing	dì	第		4
	prepare, to	yù.bèi	預備	预备	5
	pretty, (to be)	piào.liàng	漂亮		11
*	previously	yǐqián	以前		9
	price	jià.qián	價錢	价钱	12
*	price reduction	jiǎnjià	減價	减价	12

pull, to	lā	拉		8
pumpkin pie	nánguāpài	南瓜派		13
Q				
* quarter	kè	刻		6
quit kidding/joking!	shuō zhēn .de	說眞的	说真的	13
quite	tǐng	挺		9
quite (=挺)	xiāngdāng	相當	相当	11
quite good, (to be)	búcuò	不錯	不错	6
R				
ranking	dìwèi	地位		11
rather	xiāngdāng	相當	相当	11
raw vegetables	shēngcài	生菜		11
real,-ly	zhēn	眞	真	11
recently	zuìjìn	最近		11
recording	lùyīn	錄音	录音	8
register (at school), to	zhùcè	註册	注册	4
relationship	guān.xì	關係	关系	11
report	bàogào	報告	报告	13
* request, to	qǐng	請	请	7
research, to	yánjiū/yánjiù	研究	研究	11
* resemble, to	xiàng	像	象	8
respect, (in this or that)	fāngmiàn	方面		11
rest from work, to	xiū.xí	休息		5
restaurant	fànguǎnr	飯館兒	饭馆儿	10
return (something to the store), to	tuì	退		6
* return (something), to	huán	還	还	6
* return (to a place; from a trip; to original state), to	huí	回		6
rice	fàn	飯	饭	7
* right, (to be)	duì	對	对	4
right, (you are)	méicuò	沒錯	没错	7
roast duck	kǎoyā	烤鴨	烤鸭	10
S				
sad, (to be)	nánguò	難過	难过	11
salad	shālā	沙拉		11
sale, a	pāimài	拍賣	拍卖	12
* same, (to be) the	yíyàng	一樣	一样	8
sandwich	sānmíngzhì	三明治		7
* satisfied (stomach), (to be)	bǎo	飽	饱	11

	say, to	shuō	說	说	7
	scarf	wéijīnr	圍巾兒	围巾儿	12
	scarf (=圍巾兒)	wéibór	圍脖兒	围脖儿	12
*	school	xuéxiào	學校	学校	4
	seafood	hǎixiān	海鮮	海鲜	10
*	second	miǎo	秒		6
*	section, a	bù	部		8
	see (a person) off, to	sòng	送		13
	see what happens, just (VO) and	...kàn.kàn	(VO) 看看		7
	see, to	kàn	看		9
	seek, to	zhǎo	找		9
	seems the same as... (it)	xiàng...yíyàng	像...一樣	象...一样	8
	seems, (it)	kàn.qǐ.lái	看起來	看起来	13
*	sell, to	mài	賣	卖	6
	semester	xuéqī	學期	学期	6
	set, a	tào	套		12
	seven	qī	七		4
	several	hǎojǐ-	好幾-	好几-	13
	shall	yào	要		6
*	she	tā	她		4
	shirt	chènshān	襯衫	衬衫	12
	short	ǎi	矮		8
*	short of, to be	chà	差		6
	should	yīnggāi	應該	应该	8
	sing, to	chànggē	唱歌		8
	sit, to	zuò	坐		7
	six	liù	六		4
	size	dàxiǎo	大小		12
	size (clothing only)	hào	號	号	4
*	skill	gōng.fū	功夫	工夫	9
*	skirt	qún.zi	裙子		12
	skort	qúnkù	裙褲	裙裤	12
*	sky	tiān	天		4
*	small (size/age), (to be)	xiǎo	小		4
	smoke	yān	煙	烟	10
*	smoke (cigarettes), to	xī	吸		10
	smoke (cigarettes), to (=吸)	chōu	抽		10
	society	shèhuì	社會	社会	11

soft drink	qìshuǐr	汽水兒	汽水儿	10
sold out	màiwán	賣完	卖完	7
* some (+ N)	yǒu .de	有的		7
some (+M+N)	jǐ	幾	几	6
some (of plural N)	xiē	些		7
* son	ér.zi	兒子	儿子	11
soon	kuài(yào)	快(要)		6
sorry, (I am)	duì.buqǐ	對不起	对不起	6
soup	tāng	湯	汤	10
sour, (to be)	suān	酸		10
south, the	nánfāng	南方		10
* specialty	zhuānyè	專業	专业	6
spicy, (to be)	là	辣		10
splendid (=華麗)	huá	華	华	12
* stand, to	zhàn	站		7
start school/classes, to	kāixué	開學	开学	4
start, to	kāishǐ	開始	开始	11
status	dìwèi	地位		11
stern, (to be)	yán	嚴	严	8
still	hái	還	还	6
* stomach	wèi	胃		11
stomach (belly)	dù.zi	肚子		13
strict, (to be)	yán	嚴	严	8
* student	xué.shēng	學生	学生	4
study (a subject), to	niàn	念		6
* study, to	xué	學	学	5
* study, to (=學)	xuéxí	學習	学习	5
style	yàng.zi	樣子	样子	12
style (Suf)	shì	式		13
suffix, experiential	.guò	過	过	10
sugar	táng	糖		10
suitable, (to be)	héshì	合適	合适	12
supermarket	chāojí shìchǎng	超級市場	超级市场	13
suppose	yào.shì	要是		11
surname, a	Gāo	高		4
surname, a	Lǐ	李		4
surname, a	Lín	林		8
surname, a	Wáng	王		9

	surnamed, to be	xìng	姓		8
*	surround, to	wéi	圍	围	12
	sweater	máoyī	毛衣		12
	sweet, (to be)	tián	甜		10
T					
	take (a course), to	xuǎn	選	选	6
	take (a vehicle, an airplane, a ship), to	dā	搭		13
	take (someone to some place), to	sòng	送		13
	take a rest, to	xiū.xí	休息		5
	talk about, to	tándào	談到	谈到	11
	tall	Gāo	高		4
	taste	kǒuwèir	口味兒	口味儿	10
	taste (=口味兒)	wèidào	味道		10
	tea	chá	茶		10
*	teach	jiāo	教		5
	teacher	lǎoshī	老師	老师	8
*	telephone	diànhuà	電話	电话	9
	tell, to	gào.sù	告訴	告诉	13
	ten	shí	十		4
	thank (you)	xiè.xie	謝謝	谢谢	7
	Thanksgiving	Gǎn'ēnjié	感恩節	感恩节	13
	that	nà/nèi	那		6
	them	tā.men	他們	他们	4
	then	jiù	就		7
	then	zài	再		7
	there	nàr	那兒	那儿	7
	therefore	suǒ.yǐ	所以		11
	these	zhèixiē	這些	这些	7
	they	tā.men	他們	他们	4
	thing	dōng.xī	東西	东西	7
	think (when expressing one's opinion), to	kàn	看		9
	think, to	jué.de	覺得	觉得	7
	think, to (=覺得)	xiǎng	想		8
*	this	zhè/zhèi	這	这	6
	this way (as…)	zhè.me	這麼	这么	8
*	this year	jīn.nián	今年		5
*	those	nèixiē	那些		7

	three	sān	三		4
	tight, (to be)	jǐn	緊	紧	12
*	time	shí.hòu	時候	时候	6
*	time	gōng.fū	功夫/工夫	工夫	9
	time (=功夫)	shíjiān	時間	时间	9
	time-consuming, (to be)	huā shíjiān	花時間	花时间	8
	tired, (to be)	lèi	累		6
	today	jīn.tiān	今天		4
	together	yíkuàir	一塊兒	一块儿	8
	tomorrow	míng.tiān	明天		4
	tone	shēngdiào	聲調	声调	8
	too	yě	也		4
	too much, (something is) a little	zhēnshì.de	眞是的	真是的	12
	touched, (to be)	gǎndòng	感動	感动	11
	tragedy	bēijù	悲劇	悲剧	11
	treat, to	qǐng	請	请	9
	tree (=樹木)	mù	木		8
	trouble, (to be) troublesome	má.fán	麻煩	麻烦	9
	try (garments) on, to	chuān.chuān.kàn	穿穿看		12
	try, to	shì(.yí)shì	試(一)試	试(一)试	10
	turkey	huǒjī	火雞	火鸡	13
	turn in (homework), to	jiāo	交		13
	TV	diànshì	電視	电视	12
	two	èr	二		4
	two (only occurs before a measure word)	liǎng	兩	两	5
U					
	understand, to	míng.bái	明白		11
	understand, to (=明白)	dǒng	懂		11
	undertaking	shì	事		9
	United Nations	Liánhéguó	聯合國	联合国	8
	university	dàxué	大學	大学	12
*	unoccupied time or space	kòngr	空兒	空儿	9
*	unusually	fēicháng	非常		6
*	us	wǒ.men	我們	我们	4
	us (including the person addressed)	zán.men	咱們	咱们	9
	use (time/tool/chance), to	lìyòng	利用		13
	used	jiù	舊	旧	7

	utilize, to	lìyòng	利用		13
V					
	van	xiǎobā	小巴		13
	vegetables	cài	菜		9
	vehicle	chē	車	车	10
	very	hěn	很		6
	very (=很)	tǐng	挺		9
	vinegar	cù	醋		10
	V-ing	(zhèng)zài	(正)在		8
	violin	xiǎotíqín	小提琴		8
W					
	wait, to	děng	等		9
	walk, to	zǒu	走		8
	Walkman	suíshēntīng	隨身聽	随身听	7
	want, to	yào	要		6
*	we	wǒ.men	我們	我们	4
	we (including the person addressed)	zán.men	咱們	咱们	9
	weak or thin (tea, coffee, etc.), (to be)	dàn	淡		10
*	wear (garments and shoes), to	chuān	穿		12
*	wear (glasses, gloves, jewelry), to	dài	戴		12
*	wear (scarf), to	wéi	圍	围	12
	weather	tiān.qì	天氣	天气	12
*	week (colloquial)	lǐbài	禮拜	礼拜	4
	week (literary)	xīngqī	星期		4
	weekend	zhōumò	週末	周末	5
	western (America)	xībù	西部		8
	what is there to see window shopping?	yǒu shén.me hǎo guàng .de?	有什麼好逛的	有什么好逛的	12
*	what time?	jǐ diǎn zhōng	幾點鐘	几点钟	6
	what?	shén.me	什麼/甚麼	什么	5
*	when? /what time?	shén.me shí.hòu	什麼時候	什么时候	6
	where?	nǎr	哪兒	哪儿	6
*	where? /what place?	shén.me dì.fāng	什麼地方	什么地方	6
*	which	nǎ/něi	哪		4
	which day	nǎ yì tiān/něi yì tiān	哪一天		4
*	who	shéi	誰	谁	4
*	whoever	shéi	誰	谁	4
*	whom	shéi	誰	谁	4

* whomever	shéi	誰	谁	4
* whose	shéi .de	誰的	谁的	4
* why	wèishén.me	爲什麼	为什么	8
* will	huì	會	会	9
will (=會)	yào	要		6
winter (season)	dōngjì	冬季		12
* wish, to	zhù	祝		4
with (person)	gēn	跟		10
with one's self	shēn.shàng	身上		7
withdraw (from school), to	tuì	退		6
woman (derogatory)	nǚláng	女郎		12
woman, women	fùnǚ	婦女	妇女	11
wonderful	hǎojí.le	好極了	好极了	8
* work	gōng.fū	功夫/工夫	工夫	9
work (for a temporary job), to	dǎgōng	打工		5
* work, to	gōngzuò	工作		5
would like to	xiǎng	想		8
write, to	xiě	寫	写	8
Y				
* year	nián	年		4
* yesterday	zuó.tiān	昨天		4
* you (pl.)	nǐ.men	你們	你们	4
you (sing.)	nǐ	你		4
* you're welcome	búxiè	不謝	不谢	7
* young (for age), (to be)	xiǎo	小		4
your	nǐ .de	你的		4
Z				
* zero	líng	零		4

Index 2. Characters

◎ **By Pinyin**

Pinyin	Character		S No.	L
A				
* ǎi	矮		13	SC13
* ài	愛	爱	13	SC21
B				
.ba	吧		7	L7
bàn	半		5	L9
bāo	包		5	L11
* bǎo	飽	饱	13	SC27
* bēi	杯		8	SC20
běi	北		5	L10
bǐ	比		4	L10
* bǐ	筆	笔	12	SC6
bié	別		7	L11
* bīng	冰		6	SC19
bù	不		4	L4
* bù	部		11	SC25
C				
cái	才		3	L7
cài	菜		12	L10
chá	茶		10	L10
cháng	長	长	8	L12
chē	車	车	7	L10
chī	吃		6	L7
chóng	重		9	L10
* chōu	抽		8	SC22
chū	出		5	L9
chú	除		10	L12
chuān	穿		9	L12
cì	次		6	L11
cóng	從	从	11	L8
cuò	錯	错	16	L10
D				
dǎ	打		5	L9
dà	大		3	L4
* dài	戴		18	SC30
dàn	但		7	L8
dào	到		8	L6
.de	的		8	L4

Pinyin	Character		S No.	L
.de	得		11	L6
diǎn	點	点	17	L6
diàn	店		8	L6
diàn	電	电	13	L9
dōng	東	东	8	L7
dǒng	懂		16	L11
dōu	都		11	L5
duǎn	短		12	L12
duì	對	对	14	L9
* dùn	頓	顿	13	SC10
duō	多		6	L6
E				
è	餓	饿	15	L11
ér	而		6	L8
ér	兒	儿	8	L6
F				
fàn	飯	饭	12	L7
fāng	方		4	L10
fàng	放		8	L13
fēn	分		4	L6
G				
gāo	高		10	L8
.ge	個	个	10	L5
gěi	給	给	12	L7
gēn	跟		13	L5
gōng	工		3	L9
* gōng	公		4	SC33
* gōng	功		5	SC18
* guān	關	关	19	SC24
guǎn	館	馆	16	L10
guì	貴	贵	12	L12
guó	國	国	11	L5
guò	過	过	13	L8
H				
hái	還	还	17	L12
* hàn	漢	汉	14	SC15
hǎo	好		6	L6
hào	號	号	13	L12
hē	喝		12	L10

	pinyin	繁	简	画	课		pinyin	繁	简	画	课
		R					wèn	問	问	11	L7
*	rén	人		2	SC2		wǒ	我		7	L4
	rì	日		3	L4		wǔ	午		4	L5
	ròu	肉		6	L10			**X**			
		S					xī	西		6	L7
	shàng	上		3	L4		xǐ	喜		12	L10
	shǎo	少		4	L6		xià	下		3	L4
*	shào	紹	绍	11	SC12		xiǎng	想		13	L8
	shè	舍		8	L13		xiàng	像	象	14	L11
	shéi	誰	谁	15	L6		xiǎo	小		3	L4
	shén	什	什	4	L5		xiào	笑		10	L13
	shēng	生		5	L4	*	xiào	校		10	SC36
	shī	師	师	10	L8		xiě	寫	写	15	L12
	shí	時	时	10	L9		xīng	星		9	L13
	shì	市		5	L13		xíng	行		6	L13
*	shì	式		6	SC39		xìng	姓		8	L8
	shì	事		8	L9		xué	學	学	16	L4
	shì	是		9	L4			**Y**			
	shū	書	书	10	L6	*	yā	鴨	鸭	16	SC38
	shuǐ	水		4	L10	*	yān	煙	烟	13	SC23
	shuō	說	说	14	L7		yàng	樣	样	15	L8
*	sī	司		5	SC34		yào	要		9	L6
	sòng	送		10	L13		yě	也		3	L5
	sù	宿		11	L13		yī	衣		6	L12
	suǒ	所		8	L11	*	yí	宜		8	SC29
		T					yǐ	以		5	L7
	tā	他		5	L4		yīn	因		6	L8
*	tā	它		5	SC4	*	yīng	英		9	SC14
*	tā	她		6	SC3		yóu	油		8	L11
	tài	太		4	L6		yǒu	友		4	L5
	tán	談	谈	15	L11		yǒu	有		6	L5
	tāng	湯	汤	12	L10		yú	魚	鱼	11	L10
	tiān	天		4	L4		yuè	月		4	L4
*	tiào	跳		13	SC17	*	yuè	越		12	SC40
	tīng	聽	听	22	L12			**Z**			
	tóu	頭	头	16	L12		zá	咱		9	L9
		W					zài	在		6	L7
	wài	外		5	L12		zài	再		6	L7
	wán	完		7	L7		zǎo	早		6	L5
	wán	玩		8	L13		zěn	怎		9	L8
*	wǎn	碗		13	SC32		zhǎng	長	长	8	L12
	wèi	爲	为	9	L8		zhǎo	找		7	L9
	wén	文		4	L5		.zhe	著	着	12	L10

	Pinyin	Character		S No.	L
	zhè	這	这	11	L6
	zhèi	這這	这	11	L6
	zhēn	眞/真	真	10	L11
	zhèng	正		5	L8
	zhǐ	只		5	L13
*	zhǐ	紙	纸	10	SC7
	zhōng	中		4	L5
	zhōng	鐘	钟	20	L13

Pinyin	Character	S No.	L
zhòng	重	9	L10
zǐ	子	3	L11
zì	字	6	L8
zì	自	6	L11
zǒu	走	7	L8
zuì	最	12	L11
zuò	坐	7	L7
zuò	作	7	L9
zuò	做	11	L5

◎ By Stroke Number

	S No.	Pinyin	Character	L
			2	
	2	.le	了	L6
*	2	rén	人	SC2
			3	
	3	cái	才	L7
	3	gōng	工	L9
	3	jǐ	己	L11
	3	kǒu	口	L13
	3	nǚ	女	L11
	3	rì	日	L4
	3	shàng	上	L4
	3	xià	下	L4
	3	xiǎo	小	L4
	3	yě	也	L5
	3	zǐ	子	L11
			4	
	4	bǐ	比	L10
	4	bù	不	L4
	4	fāng	方	L10
	4	fēn	分	L6
*	4	gōng	公	SC33
	4	huǒ	火	L13
*	4	jiè	介	SC11
	4	jīn	今	L5
	4	máo	毛	L12
	4	niú	牛	L11
	4	shǎo	少	L6
	4	shén	什	L5
	4	shuǐ	水	L10
	4	tài	太	L6
	4	tiān	天	L4
	4	wén	文	L5
	4	wǔ	午	L5
	4	yǒu	友	L5
	4	yuè	月	L4
	4	zhōng	中	L5
			5	
	5	bàn	半	L9
	5	bāo	包	L11
	5	běi	北	L10
	5	chū	出	L9
	5	dǎ	打	L9
*	5	gōng	功	SC18
	5	jiào	叫	L8
	5	kě	可	L7
	5	qiě	且	L12
	5	qù	去	L6
	5	shēng	生	L4
	5	shì	市	L13
*	5	sī	司	SC34
	5	tā	他	L4
*	5	tā	它	SC4
	5	wài	外	L12
	5	yǐ	以	L7
	5	zhèng	正	L8
	5	zhǐ	只	L13
			6	
*	6	bīng	冰	SC19
	6	chī	吃	L7
	6	cì	次	L11

	6	duō	多	L6
	6	ér	而	L8
	6	hǎo	好	L6
	6	huí	回	L13
*	6	jiàn	件	SC31
	6	lǎo	老	L8
	6	máng	忙	L6
	6	míng	名	L8
	6	nián	年	L5
	6	ròu	肉	L10
*	6	shì	式	SC39
*	6	tā	她	SC3
	6	xíng	行	L13
	6	xī	西	L7
	6	yī	衣	L12
	6	yīn	因	L8
	6	yǒu	有	L5
	6	zài	在	L7
	6	zài	再	L7
	6	zǎo	早	L5
	6	zì	自	L11
	6	zì	字	L8

7

	7	.ba	吧	L7
	7	bié	别	L11
	7	chē	车	L10
	7	dàn	但	L8
	7	jiàn	见	L9
	7	kuài	快	L6
	7	lěng	冷	L12
	7	méi	没	L5
	7	měi	每	L11
	7	nà	那	L7
	7	nán	男	L11
	7	nǐ	你	L4
*	7	qì	汽	SC26
	7	wán	完	L7
	7	wǒ	我	L4
	7	zhǎo	找	L9
	7	zǒu	走	L8
	7	zuò	坐	L7
	7	zuò	作	L9

8

*	8	bēi	杯	SC20
	8	cháng	长	L12
*	8	chōu	抽	SC22
	8	dào	到	L6
	8	.de	的	L4
	8	diàn	店	L6
	8	dōng	东	L7
	8	ér	儿	L6
	8	fàng	放	L13
	8	hé	和	L9
	8	jìn	近	L11
	8	lái	来	L8
	8	liǎng	两	L5
	8	mén	门	L13
	8	míng	明	L4
	8	.ne	呢	L5
	8	péng	朋	L5
	8	shè	舍	L13
	8	shì	事	L9
	8	suǒ	所	L11
	8	wán	玩	L13
	8	xìng	姓	L8
*	8	yí	宜	SC29
	8	yóu	油	L11
	8	zhǎng	长	L12

9

	9	chóng	重	L10
	9	chuān	穿	L12
	9	hěn	很	L6
	9	hòu	後	L9
	9	kàn	看	L7
	9	měi	美	L8
	9	nán	南	L10
*	9	pián	便	SC28
	9	qián	前	L9
	9	shì	是	L4
	9	wèi	爲	L8
	9	xīng	星	L13
	9	yào	要	L6
*	9	yīng	英	SC14
	9	zá	咱	L9
	9	zěn	怎	L8
	9	zhòng	重	L10

10

	笔画	拼音	繁体	简体	课
	10	chá	茶		L10
	10	chú	除		L12
	10	gāo	高		L8
	10	.ge	個	个	L5
	10	jiā	家		L13
	10	jiǔ	酒		L10
*	10	kū	哭		SC37
	10	.men	們	们	L9
	10	nǎ	哪		L4
	10	něi	哪		L4
	10	néng	能		L9
	10	qǐ	起		L9
	10	shī	師	师	L8
	10	shí	時	时	L9
	10	shū	書	书	L6
	10	sòng	送		L13
	10	xiào	笑		L13
*	10	xiào	校		SC36
	10	zhēn	眞/真	真	L11
*	10	zhǐ	紙	纸	SC7

11

	笔画	拼音	繁体	简体	课
*	11	bù	部		SC25
	11	cóng	從	从	L8
	11	.de	得		L6
	11	dōu	都		L5
	11	guó	國	国	L5
	11	jià	假		L13
*	11	jiē	接		SC35
*	11	nín	您		SC1
	11	qiú	球		L12
	11	shào	紹	绍	SC12
	11	sù	宿		L13
	11	wèn	問	问	L7
	11	yú	魚	鱼	L10
	11	zhè	這	这	L6
	11	zhèi	這	这	L6
	11	zuò	做		L5

12

	笔画	拼音	繁体	简体	课
*	12	bǐ	筆	笔	SC6
	12	cài	菜		L10
	12	duǎn	短		L12
	12	fàn	飯	饭	L7
	12	gěi	給	给	L7
	12	guì	貴	贵	L12
	12	hē	喝		L10
*	12	huà	畫	画	SC5
	12	jǐ	幾	几	L4
	12	jiān	間	间	L9
	12	jiù	就		L7
	12	kāi	開	开	L10
	12	mǎi	買	买	L6
*	12	pǎo	跑		SC16
	12	qī	期		L13
	12	tāng	湯	汤	L10
	12	xǐ	喜		L10
*	12	yuè	越		SC40
	12	.zhe	著	着	L10
	12	zuì	最		L11

13

	笔画	拼音	繁体	简体	课
*	13	ǎi	矮		SC13
*	13	ài	愛	爱	SC21
*	13	bǎo	飽	饱	SC27
	13	diàn	電	电	L9
*	13	dùn	頓	顿	SC10
	13	gēn	跟		L5
	13	guò	過	过	L8
	13	hào	號	号	L12
	13	huà	話	话	L9
	13	huì	會	会	L11
	13	kuài	塊	块	L12
	13	lǐ	裏	里	L12
	13	.ma	嗎	吗	L4
*	13	tiào	跳		SC17
*	13	wǎn	碗		SC32
	13	xiǎng	想		L8
*	13	yān	煙	烟	SC23

14

	笔画	拼音	繁体	简体	课
	14	duì	對	对	L9
*	14	hàn	漢	汉	SC15
	14	.me	麼	么	L5
	14	shuō	說	说	L7
	14	xiàng	像		L11

15

	笔画	拼音	繁体	简体	课
	15	è	餓	饿	L11
	15	jié	節	节	L13

			繁	简	
	15	kè	課	课	L4
*	15	mài	賣	卖	SC9
	15	qǐng	請	请	L7
	15	shéi	誰	谁	L6
	15	tán	談	谈	L11
	15	xiě	寫	写	L12
	15	yàng	樣	样	L8
16					
	16	cuò	錯	错	L10
	16	dǒng	懂		L11
	16	guǎn	館	馆	L10
	16	qián	錢	钱	L12
	16	tóu	頭	头	L12
	16	xué	學	学	L4
*	16	yā	鴨	鸭	SC38
17					
	17	diǎn	點	点	L6
	17	hái	還	还	L12
18					
*	18	dài	戴		SC30
	18	jī	雞	鸡	L13
19					
*	19	guān	關	关	SC24
*	19	huài	壞	坏	SC8
20					
	20	miàn	麵	面	L12
	20	zhōng	鐘	钟	L13
22					
	22	huān	歡	欢	L10
	22	tīng	聽	听	L12

Index 3. Sentence Patterns

Index 4. Measure Words

This list includes measure words that are not listed in lesson vocabularies but appear as explanatory notes to new words.

◎ By Pinyin

Pinyin	Character	English	Example	L
bàng	磅	pound	牛肉	13
bāo	包	pack	煙	
bēi	杯	measure word for tea, wine, coffee	茶、啤酒、咖啡、汽水兒	7
běn	本	measure word for books, notebooks	書、本子、小說、字典	6
bù	部	measure word for films, cars, etc.	電影兒、片子、車、公共汽車、公車、小巴	11
cì	次	measure word for frequency	看電影兒	11
dào	道	measure word for dishes	菜	10
dǐng	頂 顶	measure word for hats	帽子	
dòng	棟 栋	measure word for buildings	宿舍	
dùn	頓 顿	measure word for meals	飯	13
* .gè	個 个	measure word for persons and things	籃球、麵包、電腦、電話、隨身聽、漢字、學分、學期、餃子、漢堡、三明治、圖書館、商場、飛機場、超級市場、女兒、兒子、婦女、演員	5
gēn	根	measure word for cigarettes, hair	煙、頭髮	
guàn	罐 罐	can	汽水兒	
hú	壺 壶	pot	茶	10
* jiā	家	measure word for stores, restaurants, cinema	書店、公司、百貨公司、百貨大樓、飯館兒	6
jià	架	measure word for airplanes	飛機	
jiān	間 间	measure word for rooms and building	宿舍、實驗室、大學	
jiàn	件	measure word for upper garments and coats, affairs	衣服、大衣、毛衣、外套、襯衫、事	12
* jié	節 节	measure word for classes	課	5
jīn	斤	catty	牛肉	

juǎn	卷		measure word for audio tapes	錄音帶	
liàng	輛	辆	measure word for vehicles	車、小巴	
mén	門	门	measure word for courses	課	6
pán	盤	盘	measure word for audio tapes and dishes	磁帶、菜	
piān	篇		measure word for articles and compositions	作文、報告	
piàn	片		slice	麵包	
píng	瓶		bottle	汽水兒	
qún	群		measure word for a group of people or animals	人	12
shuāng	雙	双	pair	靴子、手套	8
táng	堂		measure word for classes	課	5
tào	套		set	衣服	12
tiáo	條	条	measure word for long and soft things	魚、褲子、圍巾兒、圍脖兒、裙子、裙褲	
wǎn	碗		bowl	湯	
wèi	位		measure word for people (polite)	老師	10
xiē	些		measure word for plural nouns	東西	7
zhī	隻	只	measure word for birds, dogs, eyes, and a shoe	雞、烤鴨、火雞	
zhī	枝		measure word for branches and pens	筆	
zhǒng	種	种	kind	語言	